vulgar beauty

vulgar

beauty

ACTING CHINESE IN
THE GLOBAL SENSORIUM

MILA ZUO

DUKE UNIVERSITY PRESS   Durham and London   2022

© 2022 DUKE UNIVERSITY PRESS
All rights reserved

Designed by A. Mattson Gallagher / Project editor: Annie Lubinsky
Typeset in SangBleu Empire, SangBleu Republic,
and SangBleu Sunrise by Westchester Publishing Services

Library of Congress Cataloging-in-Publication Data
Names: Zuo, Mila, [date] author.
Title: Vulgar beauty : acting Chinese in the global sensorium / Mila Zuo.
Description: Durham : Duke University Press, 2022. | Includes bibliographical references and index.
Identifiers: LCCN 2021030481 (print) | LCCN 2021030482 (ebook)
ISBN 9781478015475 (hardcover)
ISBN 9781478018117 (paperback)
ISBN 9781478022718 (ebook)
Subjects: LCSH: Asian American women in motion pictures. | Feminine beauty (Aesthetics) in motion pictures. | Feminine beauty (Aesthetics)—China. | Motion pictures—United States. | Motion picture actors and actresses—China. | Actresses—China. | BISAC: PERFORMING ARTS / Film / History & Criticism | SOCIAL SCIENCE / Women's Studies
Classification: LCC PN1995.9.C48 Z866 2022 (print) | LCC PN1995.9.C48 (ebook) | DDC 791.43/6522089951—dc23/eng/20211021
LC record available at https://lccn.loc.gov/2021030481
LC ebook record available at https://lccn.loc.gov/2021030482

Cover art: Yingxue Zuo, *Twin Image*, 2021. Digital manipulation. Based on a still from *Twin Peaks* with Joan Chen as Josie Packard. Courtesy of the artist.

contents

Acknowledgments   vii

INTRODUCTION: **Tasting Vulgar Beauty**   1

1   **Bitter Medicine, Racial Flavor:** Gong Li   39

2   **Salty-Cool:** Maggie Cheung and Joan Chen   73

3   **Pungent Atmospheres:** Bai Ling and Tang Wei   113

4   **Sweet and Soft Coupling:** Vivian Hsu and Shu Qi   152

5   **Sour Laughter:** Charlyne Yi and Ali Wong   193

CONCLUSION: **Aftertaste**   234

Notes   241
Bibliography   267
Index   289

acknowledgments

This book critically imagines beauty as animate and flavorful, and the taste for beauty as a pleasurable problem for the senses. However, I could not have written it without a plenitude of alimentary fellowship and support.

When I began exploring the idea of the mediated Chinese body in graduate school, my advisor Kathleen McHugh inspired and elevated me at every turn. I am thankful to John T. Caldwell, Jasmine Trice, Michael Berry, Sean Metzger, Chon Noriega, and the late Teshome Gabriel for their gracious and expert guidance. Vivian Sobchack ignited my appetite for film theory and philosophy, and I'm continually inspired by my enduring friendships with Vivian, Kathleen, and Jasmine. I thank the faculty and students at the Beijing Film Academy and the Central Academy of Drama, especially Sarah Munroe and Li Duona, as well as the staff at the Taipei Film Commission for assistance with my field research. I'm grateful to UCLA colleagues and friends for the propitious conversations and LA adventures: Ben Sher, Brian Hu, Michelle Ton, Aynne Kokas, Dennis Lo, Li Li, Chris Carloy, Bryan Hartzheim, and Heather Collette-VanDeraa.

Writing this book began during my time at Oregon State University as an assistant professor of film studies, and it was enabled in part by a Center for the Humanities fellowship. The center, directed by Christopher Nichols, also funded a manuscript workshop during which Celine Parreñas Shimizu, Peter X. Feng, Jon Lewis, Iyunolu Osagie, and Elizabeth Sheehan generously gave their time and energy to impart invaluable feedback. I also wish to thank Celine and Peter, in addition to their excellent suggestions, for their galvanizing and pioneering work in Asian American film and media. Tamás Nagypál, Tekla Bude, Sebastian Heiduschke, and Nabil Boudraa kindly gave helpful suggestions on chapter drafts. The camaraderie forged in our junior women's writing salon with Lily, Tekla, Ana Ribero, Trina Hogg, Megan Ward, and Rena Lauer bolstered me during the drafting stage.

I extend gratitude to the organizers and attendees at the various institutions at which I was invited to present excerpts: Tina Campt and Nancy Worman at the Barnard Center for Research on Women's Scholar and Feminist Conference, Daniel Eisen at the Pacific University, David Fleming at the Scottish Graduate School for Arts and Humanities, Todd Kushigemachi at UCLA, and Christina León and the Department of English at Princeton University. I am heartened by the brilliant Christina for her generous and supportive friendship, as well as for illuminating a key point about minoritarian deconstruction. During my time in Oregon, the multitalented Dougal Henken, whose partnership has been instrumental in my creative praxis, read early drafts and helped me discover the book's structure. Lovely friends Melissa Melpignano and Jen Moorman opened their homes to me when I returned to Los Angeles for manuscript revisions. The resplendent Rizvana Bradley whisked me away for an inspiring interlude. I have been replenished by Samantha Sheppard's spirited friendship and magnificent life advice throughout the years since our graduate days. I thank Summer Kim Lee, Jason Coe, and Vivian Huang for their dazzling insights and for their stimulating engagements with my work. I am fortunate to have encountered many scholars with whom I have shared beneficent exchanges and lively conversations about this book and related research, especially Valerie Soe, David Roh, Vincent Pham, Andy Wang, Victor Fan, Lily Wong, Feng-Mei Heberer, Anne Cheng, Yiman Wang, Beth Tsai, Sofia Varino, Mariamne Whatley, Elissa Henken, Elena del Río, Daniel Steinhart, Masami Kawai, Renee Tajima-Peña, Shu-mei Shih, Crystal Baik, Kristy Kang, Laura Kina, Shi-Yan Chao, Anita Chang, Jun Okada, Ma Ran, Ralph Litzinger, Alex Juhasz, Eve Oishi, Lakshmi Padmanabhan, Marisa Hicks-Alcaraz, Wendy Larson, Russ Leo, Paul Nadal, Baki Mani, Natchee Barnd, LeiLani Nishime, Salma Monani, Melissa Phruksachart, Philippa Lovatt, Hunter Hargraves, Brandy Monk Payton, Michael Gillespie, David Martin-Jones, Matt Holtmeier, Chelsea Wessels, Jonathan Cohn, Jaimie Baron, Amber Musser, Ken Provencher, Mike Dillon, Terrance McDonald, and Allison de Fren. My appreciation to the editors of *Celebrity Studies* journal for permission to reprint sections from an earlier article. I am also creatively vivified by my filmmaking friends and collaborators, which in turn feeds my scholarship. Among those who have supported my film practice, I thank Joy Schaefer for her contagiously good mood and ongoing enthusiasm for my work.

The manuscript was completed during my first few years at the University of British Columbia. The incomparable William Brown carefully read this book several times in its final stages, offering nutritive thought, wonderful edits, and magnanimous support. Laura Marks, Chris Patterson, Y-Dang Troueng, Olivia Gagnon, Danielle Wong, JP Catungal, Christine Evans, and Chelsea Birks are among those who make Vancouver a vibrant place for intellectual and creative rapport. Many thanks in particular to Laura for pointing me to Carolyn Korsmeyer's work. My theatre and film colleagues and students make UBC a delightful place to live and a capacious place for thinking. I appreciate my film colleagues Ernest Mathijs, Lisa Coulthard, Brian McIlroy, and Christine for graciously welcoming me into the program, and I'm grateful to our department Head Stephen Heatley for enabling me to have the flexibility and time to complete this book. Thanks to Dmitri Lennikov at the UBC Visual Resource Centre for assistance with images.

This book takes its final shape as a result of the spacious yet incisive guidance by Courtney Berger at Duke University Press, to whom I am tremendously thankful for supporting an unusual idea about tasting bodies, from beginning to end. I am indebted to the book's peer reviewers, who helped bring out all the book's flavors. The Duke editorial board, Sandra Korn, and team have made the editorial process smooth and enjoyable.

I now know that I wrote this book for my family of origin as well as for my family to be/come. I aspire to the vast courage and resiliency of my parents, Mei and Ying, who brought me to the United States with a little cash in their pockets and two English words ("no problem"). And as I write enveloped in the haze of new motherhood, I am filled with gratitude to Will for all the nourishing gifts he shares with us. Finally, this book is for my heart, Radian: thank you for allowing me to remake the world with you every day, and for teaching me that otherworldly beauty is boundless love.

introduction

Tasting Vulgar Beauty

A young woman in a tight cheongsam saunters languidly past a handsome man in their shared apartment hallway, granting him a canted profile as she glances at him. His eyes glisten with interest. Later, when the man apologizes to her for a misunderstanding, he enters her apartment, bearing a wrapped gift. Arms folded, hips swaying, the woman feigns disinterest, a fatigued annoyance. She avoids eye contact, repeatedly pushing the man's hands away and saying *buyao* (I don't want it). Yet the familiarity she generates through impertinent gestures, paired with a distinct vocal whine, drive him to insist. She finally accepts. In the next scene, when she is alone and unwrapping the package (a pair of sheer stockings), her glee confirms the speciousness of her earlier resistance. Mainland film star Zhang Ziyi, playing an escort, is vibrantly performing the Chinese flirtation style known as *sajiao* (unleashing tenderness) in Wong Kar-wai's sumptuous *2046* (2004).

Sajiao refers to the childish behavior, edging on tantrum-throwing, that women exhibit with their romantic, presumably male, partners. Acting like a spoiled child, the woman makes her demands through aggressively cute behavior, making it clear that her partner must dote on and attend to her. Constituting a behavior that could be described as vulgar, or what the *Oxford English Dictionary* defines as "lacking in refinement or good taste;

uncultured, ill-bred," particularly to cultural outsiders unfamiliar with it, sajiao enacts an overflow of desire encoded through demand.[1] As a vulgar grab for attention and legitimacy, sajiao exhibits a form of bad taste inasmuch as childish behavior is regarded as immature and unripened.

This scene in *2046* may baffle western audiences, even challenging models of feminism that might understand this sequence as a woman's complicity in her own oppression through self-infantilization. What we overlook in such an assessment, however, is that such performativity constitutes a woman's negotiation with entrenched, gendered power dynamics. It is a ludic act of seduction whereby one plays within a system of power, not to overthrow it but rather to exploit it, a process that resonates with Jean Baudrillard's theory of seduction wherein "one can 'play' with networks, not in order to establish alternatives, but to discover their state of optimal functioning."[2] With Baudrillard in mind, what interests me are the ways in which Bai Ling (played by Zhang), in unleashing tenderness, engages in a beauty act, whereby her seduction of Mr. Chow (Tony Leung Chiu-wai) and of the viewer depends on stimulating moods, or the exploitation of affective-aesthetic agitation, for maximal attention.

Bai Ling's tensile flexibility, in spite of the constricting tightness of her dress, is conveyed through her restless energy (lightly swaying shoulders and hips), refusals to hold Mr. Chow's gaze (let alone his hand), and the way her head slackens like a floral pistil in a breeze (thereby giving us access to multiple, moving angles of her face). Such details become pervious bodily signals provoking response from both Chow and the spectator. Zhang's corporealized boredom, the ways she keeps spilling out of stillness, in turn produces irritation in the viewer, an effect heightened by the film's aural textures. Bai Ling's theme song, Connie Francis's haunting 1960 version of "Siboney," originally a 1929 Cuban song by Ernesto Lecuona featuring echoing vocals and bongo drums, inflects Zhang's body with piquant promises of foreign dislocation and exotic Latin sexuality. Through an assemblage of minor gestures, Zhang's performance of dissatisfaction is an invitation to play a seduction game of artifice, appearance, and surface. Although Bai Ling's beauty game arguably ends in loss as she falls into unrequited love with Mr. Chow, this segment nevertheless stands as the film's most memorable sequence for unleashing volatile tenderness onto its spectator, beguiling us with temperamental outbursts. Indeed, the beauty aesthetic of sajiao, forged through stirring angles of Zhang's moving face and body, grips our attention, as our eyes dance to her agitated form. The turbulence of affect in these scenes indicates that beauty is not sedative, but rather comprising and evocative of undulating intensifications of excessive feeling. Appositely, Mr. Chow and Bai Ling's affair takes place during the Hong Kong communist-led protests of the late 1960s, a volatile historical backdrop that coincides with, and is allegorized through, the lovers' inflamed sexual affair (and it is worth noting that Mr. Chow is Hong Kongese and Bai Ling is from the mainland).[3]

What this sequence demonstrates is that beauty performativity, or the unleashing/acting out of feminine beauty through embodied behavior, engages in *worlding*, by which I refer to Donna J. Haraway's concept of "becoming with" wherein "partners do not precede their relating."[4] In this way, partners are symbiotically coconstituted, becoming relative or kin through the *beauty encounter*, a concept I address shortly. Extending Haraway's concept of relationality, an ethics of making "a mess out of categories in the making of kin and kind," this book discovers a worlding that not only cosmologically reimagines nonhierarchical relations between objects and subjects, but also forges human community and belonging through such intimate encounters.[5] The worldly beauty with which this project is concerned discovers the Chinese female body in assemblage with the vulgarity of other material objects, including clothing, foods, colors, atmospheres, and animals. Such assemblages generate new worlds by way of beauty's affective shocks.

As the above reveals, a beauty encounter describes an affective response to an aestheticized gesture or movement. Affect, which is "asocial" and "autonomic," as Brian Massumi informs us, can transmute into "perception of one's own vitality, one's sense of aliveness, of changeability."[6] Following this moment of self-reflection, or "perception of this *self-perception*," we may turn our thoughts to others like us; affect can seed feelings of relation and kinship with other lives.[7] In this book, I explore how beauty affects can in particular produce feelings of Chineseness, especially as they are provoked by mediated encounters with cinematized star beauty. What is more, I argue that global identity (racial, gendered, cultural) is imagined precisely through the affective sensorium, and should therefore be understood through *vulgarity*, which draws together material, aesthetic, and racialized conditions and significations. In this way, *Vulgar Beauty: Acting Chinese in the Global Sensorium* offers a new theoretical framework for understanding the affective consumption of screen stardom and in particular, the racioaesthetics (aesthetics that cannot be disassociated from racialization) of performance. Departing from transcendental assessments and definitions of beauty, I deploy vulgarity as a critical methodology through which we can better understand beauty's materiality, its objecthood, and the ways in which we (as film spectators) consume beauty. This project challenges the ocular-centrism in film, visual studies, and western philosophy by demonstrating the centrality of one modality of vulgarity, that is, *taste* in the cinematic consumption of racialized-sexualized bodies, and demonstrates how flavor functions as a theoretical analytic. Flavor, from the Chinese concept *weidao*, enables us to examine the nonrepresentational qualities of cinema in conjunction with the ways in which sociocultural tastes are "cooked" into representation, becoming inextricable from, and absorbed into, our experience of on-screen figures. Weidao is a textural additive to the filmic engagement, one that operates phantasmatically as affective intensity and conscious feeling. As such, *Vulgar Beauty* thinks with and through the intimacies of tasting vulgarly beautiful bodies.

Star images circulate in visual economies as aspirational embodiments of lifestyle, conspicuous consumption, and gender and sexuality, positioning them as flavorful objects within cultural, national, racial, and global imaginaries. To this end, "acting Chinese" gestures to the fluid and slippery signifier of Chineseness, which is affectively renewed through embodied performativity. Such acts, which evoke flavor affects, in turn generate tastes and appetites for a sensorial formation of Chinese identity and feelings of belonging. If the body has a flavor, there thus remains the question of its edibility, which is historically situated—that is, shaped by cultural, political, and social axes that define the coordinates of race, gender, and sexuality. Crucially pointing out that there are the eaters (the white body) and the eaten (the Black body) in nineteenth-century literary productions, Kyla Wazana Tompkins notes that "the fantasy of a body's edibility does not mean the body will always go down smoothly."[8] Meanwhile, Minh-Ha T. Pham uses the term "racial aftertastes" to describe the limitations of racial tolerance toward Asian style bloggers, noting the threatening quality of raciality that lingers upon a reluctant white palate.[9] Tompkins's and Pham's work exposes the violence undergirding the eroticism of racial tasting and eating, a prominent motif in the following case studies of Chinese women in multicultural, transnational fantasies of sexual assimilation. Digestion of such figures depends upon the limits of racial and national toleration and the bounds of ideological-political sensibilities. Moreover, the enjoyment of beauty is not simply sweet. Like the complex palates of love and romance, beauty routes us through the affective dimensions of not only the sweet, but also the "bad tastes" of the bitter, salty, pungent, and sour—the aesthetic-affective flavors that form the structure of this book.

Because of the prodigious and long-winded legacy of beauty in aesthetic theory, any study of beauty calls for spinning ideas and centripetal force in order to pull us closer to beauty's elusive and slippery center. Within the forthcoming sections, we constellate and bring into orbit a creative skein of salient terms, keywords, and digressions including femme, flavor, seduction, shock, passion, charisma, and face in order to gravitate toward an open system of conceptual and cosmological possibilities of feminine beauty.[10] In what follows, I examine the key terms of the book's title, *Vulgar Beauty: Acting Chinese in the Global Sensorium*, beginning with the notion of acting Chinese, before returning to a conceptualization of vulgar beauty and a flavorful theory for analyzing film and media performance within a global sensorium.

Acting Chinese: Seduction, Staring, and the Feminine

Like other immigrant, ethnic children growing up in the United States, I did not often encounter in dominant visual cultures persons whom I or my family members physically resembled. However, when on rare occasion I did see an Asian woman's face on television, a blush of shame and fascination blanketed me, a cathexis wherein a libidinal attachment was forged through a longing for identification. Celine Parreñas Shimizu similarly describes the intense pleasures in viewing hypersexual representations of Asian women as "coexist[ing] with a terrible pain regarding racialized hypersexuality," a realization that enables her to retool the "productive perversity" of such enjoyment to recuperate Asian/American women's formation of "bad subjectivity" through performativity and representation.[11] Shimizu's rehabilitation of perverse enjoyment permits minoritarian subjects to move beyond moralistic judgments of image making, as her work interrogates the entangled powers and pleasures of shame-in-identification. We can test the applicability of this concept with a sexist colonial fantasy like *The World of Suzie Wong* (Richard Quine, 1960), which Peter X. Feng suggests is one that Asian/Americans "love to love" because Nancy Kwan's rupturing star performance exceeds the narrative's efforts to contain and subjugate her character, the titular Hong Kong prostitute.[12] If ethnic self-love offers a fraught prospect, our love of stars like Kwan can nevertheless become an externalized projection of loving ourselves, and loving (to love) Chinese/Asian/American women stars can offer a mediated stage wherein thwarted self-love transforms into transpersonal affection. As one negotiates one's own social position through a kind of nonreciprocal devotion to another, this can in turn nurture affective belonging to a global ethnic and racial community. The phrase "acting Chinese" therefore suggests intersubjective slippages between spectatorship and performance, and on- and off-screen bodies, in order to account for a mediated bodily contact within cinematic and televisual engagements.

Following and modifying David Palumbo-Liu's example, I employ the slash in Chinese/Asian/American to denote the uncertain status of "Chinese," "Asian," and "American," which mark each of these categories as unstable and always-becoming in the context of global visual cultures.[13] Although Palumbo-Liu interrogates the "dynamic, unsettled" assimilation of Asians in the United States, I find that the slash is particularly useful when discussing transnational and immigrant stars who frequently travel to live and work in multiple countries (including the United States), and whose identities suggest the split, sliding, and flexible nature of their global citizenship. On other occasions, I suspend the slash with regard to Asian American stars based primarily in the United States, in order to situate and localize my concerns around the marked racialization of Chinese and Asians within a distinct American context. The critical term "acting Chinese" lets me draw together these two groups, as it signifies the performative, contingent, and nonessentializing nature of Chineseness, which concerns a global, transnational identity. Moreover, as "acting" connotes the slipperiness and instability of the sign "Chinese," it also foregrounds the pressures under which Chinese women negotiate their public performativity under a persistent state of gendered, sexualized, and racialized uncertainty and contingency within trans/national contexts.

Within the mode of acting Chinese, *Vulgar Beauty* in particular rethinks femme heteroperformativity, defining "femme" as apparently consenting to conventional, stereotypical, and even normative beauty image making. Femme is not about sexual allure per se, but rather a ludic play with coded appearances and their significations. Femme can destabilize, if not subvert, heterosexist, phallocentric order through feigned complicity. Lisa Duggan and Kathleen McHugh offer an apt description that also returns us to Zhang's bored performance in *2046*: "Fem(me) is put on, a put-on, fetish production at the hands of subject becoming object, becoming fetish, while always retaining a sense of the performance, always amused yet (here is the challenge, the gauntlet she throws down) possibly *bored* by its effects."[14] The seduction that interests me therefore cannot be regarded as subversion or resistance in toto. Instead, it must be understood as the reversibility of power through the appearance and disappearance of signs, outside the realm of law qua production. Baudrillard writes, "Seduction does not consist of a simple appearance, nor a pure absence, but the eclipse of a presence," noting that "absence here seduces presence."[15] Seduction is the play of appearances and signs, which is to say that rather than aiming to reveal meaning, truth, or reality, it engages in an "aesthetics of disappearance."[16] Seduction is interested in seducing the real through a mode of nonlinguistic artifice, not in service of constructing a stable subject, but only to persist as seduction. The acts of vulgar beauty by femme stars, like Zhang's performance of sajiao, may therefore exhibit an apparent apathy toward autonomy, agency, subjectivity, and desire, foregoing such tokens of liberation insofar as the acquisition of such objects is geared toward accumulative production, a capital formation of subjectivity premised upon transparency, visibility, and proliferation. In relation to the threatening femme fatale, who, as Mary Ann Doane notes, overrepresents the body "because she is attributed with a body which is itself given agency independently of consciousness," the femme star's superficial embodiment (just the right amount of body and beauty) appears to placate masculine anxiety through acquiescence to the gaze.[17] This tractability, however, belies the complex force fields of meaning and affect that reside in the aesthetic encounter between women spectators and women's screen bodies, an engagement that is always already an understanding of feminine glamour as deception, or rather as a Baudrillardian seduction that "lies in the transformation of things into pure appearances."[18] Seduction erupts through the nonspaces of the visible, wherein affective surplus and agitation are discharged through the interplay between presence and absence. Moreover, although feminine seduction cannot be produced, in the aforementioned sense of productive or capital subjectivity, filmic beauty is coproduced, not only through cosmetic transformation but also through cinematic technique and the luminescent majesty of screen projection. Through the parallels between feminine beauty and film, film reveals itself to be a mode of beauty and a dis-appearing seduction.

It can also be said that cinema beckons a different regard of stars; stargazing elicits a different look than what Laura Mulvey famously characterized as the "male gaze," which is situated and emplotted in films that reinforce male/active and female/passive roles.[19] It would be more apt to say that stardom, an amplification of the actor as mythic and exceptional, engages the eye through an incitement to stare and an intensification of the gaze—although not always, as I contend, toward the direction of voyeuristic mastery. Stardom, or what we could call *stare*dom, replicates the medium of cinema, which encourages continuous looking through the persistence of vision and the illusion of relentless continuity. Insofar as film stars appear to invite staring as a perfectly acceptable mode via such a look (whereas in everyday contexts, staring is often regarded as unmannerly and rude), this provocation (seeing without being seen) only increases the star's disarming possession of charm, a term to which we later attend. Nevertheless, whereas the gaze connotes mastery, as 1970s feminist and apparatus theory inform us, staring produces both power and powerlessness in the beholder. As Rosemarie Garland-Thomson explains in regard to the stares received by differently abled and other nonnormative bodies, staring can create apertures that enable deeper contact between two subjects, as staring is an act that seeks and attains knowledge and higher learning.[20] When one party is unable to stare back, and permission to stare is always already operationally permitted by the apparatus, the unrequited stare enhances the sense that voyeurism is enabled by the generosity of the star—a gift bestowed. Moreover, when one encounters something novel, the impulse to stare intensifies. Due to underexposure and underrepresentation, racial beauties can elicit such staring, which can also take the form of curious gawking, and accompanied by a looking away in embarrassment, or perhaps a tentative look askance.

Nevertheless, since seduction "removes something from the order of the visible," the more one stares at a seductive image, the less one knows about it.[21] A project of staring at the Chinese femme therefore grapples with the ways in which she unsettles dominant modes of seeing and knowing. With this in mind, Rey Chow, Anne Anlin Cheng, and Olivia Khoo all address the centrality of Chinese female bodies in cultural constitutions of nationhood, modernity, gender, and race.[22] Chow, for example, remarks on the ways in which the production of the modern Chinese subject resounds in the interstices of western theory and Chinese tradition, erupting most graphically through the representational problems of Chinese femininity. For Chow, the feminine detail, located throughout the works of modern fiction writers like Lu Xun, Ba Jin, Mao Dun, and Eileen Chang, reveals the crisis point within transparent, narrative, and unified attempts to construct nationhood. This literary detail is a type of feminine ornamentation and what Chow refers to as a "cinematic blowing up," deploying negative affect and acting destructively upon the idealistic, moralistic notions of humanity that ground modern ideological rhetoric.[23] It is the fetishistic attention paid to the detail that can redirect our attention to the small, the minor, and the overlooked, which opens onto new worlds of meaning and inhabitance. A "cinematic blowing up" of feminine detail in particular opens onto a sensual worldliness that is always incomplete and in the making, and it is, as we will see, via the feminine through which we may glimpse this unfinished, nontotalizing world. Expanding upon such reflections of the feminine detail, not as observation by typically male authors but rather as women's performance, I observe how film beauty takes form in corporeal details and what I refer to as "minor acts," those micro and macro expressions of the face and body that edge along the performative and the natural: eyes tearing, skin perspiring, smiles cracking, fingers pointing, legs waddling, to name a few. Related to Erin Manning's conceptual "minor gesture," which attends to the ways nonneurotypical minor gesture can produce "germs of experience in-forming, opening the act to its potential," the "minor act" can similarly be thought of as the non/volitional movements of the performing, on-screen body that graze new possibilities of being.[24] Limning the boundary between the performative and the biological, such acts glimpse the sensual curvature of feminine signs, splintering away and disappearing into the horizon as soon as they are perceived. Such acts of beauty are located in their vanishing, which underscores the ephemeral (non)basis of their subject making.

As I have suggested thus far, staring at Chinese femme stars is not a process of gaining mastery, even as its apparent fixity and fetishization may suggest otherwise. Not only does staring destabilize power relations, it can allow us to engage in a practice of noticing how the minor opens onto new definitions of Chineseness. The concept of acting Chinese is also therefore a refrain or a rephrasing of the problems of Chineseness as an open signifier, a discussion beginning with Ien Ang, Allen Chun, Chow, and others in the 1990s.[25] Chow, for instance, elaborates upon the selfsame split within the performativity of Chineseness by reflecting upon the modern formation of Chinese subjectivity fractured by technologies of visuality (and film in particular) into seeing and being seen: "National self-consciousness is thus not only a matter of watching 'China' being represented on the screen; it is, more precisely, watching oneself—as a film, as a spectacle, as something always already watched."[26] If for Chow it is the feminine detail that brings readers of modern Chinese literature to the limits of intellectual thinking, it is in her treatment of Fifth Generation cinema the *"ethnic* detail" that marks China's fascination with "its own datedness, its own alterity."²⁷ Where Chow interprets women in Fifth Generation cinema as the invention of the primitive—China's internal other—in order to sustain such visual fascination, *Vulgar Beauty* demonstrates how women stars, often recognizing themselves as Chinese representatives on a global screen, act Chinese as subjunctive self-stylization that exceeds language, nation, and culture. Doing so through agitational, vulgar acts of beauty constitutes a refusal of meaning, even as it generates novel styles of being. It is not only that seeing Chinese stars is for the Chinese-identifying spectator "watching oneself—as a film, as a spectacle, as something always already watched." Rather, the jouissance of this experience lies in the elusiveness of seeing the act of seeing oneself, as well as fantasizing about others seeing us seeing ourselves as a validating act. This narcissistic process is revealed when we feel and express pride in our imagined community, but it is also flavored by the ways ethnic subjects are barred from self-love because of the disparaged status of nonwhite race and ethnicity in white society. Reframing Chow to account for the objectifying processes of racialization, Cheng interrogates the double bind of "the yellow woman" who is perceived as "someone too aestheticized to suffer injury but so aestheticized that she invites injury."²⁸ Acting Chinese therefore accounts for the hall of mirrors involved in regarding oneself as what Cheng terms an "aesthetic being." Cheng however rethinks the possibilities of objecthood, or "synthetic personhood," and augments Chow's earlier remarks about watching oneself with an observation of enjoyment: "Watching the object allows us to enjoy the fantasy of being objects."²⁹ In other words, the ways in which Asiatic femininity slides into objectness, what Cheng refers to as "ornamentalism," can enable pleasures found outside of exclusionary, violent, and colonial conceptions of the human. I examine this possibility in chapter 2, when Maggie Cheung plays "herself" (the Hong Kong film star) and becomes latex in the French film *Irma Vep* (Olivier Assayas, 1996). Through her elastic, superficial accommodations of French erotic desire, Cheung remains cryptic and unknowable, a preservational racial condition I conceptualize as "salty-cool." Cheung demonstrates through performances of racial deference and gentility how disavowals of subjectivity allow the Chinese femme to deflect acts of racism by retreating into object seductions.

Because of the complexities of the signifier "Chinese" and its multivalent meanings in relation to geopolitical territories, languages, and cultures ("Chinese" can refer to people who live in Hong Kong, Macau, Taiwan, Malaysia, and Singapore, in addition to Chinese diasporic and mixed-race individuals in other parts of the world), "acting Chinese" recedes further into an abstract fantasy of being (Chinese*ness*), rather than fulfilling an indexical function. A Hong Kong or Taiwanese actor may act Chinese in a way that differs meaningfully from a Chinese mainlander, in deliberate and unintended ways. For example, the duplicitous performances of Chineseness by Taiwanese stars Shu Qi and Vivian Hsu sunder the monolithic mythology of One China in cross-strait romance films directed by mainland male directors, even as the myth of the unified Chinese state looms over such texts, threatening to eclipse such performances as the real star of the show. As we see in chapter 4, Hsu's embodiment of aboriginal Taiwanese beauty and her performances of cute aggression soften and defer the question of hard-line Chinese politics while Shu's minor acts of hesitation betray a Taiwanese refusal to unify with China. Such acts of refusal and waiting reveal the multidimensionality of performing Chineseness, not only appealing to diverse taste cultures, but also in revealing screen performance as deferral and postponement. Screen acting, because it is recorded well before it is seen by audiences, is always conceptually elsewhere and later and simultaneously here and now, a kind of quantum entanglement. Acting Chinese in particular discloses this always-already mode of simultaneity *and* displacement and delay (a spooky action at a distance)—for other places and times—as its phenomenal fantasy resides in the ticklish elisions of subjectivity.

Beauty and the Vulgar: Moving Images and Shocks

Acting Chinese is a deixis both in the sense that Chineseness points to multivalent geopolitical, cultural, and linguistic contexts, and insofar as screen acting points to action that has occurred elsewhere and earlier. Nevertheless, acting Chinese also affectively hails its subjects into feeling Chinese; as the Chinese femme film performer slides into objectness, the Chinese-identifying spectator drifts into a shared kinship with the performer, affectively sparked. So, to return to affect, what role does beauty play in this interpellation of the feeling of one's own "vitality" and "aliveness"? We are always caught off guard by beauty, its breathtaking effect perforating our mundane rhythms. In this way, beauty throws us into small crisis, and the ways in which it startles us into being are crucial for subject formation. For Cheng, beauty "as a phenomenon calls into being in the viewer an instantaneous, complex process of identification, disidentification, projection, and rejection." It is a project of self-making, as there "can be no untouched, discrete 'self' contemplating a beauty without; the experience of beauty has always already called that 'self' into profound relation with beauty."[30] However, where Cheng in particular addresses the woman of color who is interpellated into selfhood through beauty, Elaine Scarry, via Iris Murdoch, describes a universal beholder of beauty who does not return to the self but who indeed "unselfs" and who is decentered in an encounter with beauty.[31] Furthermore, based upon an analogy between beauty's formal symmetry and distributive justice or equality, Scarry argues that because we strive to reproduce beauty, we also seek to redress the imbalance of inequality and unfairness, which movement toward justice she describes as a weight or lever. Scarry writes, "In the absence of its counterpart, one term of an analogy actively calls out for its missing fellow; it presses on us to bring its counterpart into existence, acts as a lever in the direction of justice."[32] Because justice and equality are challenged in several of the historical backdrops explored throughout *Vulgar Beauty*, which begins in reform-era China and moves concentrically forward in time and outwardly to present-day western multicultural spaces, the types of beauty with which this project is concerned arouse, agitate, destabilize, and even offend their spectators—even as they unself the viewer and call out for justice. As I demonstrate, to feel Chinese involves an unselfing in our encounter with the star, which in turn facilitates a sense of self that recognizes a communal identity within what I call the *global sensorium*, a sensorial and sensuous participation in events and communities that may include but also exceed frameworks of nationality.

Although one can argue that many of the stars addressed here embody normative and ideal beauty conventions (in terms of both Chinese beauty traditions and western racial exotica), I am not interested in cataloging beauty features, but rather in asking how beauty gesticulates. That is, I am not concerned with taxonomies of physical beauty that have become *sensus communis* or, if you will, *sensus vulgaris*. Rather, I am interested in rethinking the apparent superficiality of beauty to reframe it through its gestural expression and its capacity to move in and through particular spaces. I am interested in face and body work in terms of its affective labors, and what Elena del Río refers to as the "elusive force of [a] body" that "thinks without thinking."[33] By analyzing beauty as kinesthesia, we approach beauty as fluid and unstable motion, rather than as a static object or as a still image.

Enter the moving image.

Only by recognizing the conjunctions and alignments between the shocks of feminine beauty and the shocks of cinema as an affective medium can we attend to the phenomenologically remarkable qualities in the mediated consumption of women film stars. Indeed, the spectacular appeal of the early "cinema of attractions" provoked a series of visual shocks, which in turn prompted uncanny, anxious, and agitating sensations.[34] Vivian Sobchack elaborates upon the astonishment at the new technological ability to showcase movement, noting that the spectator's gasps "at this sudden 'presencing' are not only respirational, but also inspirational—an intake of existential *breath* and an intake of existential *breadth*."[35] With regard to feminine beauty, the screen inflates, amplifies, and mythologizes human beauty by light and scalar augmentation. Photographed in ephemeral light, women's beauty becomes mythical, spatial, and virtual.[36]

Cinema's spectacularization of feminine beauty not only animates these crises of identification, but through agitation it also beautifies the spectator's desiring look. The beholder of beauty, in their surrender to the beauty image, merges with the spectacle and becomes with the beautiful. Film beauty is a grand matter; it is breath*taking* and brea(d)th-*giving*. Think about the way the eyes dilate, the face softens, and blood flows when we see someone we like. Our features round, our body yields to the other. Nevertheless, beauty, similar to technological modernities like the cinema, flirts with disaster and produces fundamental ambivalence in its beholders. As we will see, every star bursts onto the screen and scene promising unexpected fleshed ecstasy and, like early cinema itself, produces a shocking new flavor.

The Bland and the Flavorful

I would shake out the most beautiful cotton candy, and it
wouldn't be white, either. It would be a color I couldn't even
imagine.... And the flavor certainly would not be a sugary taste,
but would be a sweetness that had never existed before. It
would be better... No, I couldn't imagine what it would
be better than.
—Can Xue, "Cotton Candy"

In contrast with the Cartesian mind-body split, Chinese somatic knowledge proceeds from ancient, cosmological mind-body holism. This concept of the mind-body has inflected various body cultures and aesthetic understandings, from mundane practices of eating and sexuality to the spectacular experiences of art, beauty, and film.[37] Whereas western medicine privileges etiology, anatomy, and scientific diagnosis, Chinese medicine centers on the sensual experiences of the lived body. Through analyses of the correlations between consumable herbs and wellness, Judith Farquhar characterizes the body as understood by Chinese medicine as a "flavorful temporal formation."[38] That is, the herbal, organic flavors of Chinese medicine and medicinal meals correspond with physiological-biological changes in the body, as "flavors not only generate a fleeting aesthetic response" but also "produce bodily changes that generate experience at a more lasting level."[39] Rather than examining the aesthetic responses embedded in flavor, *Vulgar Beauty* conceptualizes flavors of aesthetic encounter with mediated bodies. Inspired by the five Chinese medicinal flavors (bitter, salty, pungent, sweet, and sour) and their bodily manifestations, I develop an original framework that draws upon the concept of flavor as a capacious material substance that traverses literal and metaphorical significations. In other words, in turning to flavor as a way to understand beauty, I theorize beauty as something of the other that is tasted, consumed, and digested in order to arrive at the extra/sensorial dimensions of aesthetic difference, and to examine the matter of beauty—its vulgarity.

Before turning to the distinction, irregularity, and shock of flavorful beauty, we should first address the prominent role of the bland in Chinese aesthetic tradition. The aesthetics of the bland predate and foreshadow Baudrillardian seduction wherein the intended outcome is not termination qua acquisition, but rather to indefinitely extend its activity, its *conatus*. François Jullien tracks the concept of "blandness" as the highest aesthetic ideal in Chinese aesthetic philosophy throughout Confucianism, Daoism, and Buddhism, describing the ways in which *dan* (blandness) does not seek to seduce through sensuality but rather to intimate an inexhaustible potentiality in infinitude. In contrast to the bland, "[individual] flavors disappoint even as they attract" since they persuade the "passerby merely to 'stop,' [and] lure without fulfilling their promise."[40] Flavor here is a metaphor for a broad aesthetic or style. The bland, meanwhile, by combining all the flavors, represents the ways in which "the strongest presence is conveyed in the greatest reserve"; that is, by encompassing all flavors, it lacks any distinct flavor. It suggests plenitude as it recedes.[41] The neutrality of blandness gestures to the infinite possibilities not outwardly expressed; thus, one of the highest manifestations of the bland aesthetic exists in the fading sound of a musical note, whereby a lingering tone rejoins an anterior, undifferentiated cosmology at the boundary between emergence and loss. In one example, Jullien offers Tang poet Li Bo's verse about a singing and dancing woman who is wrapped in "filmy robes of gauze," a feminine beauty perceived in material and aural assemblage: "A light breeze carries the songs into emptiness: / The melody entwines itself with the passing clouds and flies off."[42] The woman's beauty, conveyed through movement, song, and breeze, transmutes into atmosphere and ephemerality before ascending toward loss, a kind of bland potentiality. Similarly, in Can Xue's surreal short story "Cotton Candy," a child becomes obsessed with an old cotton candy vendor after she discovers that she cannot taste the candy. Its blandness provokes in her a deep desire to supplant the vendor, whose "breath and body both smelled sour," and whose words, if not the candy, the narrator is able to taste. Never tasting the sweetness of the candy, the narrator experiences an unrelinquishable pining toward this object, spurring her to imagine "a sweetness that had never existed before."[43] Since this thought is immediately followed by a rumination that she "couldn't imagine what it would be better than," Can Xue observes that the narrator's pleasure is located in the attempt to imagine the unimaginable. This analogously recalls the elusive process of "watching oneself—as a film, as a spectacle, as something always already watched," another pleasurable walk up to the thresholds of the thinkable.

The bland therefore delivers us to a contemplative practice that removes us from reality. The metaphysical properties of the bland prompt reflections of a transcendental infinitude, while individual flavors satiate and stop the imaginative process. Whereas blandness is Oneness and inclusion of all (what western philosophers refer to as immanence), flavor excludes by privileging one quality as distinctly exceptional. Jullien, interchangeably referring to quality and flavor, also describes physiognomy as flavor incarnating through the physical body: "All inner qualities [or flavors] possess their unique signs through which they recognizably manifest themselves in the world: through comportment, attitude, countenance, and even the more general aspect of the face, voice, or the expression conveyed in a look."[44] Jullien equates quality with flavor because both belong to terrestrial, earthly matters. Moreover, Jullien regards beauty as flavor, rather than as blandness, and suggests that beauty constitutes a terminal point. For Jullien, beauty does not reach into lingering realms of invisibility; it does not recede. Rather, "beauty 'dumbfounds,' 'terrifies,' grasps and ravishes in an instant, but it does not give rise to the sense of savor which 'flattens and fades' and so leads through a continuous process, to the 'flavour beyond flavour' (*wei wai wei*); or to the 'vague' or the 'thin' (here and there dispersed) that leads to the 'landscape beyond the landscape' (*jing wai jing*)."[45] In other words, beauty is for Jullien flavorful and terminal, its shock too instantaneous, short lasting, and unsustainable to hold great aesthetic value.

I take departure from Jullien by arguing that not only does beauty hold great aesthetic value, but that this value derives precisely from its instantaneous, short-lasting, and unsustainable terrestrial nature, or what I wish to characterize as its vulgarity. Jullien's interpretation of Chinese aesthetic theory falls short in its underestimation of the material aspects of beauty, even as it recognizes them. This can be seen in his consideration of Li Bo's poem, where Jullien conveys the notion that the aforementioned material and aural assemblage of feminine beauty generates an aperture into the lingering transcendental beyond of loss (flavor beyond flavor), before later stating that beauty is also a terminal point (full of flavor, but not a flavor beyond flavor). While this analysis contains delicate nuances and clashes between the flavorful, the full of flavor, and the flavor beyond flavor, it also betrays Chinese aesthetic theory's ambivalence toward feminine beauty, the embodied nature of which it professes to acknowledge, even as it denies it. It is the underestimation of the embodied nature of female beauty that I wish to rethink and rehabilitate. For if, in relation to passion and charisma, feminine beauty has a long-standing history of being both celebrated and disparaged not only in Chinese aesthetic theory but also in western philosophy, embodied female beauty (and embodied beauty in general) nonetheless possesses a material power that enlivens, and which materiality we have already defined as vulgar. As earlier discussed, the vulgar "lacks good taste; [is] uncultured, ill-bred." However, it also provides beauty with new forces with which to dilate and distend nonvisual realms of sense and feeling. Indeed, we will stay with the terrifying and ravishing moment of beauty in order to make sense of its vulgar flavors and their worldly, terrestrial consequences.

In this way, it is timely to recuperate and rethink the "vulgar"—a word that appears repeatedly throughout aesthetic theory and philosophy to tacitly denote the undesirable, unwanted, common, and bad—not least to sunder the canonical criteria of beauty itself, which are exploited to debase and exclude nonwhite, nonwestern, lower- and working-class, and (dis)abled bodies. As Asian American historians observe, the Chinese body has long been associated with vulgarity in western societies.[46] From distorted stories and images of depraved Chinese bachelors, infected Chinese prostitutes, and the dirty opium dens of Chinatown through to twenty-first-century concerns over hordes of Chinese immigrants and the pandemic-causing, virally loaded Chinese body, the Chinese person is persistently associated with that which is "uncultured, ill-bred": amorality, disease, contamination, contagion, and pollution. On the other end of racial hygienics, the Chinese are also associated with techno-orientalist tropes, or what Stephen Hong Sohn refers to as the threatening "Alien/Asian" or the unfeeling, hyperadvanced, and disembodied cyborgs who remain perpetual alien others in the west.[47] The Chinese body therefore has often been characterized as abject within western culture.[48] Thus if vulgarity stains and makes ugly the Chinese within ethnonationalist constructions, then we must also bring it forward in our orbital movement around the (extra)terrestrially beautiful.

Methodologically, vulgarity also aligns us with new ways of knowing beyond dominant, masterful epistemologies. Academic connotations of "going low," introduced through Eve Kosofsky Sedgwick's influential notion of "weak" or "reparative" theory, offer a methodological alternative to paranoid, phobic, and suspicious hermeneutics that favor negative affects. Sedgwick recognizes the possibilities of vulgarity in reparative theory when she refers to camp as a "variety of reparative practices" and, in particular, "the 'over'-attachment to fragmentary, marginal, waste, or leftover products."[49] My turn to the pleasurable overattachments to waste, for example, resides in a kind of sour ressentiment whereby the racial subject overperforms narcissistic self-love through loving her bodily waste (her vaginal secretions, her shit), in order to rescue her body from social disavowal—as we will see with vulgar comedian Ali Wong in chapter 5. Such evocative waste, rendered into abject comedy, creates pleasures for in-spiring existential breath and breadth, abiding by comic rhythms and delivering punchlines in order to create communal in/exhalations of laughter.

To persist with waste, G. W. F. Hegel writes that "we only smell what's wasting away, tasting by destroying."[50] In other words, taste succumbs to time, and vulgar flavor in particular marks putrefaction, rot, and disappearance. Vulgarity thus marks a particular passage of time. Returning to Farquhar's notion of the Chinese medical body as a "flavorful temporal formation," vulgarity marks the embodiment of time's decay, its movement toward death, and the destructiveness of life. In terms of this project, it is vital to rescue a vulgar beauty that demands a different taste *palate* and *palette*, as taste and vision are synesthetically conjoined in film spectatorship. Racialized bitterness, envy, pain, and anger can vivify new aesthetics into being, even as they act (femme) fatally and destructively. Moreover, such animated feelings threaten the aesthetic order in the west, where I suggest that the attention economy primarily favors, in a perverse and unauthorized appropriation of Jullien, bland (white) mainstream beauty, which is neither irregular nor shocking in its overwhelming and constant ubiquity.

If vulgar beauty lies primarily at the margins of mainstream attention, it nevertheless does make vulgar grabs for it, as demonstrated through numerous examples in this book. We could also equate these vulgar grabs for recognition to the constitutively evicted abject who must nevertheless assert the desirability of the interior, particularly in racial terms and particularly as it is cast in outsider and/or criminal roles. Our turn to racial abjection recalls Chow's reading of ethnic abjection, in which narcissism becomes a "transindividual issue of attachment and belonging" when marginalized groups like Asian Americans are prohibited from loving their Asian Americanness, precisely because their ethnicity is associated with the pathological.[51] It is an emergent paradox then that vulgar beauty must steal attention, a criminal act that serves to undermine the abject status of the Asian/American. As vulgar beauty is a property stolen, we explore its connections with lawlessness and the underworld in chapters 2 and 3, where respectively I discuss Joan Chen's illicit Cold War plots in David Lynch and Mark Frost's television series *Twin Peaks* (ABC, 1990–91), and Bai Ling's role as an incestuous femme fatale in Alex Proyas's neo-noir film *The Crow* (1994). In these examples, the powers of such beauty yield to corrosive but generative aesthetics. The crisis provoked by vulgarity is that it comes from the wound that is minoritarian suffering, but it also has the ability to wound, its disturbing effects reminding us that difference is often coded as undesirable and indigestible.

Tasting Beauty Flavors

When explaining his decision to cast Gong Li in his debut film, *Hong gao liang* (*Red Sorghum*, 1987), Fifth Generation Chinese director Zhang Yimou stated that she was chosen because of her evocative weidao.[52] A common polysemous phrase, "weidao" (味道) bears two primary, everyday usages. First, the English word closest to weidao is "flavor," commonly used to refer to the scent, smell, or taste of food and drink. Second, it also refers to the style or presentation of a person, object, or environment. There is no English equivalent to this secondary usage, although "flavor" comes closest with its multiple significations across discourses of gustation, olfaction, and aesthetics. Eluding a concrete or fixed definition, weidao denotes a fluid, contextual, and subjective process. As a phrase, weidao gestures to internal processes of imagination, judgment, and taste, as one assimilates objects through empirical encounter. Weidao is composed of the words *wei* (taste, smell, odor, delicacy) and *dao* (path, road, street, method, way), a combination of words that implicitly suggests a methodology through what Cartesian epistemologies characterize as lower, vulgar senses in contrast to the higher senses of vision and hearing.[53] According to Kantian tradition, while the distal eyes and ears perceive beauty, other sensory organs can only perceive pleasant, agreeable, or enjoyable sensations, and therefore cannot access the moral or virtuous modes of contemplation associated with beauty. As Carolyn Korsmeyer observes, taste in the western tradition "perceives neither objects of beauty nor works of art."[54] However, Chinese epistemologies follow another genealogical account of sense making whereby tasting and eating provide foundational understandings of beauty.

Chinese etymological conceptions of beauty, 美 (consisting of the words "ram" and "large" in vertical formation) are tethered to notions of food and eating (the ram is large and is therefore tasty/beautiful) and reinforce taste as a mode of perceiving beauty.[55] Li Zehou points out that, similar to the German *geschmack* and the English word "taste," the Chinese etymology of "beauty" indicates that "early experiences of beauty, whether based upon practical utility or moral goodness, were inseparable from the sensory pleasure associated with taste, sound, and color."[56] In contrast with the Kantian regard of pleasure as degraded, uncontemplative comfort, weidao as sensory pleasure was directly connected to beauty as a moral education. Such notions of eating beauty extend as well to notions of gender and sexuality, as contemporary Chinese vernacular attaches metaphors of taste to desirable bodies. For example, young women are "tender" (*nennü*), while older women are "ripe" (*shunü*); young effeminate male stars are "little fresh meat" (*xiao xianrou*), and an erotic desire for the strange and unconventional is referred to as a "strong appetite" (*zhong kouwei*). Beauty and sexuality are thus sensed holistically through the tongue, nostrils, and stomach.[57]

Nondistal senses, including taste, reveal intimacies that radically break down the distinction between subject and object. Nicola Perullo, linking film and taste in his analysis of food, identifies how, for Gilles Deleuze, cinema provides a "vivid and direct relationship with objects" before then suggesting that "this is even truer with taste, where there is a tight and very personal relationship between subject and object, a bond where the object is consumed in the body in order to sustain or transform the subject."[58] Not only does tasting thus succor and alter the subject by incorporation of the food object, but, Perullo also notes, "I can derive enjoyment from being in a beautiful and hence satisfactory situation (for example, I am in the company of the person I am in love with) in such a way that the taste of the sandwich is completely charged with my amorous energy."[59] If, for Perullo, love is an example of beauty, I wish to reverse his argument and suggest that beauty evokes love, and that this has a material basis, permeating atmospherically and transforming taste. Thinking in associative reciprocity, taste also transmutes into beauty affects.

If beauty is a *feeling* of taste, how do we ground our critical inquiry in the tangible and observable? To put the problem differently, if one of the objections to the study of beauty is that it is all a matter of subjective taste, then perhaps an inquiry into taste and its affective-aesthetic implications is in order. Eating with a loved one may infuse food with "amorous energy"; however, insofar as love feelings are complex, colorful, and manifold, an analysis of love's affects requires closer, thicker description in order to avoid reproducing what Eugenie Brinkema, in criticizing affect studies, describes as "the same model of vague shuddering intensity."[60] Thinking beyond the shudder requires us to draw upon epistemological traditions of embodiment and aesthetics outside of continental philosophy, necessitating inquiry into what Jullien refers to as the "unthought" of European philosophy and reason's prejudices by facilitating intracultural epistemological rendezvous.[61] Such promiscuous cross-cultural encounters can generate new lines of flight in cultural studies. Weidao as an embodied, sensed quality offers new and vital understandings of our consumption of on-screen bodies, the sustenance of star cultures, and the ways in which social tastes, habits, and politics wrap around public figures in performative, affective, and sensational ways. As a charismatic and excessive modality, flavor/weidao minimizes the distance between subject and object while maintaining the alterity of "difference." If, as Jullien states, flavors "lure without fulfilling their promise," weidao can be said to be a form of embodied allure.[62]

Using the cosmological aspects of Chinese elemental thinking, not as objects of historical or anthropological concern but rather as a methodological/theoretical frame for analysis, we can differentially and meaningfully apprehend aesthetics and embodiment through epistemologies relevant to the formations of China (and Asia by proxy and influence).[63] We could, for instance, apply as a classificatory system the related traditional cosmology of Wuxing (Five Elements or Five Phases), which is based upon the notion that the world is composed of water, wood, fire, earth, and metal, positing that the manifold manifestations of these elements reveal the cyclical and interactional correspondences between cosmic movement, elements, odors, tastes, colors, tones, seasons, and directions. Within the realm of traditional Chinese medicine, elemental thinking identifies linkages between the body's inner processes and changes in the material world. The boundary between interior and exterior is pervious and even illusory. For example, a bitter taste in the mouth denotes a disturbance of the element wood in one's body, which is internally related to nerves and locomotion, and externally related to the season of spring, the direction of east, and the period of dawn. Such connections account for the development of forms, systems, and events as interconnected aspects of a holographic paradigm, whereby each part reflects the whole, and all movements or phases are part of a continual cosmic unfolding. In a similar vein, *Vulgar Beauty* reveals how flavor affective-aesthetics, in addition to their embodied, performative expressions, are laterally related to properties like viscosity, dosage, temperature, texture, duration, atmosphere, and rhythm. In other words, *Vulgar Beauty* provides us with a *cosmoaesthetics* that draws together qualia and objects in order to analyze the entangled assemblages of the beauty experience. A principle of classical Daoist thought is that the world is harmonious and unified in totalizing ways; elements are both material and semiotic, taken as both literal and expansively interpretative and abstract. Taking a cue from this exegetic model, this book finds generative the critical slide between different analytical registers when discussing flavor/weidao, and it is precisely that the semiological and metaphorical are coproduced alongside the literal and material that we pursue such shifts. As such, this book is itself an assemblage of texts and palimpsests that foreground the unstable and volatile interconnectedness between language and matter, and between objects and events.

Indeed, this book's methodology pursues a logic of deconstruction insofar as it assembles an eclectic array of unstable terms and concepts, in order to reveal the collisions within, erasure of, and transformative becoming of language and their effects on the minoritarian subject. By so doing, we unsettle the universalist and static grounds upon which western philosophy approaches Being and, by extension, matters of identity. Rather than rehearsing Jacques Derrida or Judith Butler here, however, I wish to draw upon nonwestern theorizations of deconstruction. Arguing that Chinese philosophy was always already deconstructionist, Byung-Chul Han describes

Chinese thought as that which "does not trace essence or origin, but rather the changeable constellations of things (pragmata)."[64] Han thus traces the notion of *quan* (the weight on a sliding-weight scale) across various Chinese terms, including human rights (*renquan*), tactical course of action (*quan yi zhi ji*), and power (*quan li*) in order to demonstrate how Chinese thought believes that "power belongs not to subjectivity but to situativity."[65] That is, one's position ought always to remain mutable in order to achieve (counter) balance, like the sliding weight on a scale. Applying this approach to theory, one eschews dogmatic or faithful reproductions of philosophical masters and opts for sliding, even messy, interactions between philosophical, vernacular, casual, and cosmological concepts—"*gravitation* is replaced by *situation*."[66] For this project, I wish to emphasize Chineseness itself as a kind of quan that is processual and multiple, precisely to distinguish it from how it has historically been and is continually enframed within racist, colonialist western discourse. As such, the present study creates and pursues a theoretical engagement with stars and texts that models the ways in which, as I will argue, such texts persistently wrestle and negotiate with Eurocentric and American systems of language and knowledge through play, subversion, or conformity. Simply put, there is no existing framework within western thought and philosophy with which to approach Chinese beauty without a kind of recommitment to the very mechanisms of subject-object binarisms that subjugate the Chinese woman. Therefore, a new kind of (nonwesternized) deconstructive theory around identity grapples with the textures of linguistic indeterminacy as well as attending to ontoethical concerns within different cosmological orders.

By pursuing a kind of Chinese deconstruction such as Han describes, one perhaps more aptly called "decreation," one rejects notions of originality, authenticity, and inviolable truth, and can thus generate transformative thought. Indeed, Han points to the gazelessness, fakery (*shanzhai*), and destructiveness of Chinese aesthetics. Following Han, the deconstructive work of this book is to offer a model of sliding critiques to reveal the processual projects of intertextual and intersubjective viewing and reading, which are themselves acts of drifting, tracing, and echoing inside the fullness of erasure, emptiness, and darkness. In this way, I hope that the reader will enjoy the slippery, even if occasionally turbulent, ride through various analytical registers from the material to the metaphorical, and from the philosophical to the vernacular and cosmological. Indeed, it is via the messy velocities of intertextual encounter that the reader (and spectator) makes sense of palimpsestic acts of interpretation and becoming. As this book reveals, the sensorium ecstatically "interrupts," to borrow Christina A. León's term for minoritarian deconstruction, the Platonic grounds upon which epistemology asserts universality and static objects of study.[67]

To reiterate, I am not suggesting that we directly, uncritically apply Chinese elemental or cosmological claims to film analysis. Nor is this project interested in recuperating what Michel Foucault terms a "subjugated knowledge" as a better or truer episteme to, and against, the powerful currents of western skepticism, strong theory, and scientific epistemologies.[68] Nor do I intend to essentialize or authenticate Chineseness. Furthermore, the historicization of cosmological knowledges within Chinese society and civilization also lies outside the scope of this project. Nevertheless, *Vulgar Beauty* finds generative the methodological impulse within Chinese cosmology and Traditional Chinese Medicine (TCM) that seeks to explain correspondences between subjects, objects, and phenomena.[69] A cosmological approach is attuned to the conditions of possibility whereby such belief systems constitute a common sense that shapes the structural ways in which Chinese audiences encounter visual culture—especially considering the ubiquity of TCM clinics, herbal pharmacies, and vernacular folk knowledge in urban and rural Chinese and Chinese diasporic communities.

An understanding of beauty wherein the recuperation of vulgarity and the lower sensorium emerge as privileged domains of knowing, thereby shifting the register of beauty away from the visual and toward the sensual, is also crucial in decentering and decolonizing western thought. As such, I pursue a reparative theory of tasting beauty that reveals the ways in which mediated Chinese bodies produce new sensational and affective spectatorial positions, as understood through what I term "abject epistemologies," which, unless they happen specifically to be the object of study, are often ejected from hegemonic western knowledges via paranoid hermeneutics. Through the medium of weidao, this book offers a model through which we bypass ocular-centric post/colonialist subject-object relations and power dynamics by highlighting the ways in which taste, scent, and flavor draw bodies into coiled entanglements.

Indeed, our comprehension of the holistic, synesthetic responses within the spectatorial process is deepened by understanding olfactory and gustatory imaginations. Just as 1960s cinephiles described themselves as being "bitten by the cinema," spectators also bite back at the screen, attempting to synesthetically taste what they see.[70] In unintended agreement with traditional Chinese epistemologies, film philosophers like Vivian

Sobchack, Laura U. Marks, Elena del Río, and Jennifer M. Barker demonstrate in their phenomenological inquiries that cross-sensory synesthesia and haptic visuality define the carnal experiences of film spectatorship—that is, we touch, taste, and smell in addition to seeing and hearing a film, imaginatively consuming cinema with all our senses.[71] Cinematic bodies are archives of flavor-feeling through which global Chinese audiences become cathected to mediating beauty acts and interpellated into the affective labors of identity. As a diasporic Chinese/Asian/American woman wherein I am the visitor to and beholder of screen beauty, I feel the fibrous pull of these images of femininity, the soft tug of racial, ethnic, and gendered recognition, and the beckoning magnetism of their seductive charisma.

We desire to be embraced by beauty, that is, to be held by its splints, the invisible phenomenal structures that spark and then ascend our attention toward it. As with cinema, much has also been written about beauty's powerful ability to capture and to captivate. When people speak of an actor's presence, they refer to a magnetic attunement to her affective energies, which offers the possibility of unseating us from our own preoccupations, anxieties, and neuroses. Beauty's seductive powers are inexhaustible, if we are to understand, after Baudrillard, that seduction is not accumulative or additive, but rather "removes something from the order of the visible."[72] Therefore, one cannot gorge or overdose on beauty, as it always withdraws from view, as was suggested earlier when we discussed Jullien's notion of the bland that recedes (and which I conversely apply to flavorful beauty). To borrow from Graham Harman, beauty is a withdrawn object that nevertheless possesses a "cloud of gaseous qualities that *are* present."[73] Therefore one cannot become sick from exposure to too much beauty. Nevertheless, beauty has been abandoned by many cultural theorists because it bears a stain, carrying patriarchal consumer capital's residues as a signifying catchall too global to mean anything. Even as we are reluctant to identify it, beauty is still perceived as a suspect object, a dubious property that harms and injures by reproducing embodied inequalities.[74] However, attempts to destroy or deconstruct beauty ideals fail to recognize the accretive force of beauty's circulation in visual realms; a more salient political project of unthinking and deterritorializing conventional beauty involves a committed attunement to beauty in Other forms, including in its vulgar (and grotesque and indecent) expressions. Embedded in representations of feminine beauty is always already a charge, an accusation of inequity, exclusion, oppression, and illusion—a lack on the precipice of exposure, a humiliation lurking around the corner. Yet, in understanding beauty as the corruption of a stable system of meaning making, we are reminded of Theodor W. Adorno's words that "every work of art is an uncommitted crime," possessing the capacity to violate convention and law.[75] Just as vulgar Chinese beauty is associated with the criminal underworld, it also contravenes the boundaries of common sense, delivers enlivening shocks to the body, and edges toward the thresholds of the visible and of thought. Therefore, while the risks of beauty are well documented, we ought also to consider the spellbinding rewards of beauty's transgressions, its corrupting and criminal aspirations—even if its crimes are uncommitted.

Beauty is not a finite resource, nor is it a zero-sum contest; one person's beauty does not deprive another's possession of the coveted property. Therefore, this book is not concerned with the trouble that beauty has caused (although when we discuss the western objectification of Asian bodies, this too becomes an unavoidable subject); rather, this project makes the argument that we have not troubled beauty enough—that is to say, in taking beauty now not as sensus communis but as sensus vulgaris, we take it for granted as something that does not require critical interrogation. The fault lies not with beauty but rather with our inability to recognize or admit it beyond conventional, categorical, and (white) western definitions. Relatedly, a focus on beauty's oppressive power can overlook the ways in which its beholders enjoy, desire, and take pleasure in their capitulation to beauty, a point repeated in psychoanalytic observations that the gaze does not seek to master or overpower its object, an idea that in turn is echoed in Deleuzian feminist arguments regarding the pleasures of submission, as examined further in chapters 2 and 3. Massumi reminds us that "force is not to be confused with power. Force arrives from outside to break constraints and open new vistas. Power builds walls."[76] By distinguishing force from power, Massumi suggests an alternative to strong theory and pessimistic accounts of power, punishment, and control. Although Foucauldian approaches and texts critiquing beauty's powerful inequities are crucially valuable, even paranoiacally incontrovertible, this project invests in different sets of questions. How do we make cultural sense of the forces of beauty? How does feminine beauty navigate space by modeling hospitality? What forms of mutual sociality are enabled between beauty's possessors and beholders? How does beauty service and subvert politico-ideological projects like tolerance, multiculturalism, neocolonialism, and work? How does screen beauty generate a space of becoming between formations of desire and love? How does beauty as affect shape our engagements with gender, race, sexuality, and nationality? Situating these questions within the global sensorium requires flexile geopolitics, productive con-fusions of local and global, and an undogmatic pursuit of sense making through the unruliness of touch, smell, and taste.

Hungry Passions and Charismatic Presence

Although many can attest to the ways in which the sight of beauty arouses passion, Kant insists that we must be wholly indifferent and disinterested in order to make a judgment about beauty, which he believes to be an absolute and unchanging Platonic object.[77] In less austere accounts, beauty is taken as a capricious and undeserved accident, and we are reluctant to raise it to the status of event, or that which shocks us such that common sense is shattered. However, even if there is no apparent logic to explain beauty's seeming uneven, unequal dispersals across bodies, it does not mean that beauty is a-signifying or meaningless. Indeed, beauty understood as sensus vulgaris not only shatters common sense/sensus communis, but it also reorients the sensorium such that the lower senses (taste, smell, touch) shift to dominance, and through their proximal dissolutions of subject and object, insist upon embodied interest and intimacy. Beauty is a relational affect, a force that we can relate to charisma, which enacts impassioned desire.

Indeed, for Nietzsche, charisma provides the means by which one seeks to "drag victim[s] down with the weight" of the stupidity of one's passions; it is explosive material and energetic form through which its possessor exerts his or her desire upon others. Exalting the *Übermensch*, Nietzsche writes, "Great men, like great epochs, are explosive material in whom tremendous energy has been accumulated."[78] History is therefore dictated by the strength of a few individuals' desires, the most felt, the most legibly expressed of the human (read white, European, male) group. Thus, as Charles Lindholm explains, "the claim made by Nietzsche is simply that if desire is all that exists, then let desire be gargantuan, and may the more powerfully passionate devour the world to fill their insatiable appetites."[79] While this vison of charismatic desire is not so much prescriptive (how does one inflate one's desire?) as a subjunctive extolment of ruthless wish, the important point to appreciate here is that desire plays a significant role in our understanding of charisma (the more a person wants, the bigger his or her charismatic expression). However, while desire is entangled with charisma, the latter is always circumscribed by expectations of gender and race, as Lindholm admits when he confesses that "the study of charismatic women is a task [he has] not been able to undertake," restricting his study of destructive charisma to three white males (Adolf Hitler, Charles Manson, and Jim Jones).[80] Indeed, if women are relegated largely to being the elusive object of pursuit and are discouraged from exerting their desire and want upon others, how do we make sense of feminine charisma? In particular, as we think of the ways in which women film stars generate on-screen charisma as an active, persistent, and grand force, then cinematic stardom and projection reveal scalar enhancement of charisma, and hence a monstrous appetite. Moreover, what of racialized charisma, whose materiality arguably incarnates through formal and aesthetic difference?

In contrast with Nietzsche's appetitive passion, Amber Jamilla Musser uses "hunger" to explain how insatiable appetite becomes part of the ongoing projects of racialized self-making, describing brown jouissance as a "fleshy mixture of self-production, insatiability, joy, and pain."[81] As beauty is one such hungry project of self-making, one always seeks to put oneself in its path. If, as contemporary internet slang suggests, we "hunger" or "thirst" for selfhood and attention from others, then perhaps we might also become expansive in our taste for different flavors. Because it does not "go down smoothly," racial beauty possesses a compulsive animacy and an energetic weight that beckons its beholder into volatile interaction. In contrast to the stupid drag of Nietzsche's passion, can racial beauty thus stand as an ethical, com-passionate counterweight or, to recall Scarry and Han, a lever with which to balance (quan) appetites for white beauty?

In the following chapters, then, unconventional vulgar beauty compels our hungry passions not only through haptic vision, but also through taste, scent, and voice. If bodily beauty is immanent, or folded into a singular plane of existence, then we can mobilize new materialist frameworks to further comprehend its ontological status in the world. Such a task prompts theorizations of beauty that reckon with emerging conceptualizations of (post)humanist ontologies and matter. Appositely, Mel Y. Chen has, among others, drawn attention to the ways in which we situate objects, things, animals, and people within biopolitical animacy scales.[82] For Chen, animacy is itself "a specific kind of affective and material construct that is not only non-neutral in relation to animals, humans, and living and dead things, but is shaped by race and sexuality."[83] Beauty occupies a contradictory position on animacy scales because it is often perceived as a passive and inert object, even as it animates its beholder (as mentioned, hearts palpitate, eyes dilate and enlarge, while eccrine glands secrete). Nevertheless, if we regard beauty as a kind of Nietzschean energetic material, with the capacity to shock, explode, and generate a shattering event, or as an accident, unselfing, disaster, or a criminal transgression, then a critical engagement with beauty's matter must also grapple with the biopolitical implications of beauty's affective detonation in cultural spheres—particularly when one accounts for racialized beauty. Indeed, questions of beauty must also engage with the animacies of racialized embodiment. As Sianne Ngai observes, the Asian stereotype is one that is "silent, inexpressive, and, like Bartleby, emotionally inscrutable," while other racially and ethnically marked American subjects are characterized by what she calls "animatedness," or hyperemotional expressivity qua physical, bodily exaggeration.[84] Whereas the Black body produces "overscrutable" gestural surplus in American representation, the Asian body is stoically reserved, demonstrating an economy of movement wherein no gesticulation is without its overdetermined meaning, even as its meaning is nevertheless underscored as inscrutable. However, as Vivian L. Huang observes, "the judgment of something inscrutable alerts us to the dawning articulation of a new form."[85] Thus, the inscrutable is not *devoid* of meaning but rather pregnant with plenitude, bringing inscrutability into meaningful proximity with Baudrillard's seduction, Jullien's blandness, and what I am here describing as vulgar beauty.

Pursuant to the possibilities of inscrutability, we can attend to the fact that Asian/Americans have long been portrayed as underanimated and cunning in western cinemas, regurgitating Fu Manchu and Dragon Lady stereotypes since its advent. Let us peer, for example, at the moment when Anna May Wong, the first Chinese American star in Hollywood, appears onscreen as the vengefully murderous Princess Ling Moy, daughter of Fu Manchu, in one of her most memorable films, *Daughter of the Dragon* (Lloyd Corrigan, 1931). After the advertised "celebrated Oriental dancer" finishes one of her stage performances, Wong appears in an arched recess in a white wall, adorned in a heavy metallic silver dress and matching headpiece. An off-screen man, whose shadow appears on the wall adjacent to her, compliments her: "You are incomparable, superb!" In a medium shot, Wong slowly pivots her face, giving the camera a three-quarter profile, which has been readied with a coy smirk before her swivel. In contrast with Zhang Ziyi's slackened pose in *2046*, Wong's body is taut with tension and calculation. Her smile, lips tightened across her teeth, expends no surplus energy in communicating her delight in the man's praise, and her oversignified, minimally expressive body is frugal in its prohibition of kinesthetic waste. The slow velocity of her head turn indicates her hyperawareness that the headpiece she dons, a fanlike object with dangling silver chains, hyperbolizes her feminine gesture, inflates the detail, and visually exaggerates what Cheng refers to as an ornamental personhood.[86] Framed within an oval cutout, Wong's body is inscribed as a picture within a picture, a cinematic trompe l'oeil that signifies Ling Moy's suspicious character, as well as the racialized, decorative circumscriptions that accentuate her exotic appeal.

Such prudent economies of body language indicate the ways in which the Asian female body in western cinemas carefully negotiates public space through deanimated constraint, so that its vulgar excess is contained. Adorned in platinum, Wong is restrained into a pose of inscrutable charm, rather than expressing a hungry charisma. As forces that engage and manage attention, the intelligence of mundane charm resides in knowing when to recede. In performing inscrutability, or blandness, Wong demonstrates that "plenitude is all the greater for its refusal to show itself."[87] But while charm can be pleasing, calming, or even possessing a palliative effect, it lacks the insistent intensity of charisma.[88] Indeed, charisma is vulgar precisely because it insists rather than coerces, and, much like the example of sajiao that we discussed at the start of this introduction, it makes a forceful appeal, not least because it is particularly effeminized and childish in its mode of attention grabbing. Of course, the magnificent specimens of human beauty that we regard as stars possess both charm and charisma, the ability to impress and imprint themselves, pressing or whelming their presence upon the beholder. By this token, Wong is not without charisma. But whereas charm pulls pleasant, smiling feelings from its recipient, charisma elicits a multitude of affects and reactions, including negative and, after Ngai, "ugly feelings." Unlike charm, charismatic power also operates as a repellent, and understanding charisma as a form of vulgar beauty is one of the critical moves in this book, especially because we often fail to recognize it as such—a failure that is paradoxical, since the relentlessness of charisma insists upon the possessor's unremitting presence. All the same, this often unrecognized presence helps me to suggest that Asian feminine charisma, especially in western racial contexts, often takes circuitous, undetected, or indirect paths, generating furtive and unexpected affective and aesthetic engagements, as I indicate throughout *Vulgar Beauty*.

Giving Good Face

> The face resists possession, resists my powers.
> —Emmanuel Levinas, *Totality and Infinity*

While feminine charisma can take deviant or "ugly" forms, narrative films work hard to capitalize on the presence of the star actor. Screen beauty is analogous to the close-up and to the face itself, which Deleuze describes as the "affection-image," conveying power and quality through "the compound affect of desire and of astonishment—which gives it life—and the turning aside of faces in the open, in the flesh."[89] As Doane observes, "The face, more than any other bodily part, is for the other. It is the most articulate sector of the body, but it is mute without the other's reading."[90] However, the Chinese face, articulated through epidermal, muscular, and osteological difference in a white western context, contains another kind of legible muteness that requires a reading practice (via the circuitous, undetected, or indirect paths mentioned above) attendant to the shocks of its dissemblance from underexposure. The reading of a Chinese face in such a situation is always already a misreading because of the visual legacies of discrimination and stereotype. Therefore, encountering nonwhite faces prompts a persistent confrontation and negotiation with misrecognition.

In order to contend with such misrecognition, we could briefly consider other physiognomic hermeneutics, for instance the traditional Chinese practice of *mian xiang* (face reading)—even as its musings are typically relegated in the west to the degraded, abject epistemologies of "new age" thought. We do this not in order to systematically explain spirit through facial sign, but in order to better understand a Chinese cosmoaesthetics whereby physical human form incarnates earthly desire and becomes the means by which one becomes worldly as a terrestrial social being. Cheng, referencing Gottfried Semper, reminds us that the Greek *kosmos* meant both "decoration" and "world order," drawing together "cosmetics" and "cosmology." Therefore, "ornament aims to align itself with cosmic laws," for instance, remapping space along directional paths.[91] To propose a fantastic reconciliation of this understanding with Chinese face reading, beauty as a surface ornament materializes to attract people with whom the beauty bearer has karmic business. Beauty incarnates in flesh so that its possessor (and its affected viewer) can learn the lessons and consequences of its material appearance.

While it is taboo in the west to speak about the mechanics of physiognomy, we nonetheless exercise and implement physiognomic preferences all the time. Moreover, if in the west "beauty" carries a stain, "physiognomy" bears an even more incriminating stigma because of its historical ties to racist eugenics. All the same, western philosophies on "the face" as a broad concept have motivated thinkers to address the significance of faciality in the formation of an ethical engagement with the Other, most notably Emmanuel Levinas's notion of the face-to-face encounter that instantiates an ethical and relational reckoning with the Other's irreducible difference.[92] While this unspecified face prompts ethical and moral conduct, however, the beautiful face is for Levinas superficially trivial and only "skin deep"—pure exteriority. Giving the example of a building's façade, for instance, Levinas contends that its essence of beauty is only "indifference, cold splendor, and silence."[93] Giving a beautiful face, however, has greater implications beyond "indifference, cold splendor, and silence." Indeed, the vernacular phrase "giving good face," for which Madonna credits Rita Hayworth in "Vogue" (1990), reflects upon the animated, lively labors of expression. Referring to a particular type of what Erving Goffman terms "face-work," "giving good face" suggests the responsive reciprocity of the face-as-surface, its ability to accommodate its beholder's desires.[94] Meanwhile, in the Chinese vernacular, to give or to save *mianzi* (face) acknowledges what Goffman refers to as "the traffic rules of social interaction" and constitutes a long-standing cultural tradition that makes sense of social-ethical engagements through facial encounter.[95] Rather than abiding by good traffic rules, however, face-giving in the following case studies more often than not projects enigma, inscrutability, and charismatic disturbance, qualities that bring to the fore social instabilities—thereby linking cosmetics to cosmology ("world dis/order").

For Richard Dyer, stars "articulate what it is to be a human being in contemporary society."[96] As such, the study of stars compels us to interrogate the divisions between private and public self-making, and the consumption of other selves. In this book, stars are treated as intertextual intersections of race and ethnicity, gender and sexuality, and nationality. I read stars not only as sociocultural projections of desire and un/belonging, but also as authors whose gestures, affects, and charisma impress upon us vast appetites and desires through which we examine and construct our own, even as we hold dubious space toward what Dyer refers to as "the insistent question of 'really'"—that is, our engagement with the construction of stars makes plain our commonsense skepticisms toward notions of authenticity and essentialism.

Vulgar Beauty endorses the notion that star beauty is a call to which we feel compelled to respond, an attempt to forge relationality with and through corporeal form. Star faces are thus always "for us" in a conventional narrative film, and we know this because feminine beauty is always already discovered by the camera (invention under the guise of discovery), as flattering lighting is already in place when the camera casts its look upon the star's face, signaling beauty's tautology. Such a shot, in which the face is photographed in high-key lighting, surfaces what are often the taut pillars of high cheekbones and luminous eyes (we might here refer to Wong Kar-wai's lighting of Maggie Cheung's beautifully wide, high cheekbones—talk about being held by beauty's splints!). It implicitly exposes cinema's seemingly innocent belief in love at first sight. However, our screen propinquity is crucially defined not by a mutual g(r)aze, but by frustrated eye contact and a concomitant lack of mutual contact with our beloved stars. Indeed, the impossibility of eye contact sustains cinema's unquenchable jouissance. Screen beauty is always already an incomplete project, then, an indefatigable pursuit of mutuality and relationality. We persistently stare at performers because we know they can and will never look at us. Thus the return gaze becomes *objet petit a*, the Lacanian impossible object of desire never attained or, in other words, the Barthesian punctum, the out-of-frame "blind field" that endlessly replenishes the lure that draws our desire beyond the margins of visuality. As such, the prohibitive aspect of stargazing demands that we engage with other senses and sensibilities with which to apprehend our intimately estranged relationship with stars.

Despite the lure that operates from beyond the field of vision, stars' luminescent bodies phenomenologically center a film's specular focus and attention. Even when they are photographed at the margins of the screen, their bodies magnetize our eyelines to the frame's edges and sidelines, making us aware of cinema's aesthetic constraints. Possessing charismatic luminescence, star bodies set a bio-aesthetic rhythm within a film, provoking wakefulness amid the otherwise slumbering, dreamlike qualities of cinema. In other words, when a star "lights up the screen," we feel awakened by her presence, just as morning light is our circadian cue to rise.

Five Minor Spices

Each instantiation of vulgar, flavorful beauty as affect thus offers a wakeful interruption, a rupture, and a minor shock to the major chord. In this way, beauty's flavors correlate with what Deleuze refers to as "style," or "managing to stammer in one's own language."[97] Nevertheless, to perceive beauty, particularly in bodily manifestation, is to interpret it in assemblage, a synchronicity correlated with possibilities of becoming. Therefore, it is not just that we stare at the beautiful star's face and body on display; we also simultaneously ingest her binding clothing, the insects buzzing around, the food she prepares, the nocturnal rain and glass architecture surrounding her body, and the wind in the trees—all of which animate the body-in-assemblage and atmosphere. Beauty is cosmological and world making, participating in the production of undifferentiated ecologies. Accordingly, this book demonstrates how the Chinese feminine is a cinematic invention invested in dislocating, relocating, and repopulating Chineseness throughout the world by generating imagined encounters with minor acts (performative gestures, coproduced by cinematic technique, which heighten parasensualities between spectator and performer). Adapting global optics of inquiry with regard to Chinese women stars in the contemporary era, spanning the post-Mao 1980s until the present, this book addresses national, cultural, racial, and gendered formations and (mis)recognitions of flavorful beauty. Whereas Chinese, Hong Kong, and Taiwanese stars serve a national myth-making function in Chinese and Sinophone cinemas, Chinese beauty exported to the west becomes racialized, thereby acquiring scents of alterity under different systems of signification. Racial beauty in particular operates as a minor mode, a confrontation, a stammering within the major—and it is for all such promising criminal aspirations that we should interrogate it.

Still, despite clarifications around beauty's affect and force, or what I refer to as beauty's flavor/weidao, beauty can still feel like an empty signifier suggesting abstract Venusian qualities of love and vague sensations of pleasure—or what Sigmund Freud referred to as beauty's "peculiar, mildly intoxicating quality."[98] As weidao becomes the governing principle to address beauty as feeling in form, the book is accordingly organized around the five flavors of Chinese medicine as modalities of vulgar beauty: bitter, salty, pungent, sweet, and sour. Just as different flavors are used to address various health concerns in TCM, so do aesthetic flavors function as cultural medicine, attempts both to diagnose and to treat psychic ills and dis-eases within collective, public atmospheres. However, as Steven Shaviro points out, "any theory of beauty is always inadequate to its examples."[99] As such, I begin each chapter with a personal encounter that introduces my selection of global stars and texts, objects of intimate negotiation through which I theorize vulgar Chinese femininity from the purview of a diasporic Chinese/Asian/American woman spectator. As feminist and queer scholars demonstrate, the narration of one's experiences becomes a vital and ethical means of theorizing and historicizing formations of subjectivity.[100] After Ann Cvetkovich, curating my "archive of feelings" involves gleaning popular culture images in order to sensually cull an intimately strange directory of bodies, gestures, and acts from the global sensorium.[101]

Chapter 1 begins with the first post-Mao international film star, Gong Li, and the medicinal volatilities of embittered beauty. During the late 1980s through the 1990s, Gong's bitter performances in Chinese cinema envisioned a new, feeling China and the birth of an era of wounded, bleeding nationalism. Gong sensualized Chinese pain for worldwide consumption, demonstrating the transnational mobility of indigestible flavors and the lure of wounded Chinese femininity. Cosmological rereadings of Nietzschean and Deleuzian theories of passion, bad conscience, guilt, and ressentiment anchor close readings of Gong's films *Red Sorghum* and *Hannibal Rising* (Peter Webber, 2007), as the chapter traces a shift from the porosity of leaky, postsocialist Chinese bodies to western envisionings of erotic suffering through the tasty, but indigestible, Chinese body.

Chapter 2 pursues saltiness as a postbitter disavowal ("a grain of salt") that exalts existing flavor. Following from salt's "immigrant" materiality, as it must be imported into the body, the chapter focuses on transnational Chinese/American stars Maggie Cheung and Joan Chen, who play enigmatic-exotic love interests for white, western men during the 1990s era of liberal tolerance. While narratively demonstrating the desirous mechanics of sexual assimilation, the actors also perform minor acts of deflection, drawing out salt's cooling properties as a racial technique that enacts self-preservation as the object of salty (envy-laden) desire. Jungian alchemical-psychological accounts of salt explaining how matter matters, together with considerations of proper dosage, illuminate the tempered racial ambivalences in *Irma Vep* and *Twin Peaks*, cultural texts focused on aesthetic reconsolidations of national identity through multiculturalism.

Chapter 3 further elaborates upon the affective-aesthetics of tolerance, whereby the hot, intense flavor of pungency transgresses subjective boundaries and forces communality. Constituting an undesirable atmosphere, the pungent body becomes a vexing fulcrum in dramas of Derridean "hostpitality," whereby the act of welcoming a stranger into one's home is tempered by hostility. Yet being unwelcome does not preclude a sexual invitation extended to Chinese/American women to participate in cinematic fantasies of racial cosmopolitanisms and imperial collaboration. In *The Crow* and *Lust, Caution* (Ang Lee, 2007), the reluctant birth of tolerance arrives at the expense of the Chinese femme's spectacular death. The pungent aesthetic emerges as a mode through which to manage anxiety and risk, and environments of discipline are constructed to contain the pungent body's atmospheres. However, unwelcome guests Bai Ling and Tang Wei, once in the door, reveal the limits of tolerance by enabling glimpses into the anxious death drive that undergirds liberal and colonial atmospheres.

Chapter 4 interrogates the soft power of sweetness, specifically the national politics of the People's Republic's One China policy as imagined through heteronormative romance. China is fantasized as the male partner and Taiwan as the female love interest in epic historical melodrama *The Knot* (Yin Li, 2006) and the romantic comedy *If You Are the One* (Feng Xiaogang, 2008). However, star performances by Taiwanese actors Vivian Hsu and Shu Qi reveal the soft-sweet possibilities of the artificially saccharine, the overripe, and the cute as solvent of China's hard-line politics. This chapter returns to sajiao, the technique of unleashing tenderness, as a vulgar and recalcitrant form of feminine beauty that plays, disruptively, with neocolonialist desire.

Finally, chapter 5 explores the racioaesthetics of sourness, proposing laughter as a radically open, biting condition of possibility for tasting Asian American bodies in acidic, caustic, and awkward ways. Ali Wong's star-making stand-up specials, *Baby Cobra* (Netflix, 2016) and *Hard Knock Wife* (Netflix, 2018), together with Charlyne Yi's minor stardom in mockumentary *Paper Heart* (Nicholas Jasenovec, 2009) demonstrate the racial sour as a comedic performer who disrupts hegemonic conceptualizations of gender, time, and work through effervescent hostility and astringent quirk. Where Wong's acts perform vulgar, abject materialisms through a carnivalesque body of sensual and excremental delight, Yi's offbeat improvisational quirkiness and genderqueer gawkiness introduce aesthetic arrhythmias and disorder, aligning with what Fred Moten refers to as anacrusis and Nietzschean chaos, in order to jam and to disrupt master narratives about Asian American gender, sexuality, and love.

In regarding beauty, we circle coterminous phenomena like charm, charisma, sexuality, desire, love, the gaze, and fantasy. *Vulgar Beauty* argues that an affective-aesthetic attunement to feminine beauty is an issue of survival, livelihood, and politics as much as it concerns our charismatic seductions. The question of beauty is also intimately entangled with the cinephile's delight and dilemma, engaging with fraught pleasures and bad conscience over our submission to the spectacular moving image. However, the problem is not with beauty, as biopolitical approaches may suggest. Rather, the issue is that we are sometimes unable to recognize it, let alone apprehend its unseen, phenomenal impact. Simultaneously deep and superficial, cryptic and transparent, disarming and provocative, beauty is the affective difference that captures and captivates, moving in and through us. We are undone and remade by our contact with beauty; we willingly become its passive guest, but within the wonder we hold for the beautiful, we become with and feel beautiful. If the Levinasian face-to-face concerns the ethics of otherness through a simultaneous meeting of eyes, a coincidence of seeing one another in reciprocity, then beauty stargazing is about the pleasure in never being able to see eye to eye. Indeed, to regard beauty in such a way is also to set aside the plight of voyeurism and the plague of the masterful gaze. In other words, it is about the misrecognitions and misalignments that can only arise from a spectacular and mediated confrontation with gargantuan appetites and desires. The cosmology of beauty therefore limns a world to which we fantasize an unbelonging belonging, one where we are always chasing after the object of desire's impossible gaze.

Beauty seeks our radical passivity. An appeal to pure reason in attuning to beauty via domination neglects this crucial duplicity and desirous deception. Nevertheless, if love is the mutual acceptance of one another's fantasies, the love of star beauty dreams about the impossible returning gaze from screen faces. Such longing for the impossible gaze and the mutuality of eye contact calls attention to the margins of the screen, a blind field or spot that lies just beyond it, and which accumulates and accretes the possibilities of a kind of love worlding. In *A Lover's Discourse*, Roland Barthes explains love's ecstatic fragments, conflating love at first sight with ravishment: "What fascinates, what ravishes me is the image of a body in situation. What excites me is an outline in action, which pays no attention to me."[102] Cinema teaches us how to love at first sight, becoming engulfed and ravished by beauty's basal shocks. Loving to love a movie star grants affection without a return on investment, and as such it models a kind of loving of the Other that remains in the situational margins of possibility, without expectation. Of course, I hesitate to say it is unconditional, for we know that what we receive are the seductions and desires of being bathed in beauty's radiance, even if in ecliptic form. The contested and suspect object that is beauty enables and sustains this type of love, and it is here— at the point where we embrace the risk of becoming inordinately sentimental and optimistic—that we can begin speaking about vulgar beauty's feeling and doing.

1

Bitter Medicine, Racial Flavor
Gong Li

I am thirteen years old and lying in a big bed with my favorite aunt and my favorite cousin, who is a year younger than me. They are visiting us in St. Louis, after having just immigrated to Canada from China. My aunt is teaching us Chinese slang and we learn the phrase paoniu *(picking up girls). My cousin and I giggle because the phrase literally means "to soak in girls" (*pao *as a noun means "bubbles" and as a verb refers to soaking). It is late and we are drifting off, but even as the notion of the "pickup" eludes our adolescent comprehension, something else is bothering me.*

There is only a handful of students of Asian descent in a population of over a thousand at my high school. I've been called "chink bitch," "flat-faced," and "chicken fried rice" by my young peers. Will anyone ever want to soak with me?

"I don't look like anyone! Who do I look like?"

My aunt grunts, groggily, "Gong Li. You look like Gong Li."

It is by way of a complaint in lacking identification that I first encounter China's biggest film star. Later, I watch all of Gong's collaborations with acclaimed director Zhang Yimou, realizing that I do not look like her at all. Eventually, I realize that my aunt's comment was her way of telling me not to worry about being lonely. I may stand out in the American Midwest, but I am connected to global Chinese communities via the circulation of star images.

The memory of this moment is bittersweet, and it pricks me because it is also my aunt's way of telling me that she thinks I am beautiful.

Whereas the bittersweetness with which I recall the above memory constituted an affective response both to racial injury and to my aunt's loving bandaging, the transnational mobility of (in)digestible flavors and the bittersweetness of global Chinese femininity can be seen in Gong's sensorialization of Chinese pain for international consumption during the post-Mao era. As a structure of feeling, bitterness emerges as a traumatic reckoning with the past, which becomes embodied in Gong's sensually leaky film performances. In this chapter, then, analyses of Gong's debut film, *Hong gao liang* (*Red Sorghum*, Zhang Yimou, 1987) and the Euro-American production *Hannibal Rising* (Peter Webber, 2007) demonstrate how the transnational star becomes a point of erotic translation for historical pain through aesthetics of bitter porosity. Furthermore, this chapter demonstrates how bitterness operates as an embodied, cinematic aesthetics through which to make sense of sociopolitical moods, cinematic tastes, and "racial flavor."

Bitter Interiors

Sometimes I meet one who lacks a distinctive person-scent,
and I seldom find such a one lively or entertaining.
—Helen Keller, *The World I Live In*

When a patient reports a craving for bitter foods, a TCM specialist may note that he or she suffers from an imbalance of heat or fire in the heart, the body's most crucial organ, which homes the *shen* (mind-spirit). Too much fire causes inflammation and infection. Bitterness, correlated with the element of fire, is believed to travel to the heart organ to remove heat and toxins, and, as a medicinal flavor, bitterness acts as a corrective to emotional imbalance. Similar to homeopathy's modus operandi of "like cures like," elemental disparities are homologically treated by the same element in another form. One might eat bitter melon, for instance, to treat depression or insomnia, both of which indicate that the emotion of joy (understood as agitation rather than satisfaction or contentment) is lacking, and that it is out of balance with the other core emotions (anger, fear, grief, and overthinking). Several correlations are presupposed in such a prescription: bitterness correlates with the emotion of joy, the heart organ, and with the element of fire. Such conceptualizations posit a lateral-horizontal, rather than dialectical or hierarchical, paradigm of worldly matter. It is a system privileging analogy over causality, favoring a holographic cosmology that beckons us to engage simultaneously with seemingly disparate phenomena—the "changeable constellations of things (pragmata)," as Byung-Chul Han refers to deconstructionist Chinese thought, discussed in the introduction.[1] A TCM specialist will therefore examine the patient's tongue because there are correspondences from the heart to the tongue and to taste itself; such holistic epistemologies dictate that when one cannot taste, one cannot feel.

In an analogous conception of imbalanced heat and bitterness, Friedrich Nietzsche observes the internal inflammations (fire) of European man, who, because of undergoing the self-tyranny of becoming a civilized subject, can no longer bear pain.[2] As Gilles Deleuze explains, Nietzsche proposes that "one is numbed against pain by passion" and that "pain is healed by manufacturing yet more pain.... One cures oneself of pain by infecting the wound."[3] In other words, "like cures like," heat cures heat—and in relation to this chapter's central argument, bitter cures bitter. Although both TCM and Nietzsche agree upon this curative equation, Nietzsche describes the "badness of the matter," the abject fluids and wastes ("secretion of saliva, urine, and excrement") as one's inner dirt of desire that extends outside the body to shamefully remind the individual of his or her animal passions. As his internal guilt is imaged as a horrifyingly filthy, secreting body, man punishes his animalistic impulses and desires through his self-regard.[4] Whereas Nietzsche's man of bad conscience views his bodily wastes and secretions as material proof of his guilt, contrastingly, in *Red Sorghum*, we witness a return to the earthly body that discharges from its abject interior (urine, blood, semen, tears), thereby aestheticizing vulgar ressentiment, which faults and accuses others for one's misfortunes.

Drawing upon a constellation of materialist-conceptual terms such as passions, suffering, heat, fire, and bitterness, chapter 1 considers how the latter is in particular an aesthetic mode that attempts to process historical grievance. Furthermore, bitterness is the first of the "bad tastes" explored in this book that demonstrate the ways in which the vulgar force of feminine beauty sparks passionate interest in the star body. It is the beautiful eroticization of the discharging, vulgar female figure in *Red Sorghum* that produces the affective forces for national wound healing. In other words, the terrestriality of the body, with its spectacular corporeal trembles and quivers, correlates with bitter anger as an impassioned, ecstatic (even orgasmic) mode in an attempt to reckon with trauma. This chapter in particular conceptualizes bitterness through the social, as an embodied-cinematic response to trauma. Gong's flavorful performances can be understood as animating bitterness, envisioning a new *feeling* China and the birth of an era of wounded nationalism that began in the late 1980s and 1990s, demonstrating how bitter aesthetics constitute palliative medicine in the post-Mao era. Gong's bitter beauty, however, absorbs different peripatetic connotations when she becomes a transnational star, lending her exotic Chineseness to western productions. In such cinematic contexts, Gong's aesthetic bitterness transmutes from wet secretions to racial odor, alleviating westerners in their own historical reckoning. Just as bitter foods generate stomach acids and bile to break down food, through her bitter-flavor work, Gong demonstrates how acting Chinese functions enzymatically for traumatic digestion in differing cultural contexts.

Gong was born on the cusp of Mao Zedong's Great Proletarian Cultural Revolution in 1965 in Shenyang, and grew up in Jinan, the capital city of Shandong Province. The youngest of five children born to economics instructors, Gong had childhood aspirations to become a singer. Selected by her elementary school to sing a nursery rhyme for the Jinan public radio station, Gong wished to continue studying music through high school and beyond. Although her exam scores were eleven points below university admission standards, and Gong was subsequently denied entrance to four art colleges, the persistent young woman nevertheless bought a one-way standing train ticket to Beijing, where she was finally admitted to the Central Academy of Drama in Beijing as an acting student. In 1987, after two years at the academy, filmmaker Zhang Yimou came to the school to cast his first feature film as director. Zhang's first impression of the acting student was that she was "*hen shou* (very skinny), *qingxiu* (delicate and pretty), *congming* (smart), had eyes with a highly expressive quality," but that she was not suitable as his lead.[5] It was only after a period of getting to know Gong that Zhang deduced her capacity for bitter performativity, noting that "although her outer appearance was pure and simple, not showy or overstated at all, her inner spirit and personality had a kind of *pola* [an adjectival term composed of 'pour' and 'spicy' to describe a bold and forceful quality] that could be outwardly expressed."[6] The expression of Gong's spicy personality through her apparently delicate looks generates a charismatic allure based on an ostensible conflict between interior and exterior—a manifestation of beauty that would aptly perform the contradictions of an experimental governance termed "socialism with Chinese characteristics," and the desiring impulses to aestheticize the lingering bitterness of Maoist society. Zhang's attraction to Gong was also romantic, and the pair embarked on an eight-year love affair that began during Zhang's marriage to his first wife. While Zhang patiently awaited his divorce, which his then-wife refused to grant for several years, the pair's controversial romance became tabloid fodder. Gong's stardom was henceforth tied with Zhang and his internationally recognized auteur status as one of the foremost directors of Chinese Fifth Generation cinema, even after the lovers split. The designation Fifth Generation refers to the vividly spectacular films produced by the first graduate class from the Beijing Film Academy after Mao's death in 1976. These films are credited for being the first mainland Chinese films to attract the attention of western audiences and critics. Sometimes referred to as "backward gazing" or "scar" films, a cathartic correlate to the popular "scar literature" that vividly recounted writers' personal suffering under Mao, melancholic films such as *Yige he bage* (*One and Eight*, Zhang Junzao, 1983), *Huang tudi* (*Yellow Earth*, Chen Kaige, 1984), *Lao jing* (*Old Well*, Wu Tianming, 1986), and *Lan fengzheng* (*The Blue Kite*, Tian Zhuangzhuang, 1993) use proletariat struggles during the prerevolutionary and Maoist periods as their narrative backdrops. Significantly, Gong became the first and most prominent star of this cinematic movement through her beautification of the pain and suffering experienced by individuals in China's most impoverished social classes, the rural peasants and villagers.

Zhang's assessment of Gong's seductive weidao, or flavor, reflects an attunement to her bodily quality, one also reflected in her critical national reception. Mainland film scholar Zhang Caihong, for example, contends that Gong is not beautiful in terms of traditional Chinese aesthetics, as per mythical accounts of dynastic beauties. However, he insists that she possesses *xiangtu qi'en* (a native soil-like vitality), which imparts an earthy weidao or flavor.[7] Meanwhile, Chen Xiaoyun, rearticulating Rey Chow's influential argument in *Primitive Passions*, argues that "the innate qualities in [Gong's] bones" (*qizhi zai tade guzili*) provoke nostalgic longing from the Chinese public for a self-Orientalizing, or auto-ethnographic, mythology of the past.[8] Chen's reference to bones reminds us that flavorful embodiment, much like the function of smell, summons interactions with what Constance Classen, David Howes, and Anthony Synott describe as "perceived interiorities, rather than with surfaces, as one did with sight."[9] Invoking a somatic plunging into charisma, the interiority of flavor necessitates sensuous appreciation, rather than the psychoanalytical disquisition favored by early feminist and apparatus theory, and by the pseudopsychological scrutiny and gossip found in celebrity media and the tabloid press. Rather than analyzing specular constructions of the ego ideal and sexual difference, the concept of flavor interiors approaches the coconstructions of meaning by actor/star and spectator, as flavor refers to the elusive encounters activated by cinematized gesture, or what in the introduction I referred to as the "minor act," which produces nonverbal parasensualities between spectator and performer.

Furthermore, the more often a body appears on-screen, the more accumulated meaning and flavor that body acquires within celebrity economies and visual cultures, creating what Richard Dyer refers to as "structured polysemies [which contain a] multiplicity of meanings and affects."[10] Such flavorful accretion stands in contrast to the alleged "cultural odorlessness" of global products, which Koichi Iwabuchi, in characterizing Japanese exports, describes as deliberately effacing their "cultural odor," which is "closely associated with racial and bodily images of a country of origin."[11] Japan's imperial past in Asia blemished the nation's reputation in the eastern hemisphere, but odorless Japanese products are easily assimilated in local contexts elsewhere and everywhere. The same cultural odorlessness ascribed to animated characters and electronic devices, however, cannot be said of bodies, whose alterity surfaces (among other traces) through melanin, hair, and bone structure, and sonically through language, voice, and accent. Chinese vulgarity and its soil-like vitality contrast starkly with Japanese odorlessness, insisting upon the earthy thingliness of the body. Remarks about Gong's spicy weidao and earthy nostalgic-nationalist bones demonstrate that, rather than being odorless, Gong embodies cultural fragrance, even to Chinese audiences. Here, seductive sexual difference becomes encoded as an exotic otherness perceived through the lower sensorium. Intensified by Zhang's camera, Gong's erotic-exoticness drew trans/national attention to their cinematic collaborations. Gong's tawny honeyed skin tone not only evokes a fragrant image of sun-kissed earthiness, her body, which is taller (5 feet, 6 inches) and curvier than those of many of her contemporaries, imparts a palpable rootedness and gravity, fulfilling her namesake, Gong (security and solidity). Her sensual corporeality reintroduced sensuality to Chinese cinema and public culture, and her feminine flavor attracted worldwide audiences to Chinese cinema—significantly, in a stunning departure from the restlessly energetic athleticism and de-eroticized androgyny of Cultural Revolution actors, to which we now turn.

Bland Socialist Bodies

Two decades prior to Gong's cinematic debut, actors like Zhang Ruifang embodied the strong, robust, and androgynous model of womanhood, conveying Mao's proclamation that "women can hold up half the sky" in films like *Li Shuangshuang* (Lu Ren, 1962), for which she won her first Hundred Flowers Best Actress Award, one of China's most highly visible state-sanctioned honors. Although Zhang was widely known and beloved by audiences throughout her long career, spanning from the 1940s until the 1980s, she cannot be considered a *mingxing* (star) because, as Xiaoning Lu explains, "the very word 'star'…carried a spectrum of negative connotations: corrupted lifestyles, loftiness, individualism and liberalism, all of which originate from the same source, capitalism."[12] If stardom signified capitalist corruption and the sensual degradation of the soft bourgeois body in decadent 1930s Shanghai cinema, the term "film worker" denoted the hardened, muscular bodies laboring toward Mao's vision of collectivism.

These instruments of hardened bodies assumed their most exuberant form as the gravity-defying balletic bodies in revolutionary model operas, appearing in film adaptations like *Hongse niangzi jun* (*The Red Detachment of Women*, Pan Wenzhan, 1970) and *Bai mao nü* (*The White-Haired Girl*, Yan Jinxuan, 1971). However, as Paul Clark accurately assesses, "the banality of much of this cultural production became obvious after years of unrelenting posturing."[13] Differentiated from cultural odorlessness, the scentlessness of socialist film, "empt[ied] of real substance," emanates from the ideological sublimity that undergirded state-sponsored films of this period.[14] Not only in pursuit of corporeal transcendence, that is, the apparent vanquishing of carnal desire in pursuit of political ideals, revolutionary aesthetics were generated from masculinist impulses oriented toward law and order.[15] Libido was sublimated and displaced onto the symbolic political realm, while a desexed, militarized body envisaged the communist ideal of strength and beauty. Surface constructions of feminine beauty were viewed as nefarious acts of corporeal enslavement, a notion stemming from Mao's 1919 proclamation that "women are regarded as criminals to start with, and tall buns and long skirts are the instruments of torture applied to them by men."[16] Referring to facial makeup as "the brand of a criminal," to jewelry as "shackles," and to pierced ears and bound feet as "corporal punishment," Mao made abundantly clear his belief that surface, ornamental constructions of femininity imperiled his vision of gender egalitarianism.[17] As a result, bodies became codified in genderless Maoism qua masculinity, and, as Eva Kit Wah Man describes, "female beauty was displaced from external appearance to the love of labor, the party, and the nation."[18] Women generally dressed down in plain gray or blue party uniforms with chin-length hair or up-dos, and those wearing makeup or accessories were heavily scrutinized and accused of indulging in bourgeois ideology. Nevertheless, the aesthetic concept of beauty persisted as a measure of ideological success. Women's beautiful bodies, flaunting the Communist Party's successes in ensuring health and well-being, were lifted off the ground by their ideological ebullience in balletic revolutionary operas, their natural beauty an outward measure of Maoist devotion.

A departure from the sublimated, desexualized revolutionary figure, Gong would later translate the imaginative textures and odors of lived socialist life into erotic, nostalgic flavors through her cinematic performances, playing a significant role in defining the actor not as an ideological film worker, but as a sensual star. To understand this distinction, it is useful to take a closer look at *Li Shuangshuang* and, in particular, lead actor Zhang's performative body. Adapted from Li Zhun's 1960 short story published in the communist literary magazine *People's Literature*, *Li Shuangshuang* (1962) is a comedic film about its titular strong-headed peasant protagonist and model proletarian Shuangshuang (Zhang Ruifang), who leads her village commune against moral corruption and laziness, to the detriment of marital happiness with her husband, Xiwang. After the straightforward, hard-working Shuangshuang suggests instituting a work-point system to keep track of everyone's productivity, newly elected work-point scorer Xiwang finds ways to cheat the system by giving his friends extra points, which his wife dutifully reports to the town clerk. Whereas the men in the village seek to cut corners and earn personal profit, the women, led by Shuangshuang, cheerfully work long hours harvesting wheat before returning home to make noodles for their families. Finally, Xiwang is driven to move out of their home after Shuangshuang openly criticizes his friends and becomes overly involved in her in-laws' affairs. Using a battle of the sexes plot, filmmaker Lu Ren delivers a playful vision of the socialist revolution wherein success depends upon the honest hard work and moral fortitude of all community members. Siding with his titular character, Lu Ren stated that his intention was to emphasize the *mei* (beauty) of "hard work, ideology, the times and the social system."[19] By the film's end, however, the hard work of socialist labor yields a bountiful crop and a harmonious hearth, while Shuangshuang, now rosy-cheeked in a floral-print blouse marking her feminine efflorescence, appears to have undergone a cosmetic transformation. After the couple's happy reunion, contingent on Xiwang and the rest adopting Shuangshuang's socialist prescriptions and hard work ethic, Xiwang remarks that Shuangshuang appears more beautiful than ever.[20] As Xiaobing Tang observes, "He is able to appreciate her beauty only when he identifies with the values she stands for."[21] Reiterating the priority of social duty before the personal, Xiwang jokes that the couple decided to get married and then fall in love, bucking convention. Although love is subordinate to duty, love invariably arises through duty. Although feminine conventions were seen as bourgeois and counterrevolutionary, outward beauty was regarded as a manifestation of moral correctness and upright character, transcending the visible realm. Even the floral print on Shuangshuang's blouse equated beauty with fecund socialist growth.[22] Shuangshuang's beautification, a property delinked from her individual body, functions as an ideological marker of communist achievement.

Externalizing the titular character's stubborn, hard-working, and impetuous personality, Zhang's gestures and movements throughout the film are decisive, swift, and energetic, communicated by the actor's character choices of a "loud voice" and "infectious laughter."[23] Her quick-moving body is stiffened by moral resolve and righteousness, her face often bearing a disappointed scowl or hearty, unbridled laugh, which turns her mouth into an emboldened pursed line. Close-ups of Zhang's face are sparing, although zooms and tracking shots (popular techniques throughout the Cultural Revolution era) are used throughout to signify changes in mood and subjectivity. The editing is economical in its frugality; there is no lingering upon Zhang's face, no wasted time with which to contemplate her physical beauty. Only photographing her face long enough to register her expression, the filmmaker used few close-ups because he wished to "give the audience the sense that they were watching real people live their daily lives."[24] Despite Lu Ren's claims of a proto-documentary aesthetic, however, the film is distinctly propagandistic in aligning the body with communist ideologies and material instruments of work.

For example, after the commune officially adopts Shuangshuang's work-point system at a town meeting, the scene ends on a medium close-up (from the chest up) of the protagonist, smiling with satisfaction and looking askance at her husband (figure 1.1). As this image dissolves, a close-up of Shuangshuang's work-point notebook fades into frame, juxtaposed directly over her body, suggesting that the dissolution of the individual is necessary for socialist collectivity (figures 1.2–1.4). Shuangshuang is objectified, not as a sexual or erotic image but as a recording tool with which to survey and monitor the proletariat revolution. The cinematographic construction even positions the audience closer to the notebook than to Shuangshuang, indicating the valuation of socialist labor (vis-à-vis the document and record of work) over the individual worker. Embodying the recorded accumulation of progress, Shuangshuang becomes a genderless symbol of the cooperative peasant class toeing the party line. Although gender is narrativized throughout the film, Shuangshuang does not exhibit traditionally feminine behavior until the final scene, which ends when she coyly smiles and follows her husband out of frame, notably when the political lesson concludes and domestic gender didacticism can begin, off-screen. Throughout the film, Zhang is outfitted in loose, utilitarian clothing lightly gripped by a mandarin collar, covered from neck to ankle and revealing little of a womanly figure. Following a post-1949 convention that Chen observes was "based on a universalization of desexualized body parts and an implicit masculine ideal," Zhang's on-screen body does not exude weidao as a sensual flavor of feminine distinction.[25] Moreover, we cannot visually locate the sweat beads and dampened clothing that would likely appear on faces and bodies working in fields all day. When Shuangshuang cries after her husband leaves her, her body crumples into a chair—face burrowed in crossed arms on a tabletop—and we are prohibited from seeing her tears. Secreting neither sweat nor tears, the socialist body is a self-contained vessel that navigates the world by acting upon it as a stiff socialist instrument.

Just as we cannot see Shuangshuang's tears, likewise we do not sense the sweetness of sweat produced by manual labor, as described in Li Zhun's novel: "As she pushed the water wheel, looking at the clear spring which flowed into the fields through the irrigation pipe, she listened to everybody slurping their noodles in delight, thinking they were so tasty and *sweet*. At that moment she suddenly felt that the *sweat* she and the other women had dropped in the dining hall was traveling with the spring water, into

1.1–1.4

Shuangshuang's object-ive beauty is recognized as a record of work.

the hearty, flourishing fields, turning into wheat and rice."[26] The workers' sweat feeds and nourishes the community, even as the granular foods it produces are themselves bland and flavorless, representing the highest aesthetic ideal of the "flavorless flavor," which only becomes tasty and sweet through sacrifice and labor. Here, the English translation also reveals a slippage between porosity (sweat) and flavor (sweet) whereby the imagined flavor unlocks a sensual appreciation of work. The film, however, offers a different kind of sensorial experience premised on ideologically invoking the sweat of manual labor, the tears of sacrifice, and the earthen scents of agricultural work and harvest—without visually displaying them upon a terrestrial body. Even as we see workers in the field in extra-long shot, this cinematographic distance only reaffirms distance from the earth (ballet dancers leap, defying gravitational pull in revolutionary operas, while the socialist comedic camera pulls away from the ground).

Although the party was opposed to feudal and religious thought, it inadvertently pursued the formal ideals of traditional aesthetics. The ungendered and calcified clichés of communist banality evoke the highest form of aesthetic transcendentalism or "blandness" (*dan*) in Chinese aesthetic theory, as discussed in the introduction. Related to qualities of moderation and harmony, bland flavor in Chan Buddhism refers to what aesthetic philosopher Li Zehou describes as "something that is without taste but at the same time full of flavor; in other words, 'the flavorless flavor is the perfect flavor.'"[27] In contrast to Danish philosopher Søren Kierkegaard's ontological fear of "stick[ing his] finger into existence" and "smell[ing] nothing," or to the flavorless "dull dish" of mainstream white culture bell hooks describes (a concept that appears later in this chapter), blandness in the Chinese aesthetic context concerns the transcendent, or out-of-body, mastery of carnal desire.[28] In *Li Shuangshuang*, this mastery is conveyed through Shuangshuang's subordination of marital happiness to collective socialist duty, which requires no labored thought. Nevertheless, the flavorful charm about the repetitive vernacularism of revolutionary culture may also lie in the unintended, as with the fetishization of female dancer bodies in the aforementioned model operas. As Clark observes in *The Red Detachment of Women*, "Every quiver of" our shackled heroine ripples through her red silk pajamas.[29] However, even this quiver fails to betray the body's laboring physicality. Actors, singers, and dancers in revolutionary operas and socialist comedies neither tire nor sweat (their stage makeup instead pancaked and ceaselessly retouched). The glory of socialism is breathlessly exulting, not exhausting and out of breath. In contrast with the "moral" sweat dotting Roman faces in classical Hollywood films, as Roland Barthes observes, Chinese propagandistic bodies, like "the *object of the crime*," remain "smooth-skinned, unperturbed, and watertight," figures who do not undergo agonizing internal crises because Chinese socialism is uncontestable Law.[30] Echoing the isolationism of Mao's China, the "watertight" socialist body did not interpenetrate with its surroundings.

Although socialist cinema was bland and full of flavorless flavor, the sociopolitical climate of the 1950s–70s was charged with destabilizing affective intensity. Bitterness as Nietzschean ressentiment arises from the slave's feelings of misfortune and injustice, credited to the master's will—but, as Nietzsche notes, ressentiment also produces creativity and beauty. As the preeminent philosopher of bitterness notes, the "wholly *active* bad conscience has finally (as one already anticipates)—true fountainhead as it is of idealism and imagination—produced an abundance of novel and amazing beauty and affirmation, and perhaps has really been the first to give birth to beauty at all."[31] As the following section explains, bitterness became a dominant flavor-tone in China's twentieth century, plucking at erstwhile and persistent wrongs and grudges, in pursuit of class justice and laying the groundwork for a new traumatically sensual Chinese cinema.[32] As sociopolitical aesthetic and cultural medicine, bitterness highlighted the distressing undertones and moods of revolutionary work. In his account of how an American revolutionary countermood is made, Jonathan Flatley, borrowing from Heidegger's *Dasein*, contends that "only within a mood or by way of mood can we encounter things in the world as mattering to us."[33] One might rewrite Flatley's statement, replacing "mood" with "beauty," to engage with one of this book's central arguments. As a flexible mood modality, bitterness not only revealed that Maoist nationalism mattered most in reconsolidating collective identity, it also reinforced the beauty of the Chinese virtuous work ethic (and bad taste) of *chiku* (eating bitterness). Bitterness was invoked to denounce counterrevolutionary and bourgeois cultural works that were deemed "poisonous weed," fittingly imagined as an object of bitter, toxic consumption. Even the beloved actor Zhang Ruifang, who played Li Shuangshuang, was unable to escape such persecutions. Because of her prerevolutionary success, she was imprisoned for being an established filmmaker in December 1967 for six months.

Bitter (*Ku*) Tears

Revolution is a bitter thing…not as romantic as the
poets think.
—Lu Xun, "Thoughts on the League of Left-Wing Writers"

Unlike the odorless exhilaration of socialist cinema, the sociopolitical milieu under Mao was steeped in bitter feeling. Mao implemented his notion that "good medicine is bitter to the taste but beneficial for the sickness" by institutionalizing public practices of "speaking bitterness" (*suku*) in order to eliminate old ideologies of "clan, family, conscience, and fate."[34] Seeking to awaken political consciousness in the peasant class and to increase conscriptions to the People's Liberation Army (PLA), work teams consisting of "educated outsiders" galvanized the poorest and most oppressed peasants in rural villages to publicly denounce their oppressors, setting off a discursive chain reaction known as "inducing bitterness with bitterness." Peasants were invited to "pour bitter water," "dig poor roots," and "speak bitterness by pointing to the objects [which landlords took from them]" during meetings.[35] Meanwhile, PLA conscripts were invited to assign blame and project ressentiment toward wide-ranging political entities, including Chiang Kai-shek and his Nationalist Party, Japan, and the United States.[36]

Playing a fundamental role in nationalizing consciousness under Mao, speaking bitterness continued to serve political needs after the 1950s, as acrimony toward past wrongs and suffering were publicly ritualized as a means with which to mobilize mass feeling toward revolution. Meanwhile, even as flavors metaphorically reinforced and upheld the doctrinal, state-sponsored mythos about the sweetness of liberation, discourses about food and hunger were carefully policed. Felix Wemheuer, drawing on the work of Gang Yue and Judith Farquhar, explains that "social inequality was often expressed in terms of eating and drinking," and that "the CCP represented the hungry peasantry's desire for food and justice."[37] Mao even described his socialist ideology in terms of food: "Eating for free is communism." Despite Mao's stated intentions, it is estimated that between 15 and 45 million peasants died of starvation as a direct result of Mao's Great Leap Forward Campaign between 1958 and 1961, an experiment intended to accelerate China's communist industrialization and modernization through large infrastructure projects, deprivatization of land, and collectivization of quotidian life (cooking at home was prohibited). However, speaking about this bitterness was verboten, as it was "taboo to express the idea that the peasants were hungry."³⁸ Following this failed experiment, new campaigns of "recalling bitterness" redirected grievance and reshaped collective memory. The Recollecting Bitterness and Pondering Sweetness campaign, for example, encouraged peasants to recount their suffering during the preliberation old society and contrast it with current happiness, framed as sweetness. Many audiences of "recalling bitterness" meetings were affected/infected by the fervor of the experience, and individuals were compelled to cry out slogans like "Down with the old society!" thereby affirming Deleuze's observation that *"ressentiment* is really only appeased when its contagion is spread."³⁹

Beyond its life as a political metaphor for society's perceived ills, bitterness was mobilized into affective world building, through which grievance and resentment were engineered into public culture. Overtly linking matter (bodies, objects) with meaning (experience, affect, memory), one ritualistic grievance included "eating a recalling-bitterness meal," in which young people were compelled to eat near-indigestible materials like "tree leaves, potherb, bran, and white mud" in order to temporarily inhabit the impoverishment and starvation of the poor masses during prerevolutionary times. As a catachrestic act linking language with bodily event (the words fail to fully capture the event, and thus an event is enacted), blandness as a quality of the ingested object, not as aesthetic ideal, served as an approximation of suffering wherein the difficulty of ingestion and bad taste signified the hardships and ideological mistakes of preliberation life. Rather than Nietzsche's civilized man who secretes in the image of bad conscience (secretions that shamefully remind him that he is animal), the bitter socialist absorbs "bad matter" to remind him that he is civilized only by communism.

The contagion of bitterness therefore became an embodied and deeply felt orientation through which to sense the world. Whereas imagined sweat ushers in sweet socialist futurity, performative tears recall the suffering past, and affect accretes and gains momentum through contact. Moreover, women were the preferred spokespeople for speaking bitterness, because, as mainland scholar Li Lifeng recalls, "they were emotionally vulnerable and easily shed tears. Their memories are good, and their tears can bring tears of more people."⁴⁰ Indeed, the feminization of emotional labor benefited women as marginalized subjects who became prominent historical actors for the first time. Bitterness, as the dominant flavor of Mao's socialist revolution, thus also became the taste of feminine empowerment.

Bitter feeling as a lingering aftertaste spilled into China's Reform era after Mao's death in 1976. Along with a sense of optimism during the Cultural Fever (Wenhua Re), bitterness helped to usher in a transitional period in which the old and the new repeatedly collided, generating new frictions and heat. Old toxins were purged from the social body by various cultural productions of bitterness, as influences flowed in from the west to inject passion and excitement into intellectual spheres. Memories of bitterness under Mao began to emerge in new vernacular and modernist forms in "scar" and "wounded" literature, arts, and films, which became the first post–World War II Chinese cultural productions to be internationally consumed. However, despite the international critical acclaim of earlier Fifth Generation films (*The One and the Eight*; *Yellow Earth*; *Old Well*; *The Horse Thief*), Chinese cinema had no star prior to Gong Li. The young actress would beautify bitterness and convey the feverish mood of Reform-era China throughout her six collaborations with director Zhang Yimou between 1987 and 1995.

The Body That ~~Speaks~~ Leaks: *Red Sorghum*

There are times when everything on earth spits out the stench
of human blood.
—Mo Yan, *Red Sorghum*

After working as a cinematographer on *The One and the Eight* and *Yellow Earth*, Zhang turned to his own directorial pursuits. He adapted Mo Yan's critically lauded novel *Red Sorghum*, published a year prior to the film's production. Set in a place called Slope Shibali in precommunist rural Shandong, *Red Sorghum* recounts a romance between two workers at a sorghum wine liquor distillery, and who are the grandmother and grandfather of the film's narrator, who appears in disembodied form as a baritone voice-over. The grandmother, Jiuer, inherits the distillery from her deceased husband, Li Datou, an old leper who dies mysteriously, but whose likely murderer is Grandpa, who was under Datou's employ as one of Jiuer's wedding sedan chair carriers. Grandpa aggressively tries to court Jiuer, who resists his advances, after which the scorned suitor urinates into four vats of sorghum wine, which renders the wine irresistibly delectable. Jiuer then relents to Grandpa, and the Shibali distillery begins to prosper. A few years later, the Japanese Imperial Army invades the territory and publicly flays Jiuer's benevolent father figure Luohan, who had since left the distillery to join a resistance group. Vowing vengeance, Jiuer leads Grandpa and the distillery's men to plan a counterattack on the Japanese. The film ends tragically when Jiuer, taking food to the men in the trenches, is shot by friendly fire and dies. At that moment, Grandpa stares into a solar eclipse, and his vision becomes awash in red, as his young son chants a rhyme to direct his mother's spirit southwest to the afterlife. Similar to the ways in which embittered speakers grafted their postliberation suffering onto prefeudal fictions under Mao, the film bitterly looks backward with intent to passionately forge China's futurity.

Summoned from a buried unconscious, the film opens with twenty-two seconds of black leader as the grandson explains the mythical significance of the legend about his grandparents. A revision of "speaking bitterness," the historically burdened grandson orates his posthumous grandparents' bitterness as their traumatic inheritor. Fading from black to a close-up of twenty-one-year-old Gong's face as she stares unblinkingly below and past the camera, the narrator introduces Jiuer: "This is my Grandma." This introduction is followed by dis-membering close-ups of her head, face, wrist, neck, and ear, as the bride-to-be is groomed and decorated for her arranged nuptials to the fifty-year-old leper.[41]

The close-up advocates for nearness and intimacy as modalities of film viewing, as Bela Balázs's "physiognomy" and Deleuze's notion of "faceicity" (inspired by Balázs) instruct that the development of the close-up is born from the desire to see the face in isolation and what Balázs refers to as its "polyphonic," or multivalent or contradictory, expressions.[42] The face and the close-up are homologically interchangeable insofar as they generate similar forces of intensity. Analogously, in the hermeneutic tradition of Chinese physiognomy, which also informs traditional medical practice, the face reveals body-spirit interaction and fated events. Although neither Deleuze nor Balázs prescribe how to read a face, both thinkers nevertheless suggest that the face ought to be perceived through "tenderness," "love," and "fond attentiveness." Meeting Gong's face in close-up insists upon a mode of radical, uncompromising intimacy premised on tasting the unknown other, as the camera mimics the intimate perspective one takes before a kiss. The shot therefore allows us to indulge in the sight of Gong's face from the privileged vantage point of a proximal lover. The audience is thereby thrust into the historical scene via erotic thrownness, and the vision of Gong is one predicated on desiring nearness. Moreover, the close-up tenderizes our gaze and structures a close attention that prepares us to see that red, bitter blood is speckled everywhere—we are already cued to search for this detail by the film's opening blood-red calligraphic titles, 红高粱 (Red Sorghum).

A decorative red pin is placed in a hair bun. Red thread plucks stray eyebrow hairs and wispy facial hair. Two hands button up a red mandarin collar. Dangling earrings embedded with round red gemstones echo in miniature Gong's nearly perfectly round lips. Tasting Gong from various nibbling close-ups, this introductory sequence is composed of quick, agitated kisses or, to use Adam Phillips's turn of phrase, "aim-inhibited eating."[43] Cinematically to see Gong for the first time is thus to kiss and to taste her, revealing how tasting is, conversely, "aim-inhibited kissing." Finally, Jiuer is enshrouded in a red veil, muting her returning gaze. A graphic match then emplaces Jiuer seamlessly in the red sedan, where she removes the veil with a quick, impatient gesture and a look of indignant anger. Insisting on being seen, Jiuer performs a facial striptease (first veiled by the other, then aggressively divulging her own face to the camera). Although the apparatus is conflated with Zhang's desiring, structuring absence (the director betrays his own erotic desire for nearness to Gong), taking Gong-as-Jiuer as desirable object, in the following sequence, the film shifts to her gaze, revealing the film's nonbinary possibilities of voyeuristic pleasure and tender longing.

Jiuer's wedding sedan is carried by several male carriers, one of whom would become the narrator's grandfather. A glimpse from her point of view as she moves the red fabric membrane with her foot reveals Grandpa's sweaty (salty) backside. These are not the watertight bodies that populated revolutionary model operas and comedies. Parting her lips ever so slightly (she would also like to taste him), this shot-reverse-shot is said to constitute one of the first cinematic representations of female desire in the post-Mao era, suturing the audience to Jiuer's subjectivity. Provoking the ire of young Chinese film critics who accused this sequence of mimicking Hollywood's signifying editing structure, this sequence nevertheless demonstrates Gong's feeling embodiment of Reform-era China, described by Xudong Zhang as "a mythic moral order woven from individual frustration, collective longing, sexual shock, and the universal perplexity caused by a social-ideological reorientation."[44] Erotic desire precedes the speech act and the articulation of lust, as we have not yet heard Jiuer speak. Chromatically marked by blood, lust, and passion, Gong-as-Jiuer embodies a new kind of woman: one who will not speak bitterness but who will embody it, favoring visual (cinematic) logic over language and discourse.[45] Language, after all, became a corrupted instrument during the Cultural

Revolution, resulting in the arbitrary persecution of hundreds of thousands of innocent people who were charged with counterrevolutionary thoughts and practices. Nevertheless, speaking bitterness appears in the film as a recognized genre of disclosure and testimony of suffering, specifically prompted by the film's men.

Echoing in reverse the disembodied narrator's opening words, "Let me tell you," Grandpa tries to coax Jiuer into speaking: "Don't just peep. Say a few words to us." When the bride-to-be still refuses to speak, Grandpa leads the sedan chair carriers in song while they jolt her back and forth in an attempt to "rock the urine out of her," a punitive act for her silence and a ritual gesture of sexual aggression toward the boss's woman. Zhang emphasizes the libidinal exchange in this scene by crosscutting between medium and long shots of the men and a close-up showing Jiuer becoming increasingly nauseated. Her facial expression also betrays the throes of sexual ecstasy as her body is repeatedly thrust into the air and her lips split open to take in air, an orgasmic introduction to Gong (figure 1.5). Finally, after hearing her sobs (notably a nonlinguistic utterance), the men finally stop jolting and proceed in silence. Then, while passing through a field of wild sorghum, a bandit suddenly appears and robs the men at gunpoint, before approaching the sedan chair. After removing Jiuer's veil, a close-up on her nonchalant face cuts to a close-up of her foot, which the bandit impulsively grabs and caresses. Looking defiantly at the bandit, Jiuer inexplicably smiles. Is her smile a delayed response to having seen Grandpa's bare, wet backside? Like the floating affect, seeking attachment to an object, the smile is a belated recognition of Jiuer's voyeurism bestowed later(ally) on the masked bandit, her lips parting again at the idea of a kiss. The film's crosscutting between Gong's face and foot here collapses the two principal bodily sites by which feminine beauty has been judged in Chinese beauty history (recall the three-inch "golden lotus" that ruled for a millennium)—and Jiuer's (unbound) foot is the first body part with which Grandpa will soon make contact. After a series of silent looks exchanged between Jiuer and Grandpa, Grandpa leads the chair carriers to beat the bandit to death. The looks between the two reaffirm the film's implicit belief that seeing, not speaking, is the bitter antecedent to action. After Jiuer calmly returns to the sedan chair, she rests her foot outside the partition, the first sign of her burgeoning receptivity to, and agential expression of, sexual desire. Mimicking the bandit's desiring touch, Grandpa grasps her foot and gently places it back inside the sedan chair.[46]

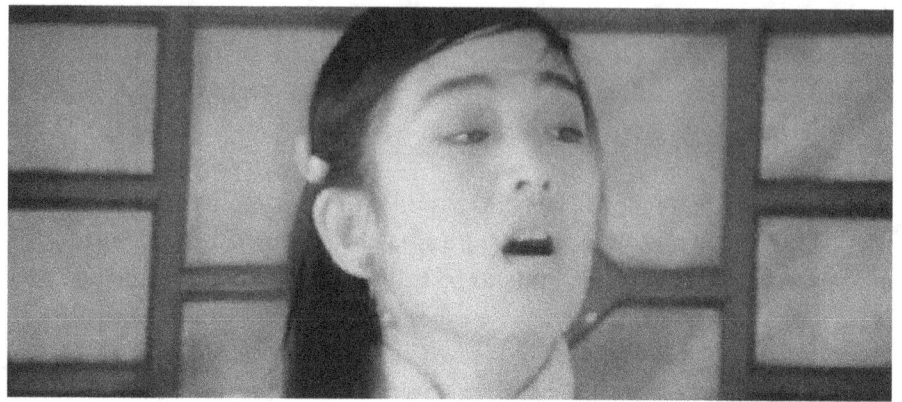

1.5

Gong's ecstatic expression generates libidinal attraction.

Red Spills

Coincidental with its depiction of bodily seductions, the film engages in a chromatic analysis of feeling and worlding through the color red, signifying embittered suffering. The brilliant shades of red are used promiscuously, conjuring intense passions across scenes of lovemaking and the production and consumption of wine, as well as images of war. Technicolor, which involves a dye transfer process that was used in this film, was sold to the Chinese film industry after the American company moved into television and relocated to the UK in the late 1970s. Signaling an ontological connection between Fifth Generation cinema and classical Hollywood through richly saturated color palettes, the film material not only helped create a sensory-based cinema in China but also helped entice western consumption: *Red Sorghum* won the Golden Bear at the Berlin International Film Festival, after which it was distributed internationally.

Associated with the Cultural Revolution and Red Guards in previous decades under Mao, the color red is cinematically resignified and recodified throughout Zhang's Red Trilogy, which, along with *Red Sorghum*, includes *Ju Dou* (1990) and *Raise the Red Lantern* (1991), bitter films set in the prerevolutionary era that each starred Gong as the suffering embodiment of China-as-woman.[47] Gong's image in her early career was continually visualized against Zhang's stunning crimson atmospheres, as one reviewer recalls with fondness: "The image of her sculptured cheekbones edged against a reddening background is perhaps one of the most recognisable from recent Chinese cinema."[48] To Zhang, red is a totalizing and holistic expression of the life cycle; he states that as it is "the colour of life, it is also the colour of death."[49] Notably, Zhang was himself "sent down" during the Cultural Revolution to work as a pallbearer in the countryside, required to wear a red sash and to carry coffins painted in vermilion, a particular Chinese shade of red concocted from toxic mercury, and a shade to which the film returns in its final sequence. Echoing the way in which words were arbitrarily used to indict counterrevolutionaries ("class," "bourgeois," "demon," "capitalist-roader"), red became a floating signifier and bitterness a floating affect that sought attachment and new meaning in the Reform era. Explaining his desire to incite passion, Zhang stated that the "Chinese have been too moderate, too reserved.... The boundless red of sorghum fields arouses sensory excitement.... It encourages unrestrained lust for life."[50] A visual corrective to Chinese modesty and reserve—perhaps also to the revolutionary generation's passive acceptance of Mao's orders—the color red in Chinese cosmology also synesthetically correlates with the bodily fluid of sweat and the taste of bitter.

We recognize that the film's redness, dispersed across Jiuer's body and the sorghum fields, references the sorghum wine as well as the forthcoming bloodshed during the Japanese invasion, nine diegetic years later. Meanwhile, the bitter wine carries with it medicinal properties. As Luohan tells her, it "can cure any sort of disease." After Jiuer's arranged husband dies, the men splash wine around in an attempt to wash away the leper's infected traces with glee in a lavish Dionysian scene, upending feudal hierarchies vis-à-vis uninhibited corporeal expression and carnivalesque celebration, meanwhile foreshadowing the tragic ending in which blood, not wine, is spilled.[51] In this scene, bitterness takes on both the liquid form of the wine and the elemental, combustible form of a fire around which the men pivot and into which Li Datou's furniture is thrown. Bitterness disinfects and purges, eschewing hierarchical boundaries and enacting a clearance for new, lateral relations. Furthermore, the bitter medicinal quality of the wine is enhanced by Grandpa's urine in the fermenting vats, initially intended as an act of petulant defiance against Jiuer's refusals to acknowledge their affair. Beholding Grandpa's defiant micturition in front of the team of distillery workers, Jiuer, again at a loss for words, finally swoons and acquiesces. Grandpa is thereafter installed as the new patriarch of the distillery via seminal consumption. As it happens, Grandpa's urine makes Red Shibali wine tastier than ever, rendering it into a profitable, proto-capitalist good. In contrast with the transcendentally sublime, watertight socialist body, the leakage of human waste as productive liquidity in *Red Sorghum* is itself a fantastic, vulgar reinscription of the Chinese body as both immanently earthbound and productive, not through asexualized socialist labor but rather through the "human brine" expelled through the man's sexual organ.[52] Through this act, the film tells us that bitterness is not only medicinal, it is also delicious.

During the film's final tragic act, during the Second Sino-Japanese War, we are reminded of the revolutionary slogan "If the past bitterness is not understood, the present sweetness will be unknown." Flavor exists relationally within a broad experiential spectrum, and sweetness exists only in relation to bitterness, an idea repeatedly invoked in the construction of national identity and affective belonging. Eliding the bitterness under Mao by setting the film during the 1920s and 1930s, *Red Sorghum* returns to an earlier moment of suffering, the Second Sino-Japanese War. The Japanese bring their own imperial connotations of red, as a symbolic red sun emblazoned on their flag contains affect within its perfectly clean borders. Through violent subjugation and colonization, however, Japanese necropolitics subjects the Chinese body to violent porosity. Rather than the orgiastic, painfully pleasurable/pleasurably painful promises of ecstatic union, the Dionysian ecstasy of individual dissolution becomes perverted in the imperialistic acting out of ressentiment, which turns to the abject elimination of the other.

Indeed, the Japanese army orders local butchers to publicly flay a local bandit and Luohan in front of the villagers. Cannibalism emerges as a trope, not of the desire to "eat the Other," to invoke hooks's description of cultural appropriation to which we will later return, but rather to constitute the site/sight of cruelty, moral disgust, and allegorical imperialism (to symbolically eliminate the nation-skin-boundary for penetration). When the knife breaks the skin on Luohan's forehead, the film approaches the abject threshold of defacement and the forcible loss of Chinese face, signifying a corpus of linguistic-cultural signification around shame and humiliation. Meanwhile, a reverse shot of Jiuer in the midst of the spectating crowd, hair matted down with sweat, illustrates the perspiring abjection of witnessing. Sweat as a stress response reroutes the body's water from the kidneys to the skin, exteriorizing anxious interiority. The viewer senses Jiuer's fear through the wet sheen that blankets her. Suddenly, the film shifts into a wide-angled perspective of the young butcher, now sitting alone and covered in his victim's blood, as the camera tracks above him to gaze upon the trampled field. The use of a fish-eye lens (the only instance

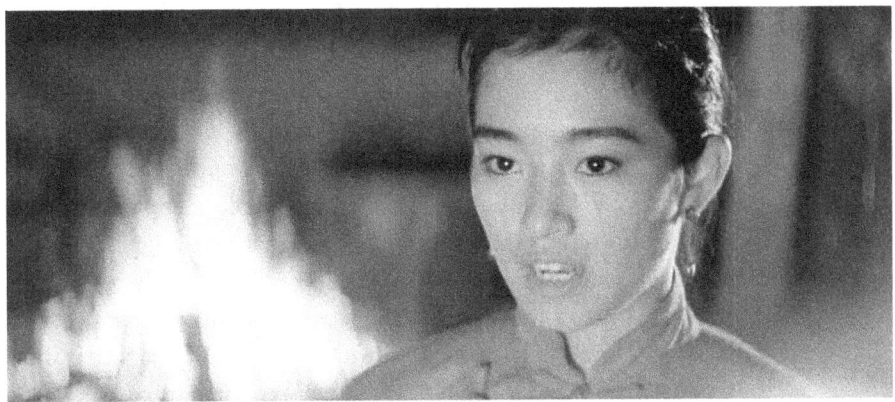

1.6

The cosmoaesthetics of bitterness are conveyed through Gong's becoming-with-fire.

in the film) opens up, wide-eyed, as if in disbelief and shock, betraying the film's own bodily response to the violence.

Red Sorghum's use of a fish-eye lens signals the bending of morality toward absurd cruelty, suggesting that to witness such cruelty demands a new mode of looking altogether. Whereas the film's opening close-up invites an erotic tasting of Gong-as-Jiuer, this warped long shot beckons a disquieted look and a queasy taste—while also insisting that we look with eyes wide open, looking in order to fully digest the trauma and the image of its aftermath. Both deferring and whetting the audience's appetite for revenge, the embittered outrage that this scene provokes finds its visual analogue in the following scene, which shows Jiuer standing before a big fire, the elemental correspondence to bitterness, as she instructs her men to sabotage the Japanese (figure 1.6). The fire demonstrates Nietzsche's notion that "something is burnt in so as to remain in his memory" with the cosmic urgency conveyed by Gaston Bachelard's observation that "all that changes quickly is explained by fire."[53] As Deleuze notes, fire is the only transformational element in Nietzsche's dice throw of becoming, enabling chance and multiplicity to be cooked and (re)heated into being.[54] *Red Sorghum* demonstrates the ways in which trauma, seasoned by bitterness, is cooked into esculent condition and changes quickly into vengeful chance. That is, surely the Chinese know they will lose to the Japanese, but they will take the chance because of the metaphysical charisma of fire's searing qualia. Within the elemental cosmologies of TCM as well as within western materialist philosophies, heat is generative—heat cures heat; fire cures fire; bitter cures bitter.

Conveying her anger through furrowed brow and narrowed eyes, it is Gong-as-Jiuer's fiery commanding directive to the group of men to avenge Brother Luohan that emboldens them to plan their counterattack. In this moment, Gong facializes the anger that Chinese viewers might feel about their national violation, and they are able to sense their own anger projected and performed on-screen. Jiuer, in turn, moved by the men's anthem celebrating the good wine, sheds a single tear as she gazes upon their show of masculine strength. Here again, it is the naked male torso on display for her purview as her libidinal impulses are sublimated into retaliating passions. A close-up of her face, softly illuminated by red-orange flames, reveals a tear as it slips down her cheek, reaching out for mimetic reaction and visualizing the asymmetries of bitterness as fluctuating fragments of anger, melancholy, and proud ressentiment. This close-up mirrors the opening sequence's hungry gaze at Gong's face, satiating the desire once more to draw near to her body. This image, demonstrating Elaine Scarry's concept of beauty's justice-orientating effects, effectively joins together a viewing position of eros, which desires and "is seized by" Gong's beauty, with a caritas or a politics of care, which the film finally redirects toward righteously indignant revolt.[55] That is, Gong's embittered beauty functions as a hinge that translates erotic desire into an intensity for justice. If beauty "intensifies the pressure we feel to repair existing injuries," then vulgar, bodily beauty cauterizes an internal burning resentment within the spectator-as-witness.[56]

In contrast with the boundless bodies of model operas and stiff, watertight socialist actors, *Red Sorghum*'s porous, terrestrial people piss, cry, bleed, ejaculate, and sweat. Whereas semen propagates and populates, piss expresses revolutionary contempt, as later Grandpa makes his heir, the narrator's father, urinate into a vat of red wine used to ambush a Japanese convoy. Men's leaking bodies nudge historical narratives toward their inevitabilities, while Jiuer's secreting body performs the melancholic loss of nationhood. *Red Sorghum*'s leaky bodies, wet from having been turned inside out, as the nation turns upside down, not only challenge the sublimity of socialism, but also the ways in which castration anxieties of national trauma are sublimated into obsession with surfaces. Betraying interior flavors, the wet postsocialist female body stands in contrast to the poreless perfection of scopophilic commodification and socialist sublimity. Vulgar beauty summons us to the body's interior excesses beyond the surface. As Jiuer's leaking body strengthens the phallocentric nationalism at the film's core, Gong as a film star would quickly thereafter become the most glamorous surface upon which China envisioned itself.

From Kissing to (Not) Eating

In the film's final scene, which involves a retaliatory effort to repair injuries inflicted by the Japanese, Jiuer prepares a grand, delicious feast (good taste to reward bitter actions) in anticipation of her men's triumphant counterattack. Flies swirl around extravagant meat and vegetable dishes, first shown in a montage composed of close-ups, echoing the nibbling kisses of Jiuer's face and body in the opening scene. But it is the swirling flies—a visualization of unrelenting, cyclical oppressions and defeats during China's Century of Humiliation—in the subsequent long shot that generate a Barthesian punctum, a bitter wounding, as we realize by melodramatic convention that the film's loving display of delicious food precludes the possibility that the food will be eaten.[57] We are bruised by the fact that Jiuer does not bother to wave off the flies, using her hands instead to flatten the wayward strands of hair that index her sweaty labor. Flies are not a bother in this world, because the Chinese have been violently reduced to the status of flies, summarily executed and disposed of as pests. As Jiuer brings the food to the men, who are hiding in dirt trenches, she is shot by friendly fire, and her dying body crumples to the ground. Without a moment to digest this image, we see a Japanese convoy drive down the road, which the men rush to ambush. Jiuer's spilled red wine intermingles with blood, and suddenly everything becomes awash in red as the film enters into Grandpa's ocular subjectivity. Shocked at the momentous upheaval of his world, Grandpa stares into a coincidental solar eclipse and loses his ability to see any color other than vermilion, a new worldview awash with the bloody imperialism of Japan, as a nondiegetic drum rhythmically sounds his rising bitterness. If black and blue are "sad colors" or bruises in Carol Mavor's account of cinematic chromatic feeling, red is energetic, hateful, passionate, and lusty.[58] It is the vivid color of extremity, the taste of bitterness, and the feeling of angered heat burning and raging inside one's chest. Moreover, it is this particular deep and intense shade of vermillion red at the film's end that finally enfolds the spectator into its ecstatic Oneness.

Vermilion, also known as Chinese red, was first derived from cinnabar pigment, the common ore of mercury, and popularly used in Chinese lacquerware to represent blood, life, and eternity in Daoism. Both the pigment and the lacquer, acquired from *Toxicodendron vernicifluum* (Chinese lacquer tree), are toxic by nature. Notwithstanding the ways in which toxins are mobilized to reinforce individual and national security, which also apply here, Mel Y. Chen contends that there is value nevertheless in redeeming the "queer productivity of toxins and toxicity" that could be oriented toward "desiring the canonically undesired: desiring disability, desiring queerness, desiring objects."[59] What this vermilion red allows, as it washes over us, is for audiences to desire the feeling of bitterness itself, to dwell in emotions of resentment, anger, and sadness as an ethical form of worldly enfolding.

The desire to taste bitterness preceded its cinematic productions because it was historically engineered into Maoist and post-Maoist culture, and Gong and Zhang's following collaborations continued to pivot around this feeling-taste. Gong's characters often perish or succumb to insanity, a pattern scholars note to discuss the fetishization and objectification of the actor's body.[60] Chow, for instance, contends that in the hands of a filmmaker like Zhang, women's stories are "a means for putting on display both the glorious and barbarous aspects of Chinese culture."[61] However, the affects of bearing witness to Gong's repeated reproductions of death also reinforce an abstract but vital concept that sustained the flavor-tone and mood of Reform-era China, one that entwines death and seduction to give birth to a new national consciousness premised on bitterly re-membering the past. Generating a catalog of bitter and symbolic deaths, Gong embodied the charismatic intersections of eroticism, beauty, and death. As an archived, deictic image, one that is discussed in the introduction as "earlier and elsewhere," Gong's bitter allure points to an impassioned and turbulent moment in the transition to market socialism throughout 1980s and 1990s mainland Chinese cinema. However, the tragic culmination of the 1989 democratic protest movement in the Tiananmen Square incident of June 4 demonstrated the state limitations of tolerance toward the people's bitterness. As Gong and Zhang were thrust into the international spotlight, they also became objects of surveillance by the post-Tiananmen government, who banned their subsequent bitter collaborations *Ju Dou*, *Raise the Red Lantern*, and *To Live*, each of which depicts the oppression and suffering of woman-as-nation during China's feudal and communist periods. Turning away from the sweetly fragrant botanical metaphor of the 1980s Cultural Fever of letting "a hundred schools of thought contend" and a "hundred flowers bloom," the Chinese state turned to its own bitter feelings and began clamping down on artistic expression. From olfactory sweetness to malodor, the wary Communist Party cautioned, "Jia chou bu ke wai yang" (Don't air your dirty laundry in public). In other words, don't focus on China's shameful problems and tarnish its national image on the global stage. The literal translation of this warning—"If your home stinks, don't flaunt it"—draws on scent and smell to indict such films as cultural trash and a hazardous waste of talent.[62]

Nevertheless, bitterness dispels toxins, and *Red Sorghum*'s lingering odors of blood, wine, urine, tears, and flayed skin powerfully endure in the film's aftertaste. *Red Sorghum* also marked the birth of international Chinese film celebrity in the post-Mao era, and Gong began to rise to global stardom. As the new face of China's cinematic internationalization, Gong feminized and beautified the image of the nation, earning a place in the American tabloid *People* magazine's Most Beautiful People list in 1993, and becoming the first Chinese celebrity on the cover of *Time* magazine in 1996. Gong's beauty also became a critical point of erotic translation for western audiences. Criticizing the 1993 Cannes Palme d'Or winner *Ba wang bie ji* (*Farewell My Concubine*, Chen Kaige) as "ineffably 'other,'" reviewer John Griffin was nevertheless taken by Gong's allure: "Gong is a beauty of celestial proportions, with talent and empathy to match. When she is on camera, the film makes sense to the dead. When she's not, it's just intrigue in an enigmatic art form."[63] Griffin's description of Gong's on-screen presence reveals the lively dimension within mediated bodily contact with feminine beauty, which not only vivifies its beholder—we wake up to her presence; we are revived from the dead—but also functions as a translation device. Moreover, while aesthetic flavors like bitterness may not retain a static meaning or signification across national and cultural boundaries, the beautiful star transliterates meaning and generates curious and erotic attachments, thereby fulfilling Walter Benjamin's prescription that the translator "must *lovingly* and in detail incorporate the original ways of meaning."[64] Such observations return us to the hermeneutics of the face and the close-up, revealing that spectatorship is flavored by desires for nearness, intimacy, and love, even when encountering pain and bitterness. As an exotic point of embodied translation, Gong's border-crossing career in western cinema would demonstrate the mutable qualities of bitter flavor when the alterity of race becomes an ingredient in the admixture of transnational performance.

Inhaling the Other's Bitterness

After Gong's reputation became well established throughout China and other parts of Asia, she began receiving offers to star in American films in the late 1990s and early 2000s, beginning with Chinese/American director Wayne Wang's *Chinese Box* (1997). After playing a vindictive aging geisha in *Memoirs of a Geisha* (Rob Marshall, 2005), the forty-one-year-old Gong was again cast as a Japanese femme fatale in the European-American coproduction *Hannibal Rising* (Peter Webber, 2007), prequel to Jonathan Demme's prestige horror *The Silence of the Lambs* (1991). Aptly, in "Eating the Other: Desire and Resistance," bell hooks describes the exploited value of ethnicity as a "spice, a seasoning that can liven up the dull dish that is mainstream white culture."[65] hooks's observation is felicitous considering that *Hannibal Rising* centers on the psychopathic taste formations of western cinema's most beloved cannibal, Hannibal Lecter. Cast to sate the diegetic and extradiegetic white male "transgressive desiring subjects," as hooks characterizes white men who seek transgression through interracial sex, Gong's embittered allure reveals the ways in which hypersexualized race flavored a narrative centered on World War II eastern European Holocaust trauma, making its subject palatable for western audiences.

The origin story begins with young Hannibal (Gaspard Ulliel) witnessing the deaths of his aristocratic Lithuanian parents and the cannibalism of his infant sister by Nazi collaborators. Fleeing an abusive Soviet orphanage, postpubescent Hannibal arrives in France to live with his widowed aunt, Lady Murasaki (Gong Li), who trains him in the soft and hard arts of ikebana (floral arrangement) and Japanese samurai swordsmanship. Although a romance between Hannibal and his legal aunt is intimated by longing gazes and swelling orchestral motifs, the film's latent fears of miscegenation permit only a brief, tense kiss. Sublimating his sexual desires into vengeance, Hannibal proceeds to kill and occasionally eat the cheeks of the men who ate his sister, including Lithuanian collaborator Vladis Grutas (Rhys Ifans), who at one point kidnaps Murasaki as a lure for Hannibal. By the end, Hannibal succeeds in killing Grutas, much to Murasaki's horror, and flees to Quebec to kill another of Grutas's men.

While critics discursively performed their distaste for the film ("an unfulfilling meal," "tastes like leftovers," and "not a tasty prequel"), the text performs western biases and belief systems revolving around the idea that "heightened olfactory consciousness" is a danger "to the established social order"—a proposition that Constance Classen, David Howes, and Anthony

Synnott explore in their cultural history of smell.⁶⁶ The lasting legacies of eighteenth- and nineteenth-century European epistemologies dictate that the empirical senses of smell, taste, and touch exemplified atavistic and dangerous traces of animalism, while sight became the exemplary sense of reason and civilization. Contrastingly, as smell became perceived as the most irrational and least sensible sense, frequently associated with "madness and savagery," humans who were fixated on smell were "judged to be either insufficiently evolved savages, degenerate proletariat, or else aberrations: perverts, lunatics, or idiots."⁶⁷ Both Hannibal and his nemesis Grutas fit this description, as they are perversely fixated on the lower senses of smell and taste (senses that intimately intermingle through the entangled processes of olfaction and gustation). Even the juridical Inspector, who is investigating the strange cannibalistic murders, and who serves as an actant for Hannibal's redemption, confronts him about his erotic fixation on Murasaki, surmising that "the *scent* of her took away the *smell* of the camp." Delivered as a callous aside to convey Murasaki's seductive exoticism, this comment is nevertheless loaded with politico-historical signification. The scents of death, human waste, and burning bodies from the concentration camps powerfully lingered in survivors' and Nazi officials' memories as "the last remnant of bad conscience [of] the Nazi death machine."⁶⁸ Hitler moreover deployed a racialized politics of smell by conjuring up medieval allegations of Jews' Satanic *foetus Judaius* (Jewish stench) as physical proof of moral decay. Attractive scent also became an instrument of torture in the camps. In *Five Chimneys* (1947), Auschwitz survivor Olga Lengyel describes the "aesthetic torture" brought on by a beautiful SS officer's perfume.⁶⁹ Evoking the "blond angel" with her own amnesiac effect on others—the Japanese imperialist government was allied with the Germans during World War II, after all—Murasaki's guilty characterization reflects one reviewer's partially digested causality: "'Hannibal Rising' puts the blame for a legendary serial killer where it belongs: with the Nazis. And the communists. And the Japanese."⁷⁰ While "the smell of the camp" operates as sensorial synecdoche for the Lithuanian World War II experience in *Hannibal Rising*, cannibalism becomes the structuring metaphor for the atrocities committed by Nazis, the metaphorical becoming literalized under the constraints of bare life.⁷¹

As radical Other, Murasaki's sensual presence, which we learn must smell of the clove oil she uses to clean her ancestor's swords, therefore acts as deodorant (clove oil is an anesthetic) for the west's traumatic sense memory. Whereas as Jim Drobnick observes that "odors are the means by which the boundary between self and other is demarcated, as well as the supposed basis of prejudicial extensions of such demarcation," Murasaki elicits *odorphilia*, the desiring cognate of odorphobia, and which is constructed from state or majoritarian investment in alterity as physical difference.[72] Furthermore, odors not only reinstate boundaries between self and other, they also challenge such divisions by becoming easily inhaled and ingested by another—their ontological essence is irresistible and forcibly charismatic. That is why the Nietzschean man who has overreacted in his internalization of guilt attempts to stand with "*stopped nostrils* before his own self, and, like Pope Innocent the Third, makes a black list of his own horrors ('unclean generation, loathsome nutrition when in the maternal body, badness of the matter out of which man develops, awful stench, secretion of saliva, urine, and excrement')."[73] Such bad odors reinforce the guilty man's bad conscience, in which ressentiment toward the other, notably including the mother, is internalized. Unable to feel guilt, the villains of *Hannibal Rising*, however, only display an excessive desire to consume Murasaki's (lawfully materteral/auntly) exotic odor. After kidnapping Murasaki as a lure for Hannibal, Grutas dramatically takes a whiff of her long black hair before licking the side of her face—tasting her in a gesture that echoes Hannibal's own gustatory penchants. Stopping short of eating the Other (which would be perfectly logical here), *Hannibal Rising*'s insatiable men only ingest Murasaki through other kinds of ocular and oral pleasures.

Despite its spectacular gratuity, *Hannibal Rising* ultimately upholds traditional, hierarchical sensorial epistemologies that align overdeveloped olfaction and taste senses with the irrational, the insensible, and the immoral. Meanwhile, the Japanese woman possessing "to-be-tastedness" provides assurance against the threat of homosexuality between cannibals Hannibal and Grutas. As Alain Corbin reminds us, Sigmund Freud "assigned" smell with anality, linking it with sadism and homosexuality.[74] The effeminized, infantilized, and sadistic men in *Hannibal Rising* who take pleasure in the smell of hair and the consumption of human flesh might also take polymorphous pleasure in tasting one another—were it not for Murasaki, who functions as heterosexual safeguard and as a smelly fetish object. Moreover, if taste and smell occupy the lowest rungs of the epistemological ladder of sense, they are analogously gendered as female and feminine in their subordinate position to rationalistic scopic and auditory masculine regimes.[75] Pertinently, Murasaki's racialized hypersexuality is foregrounded by an insult that reduces her to a single (odorous) anatomical part: her genitalia.

In a scene after Hannibal moves into his aunt's chateau, the two take a stroll in a busy outdoor food market, rehearsing what might be a quotidian vision of incestuous in-law romance. If they cannot taste one another via cannibalism or copulation, Hannibal and Lady Murasaki can at least curate a common palate of tasty foods that they will both ingest, an eros of consumption in the shared objects caressing their bodily interiors. This image of near-domestic bliss, however, is interrupted when a Vichy butcher luridly asks Murasaki if she possesses a "crossways pussy," repeating an Orientalist anatomical myth that performs excessive pleasure in the form of excited disgust. Visually communicated through the mise-en-scène, Murasaki's allegedly deviant genitalia are analogized through slit-open pig carcasses and chunks of animal flesh hanging in open stalls (figure 1.7). A literal "meat shot"—a term Linda Williams uses to describe "an insert of an insert" that gives visual proof of genital penetration in hard-core pornography—takes the place of the *ob/scene*, that which could only be off-scene in a nonpornographic film.[76] Replacing one ob/scene, aromatic, and erotogenic zone (the male anus) with the visual euphemism, and verbal intimation, of another region (the vagina), the film foregrounds Murasaki's "pussy" in order to sidestep the possibility of homo-anality. When Grutas later overperforms his heterosexuality by licking Murasaki's face, the film suggests that her face is a substitute for her ob/scene part—a misogynistic defacement, in contrast with, earlier, Luohan's nationalistic skin-flaying.

This graphic suggestion generates a surplus of meaning that exceeds language, and is in part *made sense* through the odoriferous mise-en-scène of fragrant precooked foods. Referring to an "olfactory imagination," Vivian Sobchack suggests that smell "occurs through the affective mediation of tonal elements that subjectively modulate and 'qualify' the...people we see onscreen."[77] The phenomenon reveals, in Deleuze and Guattari's concept of materialist correspondence, the "machinic assemblage of bodies, actions and passions, an intermingling of bodies reacting to one another," evocatively resonant in the conceptualization of human beings in what ancient Daoist philosopher Chen Tuan refers to as "an assemblance [*sic*] of energy...consisting of spirit, essence, and energy."[78] Murasaki's dehumanization is reinforced not only by language and by the spectacular juxtaposition of animal carcasses with her body, but also through an affective feeling-tone conveyed by synesthetic significations of bloody, sour meat. These qualify her image as something that is at once not yet consumable (raw and precooked animal) and already putrescent (decaying flesh). Chen's observation that "the 'stuff' of animal nature that sometime sticks

1.7

Hannibal Rising's "meat shot" odorously suggests the racialized anatomical insult.

to animals, sometimes bleeds back onto textures of humanness" aptly applies to this scene wherein Murasaki's "machinic assemblage" is proximally qualified by coterminous, bloody objects conveying animal death and unliveliness.[79] Murasaki's body is rendered here into a paradoxical object of suspicion, and her racialized alterity is sensualized and essentialized through sensorial intimations of the inassimilable, the nonhuman, and the indigestible.

Hannibal Rising demonstrates the complex and intimate entanglements between film's sensorial engagements, embodied performances, taste cultures, and racial formations. Kyla Wazana Tompkins's observation that "visual pleasure in black pain" suggests "a desire to taste it" also holds true for Asian bodies in transnational contexts.[80] Although variations in white desire and fear toward different bodies of color have produced separate yet sometimes intersecting assimilative-digestive tracts, critical food and eating scholars like Tompkins and others have compellingly demonstrated the ways in which racism is repeatedly articulated and enacted through cultures of ingestion.[81] As "eating the Other" in part constitutes a method for destroying the Other, tasting the Other's racial flavors also takes into account the complexities of desire within aesthetic encounters with beauty. If taste functions as a precursor or foreplay to eating and digestion, such aim-inhibited kissing in its cinematic analogue is also a practice in the erotic assimilation of the other. Murasaki's racial scent is both overwhelming and deodorizing, alluringly tasty and abjectly genital. The savoring/tasting of suffering images becomes a haptic act, defined by Laura U. Marks as an erotic engagement premised on oscillating proximities and enmeshing intersubjectivities with the visual object.[82] The spectatorial self thus becomes folded into the act of seeing, an autoerotic, autosarcophagic engagement when we understand that seeing and gazing are also tasting and smelling.

Coda: Psychic Medicine

The national body under Mao, closed to extranational and territorial influences, was imagined as a watertight corpus that jumped and glided above the earth, lacking in flavor and odor. In the Reform era, concomitant with desires to revisit historical trauma and to forge new porous futurities, bitter desires were anterior to their cultural correspondences. The urge to enfold into bitterness generated Fifth Generation cinema and engendered Gong's stardom. As an affective force that crossed boundaries, bitterness sought attachment to porous bodies and chromatic objects. Attaching itself to Gong's sensualized image, Chinese bitterness became embodied, glamorized, and globalized. Gong's role in *Hannibal Rising*, however, indicates the extent to which her racial flavor affirms ineluctable Asian difference, even as "the scent of her" is imbued with fantasies of sanitizing western trauma and deodorizing homosexual desire. Although *Hannibal Rising* uses Gong to "spice" up "the dull dish that is mainstream white culture," such racial fantasies of her deliciously indigestible body cannot make sense of Gong's embittered nationalistic weidao, a flavor borne from making sensation of Chinese historical suffering.

Let us taste a final image of Gong. In *Ju Dou*, the second of Zhang's Red Trilogy, the titular character played by the star is tortured and beaten by her husband. However, only she possesses the will to disrupt feudal order and to expose its cruelty, a fact mirrored in the film's alienating effects and fourth-wall rupture. In one scene containing such techniques, Ju Dou bares her bruised, wet body to her eventual lover, her husband's adopted nephew, who watches her bathing through a peephole. As the camera conflates with his point of view, Ju Dou looks directly at him and at the extradiegetic audience with a pained, breathless expression—her intake of breath becoming what Jennifer Barker refers to as an "in-spiring" moment in which the "film body opens onto ours and invites, even inhales, us."[83] The moment reveals the act of cinematic looking, and, following Barker, "we might even feel [the film's] pulse and breath as our own."[84] However, only through Gong's sensual embodiment of bitterness does Zhang's critique become lodged under the skin, palpitating our hearts, tearing our eyes, kindling our sweat glands, and in-spiring our bodies to move toward the flavorful image. As the ingestion of bitter foods stimulates secretions by salivary glands and digestive organs, the bitter aesthetic also stimulates and agitates us, loading our bodies with "information and energy," to invoke Audre Lorde's defense of anger as an appropriate and ethical response to racism.[85] In this case, we are angered and in-formed by the sight of patriarchal brutality. Bitterness need not only function as affective currency in the domain of bleeding, wounded nationalism and the mythos of past suffering, however. It may also move bodies toward just futurities by stirring the viewer's interior liquidity, and by inciting spillage with anxious, resentful bodies seeking reprisal. With this acknowledgment, I return to the bittersweetness of racial trauma through which I forged an adolescent identification with Gong and began to soak in the soils of odorant Chinese vulgarity.

2

Salty-Cool
Maggie Cheung and Joan Chen

I have never seen a more elegant image of a Chinese woman. Empress Wan Jung is silently protesting Emperor Pu Yi's Manchukuo coronation ceremony in Bernardo Bertolucci's The Last Emperor *(1987) by staging a minor act of insanity. In this scene, Joan Chen eats white gladiolus petals, a befitting imperial symbol of white prosperity, as tears stream down her face. But something surprising coheres between the interaction of tear duct and mouth; the saltiness of tears must flavor the flower's velvety jacket ingested by the empress. For a rebellious teenager, there's stunning honesty in the vision of a beautifully made-up woman, who, helpless and enraged, can only eat her salty sadness.*

Several years later, my college friends are talking about a "cool show" from the '90s called Twin Peaks. *Curious, I rent the DVD and begin to watch the pilot. Chen is the first face that appears. Her red lips reemerge, this time humming a soft and unsettling melody. Her expression is indecipherable, enigmatic, and cold. This does not feel as sincere as Wan Jung's exquisite rage, but it is precisely Josie Packard's inscrutable deceit that lures me in.*

Where bitterness dominates the palate for leaking, post-traumatized Chinese bodies seeking porous connection in the post-Mao era, the less intense but related modality of saltiness concerns differentials in matter and the exaltation of existing flavor. While Gong's foray into western cinema demonstrates bitter weidao's hygienic function, accented stars Maggie Cheung and Joan Chen demonstrate the postbitter aesthetic of saltiness as a means of negotiating western infatuation with the Chinese femme's object-surface. Through alchemical imaginings of salt and an aesthetic translation of salt's thermal absorption and cooling effects, this chapter reveals the conditional possibilities of Chinese cool as an aesthetic embodiment and performative posture with which to negotiate racist and misogynistic heat, as flavor collides with temperature to produce the feminine performance of salty-cool.

Whereas one does not require bitter taste to survive, the consumption of sodium chloride is vital for nerve functions, muscular contractions, and the regulation of bodily fluids, including stomach acids for digestion. Salt assists the body's functions but cannot be produced by the body. It is therefore a nonnative but necessary nutrient for survival that must be imported inside the body. Along such lines of flight, this notion of salt as immigrant substance holds particular salience with regard to the first transnational English-speaking roles for Cheung and Chen, as it illuminates the ways in which white, western imaginary worlds rely on difference and racialization in order to highlight negotiations with a multicultural national identity. Such worlds draw on ethnicity not only to add immigrant spice to homogeneity, but also to temper, trouble, and dampen visions of liberal egalitarianism on the basis of race. This chapter compares and contrasts two relevant 1990s cinematic and televisual texts: the French art film *Irma Vep* (1996) by intellectual auteur Olivier Assayas, and *Twin Peaks* (ABC network, 1990–91), the cult television series by David Lynch and Mark Frost. In both cases, the Chinese female body is instrumentalized by white male directors in accordance with superficial politics of liberal recognition—that is, to indicate through representation that every race, ethnicity, and culture is equal to another, and entitled to equal rights and access to goods, services, and opportunities. Nevertheless, as this chapter and the following reveal, the politics of tolerance, as an ambivalent and suspicious mode of passage, aestheticizes reluctance and uncertainty through the performativity of the inscrutably likable and ornamentalized Chinese woman.

Salty Dosages and Disbelief

As slang phrases like "so-and-so feels salty about x," or "so-and-so is acting salty" suggest, saltiness constitutes a muted form of bitterness, a heated anger that dissipates and is oriented in the direction of recognition. Salt is bitterness with additives of distance and time. Addressing the shared etymological root for soul, *sale* (wit), and salt, Carl Gustav Jung notes correlations between bitterness and salt: "Apart from its lunar wetness and its terrestrial nature, the most outstanding properties of salt are bitterness and wisdom.... Tears, sorrow, and disappointment are bitter, but wisdom is the comforter in all psychic suffering. Indeed, bitterness and wisdom form a pair of alternatives: where there is bitterness wisdom is lacking, and where wisdom is there can be no bitterness."[1] Saltiness vacillates between pain and recognition, mitigating bitterness with inflections of wisdom (wit) and delivering the heuristics of suffering for the sake of acquiring sagacity (soul). Salt's connection to bitterness is also supported in Chinese aesthetic theory, in which the two are corresponding flavor "others," as Sun Tzu notes in the ancient historical text *Zuo Zhuan*: "Harmony is like soup. The salt flavoring is the other to the bitter, and the bitter is the other to the salt. With these two 'others' combining in due proportions and a new flavor emerging, this is what is expressed in 'harmony.'"[2] Salt is the material indication of a harmonious wisdom that inheres in suffering, a process connected to the anima, the feminine aspects of the psyche, which Jung describes as an archetypal correspondence with the maternal eros in opposition to the masculine animus.[3] Influenced by the Chinese yin/yang dualistic model of harmonic unity, whereby the feminine and masculine form a complementary whole, Jung's notion of syzygy describes the anima/animus as a relational form that enables recognition and reckoning with one's shadow, the dark, repressed aspects within the unconscious.[4] From the bitterness of his own split with Sigmund Freud, and with a newfound sense of wisdom, Jung began to assert that sexuality was one of multiple forms of psychic energy, not the primary one, per Freud.[5] Jung's conceptualization of eros should therefore be understood through the polyvalence and multiplicities of feeling—not only through libidinal sexuality.[6] In unyoking sexuality and libido, by taking a Jungian rather than Freudian approach to drive, affective conceptualizations of libidinal force enable inquiries into unerotic affects and equivocating drives—for instance, taking into account bafflement, perplexity, and embarrassment, feelings to which we return throughout this book. In this chapter, beauty's minor forms of likability and coolness correlate with Jung's concept of saltiness as a maturation step in bitter's movement toward wisdom.

Cheung demonstrates this movement away from the bitter in the ways in which she negotiates her restrictive, objectifying costume in *Irma Vep*. Maggie, playing herself as a Hong Kong movie star, is asked to act in a modern remake of the silent French serial film *Les Vampires* (Louis Feuillade, 1915–16). To play the leading role of an underworld criminal, she wears a tight latex costume modeled after Michelle Pfeiffer's skintight Catwoman outfit in *Batman Returns* (Tim Burton, 1992). A crumpled magazine editorial displaying Pfeiffer as Catwoman appears in costume designer Zoé's (Nathalie Richard) files, which she shows Maggie in their first fitting at a "shop for hookers." Notably, Pfeiffer remarked about the physical discomfort of her costume: "It was the most uncomfortable costume I've ever been in. They had to powder me down, help me inside and then vacuum-pack the suit. They'd paint it with a silicon-based finish to give it its trademark shine. I had those claws, and I was always catching them in things. The face mask was smashing my face and choking me.... We had a lot of bugs to work out."[7] Pfeiffer's recollection of the constrictions of her Catwoman costume grants phenomenological insight into the inflections of vocal exhaustion in her memorably languid performance, revealing the somatic consequences of binding attire. Pfeiffer's feminine complaint indicates both the material restraints involved in hypersexualization, as well as the privilege that enables an A-list white Hollywood star like Pfeiffer to register such protests in the first place. Contrastingly, Maggie's grievances, if any, are unvoiced. Displaying her own agility (evocative of the lithe Chinese acrobat under a western eye, perhaps), Maggie demonstrates that she can not only move and breathe in her costume, she even smokes before every take, easing into a pose of French coolness. After Zoé remarks that the costume must be tight because it is a "bondage costume," Maggie responds defensively and perhaps even submissively, "No, I like it." Nevertheless, her rising vocal inflection, edging toward a questioning tone, seems to suggest otherwise. Along the lines of surface and skin, Maggie's latex outfit gestures through materiality the salty-cool masquerade of deflection that she must adapt in negotiating her place. Moreover, like the latex encasing her body, Maggie's racial body becomes a formal property through which the elasticity of French identity is tested.

If Pfeiffer's experience of the latex catsuit was extremely uncomfortable ("smashing" and "choking"), Maggie's discomfort when she initially tries on her costume passes through a brief wince that quickly folds into a smile, as she turns away from Zoé and faces the camera. Glimpsing her wince, only the audience becomes privy to her charming machinations, insofar as she then lies to Zoé that she likes the costume (her face says otherwise). Maggie's expression, one that quickly dissolves a look of pain into friendly acceptance, therefore distills a kind of disciplinary raciality that Maggie has adapted from acting, always ready and willing to accommodate. This "racial cheer," to borrow Vivian Huang's term, constitutes Maggie's salty-cool affective masquerade, a performance that draws upon the powers of friendly deflection, which generates a cryptic mask that ultimately forestalls deeper understanding of her personality.[8] Acting Chinese here is the art of elision and elusiveness, a seduction of inaccessibility. Salty cheer becomes a trick whereby the cool remains disinterested in making truth claims.

Less about what is true than about how much something matters, alchemical psychological understandings of salt are informed by Jung's aforementioned metaphysical-material musings on the substance. James Hillman defines alchemical psychology not as a "literal return to alchemy" but rather the "restoration of the alchemical mode of imagining."[9] In such a mode of imagining, salt "acts like the ground of subjectivity," and, by extension, the flavor of saltiness is that which gives us "a sense of the personal—my tears, my sweat and blood, my taste and value."[10] Whereas leaking bodily fluids constitute lubrication for bitter recognitions of traumatic inheritance, such fluids also encase the corporeal brine that emotes in mattering moments. Wherein the spectator perceives bitterness throughout *Red Sorghum*'s chromatic, porous world, Jiuer tastes salt in her tears, sweat, and blood within a somatic, narcissistic feedback loop grappling with the collective traumas of war. Saltiness is a becoming of the body that reaffirms psychic duress, confirming the extrapsychic dimensions of suffering through the body's leaky productions. Salty fluids extend the body in order to intermingle with the world, delivering inside contents to the outside and, conversely, to absorb nonnative salty objects into the body, churning internal systems. A migrant substance of subjectivity, salt thereby grounds us in the firstness and feltness of experience, the "wetness of the encounter," to adapt Laura U. Marks's vivid phrase about translation—and the taste of aliveness.[11]

Saltiness is also about timing. Hillman writes, "*Sal* describes one of our matters, something that is mattering in us and is the 'matter' with us—too much, too little salt, or salt at the wrong times and places, or combined wrongly."[12] Salt therefore not only describes how much we value something, but also characterizes errors in judgment and circumstance that we deem unlucky or unfortunate (salt at the wrong time and place). As contemporary discourses surrounding the police shootings of unarmed Black Americans testify, the often-repeated phrase "wrong place at the wrong time" has become a resounding defense of the officers. This notion of displacement and untimely coincidence is subsequently internalized by victims of random violence, as John A. Rich observes that "[at the] wrong place, wrong time" is a phrase "commonly spoken by injured young [Black] men struggling to uncover the meaning behind their trauma."[13] However, race does not appear in alchemical psychology or Jungian analyses, even as acts of racialized violence are often described as occurring at "the wrong times and places, or combined wrongly." Race is also elided in affect and materialist theories, as Colin Patrick Ashley and Michelle Billies note that "questions of race and racial matterings are often demonized as inherently nonmaterial and sidelined to the field of representation—the very field that affect theory often seeks to avoid or circumvent. This often leaves under theorized questions of race within affect studies."[14] Addressing this oversight, the following demonstrates that racial matter sensorially gestures to something being amiss or wrong. In *Irma Vep* and *Twin Peaks*, race becomes a salty issue, involving proper dosages of charm (beauty's minor seduction as opposed to charisma) and a savoring of geopolitical matters that often doubles back upon its own premises of inclusion, with hesitation and doubt—in other words, matters taken with a grain of salt.

Indeed, within the idiomatic logic of taking things with a grain or pinch of salt, we find that salt acts as a caution against literality. The salty orientation enables belief itself to be split and partial, not only encouraging us to be skeptical but also allowing us to embrace alternate or even degraded ways of knowing. One might think of epistemologies that have been denounced as pseudoscience, like TCM (in the west), alchemy, astrology, or witchcraft, minor formations of belief and information often taken with a grain of salt by nonpractitioners. It is precisely because they are bad ideas that such forms of abject epistemology—information and belief systems ejected from dominant productions of knowledge—are unexpectedly eased or imported into mainstream discourse. Because "bad ideas" refers to fragmented, misguided, and partially formed judgments, we are thereby free to elect belief to varying (salty) degrees and dosages while simultaneously maintaining a reasonable suspicion. Alchemy, for example, was "dogged by the reputation of being an especially bad idea," and yet it offered early modern western societies "a treasure trove of metaphors for metamorphosis, or purification, or falsehood, or capitalism," according to Katherine Eggert.[15] Eggert's term "disknowledge" thus describes a phenomenon whereby we believe even if we know better. Thinking alchemically then is to follow the logics of various "obfuscations, misguided learning practices, and scams" associated with the instability of identity and performance, elsewhere theorized in queer studies as disidentification and camp.[16]

Indeed, thinking alchemically is prototypical of thinking campily. As Susan Sontag asserts appositely in her "Notes on 'Camp,'" camp "is good for the digestion," as "camp taste supervenes upon good taste as a daring and witty hedonism. It makes the man of good taste cheerful, where before he ran the risk of being chronically frustrated."[17] Intimating a somatic parallel between chronic frustration and constipation, Sontag's alimentary metaphor of camp can also be extended to salt, as salt aids in maintaining proper stomach pH and is also "good for the digestion."[18] A salty aesthetic, like camp, enables one to indulge in bad taste, without a governing sense of guilt or shame. Moreover, a salty performance is one that is marked by hesitation, doubt, and equivocation; it is held in dubious relation to the truth. Salt is therefore connected to superstition, bad ideas, and deceit, making it easier to taste and savor bad ideas, the transgressive and the taboo, which, as this chapter demonstrates, are implicitly entangled and associated with what is cool.

Passing through various reparative theories and subjugated knowledges then, the following extrapolates from salt's thermal properties its own archetypal/stereotypical conceptualization of the Chinese feminine salty-cool through the minor acts of Cheung and Chen. Drawing upon multiple contact points between saltiness and coolness, a thermal theory of the salty aesthetic enables us to take a cultural temperature of the ways the Chinese woman is situated within two cool (art-house film and cult TV series) western cine/televisual constructions of nationality, race, gender, and performance, and posits a framework for disknowing the Chinese femme (to believe Maggie's false front and friendliness, even as we know better) in order to delight in, and cheer on, her racial saltiness.

Cool Bondage, Salty Likability

The child of a globalized upbringing, Maggie Cheung (Cheung Man-yuk in Cantonese, and Zhang Man-yu in Mandarin) was born in Hong Kong but relocated to Bromley in the UK with her parents at the age of eight. As the "only Chinese kid on the block," Cheung dyed her hair blonde in an attempt to fit in with white students, although she recalls that she was unsuccessful in her attempts at assimilation.[19] After returning to Hong Kong at age eighteen, Cheung participated in the Miss Hong Kong Beauty Pageant, earning first runner-up and "Best Photogenic Face." With exceptional "faceification" (*visagéification*), a term Deleuze uses in part to refer to the full face and its features, Cheung's wide-eyed, moon-shaped face homes soft and welcoming features—a physiognomy revealing receptivity and sensitivity. Her looks quickly earned Cheung several girl-next-door film roles in Hong Kong genre films, beginning with the role of Jackie Chan's girlfriend in *Police Story* (1985), the breakout film credited for Cheung's sudden fame in Hong Kong cinema and, by proxy and distribution, Asia and the eastern hemisphere. Over the next three years, Cheung made fifteen films, mostly comedies. Cheung was then selected by Hong Kong New Wave auteur Wong Kar-wai to star in *As Tears Go By* (1988), the first of many collaborations with Wong that would render the actor a recognizable figure on the international film festival circuit. A few years later, Cheung gained critical attention in Hong Kong director Stanley Kwan's metatextual *Center Stage* (1991), a film within a film wherein Cheung the actor plays classical mainland film star Ruan Lingyu, who killed herself at age twenty-five in response to tabloid gossip surrounding her extramarital affair. For this role, Cheung became the first Asian actor to win an international acting award, with the Silver Bear Best Actor Award at the Berlin International Film Festival, and during the ensuing height of her career she starred in other notable Hong Kong New Wave films like *Song of the Exile* (Ann Hui, 1990), *Farewell, China* (Clara Law, 1996), *Comrades, Almost a Love Story* (Peter Chan, 1996), and *The Soong Sisters* (Mabel Cheung, 1997). Often described with terms like "icon of modernity," "transnational," and "cosmopolitan," Cheung embodies the modern, global Chinese woman of the late twentieth century. Just as diasporic and exilic filmmakers infuse film's deep structure with their displacement within what Hamid Naficy terms "accented cinemas," accented performers also flavor their roles with "foreign-ness."[20] A "foreign" identity is encoded not only in the deviant enunciations and twisting of words and phrases, but also within visual embodiment—through ethnic difference, as well as through gesture and movement. As a material accent for food, salt bestows an extra dimension of spice and inflection intended to enhance the flavor of what is already there.

Roland Barthes notes that "where knowledge is concerned, things must, if they are to become what they are, what they have been, have that ingredient, the *salt of words*. It is the taste of words which makes knowledge profound, fecund."[21] The Asian female Other, in particular, helps to render fecund the buffet of multiculturalism and make palpable the implicit dictates of tolerance, in which one has to withstand (but not necessarily to enjoy) difference. Food tolerance, after all, denotes not a desire for a certain food, but an acceptance of what is or is not acceptable for intake. The salt of ethnic bodies enhances the flavors of racialized nationalism and renders digestible the exotic Other. Similar to Naficy's observation that "the accented style is itself an example of free indirect discourse in the sense of forcing the dominant cinema to speak in a minoritarian dialect," the minority Chinese body in an otherwise predominantly white European or American cast bends and accentuates the film with racial flavor. Salt is a swerve of affect, an embodied difference.

Infatuating (Sur)faces

In *Irma Vep* (1996), aging New Wave director René Vidal (Jean-Pierre Léaud) selects Maggie to star in his remake of *Les Vampires* after watching her in the Hong Kong martial arts science fiction film *The Heroic Trio* (Johnnie To, 1993). Desiring a modern Irma Vep who is also beautiful and magical, René casts the star and instructs her just to be herself. During the shoot, costume designer Zoé develops an unreciprocated crush on Maggie, and various crew members gossip with Maggie about the others. Eventually, René's inability to deepen his fantasy of Maggie as a superficial Other results in his nervous breakdown and subsequent departure from the film, which also precipitates Maggie's exit from the remake as another French filmmaker, José Mirano (Lou Castel), takes over directing and recasts white French actor Laure (who had been playing Maggie's diegetic double in the remake, and who is played by Nathalie Boutefeu) in the lead role.

After meeting Cheung at the Venice Film Festival, Olivier Assayas recounts how he became inspired to work with her. Echoing René's comments in the film, Assayas remarked, "As a film star she was radically different from anything I had experienced with French actors. She had this modern version of glamour and it started me thinking along the lines of, would I make different films if I was working with different actors?"[22] Jonathan Romney suggests that *Irma Vep* became an "infatuation film" for the director and his lead, as the two fell in love on set and subsequently married. Infatuation, however, is all about fantasy and surface; relevantly, Assayas remembers the film as "very much about the fantasies you build on the surface of movie stars."[23] A self-proclaimed fan of Wong Kar-wai and Hong Kong action cinema, Assayas was familiar with Cheung's work but believed that her potential had been restricted by the dictates of genre films. *Irma Vep* and *Clean* (2004), a collaboration between the two that followed eight years later, demonstrated Assayas's expressed interest in reimagining the French auteur cinema of *petits sujets* (minor subjects) to include the lives of non-European transnational characters.

The fantasies that Assayas built upon the surface of Cheung's stardom result in the doubling of "Maggie," the star of the film-within-the-film (the remake of *Les Vampires*) and Cheung the actor playing "Maggie," creating a *mise en abyme* of continual displacements of identity and manifold points of referentiality. Although Maggie's stardom is foregrounded as mediated access to another cinematic-mythological reference (also in a way repeating Stanley Kwan's *Center Stage* [1991], in which, as mentioned, she plays Ruan Lingyu), it also becomes a false façade, as her performance is multiply mediated by Assayas's direction, René's direction, and the layers of cinematic technique on display in *Irma Vep* and *Les Vampires*. After José is installed as the film's new director, he delivers an angry diatribe questioning Maggie's casting to Laure in a crowded French café ("Pourquoi une Chinoise?"). He then promptly replaces Maggie with the latter, who had been playing a minor role as Irma Vep's diegetic double. Falling into the trap of unsalted literality and eschewing the exciting, deconstructive possibilities of catachrestic racial recasting, José angrily says, "Irma Vep is Paris. She's the Paris underworld. She's working-class Paris. She's Arletty! Irma Vep is street-thugs and slums! 'Les Vampires' is not Fu Manchu." Fu Manchu, the mythological Chinese villain caricatured by British author Sax Rohmer, became a fixture in western popular culture and elaborated upon the stereotype of Chinese as cunning, evil, and arcane. José's bitterness about René's casting choice erupts through an angry tumble of words spat with revulsion. "Fu Manchu"—a willful misgendering of Maggie—reinforces the fact that to José, who represents French nationalism, her racial odor overpowers her femininity. José's blue-eyed brunette interlocutor then responds by bursting into laughter, a release valve from the pressures of political correctness on René's multicultural set. Assayas, however, subtly reveals Laure's unfitness for the role through several gestures: first when she complains that she cannot breathe in her costume, and second in a scene in which she ruins twenty-five takes by laughing as an ill-fitting mask is placed over her head. Later, a tear in Laure's latex costume, which would require Zoé to creatively deploy gaffer tape, signals the inappropriateness of Laure in the role. The costume signals that the role is a literal-figurative bad fit for Laure, and yet, because she possesses what José believes to be the surface French look, the new director will assert his interpretation of literal and predictable racial correction in casting and restoring whiteness to Frenchness. Nevertheless, Assayas also reveals José's unsuitability by showing the righteously angry director asleep in front of Feuillade's *Les Vampires* as it plays on his television set.

Scholars writing on *Irma Vep* remark upon the film's concern with French national cinema as well as upon Maggie's failures to pass. As Dale Hudson points out, Assayas uses Cheung as a transnational cosmopolitan archetype (another Jungian concept) through whom to critique the latent racism embedded in French national cinema. Hudson writes, "For Assayas, Vidal is remaking a cinematic 'archetype,' the character of Irma Vep, not *Les Vampires*, so that *Irma Vep* becomes a film about 'how an archetype is discovered' and 'how it has to be remade for every generation.'"[24] In *Irma Vep* and *Clean*, both starring Cheung, Assayas's archetype for cinema necessarily involves including a new racial archetype to express the growing realities of a multicultural west, one that foregrounds diversity as a model for post/national tastemaking. It bears noting, however, that distinctions between archetype and stereotype are haphazardly incidental; archetype may only require a proper dosage of sensitivity, an appropriate salting and demonstration of social grace "at the right time and place" to evade accusation as its degraded counterpart.[25]

This productive slippage between archetype and stereotype finds critical grip in Rey Chow's explanation of stereotype as a reduction to surfaces and exteriors, which can nevertheless be productively and creatively mobilized—as with Jacques Derrida's theory of deconstruction, which relies on the stereotype of the Chinese language as pure ideogram—to produce new hermeneutic and interpretive practices. Critically, the stereotype is reinforced by visual signifiers of difference, as Chow explains that "although stereotypes are not necessarily visual in the physical sense, the act of stereotyping is always implicated in visuality by virtue of the fact that the other is imagined as and transformed into a (sur)face, a sheer exterior deprived/independent of historical depth." Therefore, the stereotype of the inscrutable Chinese is derived from the violence of regarding the "other's language as (pure) image and of an entire people as (mere) face."[26] In contrast with the vivifying force of beautiful stars through the affective labors of giving good face (as discussed in the introduction), what is germane about Chow's argument is the idea that stereotypes are encounters with shallow "(sur)faces." In regard to the stereotype of Chinese inscrutability in particular, it is the exterior, the costume, and the indecipherable face that acts as an elastic outer skin, rebounding attempts to comprehend, master, and contain the Chinese feminine subject. To regard an entire people as mere face is another form of epidermalization. Flattening the "face of a person" as "surface" and "exterior" through stereotype dispels the need, desire, or lure for interior excavation. Acting as an abbreviated, flat symbol, the stereotype deters its beholders from the deep processual dives required in intimacy and love, what Alain Badiou characterizes as "always the possibility of being present at the birth of the world."[27] The stereotype is itself an infatuation with (sur)faces, fatal thresholds, and limit points, rather than beginnings and births; it is the fantasy of a finished product.

Turning Cool Racial Tricks

As mentioned above, the racial trick surfaces through Maggie's disguise of her bodily discomfort in latex, demonstrating through materiality Celine Parreñas Shimizu's recuperative concept of racialized-sexualized subjection. Shimizu contends that hypersexual representation folds Asian/American women into identification, suggesting that the recognition of the pleasures in one's stereotype holds emancipatory potential for Asian/American women to forge new social and political subjectivities through an engagement with, rather than dismissal of, their containment. In contrast with the physical choking Pfeiffer experienced in her Catwoman mask, Shimizu writes, "The fear of sexual perversity, pleasure, and badness can *choke* the voicing of complex experiences of sexuality and curb the beauty emergent from the chronicles of our sexual histories and the survival of sexual subjection."[28] It is the fear of hypersexuality that restrictively chokes the possibilities for Shimizu's perverse enjoyment of the bondage of race-positive sexuality. Maggie's proclamation that she "likes" the costume therefore reveals not only a tolerance for restriction but also an identifying pleasure with hypersexuality. When Maggie defends Irma Vep as a strong character, the distressed director René grouses, "No, no, she just gets fucked. That's all," mimicking the act of "getting fucked" with a hard slap to the top of his forearm. Maggie retorts, "Well, she has no morals, yes. But, is that a problem?," attempting to depathologize the assumed inferiority of the bottom (the fucked object) in relation to the top (the fucking subject), echoing Tan Hoang Nyugen's recuperation of gay Asian male bottomhood and its associations with feminizing abjection as a political and aesthetic position.[29] Being cool with it here not only implies an easygoing nature, a certain glide with events and circumstances beyond one's control (what we might commonly refer to as not giving a fuck). By suggesting that Irma Vep's promiscuity is not a problem, Maggie brings forth and unsettles the sexual morality (and hypocrisy) inscribed within her character's overt, surface hypersexualization. Defining Maggie's performance through the trope of latex as that "which can stretch meanings in performance, just as translations can stretch the bounds of 'identity,'" Olivia Khoo interprets Maggie's theft of Chinese feminine exoticization as an agential act.[30] Crucially, this agential act of theft hides under the guise of a salty-cool disinterest and a secretive racial knowingness that one must take what is not given via charm subterfuge, as it involves deception, being cool, and getting fucked—all the while coolly not giving a fuck.

Scholars of cool agree that coolness as an aesthetic and embodied style originates from diverse African cultures as a method of encounter.[31] Robert Harris Thompson's work traces western, central, and eastern African ancient, linguistic, and artistic traditions of cool to describe the techniques of "transcendental balance" and an aesthetic that imparts order "by means of ecstatic unions of sensuous pleasure and moral responsibility."[32] Thompson further explains that "the data, as a whole, communicate their own insight, a notion of black cool *as* antiquity, for as Ralph Ellison has put it, 'We were older than they, in the sense of what it took to live in the world with others.'"[33] Adapted by Black Americans in the United States as a mechanism for survival, coolness became a technology of self that whites and non-Blacks appropriate. Alexander Donnell writes, "Cool, the basic reason blacks remain in the American cultural mix, is an industry of style that everyone in the world can use."[34] Whereas cool style, as an industrial product, has assimilated into the American cultural mix, the cool pose itself is a way to withstand and endure the heat of liberal multiculturalism's hot, pressuring demands—most remarkably framed through the metaphor of cultural identities melting together into one large pot. Coolness is not only an outward pose and posture, it also carries an affective intensity, even if perceived as withholding or reserved. Describing affect through thermal metaphor, Deleuze writes that affects "have singularities which enter into virtual conjunction and each time constitute a complex entity. It is like points of *melting*, of *boiling*, of *condensation*, of *coagulation*, etc."[35] Gesturing to phase changes of matter through liquid, solid, and gas, Deleuze clarifies affect's processual, ever-changing, transitional nature as that which does not "blend into the indifference of the world." Melting, boiling, condensation, and coagulation are not impartial or neutral processes, but rather, loaded with thermal interest and ontic excitability. Indeed, when Maggie is called in to cool down an overheated René in the middle of his neurotic panic attack, her performance demonstrates the effects/affects of a cool posture that deintensifies René's hot temper and overheated ego.

When Maggie is summoned to René's home, she asks why he wanted to remake the film in the first place. He confesses, "I had this idea of you in this part in this costume. I thought it was very exciting. No, it's like a fantasy." As he looks down at the ground in embarrassment, a high-angle medium close-up of Maggie's face, softly illuminated from below, offers the director formal absolution (figure 2.1). Speaking alchemically, Maggie comforts René: "That's desire, and I think it's okay because that's what we make movies with." Seeking permission for his libidinal desires for Maggie through his on-screen ego, Assayas seeks forgiveness in his own desiring pursuit of exotic (sur)faces. As the director states in an interview, "Even when I made 'Irma Vep,' I hardly knew her. I used her as a Hong Kong movie star, not as the actual person she is. She's made a career being someone else, not herself."[36] During this shot-reverse-shot exchange, Maggie's close-up is for all intents and purposes a beauty shot insofar as, luminously lit from the front and below, it showcases her stunning bone structure, in stark contrast with René's dimly lit and flat reaction shot. Maggie's shot thus offers an aesthetic response to an intellectual question—answering that it's not only "okay" to use desire to "make movies" but demonstrating via cinema precisely how this is so. Feminine beauty as a glamour conjures a spell that suspends its desiring male beholder in attention, interest, and waiting, which he caches away in Platonic cave shadows (René is here leaning against a closet bursting with paperwork). Evoking the Derridean strange-making of Chinese inscrutability as surface, René remarks, "You think you're at the core of the thing, but in fact, you are just at the *surface*." Reducing Maggie to mere face (a stereotype in Chow's conception), René cannot proceed with the film because he cannot deepen his own superficial desire. He says that he "feel[s] nothing"; he is "just interested" in Maggie and no longer in the film. Seeking depth in the stereotype's (sur)face, René's breakdown occurs at the very point at which he cannot relinquish the idea that fantasy itself as a psychic operation is not serious. René fails to realize that the fantasy of courtly love is itself a masochistic game that renders love into what Slavoj Žižek describes as a "pure surface event" wherein the Lady "functions as a unique short circuit in which *the Object of desire itself coincides with the force that prevents its attainment*—in a way, the object 'is' its own withdrawal, its own retraction."[37] Therefore, when Maggie all too willingly suggests to René that having fun is a valid means through which to inhabit her role, she expresses enjoyment in preventing what is truly valued by the desiring male subject, which is, in fact, the perpetual postponement of sexual conquest and thus of enjoyment. René snaps back with annoyance, "No, it's not a game. It's very important," maintaining the de rigueur position that the meaningfulness of art is proportionate with its difficulty and inaccessibility.[38]

Predictably then, at the end of *Irma Vep*, we see René's final cut of the film, which features physical scratches upon the celluloid, a failed attempt to scratch and deepen Maggie's seductive surface and to erase the all-too-willing object of his desire, even as the director inscribes seriousness vis-à-vis formal experimentation. In René's film, Maggie's eyes, the ethnic marker of difference, are notably scratched out and replaced with white lightning bolts, turning her face into a sight/site of offensive protrusion. René's cut evokes a sequence in Jean-Luc Godard's *Le Vent d'Est* (1970), in which an entire celluloid sequence featuring workers is marked and scratched, which Peter Wollen explains as "a way of expressing negation."[39] Similarly, as a Godardian figure, René ensures that his final film becomes an "erasure, a virtual negation"; however, it is one that is specifically focused upon Maggie's racial body. The textural manipulation betrays René's/Assayas's anxious concerns over the loving depth beneath Maggie's mask of seduction, and a negation of Maggie's own ocular pleasure in gazing back. The "eyes that fascinate," the mantra that puts Irma Vep in a spell in *Les Vampires*, are here punitively negated and remade as killer eyes from which she shoots electric bolts. Nevertheless, where René fails, Assayas succeeds in his remake of *Irma Vep*, by allowing Maggie to become a desirous, cryptic surface—in turn enabling Maggie to performatively adapt the cool, resistant surface of latex for her relational interactions with the French others.

Shimizu observes that "because the Asian woman cannot be imagined outside of sex, her resistance is also found in sex."[40] In the case of *Irma Vep*, Maggie sublimates her sexual allure into less intense forms of lure and likability, a dissolution of hypersexuality into saline cool.[41] Although Maggie's persistent agreeableness and affability at first portray her as a stereotypical docile Asian woman, we have much reason to doubt her sincerity, as a series of deflecting acts of conciliation betray racialized tactics of coolness, which, rather than being steeped in bitterness, take on

2.1

The soft lighting upon Maggie's face serves as formal absolution for René's/Assayas's desires for her sur(face).

the salty orientations of a wisdom-in-formation that exploits being liked as a racial object. Maggie, in other words, demonstrates a mastery of the psychopolitics that Byung-Chul Han assigns to neoliberal likes.[42] Where Han is cynical about any possibility of a recuperative model of likes within neoliberal affect economies, Cheung demonstrates the utility of charm and pleasantness, appropriating minor affects and felinic seduction for deflection, avoidance, and indirection.

Through the film's multiple gestures to Catwoman and cat burglary, we see that Maggie's salty-cool is forged through allusions to animal transmogrification. As Jean Baudrillard writes, "All seduction is feline.... For felinity is simply the sovereign unfolding of the body and movement."[43] Felinity performs the kinesthesia of power in reconciling body and movement as unifying, totalizing force. Searching for the right direction for Maggie's stunt double, the stunt coordinator tells her that the movement should be more effortless, remarking, "You have to be even more supple. A little more...what's the word? Animal. More animal."[44] Drawing together the metaphysical concept of "becoming-animal" with performativity, Deleuze and Guattari refer to Robert De Niro's account of walking like a crab for his role in *Taxi Driver* (Martin Scorsese, 1976), explaining that "it is not a question of his imitating a crab; it is a question of making something that has to do with the crab enter into composition with the image, with the speed of the image. That is the essential point for us: you become-animal only if, by whatever means or elements, you emit corpuscles that enter the relation of movement and rest of the animal particles, or what amounts to the same thing, that enter the zone of proximity of the animal molecule."[45] In Deleuze and Guattari's estimation, becoming-animal is a crucial step in the transformation from the molar (conscious identity) to the molecular (multiplicity), but significantly, it is the velocity within the act of becoming that matters. If the human was defined by/as European man, the election of becoming-cat may offer a particularly salient model for a Chinese (in)humanist (that is, animal) femininity that sneaks and burglarizes its way into white ethno-nationalist spaces, stealthily and with speed. To get into character, Maggie even steals a necklace from a fellow hotel resident (maybe she's not so nice, after all). Although referencing Pfeiffer, Cheung's Catwoman eschews Pfeiffer's uncomfortable felinic embodiment for a smooth felinity. Maggie's secondary black latex skin, into which she is "poured," as Zoé describes, enables us to see her body as a silhouette, a darkened glimmer moving across the black-and-white screen, as we see in René's dailies and in his incomplete final edit. If, as Ashley and Billies suggest, the affective capacity of Blackness as a "sticky attractor" concerns the ways in which Black phenotypes transform into social and "specific ontological material force," then Maggie's costuming in black latex skin circumscribes what the authors refer to as "black risk" as a technology of outer skin utilized by the Asian Other, a directed deflection away from Blackness to a superficial appropriation.[46] Transforming risk into trick, Maggie's racialized sexuality and likability demonstrate the ways in which Asianness as a sticky attractor and an ontological force manages threat by friendly circumlocution and smooth affects—a digestibility without harshness or bitterness. Maggie's "own" faux fur–lined coat that she wears off the film set, however, is a persistent reminder of her feral embodiment, evoking unkempt wilderness.

Similar to the impenetrability of latex, Cheung's performativity is one of imperviousness. Maggie's deflection occurs multiple times, and her true desires are veiled; when asked if she has "sex with girls," Maggie rebounds the question back to Zoé's inquiring friend: "What about you, have you?" Then, "Why do you ask?" The cool pose is one that deflects, resists outside information, and returns the serve into the other's court. Meanwhile, those around Maggie reveal an impulse to confide in her, as Zoé explains, "You know, I tell you everything and then you can know me a lot." As the foreign body invited inside, Maggie's role as accented salt makes the shared information more fecund; as in cooking, Maggie's saltiness enhances what is already there. Similarly, René is repeatedly compelled to confess to Maggie, to explain his desires to her, as crew members seek her out in order to gossip about others. Later when Zoé asks if she agrees that there should be more personal filmmaking, Maggie cheerily replies, "I don't know," before punting the question "Do you?" back to her. It is this equivocation as a strategically cool maneuver that reveals Maggie's ultimate detachment and refusal to intimately engage through a model minoritarian performance of politeness and friendliness. We are repeatedly privy to Maggie's yielding charms, which she is able to turn on and off. This conciliatory deflection becomes most useful when Maggie's male scene partner becomes angry with her for not seeming adequately frightened. Maggie responds with giggling and apologizing; she then resets and delivers a sincere performance. Whereas Hudson interprets Cheung's performance in the role of Irma Vep as "uncertain," reading her movements as "hesitant and perplexed," he misses the point that Maggie's reluctance to inhabit the role is part of her opaque racial trick.[47] This racial trick, drawing upon salt's postbitter mediations and cool's method of detachment, deintensifies, lessens, diminishes, and withdraws from what might otherwise turn into a racial battle and its fatiguing consequences, particularly in light of the broiling ethno-nationalist sentiment beneath the surface, which finally erupts through José's racist tirade. Maggie's cool is therefore an indefatigable act of life preservation.

As a form, cool's attractive quality lies in its active solicitation of the beholder. Rather than imposing itself upon others, cool resides in waiting to respond. In Marshall McLuhan's classic distinctions between hot and cold/cool media, hot media creates an all-encompassing experience, requiring little participatory labor from its audiences, whereas cool media, fragmented and incomplete, requires fulfillment and completion from spectators. Of celebrity embodiments, McLuhan observes that "Calvin Coolidge was so lacking in any articulation of data in his public image that there was only one word for him. He was real cool."[48] Similarly, Maggie refrains from data sharing, simply allowing herself to become a projection surface for the desires and fantasies of the French crew, including Assayas himself, who would shortly thereafter marry Cheung for a period of years, before perhaps determining too that she, like *Irma Vep*'s Maggie, was ultimately unknowable. Materializing inscrutability, the costume therefore models a way of being, a container for desire, which remains unknown throughout the film through deft, discursive sleights of hand and agile performances of civility. As Zoé observes, "[Maggie] shuts up and does her job.... She keeps to herself." Moreover, "during her costume fitting, she seemed to get into it. Her costume is pretty tight.... It's like she was poured into it...but she's pretty, so she wears it well.... You want to touch her. Play with her. She's like a plastic toy." After hearing about Maggie's narcissistic pleasure, Zoé's friend Mireille (Bulle Ogier) encourages Zoé to seduce Maggie. Zoe responds, "I don't know if she'd want to," before surmising nevertheless that "the costume, the tight fit, the latex—it seemed to turn her on." Zoé and Mireille confuse and conflate the erotic signifiers of latex (kink, S&M, sex) with Maggie's own sexual desires. The isomorphic equation Maggie = latex = a plastic sex toy suggests to the French women other equations including, "Wanting the costume is a way of telling you she wants you [Zoé]." This is the domain of desire through the fetish whereby the Asian woman, as pure surface, becomes-latex to accommodate the flexible erotic fantasies of her white admirers.

As China is the biggest Asian Pacific consumer of synthetic latex polymers, as well as the world's largest manufacturer of plastic toys, these comments illuminate the ways in which Chinese industrial production is here reconfigured through the Maggie character, a Chinese actor, offering to the French an image of a transgressive, sexualized, racial plaything. Nevertheless, Maggie's refusal of Zoés advances constitutes the star's final act of salty-cool, that is to say, her enigmatic refusal disguised as accommodation. After René has left the project for rehabilitation in the French countryside, Maggie and Zoé are in a taxicab headed to an electronic rave. Maggie changes her mind at the last minute, claiming that she is "just not in the mood" and "wouldn't be any fun." Asserting her refusal with a pleasant-yet-platonic kiss on Zoé's cheek, Maggie reclaims the sovereignty of a hypersexual surface that is at once hypervisible and not to be toyed with, after all. Eliding the entrapments of visibility, Maggie demonstrates how a deployment of surfaces and superficial pleasantry offers the Asian woman, always already inscribed by racial docility, a tactic of cool detachment and deflection—even if it does not satisfy the more overt manifestations of resistance as an oppositional force. Maggie's final act of disappearance from the cast and crew's screening of René's edit foregrounds the ways in which the feminine surface willfully engages in dis-appearance, the illusion of femininity that reveals appearance as a trick. Two assistants inform the production manager that, in fact, Maggie has already left for a meeting with Ridley Scott in New York, after which she will meet her agent in Los Angeles. Flaunting Maggie's cosmopolitanism to French film navel-gazers, Assayas allows Maggie's final act of dis-appearance to stand as her final negation in response to René's materialist erasure of the global star.

Twin Peaks' Salty, Cold Ornament

As a flavor enhancer, salt functions ornamentally. Salt adorns taste, dressing up oral encounter. As Anne Anlin Cheng contends, ornamentation, conjunct with and produced by orientalism, assembles the Asiatic woman whose difference is highly visible and superficial. Drawing attention to the racial materiality of skin, clothing, and accessories through which nonwhite subjectivities are envisioned, Cheng considers how such matters reassert ontological difference within visible realms, which in turn reinstates visuality as the dominant means through which social beings establish racial epistemological certainties. Proposing "ornamentalism as a feminist theory for the yellow woman," Cheng writes, "simultaneously consecrated and desecrated as an inherently aesthetic object, the yellow woman troubles the certitude of racial embodiment and jeopardizes the 'fact' of yellowness, pushing us to reconsider a theory of person thingness that could accommodate the politics of a human ontology indebted to commodity, artifice, and objectness."[49] Like Cheng, I am concerned with the ontological, epistemological, and affective implications of Asian women's objectification via ornamentalism and decoration, inquiring after the materiality of Chinese inscrutability that gives shape and form to the object-ornament conflated with Chinese femininity. As ornamental aesthetic, salt creates the occasion to generate a distancing or cooling effect that enables the nonwhite body, like that of Maggie, to maintain its secrecy and mask its racial bitterness beneath a surface of cool. Salt produces an outlet with which to escape capture; we must not forget salt's preservative function. An affective-aesthetic consideration of the object's thermality further extends the materialist inquiry into racialized form and style. If yellowness connotes the chromatic thingness of Asiatic ornamentation, coldness suggests the thermal-affective quality of the racial ornament. Think about the chill of the ornamental object of Chinese porcelain, for example. Extending the metaphorical thermality of cool within the geopolitical, the following analyzes Chinese/American actor Joan Chen's minor acts as fantastic gestural elements within what Jodi Kim refers to as the "gendered racial political unconscious" of the "protracted afterlife of the Cold War."[50] Whereas Cheung performs the cooling property of salt to generate a deflecting-yet-pleasant enigma, Chen's role in the American cult television series *Twin Peaks* (1990–91) reveals Asiatic femininity's operations as a salty signifier, whereby the something amiss and the "wrong time, wrong place" signification of salt refers to a Cold War orientalism uneasily circulating within an intimate suburban soap opera set in the northwest American Pacific Rim.

The show, debuting a few months after the 1989 fall of the Berlin Wall, notably references the 1950s through its mise-en-scène (set design, costuming, and makeup); character types (high school cheerleaders, greasers, and seemingly wholesome nuclear families); and musical cues (Angelo Badalamenti's cool jazz musical score). The series both fondly nostalgizes the American midcentury and disturbingly unveils the era's latent perversions, scratching beneath the surface of domestic happiness to resurrect repressed and hidden crimes from suburban burial sites. Whereas the likability of the Asian femme cool resides in enigmatic geniality, denoting the salty wisdom of its possessor, *Twin Peaks*' cruel secrets generate an overarching feeling-structure of cold masochism. The Asian fetish, embodied by Chen's character by the series' end, surfaces through coldness, and in becoming thing, artifice, and object, produces a masochistic engagement with its viewer, which Deleuze describes as the experience of "waiting in its pure form," in which masochistic anxiety is split into "an indefinite awaiting of pleasure and an intense expectation of pain."[51] Although the connection between masochism and melodrama has long been established, the focus has largely been on masculine masochism, whereas, as Linda Williams notes, "masochistic pleasure for women has paradoxically seemed either too normal—too much the normal yet intolerable condition of women—or too perverse to be taken seriously as pleasure."[52] The soap opera, associated with what Lauren Berlant terms "the complaint genre of 'women's culture,'" which nevertheless provides thrilling, even if conventional, encounters with pleasure and disappointment, seems to offer particularly masochistic engagements with its women viewers through its continuous replenishment of stories featuring fraught entanglements and vignettes of domestic suffering.[53] Despite Berlant's compelling account of feminine sentimentality as a form of bargaining with the invariably disappointing "*as-suchness* of the world," *Twin Peaks*, a perversion of the soap opera through self-reflexive hysterical gesture, can be better understood through a masochistic disavowal of sentimentality—particularly if we examine the enigmatic fetish figure of its Asian woman character.[54] Deleuze's concept of masochism remains useful in its clarification of the relationship between masochism and sentimentality, as he writes that "masochistic coldness represents the freezing point, the point of dialectical transmutation, a divine latency corresponding to the catastrophe of the Ice Age. But under the cold remains a supersensual sentimentality buried under the ice and protected by fur; this sentimentality radiates in turn through the ice as the generative principle of new order, a specific wrath and a specific cruelty. The coldness is both protective milieu and medium, cocoon and vehicle: it protects supersensual sentimentality as inner life, and expresses it as external order, as wrath and severity."[55] Cruelty is sentimentality frozen, sheathed beneath ice and irradiating a wrath born not from melting fire but from compressing earth. Nevertheless, this sentimentality is super, that is, excessively sensual, by virtue of its restraint. Still waters run deep; frozen waters run abysmally.

Joan Chen (née Chen Chong) was born in Shanghai on January 3, 1961. Fourteen-year-old Chen was scouted to train as an acting student at the Shanghai Film Studio by Mao Zedong's wife, Jiang Qing, before being cast at age sixteen in her first film, *Qingchun* (Youth, Xie Jin, 1977). Chen remarked that her sudden fame as a result of this role felt "dangerous," recalling that the adoration and admiration she received only provoked dread and aversion.[56] The following year, she was admitted to Shanghai International Studies University, and within half a year of attendance she was selected to play the titular character in *Xiao Hua* (*The Little Flower*, Chang Tseng and Huang Jian-Zhong, 1979), a role for which many mainland Chinese still fondly remember the actor. Although she became a big star in China, twenty-year-old Chen chose to relocate to the United States to study filmmaking at the California State University at Northridge during the height of the Reagan era. Following her parents and grandparents in studying abroad (they had attended Harvard and Oxford, respectively), her international movement was motivated by the imagined processes of what Arjun Appadurai describes as the "shifting world" of ethnoscapes, composed of "tourists, immigrants, refugees, exiles, guest workers, and other moving groups and individuals."[57] Chen was allegedly thereafter discovered by film producer Dino De Laurentiis in a Los Angeles parking lot and cast in her first major Hollywood role as the desirable and exotically beautiful "China Lady" in *Tai-Pan* (Daryl Duke, 1986), which in turn led to Chen's memorable role as the final Empress Wan Jung in Bernardo Bertolucci's internationally acclaimed *The Last Emperor* (1987), a film that wrapped Chen-as-ornament in vibrant silks, diaphanous fabrics, and pigmented cosmetics. A decade later, Chen directed the devastating Cultural Revolution film *Tian Yu* (*Xiu Xiu: The Sent Down Girl*, 1999) about a young woman who during the Cultural Revolution is "sent down" to the countryside for reeducation, and who while there who is repeatedly abused sexually by men, a traumatic subject that signals Chen's own interest in sexual subjection. Prior to Chen's transnational career in directing, she became through *Twin Peaks* the first Asian/American actor to star as a regular character in an American prime-time television show since Anna May Wong's leading role in *The Gallery of Madame Liu-Tsong* (DuMont Television Network, 1951), which was canceled after one season.

Twin Peaks set a new standard for cool in 1990, evinced by a *Newsweek* review declaring that "trendiness had become as simple as turning on the TV each Thursday evening—and then, at work the next day, pretending you understood what the hell was going on."[58] The show follows Detective Dale Cooper (Kyle MacLachlan) in his attempts to solve the murder of the town's beloved homecoming queen, Laura Palmer (Sheryl Lee). Beneath the face of suburban normalcy lurk dark and sinister truths, one of which is that the man who raped and murdered Laura was none other than her own father, Leland Palmer (Ray Wise), who was at the time possessed by an evil spirit simply called BOB (Frank Silva). The surreal serial soap performs a symbolic autopsy on small-town American lives and secrets, with a metaphysical bent. Among the preternatural situations in Twin Peaks is a series of twinning personas: BOB and Leland; BOB and Cooper; Laura and her identical cousin, Maddy (both played by Sheryl Lee); and Laura, the blonde white teenager, who is twinned with Josie, the young Chinese/American woman. Josie was a Hong Kong prostitute who immigrated to the United States to live with her husband, Andrew Packard, in Twin Peaks. After her husband presumably dies in a boating accident (he is later revealed to be alive and in hiding), Josie takes ownership of Packard Sawmill, living off the sale of local native lumber and becoming an influential member of the township. Josie's lovers are also twinned: her ex-husband, Andrew (Mark Frost), and Andrew's former business associate, Thomas Eckhart (David Warner); and Josie's present lover, Sheriff Harry S. Truman (Michael Ontkean), who shares a name with the first Cold War president, with Josie's avuncular admirer and roommate, Pete Martell (Jack Nance). Vain and beautiful, Josie plays the exotic neighbor, tasked with acting out the fantasy of assimilation vis-à-vis heterosexual encounters with multiple white male lovers. This sexual allegory, harkening back to the hot wars of European imperialism and colonialism, re-members and re-animates the Asiatic Cold War (which includes the Korean and Vietnam wars, in which there were no agreed-upon winners or losers) through Josie's hypersexual mediation. The show displays through Josie's sex appeal what one American male character remarked of another Chinese beauty on the midcentury American television adventure show *Hong Kong* (ABC network, 1960–61), "That's a communist? The Cold War is heating up."[59] Christina Klein argues that American midcentury middlebrow culture, in an attempt to wrestle Asia out from behind the Soviet Union's "iron curtain," or in the case of Hong Kong from behind China's "bamboo wall," sutured the United States and noncommunist Asia by translating alliances "into personal terms and imbuing them with sentiment, so that they become emotionally rich relationships that Americans could inhabit imaginatively in their everyday lives."[60] One such "emotionally rich relationship" was the taboo, interracial white-Asian romance. While a few films, including D. W. Griffith's 1919 cautionary tale *Broken Blossoms* and *The King and I* (Walter Lang, 1956), explore the Asian man–white woman relationship, the white man–Asian woman couple, seen for instance in *The World of Suzie Wong* (Richard Quine, 1960) and *Sayonara* (Joshua Logan, 1957), was far more common for Cold War middlebrow warming. Susan Koshy observes that while the Asian man–white woman "dyad" suggested the impossibility and danger of assimilation, the white man–Asian woman couple in both film and literature "has historically been more serviceable" to assimilation and integration efforts.[61] As an Asian immigrant who becomes the object of desire for white and European men across two love triangles, Josie participates in a sexual allegory that performs what Kim notes as "the Manichaean U.S.-Soviet Cold War rivalry…triangulated in Asia."[62] Nevertheless, *Twin Peaks*' (post-)Cold War heating is yet another of the show's misdirections, ultimately exposing Chen-as-Josie's cold, inscrutable cruelty beneath a sultry exterior (inverting Deleuze's image of the supersensual masochism of heat beneath the cold). For Lynch and cocreator Frost, the Cold War remains a chilly specter, synchronously and atmospherically conveyed by the brisk, damp Pacific Northwest climate of the fictional Twin Peaks. Josie's characterization as the racial object of desire also embodies this chilliness. For all of Josie's hot superficial appeal, the series progressively reduces her to a cold decorative object until, at last, Josie's soul is consigned to eternal, frozen damnation inside a wooden knob.

Aptly, the cool as an epistemological technology also arose in the American postwar era. Alan Liu's work on the rise of postwar coolness in informational networks brings together ironic detachment and new ways of knowing, as he describes cool as the "aporia of information," whereby cool is *"information designed to resist information*—not so much noise in the information theory sense as information fed back into its own signal to create a standing interference, a paradox pattern."[63] As the aporia of information, cool is an expression of doubt, bringing it into synonymous alignment with salt as material dubiousness. Cool is thus a solipsistic epistemology. It is a pose of narcissistic pleasure and self-satisfaction. Thus, Liu argues that "cool is precisely the incest of information (information fed back into its own signal)," a form of informational cannibalism.[64] As a form of refusal, cool offers the possibility of disrupting knowledge work through ceaseless regurgitation and reabsorption of its own output. This version of cool accords with Dick Pountain and David Robins's attitudinal definition of "cool" centering on narcissism, ironic detachment, and hedonism as the trifecta of its pathological characteristics.[65] Where Sianne Ngai's definition of "cool" in relation to "interesting" specifies the ways in which it delays and defers judgment—one needs a longer digestive period for "interesting"—here, "cool" is the refusing glimmer of unkept promises. Unlike the rhetorical bookmarking of "interesting," which accepts the other's insight and defers judgment until a future time, the cool aesthetic simply refuses the wisdom of others, insisting rather upon autodidactic erudition. And if cool forestalls, coldness pressurizes the refusal of outside knowledge. Not only does cold endlessly cannibalize its own informational output, but its suspicions also fold back upon itself. As the Cold War itself was sustained by the endless cannibalism of nationalistic propaganda, it constituted a form of disknowledge wherein the falsity of information does nothing to prevent belief in Manichean logics and reductive perceptions of "us" and "them." In other words, wars are ostensibly propagated by eliminating the grain of salt that is doubt.

With the extensive coverage of the Vietnam War on television throughout the 1960s and 1970s, Asian faces in a mediated domestic environment were familiar and evocative of America's protracted, failed wars with the eastern Other. *Twin Peaks* was the first American television show to index Asian faciality in a soapy melodrama, as Chen's face repurposed the image of Asianness and situated it within the home space.[66] Rather than warmly welcoming the foreigner, however, the show reveals a chilly and eventually envious (the slang connotation of which is also salty) hesitation toward the exotic-girl-next-door. Furthering our inquiry into the thermality of racioaesthetics, the following analysis tips the analytical frame from the cool to the cold, from likable deflection to frigid ornamentation. Revealing the coldness of the fetish and the saltiness of, and toward, its racial bearer, the following analyzes triplicate scenes that illuminate Chen-as-decoration through cosmetics, apparel, and performance in her American televisual debut: the gaze of Josie's mirrored reflection, which opens the series; Chen-as-Josie's performativity as a salty housemaid; and finally, Josie's dis-appearance into frozen objecthood.

Scene One: The Lost Gaze

Chen opens the entire *Twin Peaks* thirty-episode series via the Lacanian mirror stage (figure 2.2). The scene begins with a black onyx table lamp with two canine figures facing screen right on the base (one dog stands as another lies on the ground). In contrast with the felinic as singular, individuated, and secretive in *Irma Vep*, here we have the pack, the hunt, the multiplicity of two. Like the luster of Maggie's latex, the burnish of onyx gleams with salivating hunger. The cat seduces, but the dog hunts. This is the first affective-thermal shift from Cheung to Chen, cool to cold, saline desire to oversalted excess. Nevertheless, Lynch opens with misdirection when the camera pans left, away from the black dogs' eyeline. We see the edges of a mirror and Chen's face, tilted left, as she holds a thin lipstick brush to her mouth. Gazing at her perfectly made-up face, Chen hums to herself as she gently rolls her head to the right, giving us multiple beauty angles. If the Lacanian mirror stage establishes a false coherence of self, this facial mirror shot further dis-locates the ego as facial mask, adorned by a cosmetic layer that foregrounds the manipulated feminine surface. The self-in-totality perceived in this mirror is dis-illusioned by narcissistic gesture and pigmented decapitation. As Mladen Dolar clarifies, the Lacanian mirror stage, and the doubling it produces, "entails the loss of that uniqueness that one could enjoy in one's self-being, but only at the price of being neither an ego nor a subject. The doubling cuts one off from a part, the most valuable part, of one's being, the immediate self-being of *jouissance*."[67] The mirrored reflection therefore contains the loss of the *objet petit a* whereby, following Dolar, "one can see one's eyes, but not the gaze which is the part that is lost."[68]

Several equivalences, or doubles, are envisioned in place of the lost gaze. The mirror as surface mediates the image of skin as mediation of interiority, and Chen's faceicity in close-up, the affection-image, becomes the affective skin of the film. We are drawn to Chen's scarlet red lips, "the most luscious mouth on either side of the Pacific," according to *Time* magazine, as

2.2

Josie's Lacanian mirror dis-locates the ego and sets off *Twin Peaks'* elusive search for feminine jouissance.

the sound of Josie Packard's close-lipped humming initiates the series' fixation on elusive utterances irreducible to language, which exceed rational comprehension and can only be felt through affective vibration.[69] Indeed, hysterical crying and laughing dominate the show's aural soundtrack. Josie's minor act of humming mixes with Badalamenti's nondiegetic score, which creeps into the shot through an eerie drone sound followed by repetitive synthesized notes rising and falling into twin sonic peaks (C, A-flat, G, B-flat, E), the flat notes portending deviance and doom. The ominous electronic music associates Josie with the inhuman by way of technological, artificial synthetic sounds, aurally supplementing her animal association with the onyx canine lamp. Moreover, Josie's humming, operating outside the confines of language, ambiguates her social identity. Relatedly, Josie's idiosyncratic accented English and malapropisms throughout the series constitute the reoccurring theme of misalignments and slippages between speech and intent, word and body. Josie's speech acts therefore engage in the deconstructive work of identitarian catachresis through the misuse and abuse of language that Christina A. León describes as a crucial step in recognizing "the pressures of signification for those who are overdetermined by their sign as referent, as evidence," as I discussed in the introduction.[70] Still, it is Chen's face in close-up that forecasts the series' preoccupation with misrecognition and deception, marked by the dubiousness of Josie's exotically beautiful, painted features, which we first see in its inverted reflection.

Following this shot, we see Josie's in-laws and roommates Pete Martell and wife Catherine (Andrew Packard's sister, played by Piper Laurie). In long shot, Pete delivers to Catherine a kiss on the hand and an affectionate stroke of her ear, to which she responds with only an icy glance, before returning to her morning newspaper. After he leaves to go fishing, slamming the screen door behind him, the camera cuts back to Josie. Prompted by the sound to peer over her shoulder, Josie's lips part slightly as her eyebrows softly rise in pitying recognition of the middle-aged couple's loveless marriage. Cutaways to Josie's face, suggesting preternatural knowledge via proximity and gesture, color the subsequent sequence in which Pete discovers Laura Palmer's dead body on the beach, wrapped in plastic. The nondiegetic "Laura Palmer's Theme" that plays creates a sound bridge that connects Josie and Laura, who are visually bound by bearing the only close-ups thus far in the pilot's opening minutes. Moreover, both women are wrapped in artifice, and a warning is issued: the mineral ruse of cosmetic deceit eventuates in plastic burial. This we gather from Laura's inverted close-up, the blue pallor of her corpse lips as antipode to Chen's blood-red lips. Narcissistic feminine beauty is teleologically implicated in the crime of murder.

Running parallel to the investigation of Laura's murder is Twin Peaks residents' probe into Josie's murky Hong Kong past in an attempt to understand the mysterious foreigner. "Who was Laura Palmer?" and "Who is Josie Packard?" are questions juxtaposed, as both women signify epistemological limitations about what can be known. The hermeneutics of narrative and of transnational assimilation converge to pose questions about Josie's identity, particularly in regard to her Hong Kong past, a narrative accessible only through anecdotal evidence and self-testimony. After Josie's presumed death, her lover, town sheriff Harry S. Truman, asks Catherine, "What made her do the things she did? What was she after?" to which her sister-in-law replies, "Early in her life she must have learned the lesson that she could survive by being what other people wanted to see, by showing them that. And whatever was left of her private life, she may never have shown to anyone." Josie survived by always becoming in the shifting logic and desire of the Other. However, it is precisely that which is never shown to anyone, in other words, the object of desire's returning gaze that produces jouissance, or excessive-transgressive pleasures (as signaled by the opening mirror shot). As Todd McGowan notes, Lacan did not conflate desire with the desire for mastery or domination—a notion that prevails in traditional gaze theory; rather, desire stems from the loss of power, "the point of total jouissance."[71] McGowan further clarifies that the "gaze of the object gazes back at the subject, but this gaze is not present in the field of the visible."[72] It is Josie's inaccessible jouissance, that is, her returning gaze, alluded to within a performance of the enigmatic object, that demonstrates the perpetually deferred resolution on the Asian/American woman—a fact that only increases desire for the racial *objet petit a*.[73] The idea that Josie "survived" by being what other people wanted to see echoes the assimilative demands on Asian/American women, be that to conform to the model minority stereotype or to pressures of sexual assimilation via hypersexuality, to name but two persistent expectations. The unresolved narrative of Josie's mysterious demise ("Where did she go?") inverts the question of the indefinite origin of the foreign Other ("Where are you from?"). Viewed as perpetual foreigners in American society, Asian/Americans are suspended in becoming—a notion invoked by questions of origin, as well as by the legal term for US citizenship, "naturalization."

Female doubles in particular manifest the vicissitudes of coming and going. After Laura's death, her identical cousin Maddy appears, as the show makes reference to another Cold War masculinity-in-crisis classic, Alfred Hitchcock's *Vertigo* (1958), in which the collapse of male authority becomes anxiously projected onto the instability and nonessentiality of feminine identity. Josie, however, conjures up a more disturbing, chthonic notion of the double. As Laura's English tutee, Josie also mimics Laura's returning gaze from beyond the grave, one that is unapproachable yet endlessly pursued. As figural "twin peaks," or women's breasts, Laura and Josie constitute an anatomical binary of feminine seduction whereby only the dead (Laura) and the object (Josie) can generate the "interrupted love" that Deleuze ascribes to the masochistic "identification of sexual activity with both incest and second birth, a process which not only saves him from the threat of castration but actually turns castration into the symbolic condition of success."[74] Whereas the symbolic success with which Deleuze is concerned involves the possibilities of mother-son incestuous play through masochism, in *Twin Peaks*, a show about father-daughter, incest offers the image of "second birth" through the death of its women characters. The perversion of castration-as-success in the male masochist's fantasy rests on the fantastic displacement of "a child being beaten," referring to Freud's study of Oedipal desires entwining pleasure and suffering, to *"a father being beaten,"* as Deleuze observes in Leopold von Sacher-Masoch's novels. When the male masochist ensures his own beating, assuming his father's image and likeness, he therefore "liberates himself in preparation for a rebirth in which the father will have no part."[75] This in turn releases him from the paternal symbolic order, and therefore, castration and "interrupted love" (reconfigured as success) enable a maternal relationality-as-law, and hence also the possibility of a parthenogenetic second birth in the domain of masochism, which is "cold—maternal—severe, icy—sentimental—cruel."[76] Embodying the maternal figure as the one who beats (instead of the father), Laura and Josie disavow the superego and imbue the female sadist with immense power through the cruelties of inanimacy. Laura's cold, dead corpse and Josie's descent into cruel object-ification force upon their male suitors an indefinite waiting and withholding of pleasure. Consequently, the masochistic men who love them hysterically weep over them, a rerouting of salty seminal fluids into salty feminized tears. In *Twin Peaks'* melodramatic universe, men spill tears, not semen, over their beloved femmes fatales, and it is this abject salty inversion that, in revealing the upending of the superego, demonstrates the show's overarching preoccupation with the decay and decline of the masculine: a world in which fathers, boyfriends, and the law fail to deliver their promises of protecting women from the threat of themselves, a realization that only unmotherly maternal sadists like Laura and Josie, through their cold cruelty, can unearth.

Scene Two: Domestication

The cold enigma generated by Josie's self-gaze is certainly not like Titian's warm and fleshly *Venus with a Mirror* (1555), in which the goddess of love responds to the mirrored image of her naked torso with a gesture of modest contemplation, with one hand placed on her chest and the other clutching the velvet wrap enveloping her seated half. Whereas Titian is said to be affectionately envious (salty) of the mirror beholding the beauty, *Twin Peaks'* mirror shot draws upon Chen's startling ethnic beauty as a focal point of destabilization. The mirror is less a reflection than a refraction, intended to bend and to dis-locate the fantasies of small-town America. For the white spectator, Chen's close-up forsakes identification for exoticism, sensuality for beauty, and it disavows representation for desire. Nevertheless, Josie, an Asiatic Venus in Furs, evokes Masoch's titular character through her statuesque figure, as though cut from cold marble, frequently seen throughout the series draped in furs, lace, and silk. In the show's second season, however, Josie's decorative racialization vis-à-vis the ornament is forcibly stripped away, as her in-laws demand that she become their housemaid as punishment for her complicity in an assassination attempt on her husband, Andrew, who is revealed to be alive and hiding from his enemy, Thomas, another of Josie's suitors. This narrative punishment, encoded through a desire for a servile Asian domestic, however, rather than achieving its superficial morality lesson, instead exposes a phantasmatic anxiety provoked by Josie's costumed body. Nevertheless, Josie resists her demoted station in the household through minor acts of performance which reinstate her salty recalcitrance.

The scene opens on the Martells drinking champagne at their candlelit dining table, as a series of insincere romantic gestures between the couple ensues. Pete abbreviates W. B. Yeats's "A Drinking Song" (1916) to fit the occasion, reciting his edited version of the poem to Catherine with exaggerated performativity: "Wine comes in at the mouth. Love comes in at the eye.... I touch my glass to my lips. I look at you and sigh."[77] Catherine, ornately dressed in a white chiffon and lace ensemble, responds in turn by thanking Pete, and remarking, "That's very lyrical." Both engage in misrecognition of the other's insincere romantic attempt, demonstrating the inevitable consequence that "love is giving something you don't have to someone who doesn't want it," an observation credited to Lacan.[78] In other words, love, as with the cool, is founded on the glimmers and glamours of unfulfillable promises. Pete's recitation misses the tonal mark of romance, as the song despairs of a life spent drinking, and Pete deliberately omits the line, "Before we grow old and die." Meanwhile, Catherine's cherubic outfit in this scene is risibly infantilizing. When Catherine calls Josie over to bring their appetizers to the dining table, a new camera angle reveals that Josie had been standing a few feet away in the kitchen this entire time, bearing witness to the Martells' spurious showcase. Josie, functioning again as a triangulated point (in addition to her dual love triangles) as a spectator of the Martells' feigned domestic bliss (an attempt to mask the musty odors of their stalemated Cold War marriage), becomes interpellated as the third-party voyeur to the couple's unsuccessful and clumsy seduction act. Josie slowly ambles to the table while ostentatiously licking her fingers, the act of self-tasting as an autoerotic gesture that reinstates the Asian woman as a sensually flavorful body. Even if "love comes in at the eye," Josie's digital savoring signals the triumph of her to-be-tasted-ness over Catherine's to-be-looked-at-ness. When Catherine tells Josie that she intends to show her all the respect and affection she deserves despite her new position in the household, Josie responds with sarcasm, "Thank you, Catherine, and I will try to do the same," as she flashes her an insincere, dispassionate smile. Finally, when Catherine reminds her to put on her "little maid's cap," Josie acquiesces, pouts her lips, and proudly saunters away, irreverently modeling the outfit as a self-aware spectacle for the Martells' viewing pleasure, winkingly conveying to the televisual audience that the costume of subservience, the skin of submission, is an ephemeral farce (figure 2.3). Nevertheless, Catherine's own salty-envious feelings toward Josie are betrayed in the last lines of the scene when Pete questions Josie's unfair treatment. Catherine responds, "Josie had a hand in Andrew's death and she did everything in her power to destroy me. She's lucky she's not hanging from a tree," which recalls Lynch's own name as well as its significations of racialized brutality—unwittingly resuscitating memory of the American Pacific's historical anti-Chinese violence, for example the Los Angeles Chinatown mob lynching of eighteen Chinese immigrants in 1871. Indeed, this scene is exemplary for the ways Lynch's oeuvre deals with the near-constant eruption of memorial atrocity through placid domestic surfaces. With the threat of a racial lynching hovering in the air, Josie's parody proffers a candy-coated response that both ameliorates and nettles the menace undergirding the women's cross-racial interaction.

Notions of Chinese servitude are refigured in this scene as Josie's behavior defamiliarizes and denaturalizes the inferior social position forced upon her. Reinterpreting the desexualized maid's uniform, making visible class difference, Josie subversively embellishes the costume through hypersexualized gesture, instrumentalizing beauty to reclassify her body as one that excessively desires. This sequence is similar to one in Douglas Sirk's maternal melodrama *Imitation of Life* (1959) about a young mixed-race woman, Sara Jane (Sandra Dee), who chooses to pass as white. Sara Jane spitefully greets the guests of her mother's white employer, Lora (Lana Turner), with the caricatured affectations of a Southern mammy, much to the distress and confusion of Lora and Sara Jane's mother, Annie (Juanita Moore). Elena del Río asserts that Sara Jane's performance of "the gestures and speech of both whiteness and blackness—is perhaps the film's most subversive statement regarding the impermanence of identity, its openness to reinvention, and the non-essential ties between the body's vocabulary of gestures and movements and the particular meanings these signs mobilize in a given culture."[79] Whereas Sirk's film critically historicizes the relationship between ethnic performance and service, *Twin Peaks*' maid scene self-consciously parodies the subservient, hypersexualized performances of Chineseness, putting what del Río calls the "white fantasy of exotic femininity" on superficial display.[80] Meanwhile, Chen's short, boyish haircut undermines the conventions of these gendered fantasies, adorning androgyny as ornament, as she proudly dons long red fingernails while working, another corporeal refusal of her demoted station (figure 2.4). Revealing the double artifice of Chineseness and gender, Chen-as-Josie's embodiment provokes identification with masquerade as a form of superficial seduction. Moreover, her overperformance, the self-satisfied suckling of her fingers, a gesture of cannibal cool, reveals pride and pleasure in her impermanent position: between whiteness and Chineseness, between masculine and feminine, and between the United States and Hong Kong—a liminal space that allows for infinite reinvention and delight in tasting self. Whereas Sara Jane finds her liminality unbearable, Josie embraces these in-between thresholds. Although Catherine is salty about Josie, Josie's oversalted performance, brimming with campy sarcasm, betrays an enjoyment in excessive flavor. As with the canine lamp, Josie's housemaid attire betrays the American impulse to hygienically domesticate the foreign body so that she is permitted to enter the white American home. Within the American imaginary, the foreigner's invitation rests upon her ability to give service. Nevertheless, *Twin Peaks*' themes of becoming, rendered through Chen's performance, analogizing the indeterminate and unstable status of the Chinese body in transnational cultures, indicates, at least ephemerally, that there are flavorful pleasures to be found in a burlesque state of becoming. In contrast with Cheung's friendly and accommodating smiles in *Irma Vep*, Josie's overperformed penance and puckered lips form an overdosage of salt.

Scene Three: Object-ification

By the end of the series, Josie, like Laura, meets her tragic demise as a consequence of her indecipherable desirous nature. After shooting wholesome cherry-pie-eating hero Dale Cooper in the chest, Josie becomes *object*-ified, her soul entrapped in a wooden bedside table knob after she "dies" from fear, thus foreclosing any further possibility of comprehension. Whereas Deleuze offers the image of the "man without name…without family…

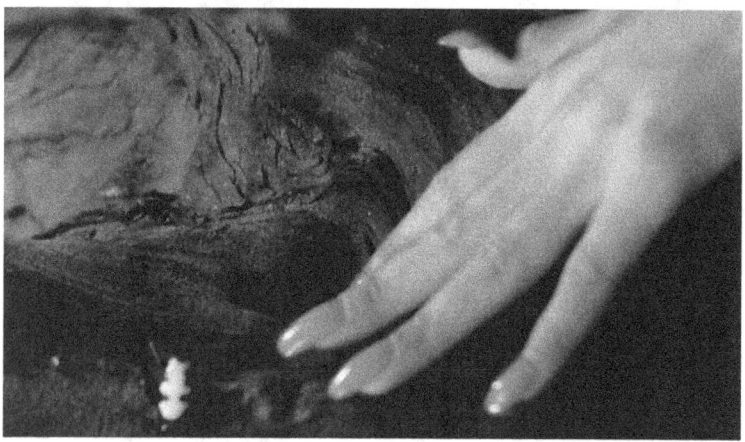

2.3–2.4

Chen-as-Josie refuses her demoted station through minor acts of ornamentation and performance.

without qualities…without self or I" as a shattering or effacing of individuality within the realms of non-sense, Lynch manifests this radically unknowable being of transformation in the evil spirit of BOB, twinned with Josie as both possess the capacity for transmogrification.[81] Exceeding paradigms of humanity and plunged into thingness, Josie can only be described as eternally becoming to the point of stasis. Nevertheless, the femme fatale's inexplicable death invokes the hysterical performances of grief and unfulfilled desire by the masochistic men who continue to love her in her absence. As McGowan explains, "[Lynch's] films...allow for a momentary experience of the gaze that occurs when the worlds of fantasy and desire intersect."[82] Not only does the intersection of fantasy and desire in Lynch's work serve to highlight the traumatic nature of desire, but this momentary contact between the two structures also enables the gaze—that is, the returning gaze of the object of desire—to emerge, not through visuality but through affectivity. As an embodiment of the undomesticated gaze, Josie, like Dorothy Vallens (Isabella Rossellini) in *Blue Velvet* (1986), is also "irreducible to any fantasmatic identification."[83] Because of the threat she poses as the elusive *objet petit a*, Josie finally becomes a fetish object, in Deleuze's characterization, a "*frozen*, arrested, two-dimensional image, a photography to which one returns repeatedly to exorcise the dangerous consequences of movement, the harmful discoveries that result from exploration."[84] Furthermore, Chen's death scene reminds us of Gaylyn Studlar's clarification that for the masochist, "orgasm is not the goal," as he is willingly bound to a pregenital sexuality of submission to the mother, premised on "suspense and distance."[85] After Dale and Harry have discovered that Josie has fatally shot Thomas in a hotel room (this occurs after Josie has shot Dale), she, with a tear streaming down her face, tightly shuts her eyes, clutches her gun, and begins to gasp for air. A vision of female ecstasy, if not orgasm per se, Chen's final minor act of animatedness shows Josie swooning to fatality, dropping onto the bed as her body twists into a position with her head hanging over the edge, legs unnaturally crossed. If Josie opens the series by evoking *Venus with a Mirror* (1555), her death scene gestures to Henry Fuseli's *The Nightmare* (1781), an oil painting depicting a woman in the throes of a nightmare with a demon sitting on her chest and a horse lurking in the background (figure 2.5). Whereas erotic attention in *The Nightmare* centers upon the protagonist's full breasts, Josie's bare legs and feet become the erotic fulcrum of a twisted, or perverse, bodily fixation (figure 2.6). Desire (not orgasm!) emerges at this point, taking over from fantasy, as we see a bright spotlight shining on BOB crawling upon the bed on all fours (the hunting dog). He howls, "Coop, what happened to Josie?" At that point, the Man from Another Place, a dwarf who moves and speaks in reverse, dances upon the bed, as Cooper (also spotlit) looks on in bewildered and masochistic suspense and distance. Both figures (BOB and the Man from Another Place) embody the Lacanian Real, a traumatic realm that we cannot access but which we endlessly pursue through desire.

2.5–2.6

Evoking Henry Fuseli's *The Nightmare* (1781), Josie's death pose suggests that her posthuman transmogrification is otherworldly.

The spotlight, an attempt to "shine a light" on Josie's elusive death scene, serves an ironic function, as we cannot acquire knowledge of the traumatic Real through luminous rationality. Nevertheless, as the Freudian fetish exists on the threshold of disavowal and discovery, when it is still possible to believe in the existence of the mother's phallus, Josie fittingly assumes this fixated point as the deflection object of a bedside nightstand's wooden knob. Therefore, even as the narrative attempts to contain Josie's inscrutability, this ending also prolongs the masochistic engagement with her image, as her inexplicable death suspends her male suitors in indefinite, fetishized submission to the unknowable object-ornament.

Although the presence of a Chinese woman in an American small town seems to collapse difference, paratextual apparatuses maintain more conventional ethno-nationalist boundaries. The deferred resolution on the Asian/American woman is nowhere more evident than in the October 1990 issue of *Rolling Stone* magazine, featuring "The Women of Twin Peaks" (figure 2.7). The glamorous cover photo captures Lara Flynn Boyle, Sherilyn Fenn, and Mädchen Amick tightly embracing one another in identical beige tank tops and jeans, their illuminated homogeny celebrating what Richard Dyer describes as "the glow of white women."[86] The *Rolling Stone* cover is no different in its attempts to show the luminescence of *Twin Peaks*' white women, as their arms latch around one another's bodies to produce a centaur of illusory nudity and denim. Despite Josie's significance on the show, no less prominent than the roles of these women, Chen is missing from the photo as well as from the feature article inside, titled "Babes in the Woods."[87] By the article's logic, Josie is neither woman/babe, nor is she of Twin Peaks. In other words, her ethnicized, racialized, and gendered difference are managed via exclusion, as the jouissance of the Other cannot appear in the field of vision.

Chen's outstanding Asian beauty is not only threatening to the visual homogeny of glowing white beauties, it is also cruelly destructive within Lynch's narrative. Over the course of the two seasons of the show, Josie's image transforms from an assimilable Chinese girl-next-door to a dangerous femme fatale whose beautiful exoticism becomes an instrument with which to obscure the deadly secrets of her enigmatic foreign past. Her lover Harry remarks to Catherine (who earlier wished to lynch Josie) that it is difficult to hate someone so beautiful, even as he learns of Josie's multiple assassination attempts. After her disappearance, Josie becomes a specter hanging over the town, as she leaves "good men" like Harry and benevolent father figure Pete in perpetual longing to "see a girl as lovely

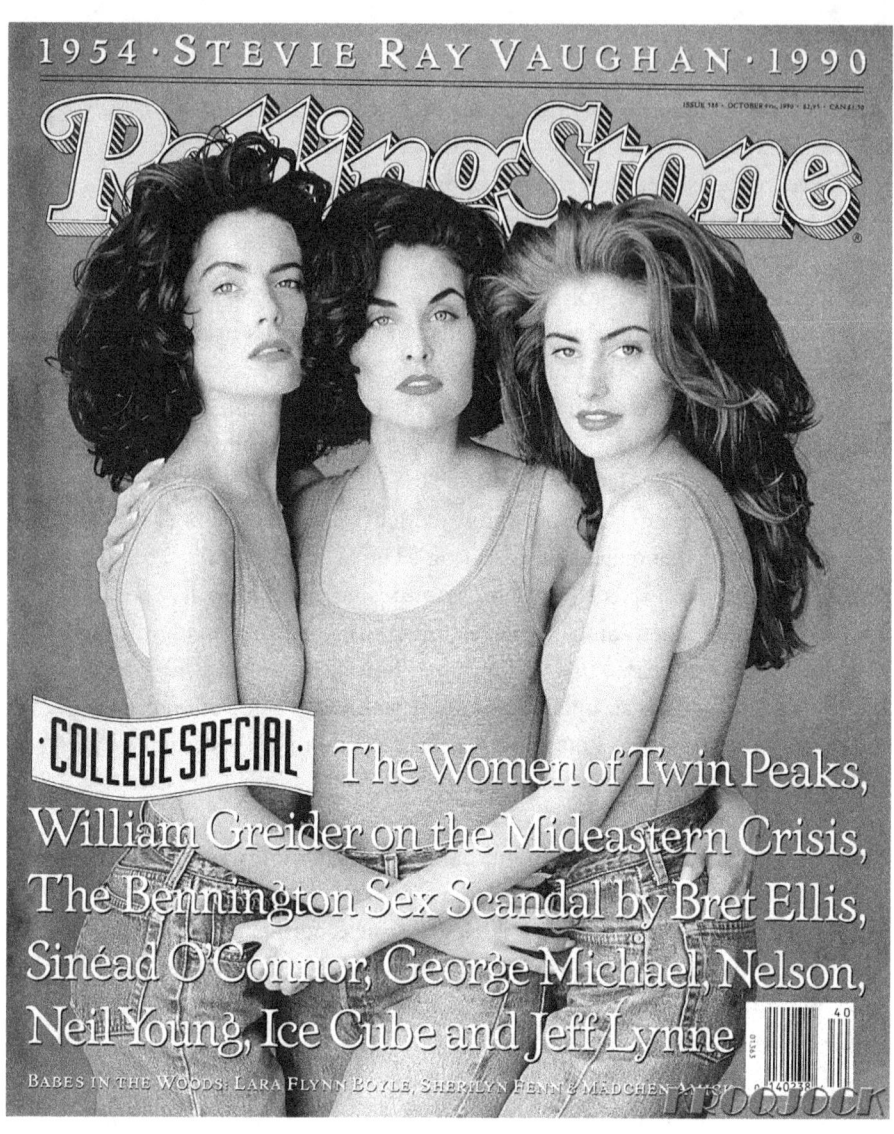

2.7

Chen is missing so that *Twin Peaks*' white women can glow.

as Josie" again. Indeed, the *Twin Peaks* Laura/Josie double reveals the affective consequences of feminine beauty, fulfilling a quasi-noir femme fatale convention. Just as Laura left a line of men who were in love with her in the wake of her death, so too does Josie leave behind a string of men both alive and dead, entranced by her exotic beauty. In interviews, Lynch resisted the impulse to explain the "disease" of Dorothy Vallens and Laura Palmer, stating, "It's so beautiful just to leave it abstract."[88] As he points out, desire and incomprehensibility are inextricably linked—this was part of the allure of Lynch's beautiful women. As an inscrutable foreigner, Chen disrupts and threatens the homogenous fantasy of idealized white women; nevertheless, as an embodiment of abstraction, Chen-as-Josie represents the point in the Other that eludes the gaze, an objectified subject of desire that provokes pleasure precisely because it is missing. Moreover, Josie's deathly jouissance, whose threat finally metamorphoses into a banal, bland object, illustrates the ways fantasy in form resembles the stereotype; both are fixated upon end points, finalities, and systems to manage one's desire for the ever-elusive gaze. In this way, fantasy and stereotype as psychic operations attempt to forge shortcuts to finitude and even to death, circumventing the processual, fragmentary, but enlivening challenges of contingency and unknowability. Rather than achieving its goals, however, neither fantasy nor stereotype are able to master or rein in desire, which only seeks to persist insatiably as desire.

Conclusion: Feeling Salty—Feeling Cool

Suggesting that the depressive position enables a politics of relationality, José Esteban Muñoz proposes that "brown feelings," attached to the Latina subject position, are fundamental to the formation of belonging to an antinormative culture through racial performativity.[89] Cheung's role in *Irma Vep* offers one response to Muñoz's "feeling brown, feeling down," by demonstrating "feeling salty, feeling cool" as a means through which to work through melancholic, dismal, and implacable positionalities of racial otherness. For if feeling brown is a depressive negotiation with minoritarian being-in-the-world, then feeling salty is the affective management of bitter, angry feelings that arise from outsider subjectivity. Saltiness as a racial technique of recognition tempers indignation and lingering bitterness that erupt from experiencing Othering, forming an affective orientation toward the acquisition of acumen, judgment, and critical distance. A salty cool enables its subject to act flavorfully and cryptically. In becoming-latex, Maggie becomes-secret. By Deleuze and Guattari's estimation, the secret as secretion of exteriority must "sneak, insert, or introduce itself into the arena of public forms; it must pressure them and prod known subjects into action."[90] The secret is thus not only a container but also a contagion which, like Gong Li's bitter secreting body, is an attempt to spread, touch, infect, and transform. Nevertheless, Maggie's performing body indicates likability, not lovability, as per the deft flavor of salty-cool. Being likable, after all, is just enough to glide in and through without too much noise or notice, allowing for minoritarian subjects to pass through white spaces and to dis-appear, at moderate dosages and undetected velocities. Whereas Cheung performs the salty-cool as a mode of likability and deflection, Chen inhabits her role through a cold and masochistic lure that both alleviates and aggravates masculine sentimentality. As characters in *Twin Peaks* repeatedly comment on Josie's self-adornment through lavish cosmetics and apparel, reinforcing Chen-as-Josie's ornamentation, the insistence on Josie's surface reveals the ways in which the Cold War's televisual afterlife and racial aftertastes are a glamour, composed of tricks of light and beauty, as a form of erasure, misdirection, and transcendence via objecthood. Josie Packard reveals that the dangers of a racial presence exceed decorative function and must recede back into the unseen field of vision, the object's lost gaze. Nevertheless, we must take a cue from salt's encouragement to doubt and dis-know, all the while enjoying the bad ideas and racial tastes of overdosage.

3

Pungent Atmospheres:
Bai Ling and Tang Wei

I am on a date in San Francisco, and we go to see Lust, Caution *at the Landmark Embarcadero Center Cinema. It is a late-night showing; besides us, there is one middle-aged couple in the theater. Each time we reach one of the film's graphic sex scenes, my face and body tingle with heat. I blush in the theater's dark cocoon, glowing with embarrassment and curious pleasure.*

Lust, Caution ends, and we sit in silence. The air is thick with sexual tension. We had been marinating in the film's atmosphere and are suddenly suspicious of one another. As we descend the long escalator down to the street, my date turns to me: "The lead actress was great."

"She was. I don't recognize her from other films."

"The film worked because she has a really innocent face.... I don't think you would be convincing in that role."

"Because I look...guilty?"

> *"You just don't have the right look for it."*
> *The mood turns acrid, and the date concludes shortly thereafter.*
> *My date believed that the film is about the sexual corruption of a young, innocent woman so enamored with her lover that she unwittingly betrays her ideals and sacrifices herself. What was incomprehensible to him was that the woman was always prepared to surrender to the fatal pursuit of her piquant jouissance.*

A mood can become tense, acerbic, and foul at the drop of a few words. Pungency enacts ephemeral boundaries between the tolerable and the intolerable. As we will discover in this chapter, the pungent limit line also describes the cinematic debuts of controversial actors Bai Ling and Tang Wei. In *The Crow* (Alex Proyas, 1994), Bai plays femme fatale Myca, who has sex with her half-brother and carves out her lovers' eyes for occult rituals. Myca's transgressive body, assembled with and against the film's dark atmospheres, envisions American liberal multiculturalism's superficial desire for representation as well as its undigested impulse to enact gothic punishment upon nonwhites. Meanwhile, Tang's debut film, *Lust, Caution* (Ang Lee, 2007), allegorizes Chinese-Japanese wartime collaboration through the violent entanglements of sex. Generating a thick environment that yokes together sexual and historical encounter, *Lust, Caution* comments on colonialism's rotting climate as it glimpses Jiazhi's jouissance as a desire to betray the nation and to welcome her own death. In both cases, desiring women are portrayed as necropoliticized objects that must be excised from the social—both characters must die so that the nation, distressed as it may be, can live. As Bai and Tang's sensational, taste-violating performances limn the boundaries of hospitality and tolerance, such pungent bodies are aligned with moral putrefaction and rot. As this chapter demonstrates, these unwelcome guests become atmospheric and environmental in their affective capacities. Nevertheless, it is precisely the anxiety provoked by death-driven perceptions of cultural decay that sustains desire. Atmospheric anxiety, in and through pungent bodies, therefore constitutes a type of nervous charisma, a lure. In their early hypersexual film roles, Bai and Tang overperform the giving/gifting of the enticing Asian female body as overcooked and overdone, at the limits of sociocultural and political rottenness.

Tolerating Spice and Racial Atmospheres

In a 2013 Pennsylvania State University study, researchers discovered that the frequency of chili consumption was associated with "sensation seeking" and "sensitivity to reward."[1] Sensation is broadly defined and measured through four factors in the experiment: thrill and adventure seeking, experience seeking, boredom susceptibility, and disinhibition. Such factors positively correlated with participants' craving for foods with capsaicin, a compound derived from chili peppers that is colorless, hydrophobic, and highly pungent. Discussing the constrained risk of seeking spicy foods, which the researchers also connect to displays of "benign masculinity" in Mexico and among American college students, they found the "strongest relationship" between desires to seek out diverse sensations and the preference for spicy foods. The researchers speculate that "the consumption of chilis is linked with an individual's perception among peers, or 'machismo' and the perception of strength."[2] What the researchers describe as a "benign masculinity" connotes a gendered performance of withstanding irritation and mild forms of pain, a type of mind over matter that accords with traditionally masculinist notions of bodily endurance (e.g., the popular gym mantra "pain is weakness leaving the body"). Moreover, the fact that a burning sensation accompanies the ingestion of capsaicin reveals a tolerance, perhaps even a desire for irritation. Spiciness captures this ambivalence, as the taste of risk correspondingly signals its perceived (gendered) reward. Unsurprisingly, spice seekers were found to be highly responsive to social benefits such as money, sex, and increased status and approval. Thus, spicy cravings correlate with sensation seeking as well as with normative desires for social success. That a certain amount of experiential irritation is concomitant with social conformity reveals the extent to which tolerance and agitation reside in close quarters. In accommodating some amount of displeasure, spice seekers exhibit a hospitality toward the strange discomforts of spice. However, as Jacques Derrida notes, hospitality contains an implicit hostility ("hospitality, hostility, *hostpitality*"), revealed in the Latin derivations for "foreigner" (*hostis*), which means "welcomed as guest or as enemy."[3] Indeed, this chapter is interested in the ways in which seemingly antirelational and pungent affects both reinforce racial socialities and offer new possibilities for Chinese and Chinese/American women to reveal and exploit the fault lines of cultural, political, and national tolerance for the foreigner, who becomes both host and guest, guest and enemy, stranger and neighbor.

As the above scientific study reveals the curious entanglements between intense sensation, tolerance, risk, and hostility—and as an opening salvo into a discussion on the pungent—its findings invite us to ponder the toleration of the unpleasant as a modality by which we acquire social normativity. Wendy Brown's work on tolerance as a form of control and aversion management illuminates this idea within liberal governmentality, as she observes that, "like patience, tolerance is necessitated by something one would prefer did not exist."[4] Would we not prefer the spicy taste without its scalding burn?

The irritant is emphatic. Think of the scorching sensation of capsaicin itself, which stresses the surfaces of the body, inner and outer, suddenly beckoning our attention to its intensities. As a focal point of sensation, resistant to our desire and will, the spicy burn inflames us. The most emphatic manifestation of spice and its irritating qualities is pungency. When pungency is experienced from the outside, it incites disidentification and unattachment to something or somebody, as the perception of pungency (generally assumed to be unpleasant and disagreeable) is implicitly accusatory. A perception of another's piquant body odor, for instance, elicits a nervous glance, an attempt to locate and attribute the scent to some (uncontainable) body. Maggie Cheung's latex secret this is not. An unpleasant smell arouses disgust, the chief affect of moral and political judgment.[5]

Besides the possibility of being embodied, a pungent smell also sharply surfaces the materialization of air, revealing how air constitutes a social atmosphere. Complaints by white Americans of the strong scents of their neighbors' "ethnic" foods, for instance, is one of the common ways in which cooking practices are racialized as unsociable and unneighborly. Thus the pungent atmosphere is inextricably bound up with race and what could be termed the atmospherics of racial ontology. Such complaints express desires for ethnic/racial segregation under the guise of olfactory discomfort, resulting in racialized-capital impulses to privatize, fragment, and segregate what may otherwise become uncontrollable publics of collective air and atmosphere. As Hsuan L. Hsu contends, "Toposmia can produce olfactory maps of environmental inequality," and atmospheric separation "distributes toxicity along racial lines."[6] Moreover, as a social aesthetic, the pungent is attached to etiological notions that noxious miasmas negatively affect health. Foul air is framed as a slow violence that poses a health threat and debilitates bodies. In response, the invention of air conditioning, with origins in the first chlorine gas attacks of World War I, as Peter Sloterdijk explains, was grounded in "disconnecting a defined volume of space from the surrounding air."[7] Thus, as Sloterdijk rightly observes, "the 20th century will be remembered as the age whose essential thought consisted in targeting no longer the body, but the enemy's environment."[8] Derived from chemical-climatological warfare, "atmoterrorisms" will also emerge in twenty-first-century culture in "new forms of expression."[9] Whereas bitterness and saltiness eroticize bodily waste and sexual fluids, the pungent, however, has difficulty transubstantiating into something palatable. Adding salt to a chili pepper only enhances its intense flavor. The pungent can only dissipate in time. Inasmuch as we pay particular attention to the way it permeates, spreads, and dissipates, it could be said that pungency is the most environmental of flavors, insofar as it surrounds and envelops us. We wait for body odor to disappear. We wait for the spicy burn to subside. The pungent is a discomforting passing-through, an atmoterrorist irritant, and its etymological roots in pain clarification ("sharp, piercing, stabbing, pricking") elucidate its startling and abrupt quality.[10] Pungency, entangling pain and spice, insists upon our endurance while we wait for its dissipation. Thus the pungent is a time-based ontology whose offensive structures must be endured during its piquant dispersions. Meanwhile, the pungent aesthetic represents a new time image in which the twentieth-century crisis of ocular epistemology following World War II (what we see is no longer indexical) gives way to a twenty-first-century crisis of time-as-waiting (we look because we cannot act). The form of looking that the pungent demands is therefore one of toleration.

Despite its insistence on enduring time's passage, there is nevertheless a willfulness in the pungent encounter that does not equivocate or mediate like salt, but rather prods and agitates. In the cinematic realm, for example, one may refer to Third Cinema's agit-prop (agitational-propaganda) documentaries like *The Hour of the Furnaces* (Fernando Solanas and Octavio Getino, 1968), in which rapidly edited montage sequences juxtapose western advertisements of white bikini-clad women and beatnik men with documentary images of terrified, anguished Vietnamese villagers during the Vietnam War. Edited to the adrenally stimulating beat of a machine gun, such vociferous displays jostle the sympathetic revolutionary into a frenzied state of righteous indignation. In Solanas and Getino's own words, the task of the guerrilla filmmaker is to make films that are "indigestible" to the system.[11] Here the doubled meaning of "rumination," one connected to contemplative thought (and in this case, revolutionary) and the other referring to the syndrome wherein one regurgitates indigestible food, are yoked together. Along other revolutionary axes, Mao Zedong's legendary craving for spicy Hunan cuisine inspired the dietary prescription for revolutionaries: "If you don't eat *la* (spicy), you are not a revolutionary."[12] That the capacity for eating spicy, and of desiring/enduring irritating sensation, becomes a vital requirement for revolution indicates the ways in which spice moves bodies toward action. Guy Debord's evocation of rot and putrefaction in 1956 metaphorically draws upon pungence as the fetid time for action as "the premises for revolution, on the cultural as well as the strictly political level, are *not only ripe*, they have begun to *rot*."[13] Whereas saltiness alerts us to the matter of something, that something is amiss because time and space are out of sync and inconjunct, pungency itself is the urgent matter. In other words, whereas saltiness is the signifier that points and gestures elsewhere (to another sign), pungency occupies the place of the signified, a meaning that is immediately felt and sensed.

Regarding pungency as signified matter returns us to one of the central questions of this book, which is to ask how Chinese women's bodies matter through the lower sensorium (taste, smell, and touch). If pungent is the most atmospheric, even atmoterrorist or revolutionary aesthetic, then how does the spectator consume a pungent body? And what is beautiful about it? Before grappling with the irritating spice of the pungent Chinese women with whom we come into contact in this chapter, it is crucial to discuss what pungent is not. As noted by Richard Dyer, Norman Mailer described the comfort and ease Marilyn Monroe's sexuality elicited in comparison with other women: "Difficult and dangerous with the others, but ice cream with her."[14] Dyer further elaborates upon the digestible seductions of Monroe: "It almost becomes the point of the films that Monroe takes the *sting* out of anything that her sexuality seems likely to stir up."[15] Lacking sting or spice in her vulnerable desirability, Monroe offered an easily digestible sexuality that went smoothly down gustatory-cultural pathways. In fact, Monroe's femininity soothed irritation, as her quivering-but-always-sexually-accessible femininity embodied the conflicting impulses of American midcentury sexual identity, itself quivering undecidedly between a post-Kinsey openness toward sexual pleasure and the sanctimonious, puritan blush of 1950s family television sitcoms. Similarly, Rock Hudson's pre-AIDS presumed heterosexual body was perceived as milky-white dairy—a mollifying, handsome mass of unthreatening good looks. A 1958 *Look* magazine article describes Hudson thus: "In the past few years too many actors have been sensitive and spooky like Jimmy Dean; the public got tired of *decay*. So now here's Rock Hudson. He's wholesome. He doesn't perspire. He has no pimples. He smells of *milk*. His whole appeal is cleanliness and respectability—this boy is pure."[16] Moreover, as Richard Meyer writes, "Hudson offered not only the visual pleasure of his form, his open-faced good looks and unparalleled large proportions, but the promise to control that big body, the promise not to pounce."[17] Attraction to Hudson's colossal "rock" body hinged on his restraint and control over his corporeal capacity. Hudson's hormonal balance, as evinced by his unblemished, antiperspirant skin, demonstrates that the hygienic fantasies surrounding the unsecreting white body is steeped in a desire for a smooth, matte surface. Although promising sex, the milky–ice cream charms of Monroe and (pre-AIDS) Hudson did not permit any evidence of sexual labor. Monroe and Hudson's watertight contained/container bodies rendered their attractively sweet surfaces into sites/sights of leisurely nonwork and play—in other words, dessert. Such antacid fantasies of easy, consumable sexuality through sweet confections, however, are not often projected upon persons of color in mainstream western media.

Returning to the opening discussion about spicy consumption as a form of risk taking, it is crucial to note the unevenness of risk and reward inscribed and dispersed across different racial bodies. Vivian Huang notes the "historical asymmetr[ies] of which bodies receive comfort and which bodies are objectified in the name of providing comfort," observing that the "Asian woman" subject is the effect of "militarized and capitalist manifestations of paternal hospitality."[18] Huang compares the work of Asian/American performance artists Yoko Ono's *Cut Piece* (1964) and Laurel Nakadate's *Happy Birthday* (2000). Under the guise of hospitality, Ono invites audience members to cut and remove a piece of her black clothing, while Nakadate invites herself to three white male strangers' houses to celebrate her fictional birthday with cake, filming each celebration with the men, all of whom first approached the artist in public. The intimacies performed (Ono's sacrificial undressing and Nakadate's fête of self) displace the focus from Asian femininity's gifts to their guests' credulous, and potentially hostile, willingness to take. Each artist respectively plays Asian hostess in ways that both expose and complicate social expectations of the Asian woman, ultimately generating an inscrutable form of hospitality. However, Huang argues that, rather than using negative affects and distancing techniques to shatter and disrupt normativity, Ono and Nakadate draw upon modes of intimacy in order to reveal the minoritarian processes that embed racialized, gendered sociality. In other words, Ono and Nakadate tolerated, even offered themselves up to, potentially irritating, pungent guests (revealing Derrida's dual-edged "hostpitality").

The pungent straddles the edges between tolerance and intolerance, acting as a taste limit for what is socially ingested and consumed. The pungent aesthetic is therefore that which threatens to puncture normativity, and too much pungence can irritate the digestive tract. Similarly, in the cultural arena, circulation routes and visual economies can themselves become reactive, seen in the public criticisms of Bai and Tang through inflammatory channels of media communication. Nevertheless, following the herbal prescription of pungent flavor in Chinese medicine, the pungent also stimulates blood circulation and breaks down accumulation in the body. In the following pungent case studies, the women's minor acts of offensive behavior ultimately boost the circulation of the contested films, as well as the texts' pungent envisionings of multiculturalism and colonialism. Bai and Tang's characters in such productions must endure death so that the nation can live, their sacrificial bodies becoming the altar upon which tolerance is endured and stretched to the limits of hospitality. If, as Sianne Ngai describes, irritation resides "in the uneasy zone between psychic and bodily experience [that] produces an oscillation between insides and outsides," then figures who provoke public irritation become points of mediation for outsiderness, which attest both to the exterior manifestations of psychic discomfort and to the zones of tenderness and sensitivity wherein social identity is most uncertain.[19]

Inscrutable Pungency

A 2016 magazine interview titled "Bai Ling Is Still Alive" opens with Bai's alleged "life philosophy": "If you're embarrassed, you don't believe you're deserving. Be shameless."[20] Mitchell Sunderland follows Bai's statement by saying, "It's shocking that [Bai]'s still alive," citing her battles with alcoholism and experiences of sexual abuse while enlisted as an "entertainment soldier" in the People's Liberation Army (PLA). Notwithstanding the incapacitations of such life-draining/negating experiences, Sunderland's remarks intimate that there is something else about Bai that renders her livability suspect, perhaps aroused by her performativity of Chinese inscrutability in films as well as in extradiegetic public spheres. If the "sticky affect" of shame, to draw from Sara Ahmed, binds its subjects to undesired objects, the shamelessness that Bai exhibits seems to shock, repel, and distance her beholders, becoming inscrutable through its alienating, shocking defiance of social norms.[21] Thus, the presumption of Bai's death operates as a kind of discursive biopower signaling not only her moral transgressions but also her illegibility as a living subject. If Bai's apparent shamelessness is tied to social death, to what extent does her bare (celebrity) life speak to the sovereignty of aesthetic economies and visual cultures?[22] Within such circulations, how might Bai's inscrutable image envision, as Huang suggests in her account of Asian inscrutability, "the dawning articulation of a new form"?[23] What does such a dawning articulation of inscrutability look like when it revolves around death and fatality?

Putrefaction, the rotting of corporeal life, is often described as pungently odorous. Nevertheless, as Joanna Radin points out, rot "is a way of thinking ontologically in reverse," as putrefaction constitutes a form of dying-as-process that enables us to make sense of disappearance in the order of things.[24] Putrefaction and rot offer particularly generative optics through which queer theory and critical race pessimisms strike meaningful correspondences between ontological disappearance and social marginalization. Critically engaging with rot and the pungent as a process rather than as finality enables us to think through the disappearing act as an especially useful performance when engaging with the moving-image histories of Asian/American (in)visibility, even as hypersexuality as a form of pungent embodiment signals fatality, a racialized femme fatalism.

A "Hot Mess" and a Crow

The ultimate locus of genital *jouissance* is a place—this is no
mystery—where you can pour torrents of boiling water, brought
to a temperature no other mucous membrane could withstand,
without provoking any immediate sensory reactions.
—Jacques Lacan, *Anxiety: Book X*

Bai Ling (White Spirit) was born in Chengdu, Sichuan Province, in 1961 to artistic parents, a musician and an actor/dancer who later divorced under the fracturing pressures of the Cultural Revolution, which forced them into separate ideological factions. Joining the PLA at age fourteen, Bai became what is known as an "entertainment soldier" or a "literary and arts soldier" (*wen yi bing*), a noncombatant position intended for the purpose of entertaining troops. In the July 24, 2011, broadcast of the reality show *Celebrity Rehab with Dr. Drew* (VH1), in which Bai was a participant, the actor recounts that during her time in the PLA, she was sexually abused by several generals during her three-year station in Tibet. Later she revealed that one encounter led to an unwanted pregnancy and termination. Following her service with the PLA, Bai returned to Chengdu, joining the People's Art

Theater to begin pursuing professional acting, after which Teng Wenji cast her in her first movie role in *Haitan* (*On the Beach*, 1985). Bai proceeded to act in several Chinese films before enrolling in New York University as a visiting scholar in 1991. Following Bai's first American film, *The Crow*, Bai landed her most significant and acclaimed role to date, opposite Richard Gere in the political thriller *Red Corner* (Jon Avnet, 1997), for which she was praised for lending "grace" and "gravity."[25] Despite the possibility of Bai becoming a "serious actress," however, as indicated by the positive accolades for *Red Corner*, she instead became notorious for her stint on *Celebrity Rehab*, scantily clad red-carpet appearances, public disclosures about her bisexuality and sexual openness, and cryptic and baffling statements about herself during interviews (frequently describing herself as "a wild animal," for instance). Within thermal considerations, Bai exemplifies what vernacular gossip and tabloid discourses refer to as a "hot mess," suggesting that she is "a person who is seemingly emotionally or mentally unbalanced who yet remains alluring, esp[ecially] one whose unbalance derives from social debauchery (excessive partying)."[26]

Although the slang usage of "hot mess" was added to the *Oxford English Dictionary* in 2014 to denote "something or someone in extreme confusion or disorder," the first appearance of the phrase dates to an 1818 "Letters on the West Indies" document, written by James Walker of the Berbice Commission in reference to a "warm meal" served to the young and the sick, as an "indispensable part of a well regulated plantation."[27] Colonialists understood that to effectively extract labor, they must also give warmth and nutrition. That the original term yokes hot food and nutrition to colonial exploitation—to promote nourishment as a best practice to maintain indentured discipline and bodily regulation—indicates the kinds of bound, racialized subjectivities forged through capitalism's totalizing and unyielding "heat." That the presentation of food was a "mess" served to remind governed bodies that they did not deserve any formality or ceremony that might individuate them. The "mess" of food thereby echoed its undifferentiated horde of laborers. In Marshall McLuhan's thermal taxonomy of national identity, "backwards countries are cool, and we are hot," the "we" referring to the industrialized, capitalist First World.[28] Analogously, the "'city slicker' is hot, and the rustic is cool."[29] Modernized, racial capitalisms are hot because of their inescapable totalization through multifaceted technologies of subject interpellation enacted by social institutions and mediated apparatuses.[30] Resultantly, racist and misogynist heat could also be a form of capitalist febricity, a feverish symptom of the production drive wherein racialized subjects must undergo heating in order to join the melting pot of multiculturalism and compete with white Americans for resources, goods, and opportunities. To paraphrase one television host, through their submission to the suffering implicit in "melting," subjects rightfully earn their status as American.[31] Moreover, gendered terms like "hot mess" and "toxic celebrity" draw upon material-semiotic metaphors of heat, toxicity, and inanimacy to police women's behavior and appearance—even as "hotness" operates as an aesthetic-behavioral performance of sexual accessibility. After all, hotness or heat, ascribed to objects of beauty, also depicts the somatic qualities produced by the increased sweat generated by apocrine glands when one feels sexual attraction, as well as to the increased circulation of blood to the face, reproducing a physiological side effect of orgasm. That the experiential characteristics of becoming sexually aroused become displaced onto the eliciting object signifies the ways in which bodies become projection screens for individuals' own phenomenological subjectivities. "Hot mess" thereby betrays its own ambivalent attraction and desire through judgment.

The racialized hot mess reveals the implications of overheating in the multiculturalist melting pot, a process that is viewed in the 1990s American cinematic imaginary as one that scorches nonwhites and whites alike. One of the most pungent films of the era, *The Crow* is the debut feature of and graphic novel adaptation by Australian director Alex Proyas, who before then directed music videos for 1980s New Wave bands like Crowded House and INXS. The film is an otherworldly revenge thriller saturated with music video aesthetics (rapid cutting with short takes, prominent rock music interludes, and unhinged cinematography). On the eve of their wedding day on Halloween, Eric Draven (Brandon Lee) and his fiancée, Shelly Webster (Sofia Shinas), are murdered by a multiracial inner-city gang, who also rape Shelly in front of Eric before she is killed. Eric resurrects one year after their deaths with supernatural powers of strength and imperviousness to pain, and is mysteriously connected to a crow that provides his link between life and death. If the bird is injured, Eric also suffers. Avenging Shelly, Eric kills off each of the gang members in a series of gruesome scenes until the film's dénouement, in which a final battle ensues between Eric and the half-Asian criminal mastermind Top Dollar (Michael Wincott), and Top Dollar's Asian half-sister and lover, Myca (played by Bai). With the help of a sympathetic Black cop, Sergeant Albrecht (Ernie Hudson), who had been investigating the couple's murders, Eric manages to kill Top Dollar and Myca in an abandoned church. Afterward, Eric says goodbye to his friend Sarah (Rochelle Davis) and returns to the grave site, where we see him reunited with Shelly in the afterlife. Sarah, a tomboyish adolescent white skateboarder, provides the film's narrational voice-over, perversely sweetening *The Crow*'s gruesome acts of depicted violence.

The Crow is not only dealing with Black identity politics through bifurcated images of good (Black) cop and bad (Black) gangster, it is also grappling with an emergent Asian/American population and the possibilities of white-Asian miscegenation, foregrounded in the lead casting of Brandon Lee (martial arts star Bruce Lee's son with Linda Lee Cadwell), and narrativized through the half-Asian character of Top Dollar. Eurasian and Asian characters, appearing as moral binaries, possess supernatural capabilities, animalistic qualities, and transgressive desires, and white-Asian miscegenation becomes part of the film's scaffolding of dystopic tolerance. As the following examines, the film reveals multiculturalism as a bad idea, both cool and morally questionable through its aestheticization of racial tolerance as a form of campy, salty disknowledge.[32] Meanwhile, the pungent atmospherics of the film, strained through Bai's minor acts of hypersexual inscrutability, reflect a hostile antagonism toward cinematic envisionings of 1990s American multiculturalism, which indicate the extent to which Chinese/American women were perceived as the unwanted guests at the messy buffet of cosmopolitanism. Accordingly, the film positions the (white) spectator as a reluctant host who must demonstrate his flexible liberalism by tolerating his pungently racial guests.

Tolerating Heat in the Dark

The Crow's dystopic view of multiculturalism reveals the structures of latent hostility in toleration, and illuminates the problems of a liberalist politics of recognition. Whereas Maggie's eyes are scratched out as a frustrated attempt to plumb her desirous surface in *Irma Vep*, similarly the motif of blinding and the impairment of sight appears not only when Myca's eyes are pecked out before her death, but also formally through the dark aesthetics of fascistic-gothic cinema, whose logic is geared toward legitimizing spectacular forms of punishment toward unruly bodies of color. Significantly, Rey Chow, arguing that fascistic aesthetics rely on transparency, luminosity, and idealistic surface projection, contends that "rather than hatefulness and destructiveness, fascism is about love and idealism. Most of all it is a search for an idealized self-image through a heartfelt surrender to something higher and more beautiful."[33] Indeed, those who believe in fascism earnestly believe they are in pursuit of a higher and "more beautiful" truth; they are not motivated by destructive cynicism and nihilism. Chow thereby provocatively locates fascism within 1990s multiculturalism, referring to fascistic tendencies within our liberal (institutional) midst as "a longing for a transparent, idealized image and an identifying submission to such an image."[34] In other words, Chow argues that the uncritical desire to submit to the authority of the nonwhite Other in the era of liberal multiculturalism only affirms models of visibility that falsify and reify difference under the guise of transparency and goodwill. Liberal practice, like fascism, does not think beyond the surface. Yet the problem is not with surface itself, but rather with fixation at the point of the surface, and specifically upon facial difference and difference-as-face to which Chow calls attention as that which immobilizes the façade and prevents "surface play." When surface is mined only for difference, it does not move. Where *Irma Vep* grapples with its desires for Maggie as a surface projection of Assayas's good liberal and courtly intentions, finally encrypting her as a cool surface secret, *The Crow* brings to light the monstrous ambivalences of American liberal multiculturalism and its fascistic-gothic aesthetics, superficially packaged in the bad-cool style of 1990s goth, grunge, and punk. However, a surface reading must also account for the interior phenomena that alter the texture of its exterior—for instance, the thermal blush flowering upon the face when one feels attraction or eats a hot pepper—these interior changes alert us to our delicate affectability and interchangeability within subject-object relations.

What also therefore emerges from this official multiculturalist politics of recognition is an ambivalent cultural and aesthetic response to tolerance as a mode of governmentality. Subcultural aesthetics and aggressive viscerality helped *The Crow* achieve cult status during the Clintonian 1990s. During the fraught racial milieu marked by the 1992 riots in South Central Los Angeles over the acquittal of the policemen who beat Rodney King and the 1995 acquittal of O. J. Simpson by a predominantly Black jury, then-president Bill Clinton's consistent public-facing commitments to racial equality, reconciliation, and dialogue, formalized in his 1997 executive order "One America in the 21st Century: The President's Initiative on Race," anchored official and political discourses in the recognition of the United States as a multiracial democracy. Advocating for a "more perfect union" and urging Americans "to lift the burden of race and redeem the promise of America," Clinton is famously remembered for his popularity with African American voters, with Toni Morrison calling him "the first

Black president." Moreover, Clinton put forth toleration as a premise for democratic government. As Brown explains, the liberal, civilized subject is expected to tolerate difference; tolerance therefore becomes "a crucial analytic hinge between the constitution of abject domestic subjects and barbarous global ones, between liberalism and the justification of its imperial and colonial adventures."[35] The aesthetics of tolerance in *The Crow* are tested by the film's abject and barbarous acts of embodied violence committed by and upon its multiracial gang, who represent the ways in which liberal promises, encoded in a grotesque flattening of difference, yield only urban decay and moral chaos. Our vengeful hero Eric, in the name of love, is therefore permitted to enact a catalog of vengeful violent acts upon his murderers, including fatally stabbing each vital organ; a forced drug overdose; scorching a person to death in a car explosion; violent defacing via removal of eyes; and a shove that ends in impalement. Flashbacks from Eric and Shelly's points of view looking upon their torturers punctuate these retaliatory scenes, galvanizing vengeance and fear, as the spectator occupies the perspective of these victims. Performing the management of hostility and antagonism toward difference through gothic spectacularity and an aesthetics of subcultural cool, the film itself tolerates violence against its nonwhite characters and, in particular, against Myca, the inscrutable Asian femme fatale, a subject to which we will soon return.

Demonstrating Chow's observation that fascistic monstrosity rests upon idealistic devotion and a belief in fascism's eminent decency, the film's twelve-year-old narrator says at the end, "Buildings burn, people die, but real love is forever." Buildings and people are temporary, but "real love," which transcends time and space, constitutes the film's devotional idealism.[36] Moreover, it is *The Crow*'s atmospherics of perpetual night, its endlessly dark, rainy environment, that further reaffirms transcendental love as the only possibility of light. This inky, nocturnal world envisions what Andrew Culp refers to as a dark Deleuzian era insofar as we willfully face the cruelty of "the demons, the sign-bearers, who bring thought to us."[37] Reading Deleuze against the grain of the joyous philosophy in which he's frequently situated, Culp draws upon a destructive-becoming of a world that ushers in the deterritorializing powers of the outside, which, quoting Deleuze, occurs when "the singing of the birds is replaced by combinations of water, wind, clouds, and fog."[38] Forecasting the coming of a communist apocalypse through metaphors of weather and extraplanetary intervention, Culp's interpretation of Deleuze concludes, "darkness advances the secret as an alternative to the liberal obsession with transparency."[39] That is, to unthink the old order is to abolish transparency as an expression of liberal progress.

The fiery, smoky atmospherics of *The Crow* also visualize atmoterrorism, or that which for Sloterdijk "voids the distinction between violence against people and violence against things: it comprises a form of violence against the very human-ambient 'things' without which people cannot remain people."[40] Indeed it is remarkable that state atmoterrorism in the form of lethal gas was first attempted on a Chinese immigrant in 1921 by the state of Nevada in the prosecution of a twenty-nine-year-old Chinese immigrant, Gee Jon, found guilty of murdering Tom Quong Kee during gang warfare. Gee, an intolerable person of color, thus became the first human subject for ambient violence within the American prison industrial complex. The experimentation of this event is underscored by the fact that the first attempt to execute Gee was unsuccessful, because they attempted to pump gas into his cell, which inevitably leaked out. This led to the innovation of the gas chamber, which also allowed witnesses to watch as a weeping Gee—his own final act of affective atmospherics—was put to death. The racialization at the heart of atmoterrorism spectrally hovers in *The Crow* through the multiracial gang's own investment in thermoterrorism, as Top Dollar commands them to set the city on fire. The film therefore spectacularizes the perversity of the subjects' own biological complicity in the making of their own death. We are forced to breathe in the particulates of highly toxic matter and usher in our fatalities within such an atmosphere. As with Sloterdijk's example of the World War II Dresden bombing, *The Crow*'s "night of fire" indicates the ways in which "the human being's being-in-the-world cannot, under any circumstances, mean a being-in-the-fire."[41] Under conditions of fire, the body's impulse to inhale ensures one's own fatal suffocation, voiding the distinction between violence against people and violence against things.

Pungent Animality

We learn early on that the gang's destructive impulse to burn buildings stems from the desires of the inscrutable Asian femme fatale. When Myca confesses to a room of delinquent men, "I like the pretty lights [of the burning city]," they erupt in laughter. The laughter is a response to what Slavoj Žižek describes as the "obscene, cruel, superegotistical, incomprehensible, impenetrable, traumatic dimension of the Voice, which functions as a kind of foreign body perturbing the balance of our lives."[42] Voice itself becomes the uninvited foreigner that pierces one's outer surface, only to become an unsettling inner acoustic vibration between the ears. Embodying the pungent object of incestuous male desire, Myca's improper figuration is therefore signaled at the linguistic, vocal register. Whereas Myca's hypersexuality can be reread as a form of subversive cool, Myca's immigrant formation of language is not rehabilitated as such. Her overdrawn red lips, clownishly framing the accented English words that escape them, visualizes the ways in which, as Mladen Dolar observes, voice constitutes "what does not contribute to making sense."[43] Myca's overattention to her lips, using red lipstick to color beyond the natural contours of her lip line, gestures to the elusive, immateriality of voice itself, unconfined to, and unable to be contained by, the body. Moreover, Myca's accent functions, as Dolar explains, as "something which brings the voice into the vicinity of singing," as "a heavy accent suddenly makes us aware of the material support of the voice which we tend immediately to discard."[44] Myca's accented speech, akin to the singing of the bird (or in this case, the cawing of the crow), not only renders audible the ways in which speech acts are mediated by the symbolic order, but also the ways in which the desiring female object confesses her own lack (by liking the pretty lights, she confesses her desire, which is, by psychoanalytic accounts, a confession of one's own lack). A desired object becomes a loving, desiring subject in a confessional moment that Žižek describes as "deeply embarrassing and truly scandalous."[45] Toward this end, we could regard the pungent scent and voice as not only scandalous, but the grounds upon which tolerance is summoned (that which we "tend immediately to discard").

In Žižek's analysis of tolerance as ideology, he adds smell to the list of psychoanalytic partial objects that elude capture:

> For the middle class, lower classes smell, their members do not wash regularly—or, to quote the apocryphal answer of a middle-class Parisian to why he prefers to ride the first-class cars in the metro: "I wouldn't mind riding with workers in the second class; it is only that they smell!" This brings us to one of the possible definitions of what a *neighbor* means today: a *neighbor* is the one who by definition smells. This is why today deodorants and soaps are crucial; they make neighbors at least minimally tolerable.... Lacan supplemented Freud's list of partial objects (breast, feces, penis) with two further objects: voice and gaze. Perhaps, we should add another object to this series: smell.[46]

Elaborating further on the ways disgust and scent work to substantiate alterity through physical difference, we can add another social persona to the doubled Derridean "foreigner" (hostis) as "guest or enemy"—Žižek's "neighbor." Such comments are useful in other ways. First, the fact of ideology as an exterior object that attaches itself to sense, here specifically to smell, enables us to connect ideology to matter. Second, as a partial Lacanian object, smell is akin to voice, holding the potential as *objet petit a*, a lure that gestures to the inaccessible Real. Once again, smell marks the Other's radical alterity, and bad neighbors epitomize the desires of reverse gentrification—instead of being hospitable, they, like Myca and her half-brother, burn people out of their homes. In this scene, Myca, who is suddenly self-conscious after her preferential admission for "pretty lights," glances around the room earnestly—the same glance that attempts to identify a bad smell to a body is here locating cruel laughter to its source. Betraying a sincere desire for love-writ-as-light through slightly broken English is not only embarrassing, it is also a confession of Myca's feminine, desiring enjoyment. Moreover, it is Bai's minor gesture here—a slightly wounded look as her smug smile droops—intended to reveal Myca's shame, that marks Myca as an utterly pungent figure operating in a post-bitter recognition of her own unbelonging (figure 3.1). Even though Myca is the favored lover of the city's top criminal mastermind, this isolating frame reminds the viewer of Myca's radical alterity and racial difference. Exceeding the demands of the narrative, the racial discomfort embedded within this shot spills over into a cinephilic domain wherein Bai's hot body generates an excessive engagement with what is beneath the surface of the skin. Yet her baffled expression, framed in medium close-up, produces an excess of meaning that escapes the men's logic. Myca's expression in this scene lies in her fecund incomprehension of others' laughter, which situates her outside the symbolic order as an inscrutable, unassimilable figure of racial jouissance.

In stark contrast with the syrupy display of Eric and Shelly's heteronormative love, on the cusp of sanctification before their untimely, brutal murders, Top Dollar and Myca's incestuous love is nonprocreative, sadistic, and violent. In the film's introduction to the criminal pair, a rapid dolly shot advances upon Myca's backside in the shower as we see that she is emblazoned with a large tattoo of an abstracted crow that descends to a triangle pointing to her voluptuous bottom. Our rear-side introduction to Myca, rather than sexualizing her maternal breast, hints at anal, pungent perversion, an idea echoed in her nonprocreative and sadistic

3.1

Myca's overdrawn lips reveal the pungent transgressions of her accented voice.

sexual practices. While Gong Li is introduced via a frenzy of tender kisses/close-ups caressing her face in *Red Sorghum*, as discussed in chapter 1, Bai makes her Hollywood debut as a body in the midst of sanitization. Myca's "unwashed [bad Neighbor] scent" is not repudiated but rather emphasized by her ornamentalized red lipstick and permanent tattoo, which indicate the extent to which her bodily dirt is fixed and permanent. Thus, in contrast with Gong's look into the camera, we meet Bai in a compromising pose, a predatory advance behind her back. As the camera dollies with rapid velocity toward her, we then glimpse three-quarters of her face as she turns her head; and there is a doubled deprivation of the illusion of eye contact because her eyes are closed. When she returns to the bedside to her half-brother/lover, we see another naked woman on her side, turned away from the camera. Apparently, the ménage à trois had worn their partner to the point of mortal expiration, and Top Dollar remarks, "I think we broke her." Indeed, the perversity of Myca's incestuous desires are matched only by her postcoital propensity to cut out her lovers' eyes, a ritualistic organ that the couple sets aflame in order to inhale its burning fumes.

As tolerance is an ambivalent, even undesirable, object, especially when it is obligated or solicited, such aesthetics of reluctance manifest through the bodily acts of violence committed by and upon its multiracial gang. The searing demonstration of a dystopic, overflowing melting pot correlates urban destruction and crime with the flattening of racial-cultural difference, leveling the city's uneven topological surfaces to the ground to help visualize the hot horrors of racial mixture. Similarly, the gangs' reversal of hospitality through violent acts of unwelcoming turn into acts of hostage. In Proyas's urban dystopia, multicultural gangs composed of single bachelors act out their ressentiment toward privileged, happy middle-class couples, whom they perceive as denying them hospitality—and in response, the gangs become hostile and take them hostage, playing out the full Derridean drama of the capriciously changeable fluctuations of the identities of both guest and *hostis* (host or enemy). Rather than a hygienic or attractive "cosmetic multiculturalism," to invoke Lisa Nakamura's term, the film instead reveals the squalid miasma of a racial cosmopolitanism that confuses and violates boundaries of life/death and human/animal.[47]

The titular critter, which forges a human's mystical connection to the sphere of the dead, brings to the surface the question of animality, which inflects the film's racialized animacies. The "humanimals" that abound in *The Crow*, to use Mel Chen's term, are monstrous metaphors for the film's male Eurasian characters, Eric and his arch nemesis, Top Dollar.[48] Just as the border between life and death becomes permeable, racial boundaries are monstrously violated in the embodiments of these two men. Such multiculturalist-miscegenation nightmares manifest through the instability of the human through its animal transubstantiations. Eric and Myca are both associated with the crow as well, and they possess a supernatural connection to the bird (while the crow is an extension of Eric's body, Myca is able to deduce the connection between the two). As a compact counterpart to Edgar Allan Poe's Raven, the crow prefers the urban habitat to wilder parts, and, aptly, the film's vision of multiculturalism is tied with notions of urban crime, particularly with the fiery destruction of buildings on Halloween (or rather, by its infernal rebrand, Devil's Night). *The Crow*'s alchemical exchanges between human and animal envision the disknowledgeable practice of multiculturalism as a politics requiring not only our suspension of disbelief but, more importantly, our tolerance. In other words, the film's violation of bodily surfaces reveals the dubious hesitation of 1990s American tolerance, transmogrifying anxiety into an aesthetic viscerality that jolts us into a cool spectatorial pose. By demonstrating that we can coolly consume the film's body horrors against its diegetic primitives, we demonstrate our capacity for self-regulated liberal tolerance, engaging in what Brown refers to as "mannered racialism," which ultimately only reaffirms white supremacy, as tolerance is virtuously bestowed upon nonwhites, and not the other way around.[49]

However, the film's virtuous tolerance is tested by the immoral Myca, with whom it can only put up for so long; her badness reveals the extent to which toleration has been stretched. Significantly, Myca's death is the most spectacularly graphic murder in the film, her overkill a sensationally punitive gesture that effaces her body (an attempt to disfigure and remove her face by eliminating its eyes), effectively erasing the inscrutable Chinese-as-face that Chow describes. As in *Irma Vep*, the Chinese femme's "eyes that fascinate" restate her physiognomic, ethnic difference, which must be removed. After the crow pecks out Myca's eyes, as karmic punishment for her own acts of eyeball procurement, she falls down the center of a staircase inside an abandoned church, clinging briefly to a bell (a nonhuman voice sounding her doom) before plummeting to her death. Nevertheless, despite the overtly pungent punishment Myca receives, what also lingers in the film's aftertaste is Bai's erotic charge. What remains are the fragmented images of Bai's overdrawn mouth signaling oral perversion, as well as the anal initiation to which we are privy in her introductory shower scene. Such are the sticky, flavored part-objects that remain in the spectator's imagination.

As a *homo sacer*, Giorgio Agamben's term referring to a body neither animal nor citizen whose biological life is suspended in state biopower, Myca's liminal body is radically vulnerable to the sovereign right to kill. To kill is one thing, but to overkill has become standard for Hollywood's darker genres and their appetite for sensational body horror. The aesthetic of the overkill suitably aligns this postapocalyptic overworld and its bone-chilling acts of spectacular violence, demonstrating the punitive logic Ethan M. Higgins and Kristin Swartz explain of the gothic paradox that "it takes a monster to kill a monster," an aesthetics used both to illuminate the monstrous nature of the marginalized and to conceal the deeds of spectacular punishment, as well as to indicate that only through a gratuitously violent response can the state express its power and authority.[50] In contrast with the underworld, which refers to a criminal underbelly that reproduces modern capitalism's drive toward accumulation through a subversion of law and order, this overkilling world is one that takes the logic of production to biopolitical extremities, toward the continuous renewal of death, disaster, and destruction for capital. As Achille Mbembe explains of colonial space, "Under a regime of vertical sovereignty, colonial occupation operates through schemes of over- and underpasses, a separation of the airspace from the ground."⁵¹ If the overpass of colonial power rests upon optical mastery over the lay of the land, it is also a defensive position that retreats into high altitude to survey the grounds. Similarly, Eric and the crow are able to ascend such heights to mimic colonial power and the necessity of precision in killing, whereas Myca's fatal descent reaffirms the necropolitics of the colonized body, which must surrender its mortality and become inert animal matter. If the plantation, following Mbembe, becomes a "state of injury, in a phantom-like world of horrors and intense cruelty and profanity," and if slave life is a form of death-in-life, this becomes aestheticized in gothic cinemas, a kind of rupture and specter that betrays the west's unconscious guilt complex over slavery.⁵² This complex, in turn, is marked by the pungent toleration within mainstream cinema's darker expressions of multiculturalism.

Dubious Paratexts

Since *The Crow*, Bai has become an infamous D-list celebrity, often appearing on the red carpet in tight, revealing outfits that draw attention to the actor's lanky figure. Bai's overwhelming off-screen performativity as a hot mess forces retasting along the lines of the hostile, bitter act of rumination.⁵³ By evacuating subtlety from her sexy act, Bai imbues hypersexuality as a kind of offensive behavior, or as first strike. Bai's self-presentation reveals that if savoring suggests a lingering enjoyment of the memorial act of retasting, then mercyism or rumination is the violent uptake of matter experienced once more in burning form. In other words, Bai's revealing, "nip-slipping" ensembles summon a double take/taste of her hot outfits and invite staring. Moreover, Bai's provocative off-screen performativity has eclipsed her film roles, while her celebrity persona engages in making dubious claims and practices of disknowledge. One assertion Bai repeatedly makes is that she possesses "eight little spirits" residing within her, an explanation she uses to justify posing nude for magazines and other media outlets.⁵⁴ Bai also repeatedly states that she has been reincarnated from a wild animal, specifically a cheetah or a leopard, and that she feels more animal than human. Other dubious (salty) claims assert that she is "from the moon," a self-proclaimed extraterrestriality that affirms what Stephen Hong Sohn refers to as the "Alien/Asian," a yoking together of terms that reveals the ways in which "the alien stands as convenient metaphor for the experiences of Asian Americans, which range from the extraterrestrial being who seems to speak in a strange, yet familiar, accented English to the migrant subject excluded from legislative enfranchisement."⁵⁵ By "nonsensically" disavowing her humanity, Bai draws attention to western humanism's exclusion of Chinese bodies. As scholars like Sohn, Nakamura, Leilani Nishime, and David Roh contend, yellow peril fantasies inscribed within techno-Orientalist narratives betray a kind of pungent saltiness—the resentful envy emanating from what Sohn refers to as "the West's desire to regain primacy within the global economy" in the wake of ascending Asian economies and technological-industrial developments.⁵⁶ However, where discourses of liberal tolerance may for Brown function "not only to anoint Western superiority but also to legitimate Western cultural and political imperialism," it is only at the extremities of tolerance whereby we may locate the west's pungent anxieties about its potential/real/imagined inferiority.

Whereas Cheung embodies just the right amount of salty flavor and racial matter (the deft touch of salt), Bai's dubious behavior and over-the-top hypersexuality approach the material-semiotics of a particular kind of salt perceived to possess pungent risks, namely monosodium glutamate (MSG). As it has become associated with cheap Chinese food in the west in particular, MSG culinarily marks Chinese difference, as Robert Ku elucidates: "MSG is routinely singled out as the embodiment of all that is wrong with the current state of human gastronomy."⁵⁷ White Americans have responded to the allegedly negative effects of consuming MSG with hostility and anger—performing the limitations of digestive and multicultural tolerance. Nevertheless, in an act of defense, similar to the ways in which the overheated body loses fluids and salts, Bai's hot mess persona offers an embodied image of heat intolerance that evaporates the multiculturalist melting pot, returning Bai's image to one of cool incomprehensibility and indigestible Chineseness.

Colonial Rot and Mainland Anxiety

The atmospheric is unbounded by society and law. Nevertheless, the pungent atmosphere as a performative event of moral rot offers a way to engage with pervasive sensibilities and judgments concerning behavior and social performance. Invoking the pungent atmospheric is a means by which we reinstate perimeters around law and sociality, and the mood that the pungent interjects is one of suspicion and, more significantly, one of anxiety. To deal with anxiety is to deal with desire or, more specifically, the deferral and unfulfillment of pleasure.

In our final encounter with pungency, we turn to Jacques Lacan's tussle with anxiety in *Seminar X*. Positing that anxiety is conjured when there is no possibility of lack, Lacan states that the insistence of infant desires being met by the mother creates an insistent model "of the demand that will never let up."[58] Lacan states, "Anxiety isn't about the loss of the object, but its presence. The objects aren't missing."[59] Anxiety thus arises from the fear of lacking lack, and it is located between the Other's jouissance and their demand. Anxiety arises from the indeterminacy of clearly distinguishing the Other's desires, needs, and wants (and whether those are even separate). Here, the m/Other is unrelenting in her gift to the infant, and demand becomes totalizing. In adult romances, the smothering behavior of a sexual partner, signaling both unequivocal love and nondesirous love, becomes an unattractive, even repellent, turn-off because such behavior no longer permits the possibility of jouissance in the pursuit of the object of desire (in both directions). Smothering is the territorializing performance of love's fait accompli, the vanquishing or melting of desire through its needy gestures of encroaching proximity. The "sm/Other" can thus be thought of as a romantic partner whose ubiquitous presence turns her into a maternal cannibal, a purveyor of totalizing consumption, on the brink of expurgation, of the rotten.[60] Within its presentation of total demand, the sm/Other's gifts are not the conventional articles of hospitality but rather the partial and abject objects that signal rot, decay, and stink. Aptly, the pungent appears in Lacan's theory of anxiety through "dejecta," "trace," and excrement, the partial object governed by the pleasures of the anal function. He states, "Among the different excretory functions, why single out the anus, if not for its decisive sphincter function which contributes to cutting an object? This cut is what gives its value, its accent, to the anal object, with everything that it can come to represent, not simply, as they say, on the side of the gift, but on the side of identity."[61] Here, the gift or hospitality becomes part of the process of identity formation. Neither the titillating gift of Ono's clothing nor Nakadate's offering of birthday cake (discussed by Huang) with which we opened this chapter, this infantile gift is—literally—shit. Moreover, it is the cut—the performance of agency and will—of excretory functions that produces the illusion of identity. As such, the successful mastery of toilet training instills in the infant an important source of pride and confidence, earning the love of m/Other by demonstrating the sociable and appropriate management of bodily waste. Nevertheless, mastering pungent acts of the body also invokes anxiety because it signals m/Other's consistent super-vision as an omnipresent surveying mode that never ceases to take her smothering gaze off her child (and his/her rear). Like a wet blanket, the gaze coincides with demand itself, thereby extinguishing *objet petit a* and desire.

Whereas a Lacanian sm/Other resembles a phallic, overbearing m/Other—a monstrous femme fatale like Myca—there is another crucial way to understand this concept with which to analyze our second pungent case study. The pungent can also be charismatically alluring, indicating the ways in which we desire transgression, violation, and irritation. As Peter Adey describes in his material-affective ecology of megacity atmospheres, "Atmosphere fills the void of media abstractions with the air of a place we can imagine inhabiting. We could go as far as to say that it is the air which has smothered such places with a kind of charisma. Smoldering away, the megacity's atmospheres lend a definite aura."[62] "Smother" and "smolder" give off an *odor di femina*, a feminine distinction. As an exaggerated m/Other figure of pungent charisma and unpermitted erotic desire, the sm/Other as a charismatic and atmospheric modality is one that insists upon and demands pungent sexual display as a means of accessing love.

As a type of pungently charismatic atmosphere, we might refer to the womb, a space Lacan deliberately a-*voids*. As corrective to this lacuna, Bracha Ettinger's notion of the borderspace within what she refers to as the prenatal "matrix," from the Latin for "uterus/womb," radically locates a type of nonrelational, processual, subjective encounter between I and non-I. In other words, it is also a space of hospitality. Writing about pregnancy and the womb as a matrixial borderspace, Ettinger describes the envelope inside a woman's body, another type of atmosphere, as a host space whereby prenatal, pre-Oedipal "relations-without-relating" can take place, and a kind of presexual incest whereby mother and child's bodies commingle and encounter otherness via jointness.[63] Therefore, although the sm/Other can constitute a psychotic archetype that "threatens us with her infinite, engulfing power," the sm/Other also suggests the possibility of Ettinger's concept of a "shareable dimension of subjectivity in which elements that discern one another as *non-I*, without knowing each other, co-emerge and co-inhabit a joint/joining space, without fusion and without rejection."[64] As a relational form, this image of pre-Oedipal, prephallic, precastrated becoming offers the potential to reverse psychoanalytic conceptions of woman as "lack," "nothing," and negation because of woman's exclusion from Symbolic phallic processes. For instance, the sm/Other can perhaps do the kind of pungent "revolutionary mothering" imagined through women-of-color feminisms by Alexis Pauline Gumbs, China

Martens, and Mai'a Williams. Pointing out the ways in which the mothering of the poor and of children of color has been marginalized and under attack in the United States, particularly under Ronald Reagan's neoliberal invention of the "welfare queen," Gumbs writes that "the radical potential of the word 'mother' comes after the 'm.' It is the space that 'other' takes in our mouths when we say it."[65] Sm/Othering, as an aesthetic modality, attempts to close that space of the "other," whether it is the gap of desire between subject and object, or that embodied void alluded to by Gumbs. Sm/Othering as an insistence of feminine desire not only fills lacunae, it overfills and overspills in ways that agitate and irritate mainstream publics. Nevertheless, what I wish to seize upon is the extent to which the appearance of matrixial desire in art and cultural production is perceived as a threat—indeed, a domestic atmoterrorism—that cannot be tolerated. As Ettinger states, "The silenced matrixial desire, on the other hand—that of linking with the unknown and bounding with unknown others in the process of becoming and transforming oneself—puts patriarchy in danger."[66] Thus, psychoanalysis has always been unable to conceive of the before/beside borderspace of pregnancy, because, as Ettinger notes with a nibble of sarcasm, "it is too dangerous!"[67]

Woman and her desire have always made great men of psychoanalysis stutter, a fact encapsulated by Freud's epistolary concern posed to his French colleague Marie Bonaparte: "The great question that has never been answered and which I have not been able to answer, despite my thirty years of research into the feminine soul, is 'What does a Woman want?'" It would seem that Lacan was no more prepared to answer this question. According to a Lacanian model of castration, feminine jouissance is unknowable, inaccessible, and unintelligible, because it exists beyond the Symbolic domain of the phallus, and only in traces, part-objects, or what Ettinger refers to as "psychic wild residues."[68] Similarly, the gaze, an elusive and illusory desire to encounter the unapproachable Real beyond the realm of appearance, is something for which we long but can never capture, another "phantasmatic trace of a traumatic trace," *objet a*.[69] Providing a new conceptual framework through which to acknowledge female jouissance, a nonphallic matrixial gaze through which touch, movement, and voice offer the possibility of a transsubjective intimacy engenders "a disturbing desire for jointness *with* a foreign world, the unknown other, the uncognized, the stranger inside the known other, a stranger who by definition is never a total stranger because it is unthinkingly known and traumatically accessed."[70]

Returning to this chapter's concerns with hospitality and strangers/neighbors conceived through political (in)tolerance, matrixial aesthetics can allow us to glimpse, if not fully gaze upon, the processes of a traumatic coemergence through the sexual relation. In other words, in contrast with the stare that stars elicit through the shock of their beauty, or with the double-take bewilderment at a star like Bai, the glimpse intimates the partial, the fragment, and the residual trace of a suppressed maternal relation, a pre-"conscious" subjectivity of the womb. Such womb phantasies, when partially inscribed through the cinematic gaze, invoke domestic terrors and anxieties, as evinced in such films' pungent reception. In what follows, glimpses of feminine desire via the matrixial sm/Other in Ang Lee's film *Se, Jie* (*Lust, Caution*, 2007) about the collaboration between the Chinese and Japanese during the Second Sino-Japanese War, performed through the graphic sexual acrobatics staged between an undercover Resistance fighter and her target (a Chinese high official of the collaborationist government), result in a pungent backlash that draws together memorial war trauma, the humiliations of collaboration, and the shame provoked by encountering a feminine jouissance that reveals the nation's death drive within colonial encounter.

First let us set the stage by briefly invoking Jing Wang's historical-thermal approach to the mainland's "high culture fever" that emerged throughout the postsocialist 1980s. Wang notes that the resurgence in neo-Confucianism, which she metaphorizes as a "wholesome Confucian spiritual diet," was intended to "neutralize the *pungent* flavors that modern Western values left on the palate of a modernizing China."[71] Western culture's overpowering pungent flavors elicited a nativist-cultural response. As the appeal of western ideologies and material cultures seemed simply too strong to resist and too pungent to ignore over time, neo-Confucianism made its reentry into Chinese society by way of a tempered, traditional, and more harmonious path to modernity in the late twentieth century. Among the pungent western values that seeped into China's porous boundaries were more open attitudes toward sexuality and explicitly feminized displays of women's bodies. The neutralization of such driving influences impelled the moral policing of women, manifesting through disciplinary discourses around celebrities. Stories about the moral deficiency of Chinese film stars are common even today; for instance, the belief that many female celebrities are upscale escorts remains largely unchallenged, as one journalist explains that "right or wrong, there's a widely-held perception in China that many beautiful actresses, singers, and dancers sleep their way to success."[72] Performance anxieties envelop mainland Chinese women film stars, who have long been objects of censorship, surveillance, and gossip—particularly when the topic concerns their sexual performances, both on- and off-screen.[73]

Desire, anxiety, and pungency are tightly wound orbs of affective relationality within the intimate publics of screen cultures, particularly when it involves women stars. As cultural flows, controversies surrounding the sexual behaviors of female stars demonstrate this triangulation. If pungent (white) anxieties surrounding Bai's star body revolve around the reluctance toward American multiculturalism, manifesting as an "atmo-Orientalism," then mainland Chinese and Sinophone audiences projected another kind of pungent anxiety upon Chinese women stars. The past century's shifting social constructions of gender in China have culminated in a great sense of anxiety about female sexuality. During the Maoist era, in Dai Jinhua's words, "desire, the gaze of desire, the language of bodies, and the signification of gender were all designated as trademarks of the class enemy."[74] However, the post-Mao era, particularly after China's 2001 entry into the World Trade Organization, has witnessed what Mayfair Yang describes as the "rapidity of the return of gender differentiation, the ascendancy of the male gaze, and masculine sexuality's domination of a public sphere partially vacated by the state."[75] Chinese women stars' hypervisible bodies and behaviors became public objects subject to neo-Confucianist moralism and social judgment, provoking both sensual pleasure and moralized anxiety. In the twenty-first century, actresses who draw the most controversy, like Tang Wei, reveal conflicted desires at the intersections of an ever-expanding globalized consumerism and the pungent formations of Chinese nationalism.

Piquant Shame

Tang Wei was born in Wenzhou city in 1979 and grew up in Hangzhou city, China, the only child of an actor and a painter. After graduating from the Central Academy of Drama in directing, Tang appeared in several Chinese television programs before debuting as the lead character in Ang Lee's adaptation of Eileen Chang's (Zhang Ailing) short story, "Lust, Caution," initially published in Chinese in 1977. After the 2007 theatrical release of a censored version of the film (various reports state that anywhere between seven and thirteen minutes were cut), and after its subsequent banning in the PRC, Tang was herself banned from working in China for several years, and her domestic modeling endorsements were immediately revoked.

Despite, and perhaps because of, the choir of (predominantly masculine) discontent, it is Tang and not Tony Leung Chiu-wai, playing her sexual partner in the film, who carried the stigma of *Lust, Caution*'s sex scenes. Tang was castigated for what was perceived as the unpatriotic and shameful sale of her body to Lee and his film. The public banning and criticisms of Tang, in contrast to the silence around Leung's performance, reveals the gendered stigmatization surrounding sexual performativity. Although the anxieties of sexual performance expressed in everyday vernacular are typically portrayed in masculinist terms of stamina, athleticism, and virility, the burden of cinematic sexual performance is often projected onto women. According to online reports, the official justification for banning the first-time film actor was that she was an "unhealthy influence" on young people, because her fame arose from "taking off her clothes."[76] Other critics took up the film's historical representation, which is severely inconsistent with the *guanfang yishixingtai biaozhun* (government's ideological criteria). What was perceived to be morally rotten revolved around the film's display of feminine desire and its pungent, deathly pursuit of matrixial jouissance. The moral outrage directed at Tang's hypersexualization coagulated with national disgrace, driving the acrid nature of the film's critical backlash.

The inherent prurience of the film's sexual representation is con-*fused* with bitter affects, as the story of collaboration between the Japanese and ranking Chinese elites during the Second Sino-Japanese War aggravates a national shame.[77] Moreover, the nationalistic performances surrounding the film's reception, conveyed in vitriolic rhetoric, correspond with frustration over a fifty-year silence and continuous denial on the part of Japanese politicians who deny the events of the war. The affective shame economy constructed around remembering China's past "century of humiliation" therefore serves as a politics of belonging "to a nation that was hurt into being," to invoke Gloria Davies's description.[78] Thus, the outrage directed toward a scapegoated film like *Lust, Caution* can also function as affective glue for Chinese diasporic communities across national boundaries, aligning the bodily space of affect-sensorial experiences with the social space of being Chinese.

Pouring salt into an unhealing wound, the film displaces war crimes committed by the Japanese military (e.g., rape and torture) onto a Chinese character. *Lust, Caution* spectacularizes the female protagonist's repeated sexual coercion as an oblique, albeit perverse, metonym for the rape that Japanese soldiers performed widely during the war, as Lee admits that the first sex scene between the two leads was meant to evoke "the brutal Japanese rape of the Chinese."[79] Representing "the body of the nation," women suffered a distinct punishment during the war premised on sexual submission and humiliation, most notoriously in Nanjing over the course of six weeks.[80] *Lust, Caution* narrativizes this distinction through its depiction of a woman who is at first seemingly raped by, then repeatedly submits sexually to, a high-ranking collaborator of the Japanese whom she is attempting to entrap for assassination.

Lust, Caution opens in Japanese-occupied Shanghai in 1942, where we see four wives playing mah-jongg in the residential compound of the Chinese collaborationist government. As mah-jongg is organized around the "eating" (*chi*) and "touching" (*peng*) of tiles, this introductory sequence gestures to the feminine relation beyond the scope of the visual. It must also be noted that "peng" describes a specific kind of touch—a collision, a bumping into—that suggests an unexpected, even undesired event. The character 碰 consists of the radical for "stone" and the character for "side by side." The valence of "peng" therefore denotes a kind of inflexible, even impenetrable encounter between two solid objects/subjects. Both hard touch and gustatory desire will become thematized through the film's sexual acts, which deliberately confuse and interweave violent conflict and desire, entangling self and Other through physical intimacy. Through a series of glances, we glean that the youngest wife of the four, a polite yet aloof Mai Tai Tai (Tang Wei), is familiar with Mr. Yi (Tony Leung Chiu-wai), the mah-jongg hostess's husband and high-ranking collaborationist. Later, we deduce Yi's initial attraction to Mai Tai Tai through the subtleties of mah-jongg game play, when he deliberately allows her to eat (chi) one of his discarded tiles, which leads to her victory. Mai Tai Tai then excuses herself to go to a café where she makes a coded phone call to a group of armed young men and women. In the following flashback, Mai Tai Tai, whose real name is Wang Jiazhi, and the other young people are revealed to be theater troupe members attending Hong Kong's Lingnan University, and who are led by the charismatic revolutionary Kuang Yu-min (Leehom Wang). After their success with a patriotic play put on to raise funds for the resistance movement, Kuang asks the others to "do some real acting," hoping to enlist their help to entrap and assassinate Mr. Yi, an official of the Republic of China (1912–49) who tortures spies and resistance fighters for the Japanese puppet government, led by Wang Jiwei.

In the film's first act, the themes of *Lust, Caution* are established: performance, politics, and betrayal. In an extended flashback that leads back to the film's opening mah-jongg scene and the telephone call, we see Wang

Jiazhi playing the role of Mai Tai Tai (or Mrs. Mai), who must seduce Mr. Yi, thereby luring him into the aforementioned assassination trap. After exploiting Tsao (Kar Lok Chin), Yu-min's hometown connection, in order to gain introductions to Mr. and Mrs. Yi (Joan Chen), Mr. Yi shortly thereafter reveals his attraction to Mai Tai Tai. In preparation to become Yi's mistress, Jiazhi agrees to lose her virginity to, and practice having sex with, one of her male colleagues. Despite their flirtations, the handsome Yu-min, all intellect and revolutionary drive, relinquishes the opportunity for intimacy with Jiazhi, instead assigning the task to another fellow troupe member who has had experience "with prostitutes." A few days after Jiazhi's sexual training begins, Mr. and Mrs. Yi abruptly announce that they're moving to Shanghai. An unexpected visit from Tsao, who discovers the group's covert masquerade, leads to a brutal murder scene when the men of the troupe take turns stabbing him. Tellingly, the sexually repressed Yu-min wounds his own hand with the knife in his first attempt. That the knifing is a metaphor for sexual penetration is evident, given that Tsao brings a loaded gun that quickly falls into the group's hands. Gazes exchanged between Yu-min and Jiazhi reveal that Yu-min wants her to see that despite the fact that his real desire is to penetrate Jiazhi, he, following the conduct of a proper revolutionary intellectual, transfers his unrealized sexual passion to a violent act of murder. Jiazhi, witnessing the murder and glimpsing Yu-min's brutal libidinal projections, runs from the apartment in horror.

Three years later, a destitute Jiazhi is in line for food rations in war-torn, Japanese-occupied Shanghai. A run-in with Yu-min persuades her to resume her undercover role-playing as Mai Tai Tai in order to entrap Mr. Yi, who has since been promoted to the head of the secret service for the Japanese. After Mai Tai Tai is invited to stay at the Yi house, Yi arranges to take her to a secluded apartment where the two have intense sexual encounters. After Mai Tai Tai finally earns Yi's trust, he sends her to choose a diamond ring as a gift. The film then returns to the present, to the opening sequence during which Jiazhi makes the coded call to the resistance group. Mai Tai Tai and Yi go pick up the diamond ring, and upon hearing sounds of the resistance group advancing, Mai Tai Tai/Jiazhi suddenly whispers to Yi, "Go, now! [*kuai zou*]." After Yi narrowly makes his escape, Jiazhi, in a daze, leaves the store. Yi then orders the capture and execution of the entire theater troupe, including Jiazhi. A final exchange of glances between Jiazhi and Yu-min as they kneel waiting to be executed suggest that it is their missed sexual encounter, this romance thwarted, that culminates in deadly consequences. In the final scene, the collaborationist wives' mah-jongg group plays downstairs while Yi ruminates on Mai Tai Tai's empty bed upstairs in the dark. Neither Yu-min nor Yi, in the good company of Freud and Lacan, was able to understand women's desires, which remain an inscrutable enigma that exists only in traces and part-objects like the un/eaten mah-jongg tiles strewn throughout the film. However, that which is tasted or eaten is not always digested, leaving one strangely empty, like Yi enveloped in shadow by the film's end.

Lust, Caution's narrative of a resistance plot foiled by a female spy's amorous feelings for her enemy target would not necessarily upset Chinese audiences. Sixth Generation filmmaker Lou Ye's *Zi Hudie* (*Purple Butterfly*, 2003), for instance, stars Zhang Ziyi as a Chinese resistance fighter who falls in love with a member of the Japanese secret police. However, it is *Lust, Caution*'s three scenes featuring near-pornographic sexual performances (adding up to around eight minutes), shot during what the first assistant director described as "eleven days in hell" with the camera rolling for 154 hours, that has incited the most impassioned criticism from Chinese and Sinophone audiences.[81] Playwright Huang Jisu wrote the widely read and influential essay "China Has Stood Up, but Ang Lee and Company Are Still Kneeling" and continued his dramatic tirade about *Lust, Caution* on his blog, where he stated that the film's conception of the bed was no longer a stage for human love but rather a "brutal arena," vocalizing the common outcry from critics that *Lust, Caution* employs *meihua* (glorification) of traitors.[82] As Hong Kong actor Tony Leung Chiu-wai, one of Sinophone cinema's most popular leading men, plays the Japanese puppet agent with whom Tang's character falls in love/lust, such assertions are not unfounded. Critical fury about *Lust, Caution* also extended well beyond China and into Sinophone communities around the world.[83] As the *South China Morning Post* reported, a Chinese/American group based in California called the Traditional Family Coalition issued a press release written in both English and Chinese urging all Chinese people worldwide to boycott the film. In it, group spokesperson Bill Tam charges Lee with being a "cultural traitor" and accuses Tang of being "worse than a prostitute" for having no "sense of shame" for her simulation of sex acts.[84]

Deviating from common tropes of nationalistic Chinese film and media dealing with the subject of the Second Sino-Japanese War, *Lust, Caution* does not feature heroic resistance fighters or helpless war victims, unlike *Red Sorghum* or Zhang Yimou's Nanjing Massacre film, *Jinling shisan chai* (*The Flowers of War*, 2011). Rather, the film reveals the fissures and failures within a political movement—namely that a woman's desire can sabotage political morality (the phallic superego).[85] As Hsiang-yin Sasha Chen observes, Yi "shifts his body through various near-impossible sexual maneuvers to penetrate Wang, which can be seen as analogous to an interrogation involving cruel torture."[86] What is more penetrative, however, is the way Yi looks at Jiazhi, with what Tang has described in interviews as Leung's "electric eyes."[87] Staring into her eyes during their sexual trysts, Yi scrutinizes Jiazhi's sexual performance, seeking the impossible gaze from the position of the Other. If Jiazhi truly enjoys having sex with him and is not faking her pleasure, then he can trust her. Whereas Yi excels in extracting the confessions of his political enemies under physical duress, his inability to fully access Jiazhi's jouissance creates an unrelinquishable desire for her. Perversely, for Yi, sexual encounter provides the space for private interrogation of desire, whereas public, colonized space enables the flow of affection and sincerity. While Yi's eyes harden during sex, they glisten, soften, and caress Jiazhi with affection in public spaces. Indeed, Yi's eyes water when Jiazhi sings to him, and it is this leakage that finally undoes him.

During one of their public trysts, Yi invites Jiazhi to a Japanese teahouse, where in the next room drunken Japanese soldiers fall over one another to the sounds of a neglected geisha's discordant, minor-laden song. After Jiazhi quietly slides the door shut, creating an intimate "womb," she, in a minor act of cultural resistance, performs a Chinese folk song complete with subtle feminine gestures and movements. The melody, from the song "The Wandering Songstress," which is featured in the leftist Chinese film *Mailu tianshi* (*Street Angel*, Yuan Muzhi, 1937), appears to stir Yi's heart, and his eyes tear up. Jiazhi's voice, birdlike and clean, penetrates his natal psyche. In another scene, Yi angrily tells Jiazhi that he can no longer focus on his duties because he keeps thinking about her, and in particular her fragrant smell. It is voice and scent, not image, that constitute the transgressively pungent part-objects and atmospheric forms that produce matrixial coemergence. Wang's relentless bodily seductions, a sensational sm/Othering through sexual consent, a form of hosting with and gifting of one's body, generates the transsubjective alliance between the two, closing the proximity between the Resistance fighter and her enemy. In *Lust, Caution*, we make sense of colonial occupation as an intimate somatic event between the gaps of Tang and Chiu-wai's porous, corkscrew bodies-in-sex. Thus by the film's end, although Jiazhi betrays the nation, it is she who heroically pursues her desire to its fatal conclusion, while Yi, traitor both to the nation and to desire, is the one left irreparably wounded (and not womb-ed) because he chooses to foreclose the infinite possibilities of feminine jouissance, which, even if it cannot fully be known, should be enjoyed and pursued in wild part and ephemeral trace.

As many reviewers and critics have pointed out, Lee embellishes Eileen Chang's only overt reference to sexual intercourse: "Somewhere in the first decade or two of the twentieth century, a well-known Chinese scholar was supposed to have added that the way to a woman's heart is through her vagina."[88] It could be said that the pathway from vagina to heart also passes through the womb. Within the fantasy of matrixial return, Jiazhi's body continually folds into a fetal position when she and Yi are together, first collapsing into that pose on the bed after their first brutal sexual encounter, when he whips her with his belt, ties her hands behind her back, and forces himself inside her (figure 3.2). The second time Jiazhi reproduces this vulnerable position occurs before she sings for Yi; she crumples and lays her head in his lap. Finally, Jiazhi's body folds into this position as she and Yi mutually reach sexual climax during the film's final graphic sex scene (figure 3.3). Whereas Jiazhi's song undoes Yi, it is the enfolding/enfolded intensity of Jiazhi's bodily surrender that enables Yi to, in Jiazhi's words, "worm his way into [her] heart." This minor act of re-creating the fetal position thereby continually evokes the womb, and the nation as womb-space. Rather than a hospitable space of encounter between I and non-I, however, the nation under siege becomes a too-porous envelope that has inadvertently invited in hostile, destructive guests. What is therefore most troubling about this sexual allegory is that colonialism, as a collaborative condition, is an intimate, even desirous affair of complicity, a will to realize a dangerous (feminine) jouissance that welcomes and enfolds the Other into its fatal embrace.

Freud described the death instinct as "an urge inherent in organic life to restore an earlier state of things which the living entity has been obliged to abandon under the pressure of external disturbing forces; that is, it is a kind of organic elasticity, or, to put it another way, the expression of the inertia inherent in organic life."[89] The death instinct in Freud's conception suggests the desire to return to an inanimate, inert state. Remarkably, however, Freud includes in his argument a biological experiment with infusoria in which animalcules perished when crowded together in their "own nutrient fluid" but "flourished in a solution which was over-saturated with the waste products of a distantly related species," an observation that applies to colonialism itself as a system that thrives in waste, decay, and death.[90] Whereas Bai's suspect livability manifests as her character's involuntary death in *The Crow*, Jiazhi is hospitable to death. Jiazhi's step

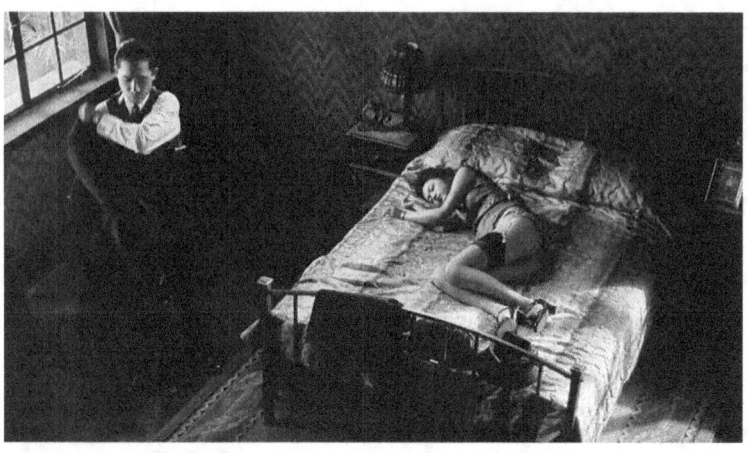

3.2–3.3

Jiazhi's repeated fetal position evokes the dangerous matrixial relation that is willing to host enemy others.

toward Thanatos is signaled in the film's final sequence at the jeweler's shop in which Yi and Jiazhi pick up his gift for her, a diamond ring. Jiazhi takes the ring from the box, asking Yi if he likes the jewel she picks out, and a point-of-view close-up frames Yi looking into her eyes with a soft look: "I don't care about jewels. I only want to see it on your finger." Jiazhi acquiesces, placing the ring on her finger, a material symbol of the pair's entangled commitment. After she attempts to remove it, protesting that she does not wish to wear such expensive jewels on the street, Yi gently instructs her to "keep it on." At this point, Jiazhi's eyes begin to well, her porosity indicating a return to the unbounded womb-space wherein subjects meet in indistinguishable, undifferentiated form. Yi then takes her hand and tells her, "You're with me." Whereas in the English translation, the feminine "you" (Jiazhi) is yoked to the location of the phallic "me" (Yi), giving off a whiff of proprietary masculine relations and egotistical desire, the Mandarin utterance more vividly expresses the coterminous, nonhierarchical qualities of matrixial encounter. Yi says, "Ni gen wo zaiyiqi [You and me are together]," indicating that beside-ness and with/ness (what Ettinger refers to as "wit(h)ness") becomes unity and oneness, precisely what the marriage ring ceremonially signals.[91] And yet, as Todd McGowan notes, the structure of a ring resembles that of the death drive, "a closed loop organized around a central absence."[92] Jiazhi's acceptance of the ring signals her embrace of the death drive, knowing that she will sacrifice her own and others' lives in order to save Yi's, for the sake of pursuing her feminine enjoyment to its fatal ends. Thus, Jiazhi finally utters her own death sentence when she tells Yi to "go quickly." Yi misrecognizes this code at first, offering only a baffled "Hm?" that reaffirms that Jiazhi's subjectivity remains enigmatic and elusive to the end. Neither a slip nor an accident, Jiazhi repeats the line a second and final time, while frantically and insistently peering into his eyes. While feminine or maternal self-sacrifice is certainly not an exceptional or extraordinary trope (particularly in a historical melodrama), what is inflammatory and pungent about *Lust, Caution* is the fact that Jiazhi's jouissance, conjunct with the death drive, offers a glimpse of colonization as a mode of perverse enjoyment and complicity with our fatal desire. Jiazhi's sexual enjoyment exceeds her desire to live; she dies so that Yi's pleasure-granting phallus could remain in the world and "flourish... with the waste products of a distantly related species." Although for Haiyan Lee this is a "feminist gesture of defiance by which a passive body speaks up as an acting and forgiving subject," or what she terms an act of "contingent transcendence" that is prompted by a Levinasian look at Yi's face, on the contrary, Jiazhi is conducting her final, active act of seduction whereby her execution, ordered by Yi, becomes the terminal penetration that persists henceforth in Yi's conscience.[93] Whereas their sexual affair begins with Yi belting Jiazhi's hands together and forcing himself inside her, it concludes with the chiming sound of a clock, signaling Jiazhi's death, which penetrates Yi's body and brings him to tears (as with *Twin Peaks*, an inversion of salty semen and tears). By proving that her sm/Othering desire can only be extinguished by death, Jiazhi's self-sacrifice demonstrates the ways in which feminine sexual pleasure is neither of this world nor of its sociopolitical atmospheres.

That the pungent desires of the body can overcome the conscious and moral mind is the most disturbing and shameful revelation of all. Here, the pungent as putrefaction directly manifests the death drive (id will always overpower the superego), and the bodies we see in the throes of sex are rotting bodies, the decaying forms of colonial encounter. As Ann Laura Stoler writes, rot "opens to the psychic and material eating away of bodies, environment, and possibilities," therefore offering a dense metaphor through which we can understand the lingering ruins of colonialism.[94] Ruins imagined as a kind of atmosphere becomes particularly poignant given that Japanese colonialism, as Paul Roquet points out, was in part justified using the atmospheric attunement of "reading the air," which was used as a "rhetorical strategy for authority figures to indirectly persuade underlings to acquiesce to the status quo, diverting attention from vertical power structures by shifting blame to an atmosphere instead."[95] Wartime atmosphere thereby relieved individuals of taking responsibility for brutally savage crimes, which included the rape and mutilation of Chinese women.

Jiazhi's jouissance thus becomes an irritant, an intolerable pungent offense, especially given China's nationalistic stance about the war. Similar criticisms, for instance, were launched at Italian filmmaker Liliana Cavani for her 1974 film *The Night Porter*, in which an ex-Nazi officer and his concentration camp prisoner resume a sadomasochistic, destructive sexual affair that began in the camp and ends in death after the two reunite by chance in Vienna after the war. Cavani was also interested in understanding the psychological bind of victim and perpetrator, as *The Night Porter* reenacts traumatic entanglement through a sexual practice saturated in violence and pain. Responding with moral outrage, Roger Ebert wrote that the film was "as nasty as it is lubricious, a despicable attempt to titillate us by exploiting memories of persecution and suffering."[96] What Ebert failed to comprehend is that desire does not abide by the rules of a good or moral conscience. If Nietzschean bad conscience is the internalization of force and guilt, which turns into pain, it also desires confirmation through suffering. In both *Lust, Caution* and *The Night Porter*, amorous feeling arises from guilt and loss (even if it is not the same guilt and loss from both parties, a point that demonstrates Lacan's observation that "there is no such thing as a sexual relationship because one's jouissance of the Other taken as a body is always inadequate").[97] Nevertheless, such guilt and loss are also the foundations from which beauty can be born. As Steven Shaviro observes, beauty "is not a recompense for anything that has been lost. Beauty is rather the pang of loss itself, its truest expression. It cannot be shared, and it cannot be preserved. It vanishes in the very act by which I apprehend it. I can only cry out, a witness to its passing."[98] If beauty is "the pang of loss itself," or the peng of hard touch, always already a mode of mourning for the ephemerality of the beauty act, lust for beauty is sustained by a fantasy that one has not yet witnessed it. In other words, the chase after beauty is premised upon doubt.

Appositely, Lee's longtime producer and screenwriter partner James Schamus comments on the performative nature of lust and its relationship to dubious caution, separated in the film's title by the tentative breath of a comma. Schamus writes:

> For the performer always, by definition, performs for someone. And that audience, no matter how entranced, is always complicit: it knows deep down that the performance isn't real, but it also knows the cathartic truth the performer strives for is attainable only when that truth is, indeed, performed. Yee [Tony Leung] doesn't simply desire Mak Tai-tai [Tang Wei] while suspecting she is not who she says she is; it is precisely because he suspects her that he desires her. In this sense his desire is the same as hers: he wants to know her. And so lust and caution are, in Zhang's [Ailing, a.k.a. Eileen Chang] work, functions of each other, not because we desire what is dangerous, but because our love is, no matter how earnest, an act, and therefore always an object of suspicion.[99]

The tension between lust and caution is not only what attracts the protagonists in the film, it is also what sustains erotic interest in Tang the actor, of whom global Chinese audiences knew little, and yet whom they saw re-creating the most intimate of human interactions. We are complicit in the film's highly graphic sex scenes, knowing that the "cathartic truth" of the intensely fraught connection between enemies can be achieved only through the film's sexual performances. However, as discussed above, complicity with the Japanese during the war is not a truth that many Chinese people wish to hear, as they feel that catharsis is not as worthy an affective encounter as ressentiment. Thus, performing their pungent critiques, Chinese critics passionately decried the film as a "sexually transmitted disease" and charged it with "using pornography to attack humanity."[100]

Violent bodily persecutions in war are indeed displaced onto bellicose sex sequences, and eleven days of shooting bedroom scenes produced the building pressures and tensions in the actors' bodies that subsequently emanate on-screen. Corporeal labor is communicated through protruded forehead veins, sweat beads, and flushing cheeks, while expressions of love and hate flicker and vacillate across Tang and Leung Chiu-wai's faces. Such expressions of erotic engagement mirror those of shame, and this complex image negates the very premise of "saying no," to evoke a particularly poignant phrase from the populist 1996 publication *The China That Can Say No*.[101] That is, Tang's bodily efforts betray the fact that indeed, she cannot "say no" to border-linking involvements of the body-in-sex, which is always a fantastic agreement to share and enjoin.

Even though her onscreen body generates a surplus of meaning, we see Jiazhi, Mai Tai Tai, and Tang as one person, particularly because Tang's face was unknown and inscrutable to global audiences when she appeared as *Lust, Caution*'s lead actor. First assistant director Roseanna Ng recalls that Lee specified that the lead actress "would not be a cookie cutter of the current movie stars: no oval face, no big-eyed Barbie, no long-limbed willowy mannequin."[102] Moreover, the director's parting instruction ("what others don't want, I'll take") also indicates that the lead actor's appearance should be undesirable in a conventional sense. Tang looked "completely unassuming" and "plain" to the production team during auditions, and yet she was chosen from more than a thousand actors by Lee less for what she looked like, and more for what she did not look like. Manohla Dargis remarked that Tang's pretty, gentle appearance was ill suited to the role, a sentiment echoed by Chinese viewers and critics who hoped to see a symbolically strong face that could demonstrate the condemnable qualities of "sacrifice, betrayal, fanaticism, [and] lust" to underwrite a reductive yet morally righteous vision that denounced the evils of collaboration.[103] Neither commercially attractive ("she has a face that doesn't sell here"), nor a "big-eyed Barbie," Tang's heart-shaped baby face became a sight of illegibility and inscrutability. Whereas the pungent racial odor of Bai relates to her thermal inscrutability in a film that envisioned 1990s American multiculturalism through gothic dystopia, Tang's illegibility as desirous woman and national traitor incited a pungent moral outcry in China and the Sinophone world. In both cases, Bai and Tang's pungent bodies became atmospheres of rot and putrefaction, evoking the scent of death in their embodiments of the seductively intolerable. Whereas Bai has remained pungently inscrutable in her career, however, Tang's mainland redemption was precipitated on the deodorant scrubbing of her malodorous associations with *Lust, Caution* after a two-year mainland ban. Through careful, strategic participations "at just a few charity campaign events, working as a volunteer without any makeup, or in bookstores, and at several top brands' fashion shows overseas," Tang became a morally hygienic star and, in demonstrating her cultural capital and "dignity and self-restraint," Tang's postfilm performance sanitized the memory of her incendiary portrayal of a wartime traitor.[104]

Pungent Remains

The nude Chinese female body in *The Crow* and *Lust, Caution* acts as a pungent atmospheric, signifying simultaneous desire and anxiety toward tolerance, matrixial desire, and the death drive. Noting the lack of a tradition of the photographic nude in China, François Jullien argues that the Chinese hold an "aversion of this *overdirectness*," as "Chinese aesthetics demand that there should always be a 'beyond': a 'beyond' to words, to shape, to the taste of things."[105] However, as this chapter demonstrates, pungent beauty, presented in the nude, rather than acting as a frozen final form, gestures to the beyond precisely by bringing us closer to the thresholds and limit points of toleration. Furthermore, the cinematic nude invokes for Jullien one of the three primary priorities of Chinese aesthetics, namely the diffusion of atmosphere (*fengshen*).[106] In both aforementioned cases, the political investment in reproducing Chinese inscrutability through the femme fatale takes form as a piquant figure that alerts its audiences to the social climates of liberalism, multiculturalism, and colonialism. The vulgar racial odor of Bai, as it relates to her thermal inscrutability and hypersexuality, helped envision 1990s American multiculturalism as a failed and scorched urban landscape engulfed in flames. Meanwhile, Tang's illegibility as a desirous woman and a national traitor incited strident condemnation in China and among Sinophones. As a means of assessing cultural temperature, pungent charismas reveal the tenuous atmospheres that trace our political subjectivities, while feminine jouissance hovers just beyond the frame, inviting our glimpse.

Sweet and Soft Coupling:
Vivian Hsu and Shu Qi

The street's flickering neon lights look dreamy under the weariness of jet lag. It is our first night in Taipei, and my partner and I stumble into Huaxi night market, also known as Snake Alley. We drag our fatigued bodies to look at snakes in glass aquariums, declining invitations from vendors to dine on them. Our hunger leads us to a small congee shop where we order bowls of sweet glutinous rice, mung beans, red dates, and sweet potato. This burst of carbohydrates floats us to the next destination, an adult bookstore where I hope to find Vivian Hsu's erotic photo albums, Angel *(1995) and* Venus *(1996).*

The shelves are lined with covers of young Asian women in various states of undress. Many of them look directly at the camera with chin pointed down, eyes looking up, mouths smiling or with lips slightly parted. They appear sweetly compliant and sexually curious. I ask the clerk if he has Hsu's books; he shakes his head no.

Later, I discover that the best method of procuring Hsu's albums is on eBay or Amazon for $40–$109. One eBay listing advertises: "Used, very good, no tears, no severe stains, no severe scratches."

That the book may have light scratches reveals how we treat our mediated objects of desire—adoring and suspicious of a surface we suppose is soft, we draw our bodies toward an imagined beneath.

Taiwanese stars Vivian Hsu and Shu Qi, both beginning their careers in soft-core pornography, broke into the mainstream to act in films that belie China's aggressive intentions toward Taiwan. Big-budget films such as those directed by mainland male directors like Li Yin and Feng Xiaogang attempt to render the Taiwanese female body pliably willing for imagined cross-strait coupling, reimagining Chinese-Taiwanese codependence through romantic heterosexuality. In such films, Taiwan is cast as a female partner who, even if she hesitates, ultimately defers to a benevolent, masculine China.[1] Whereas cinematic bitterness disseminates through leakage of interior liquids from an immanent body, sweetness and softness depend upon surface manipulations. Bodily and spatial exteriors, tender and transparent, mark a point of contact with the world, while smoothness and seamlessness homologically envisage the linear narrative of One China without fissure. The bodies of women stars, upon which such ideas are also projected, become ripe, receptive, and finally ruined in order to accommodate hardened, masculinist desires for partnership.

"Smelling Good"

During the 1997 Asian financial crisis, a series of events beginning with Thailand's sudden currency devaluation threatened to instigate a global economic meltdown. China's refusal to devalue its currency in order to maintain stability in Asia won the nation great favor throughout the region. Meanwhile, Thailand's longtime ally, the United States, provoked bitter ire for its lack of fiscal support, as effigies of then-president Bill Clinton were burned in the streets. After the crisis was averted, Rodolfo Severino, head of the Association of Southeast Asian Nations, proclaimed, "China is really emerging from this smelling good." A far cry from the bitter tastes of revolution and remembrances of suffering during the previous decade's Cultural Fever, China's international policies since the late 1990s have centered on "smelling good" through strategies of *heping jueqi* (peaceful rise), which themselves are premised on "soft power," a term Joseph S. Nye uses to describe a method of political coercion based on persuasion rather than blunt and direct force.[2]

As a result of a shift toward public diplomacy alongside efforts to spread Chinese language and culture around the globe, China has been trying to sweeten its image throughout Southeast Asia, Latin America, and Africa, particularly in territories that the United States overlooks or alienates because of their perceived lack of economic return. In his study of China's twenty-first-century "charm offensive," Joshua Kurlantzick describes China's strategy of "becoming friends and partners with neighbors," particularly with developing nations.[3] Nevertheless, as he points out, "not all of Beijing's goals follow from Peaceful Rise, though. Taiwan is a special case."[4] Despite the fact that Taiwan has instituted a liberal democratic government with a free, competitive presidential election since 1996 (a decade after the lifting of martial law), the Chinese Communist Party (CCP) still views Taiwan as its province rather than as an autonomous nation, having adopted a hard-line stance since the founding of the People's Republic in 1949 and the subsequent exile of the Kuomintang Nationalist Party (KMT), who fought with the CCP for mainland control during the first half of the twentieth century. Chinese leaders have repeatedly expressed that they would not hesitate to "use force" to maintain their One China policy, enforced by the passage of the 2005 Anti-Secession Law, and the act of aiming missiles at the territory, ever ready to respond to Taiwan's hypothetical declaration of independence. In part motivating China's stubborn stance is the state's desire to retain control over two out of four Asian Tiger economies (Hong Kong, a Special Administrative Region of the PRC, and the Republic of China, Taiwan). As a result, overt political tensions and antagonisms plaguing cross-strait relations have also generated hostility in the global atmosphere, with its bad feelings spilling over into other national politics. Donald Trump's phone call with Democratic Progressive Party president Tsai Ing-wen in December 2016, for example, broke with a long-standing convention established in 1979 when Washington forged diplomatic ties with Beijing and subsequently cut them with Taiwan. Temporarily souring relations with Beijing, the call was widely covered in American news and social media, fueling bitter postelection moods and amplifying doubts about the then-president-elect's lack of knowledge about international relations.

Taiwan's *longue durée* is much more heterogeneous, complex, and fractured than China's singular and totalizing explanation of its geopolitical identity. The master narrative that insists that Taiwan is part of China must grapple with the presence of long-standing indigenous cultures and Austronesian groups, Han immigration to the island beginning in the seventeenth century, and foreign colonization, which began with the Dutch in the seventeenth century before dynastic China reabsorbed Taiwan.[5] Following China's loss in the First Sino-Japanese War, Taiwan was ceded to Japan and underwent multiple stages of colonialism, from assimilation and incorporation to subjugation and military mobilization between 1895 and 1945. After the defeat of the Japanese in World War II, the KMT under Chiang Kai-shek took control of Taiwan and instituted a repressive one-party regime under martial law for nearly forty years (1949–87). Democracy movements of the 1970s and 1980s evolved out of growing support for Taiwan nationalism and widespread discontent with the Nationalist Party, bolstered by a well-educated middle-class majority and a strong, developing economy.[6] Today, a minority of Taiwan's population of 23 million consider themselves Chinese, whereas the Minnan majority, descendants of Han migrants from the mainland Fujian Province, and Guangdong Province descendants, the Hakka, identify as Taiwanese and support the democratic sovereignty and Taiwan's current de facto independence.

In an attempt to move the Taiwanese majority toward friendly reconciliation with China, a different and softer kind of cross-strait narrative takes place in Chinese cultural production, even as such endeavors are equally invested in reunification. Soft power manifestly conjures gendered and sexualized conventions, juxtaposing feminine charm and appeal against masculine, militaristic force. Although Nye and other political scholars avoid the gendered implications of soft power, the feminine erupts throughout the discourse, tellingly, as playful asides. Nye acknowledges that his "deepest debt" goes to his wife, whom he describes as "a woman with wondrous soft power," suggesting that soft power becomes affective and legible through personality.[7] Along with feminine connotations, scholarship concerning Chinese soft power intimates persuasive strategies through romantic rhetorics.[8] Romantic desire is invoked, yet cross-strait libidinality and the ways in which aesthetic objects (including humans) play an affective-performative role in nationalist mythologies are left out of hard, serious politics. Nevertheless, the feminine persists via denotations of softness and attraction—even if only in acknowledging puns and perfunctory synonyms.

As a result of the growing economic interdependence between Communist China and democratic Taiwan, soft power, communicated through polyvalent flavors of cinematic and embodied sweetness, underline ambivalent cross-strait attractions. As Taiwan's largest trading partner and foreign investor, China engages in a double-pronged hard and soft strategy to maintain codependence, described by Emerson Niou as "first, by threatening the use of force to deter independence and second, by fostering economic integration to induce unification."[9] The secondary approach and its utilization of soft power involves the world-making bodies of Taiwanese women film stars as affective vehicles through which femininity is mobilized to garner popular support for Chinese unification. What of such stars' "wondrous soft power"? How is the sweetness of soft power communicated across weidao through cinematic allegory, technique, and form? The construction of national soft power is itself a celebritization and feminization of state image to bestow an attractive impression upon others ("smelling good," to recall Severino's words). This chapter expatiates on that good smell as sweetness, connecting the flavor aesthetics of sweetness to textural densities of softness in the sensorial permutations of performative cuteness, conspicuous consumption, and spatial politics.

Soft, Tender Beauty

The correlation of soft power with the feminine is particularly germane to approaching Taiwanese film stars from a mainland perspective. As with the socialist film worker's ideological service, modern celebrity operates as a type of behavioral prescription, elevating aspirational goals advocated by the state.[10] In contrast to the formation of Li Shuangshuang as a proletariat proto-celebrity, discussed in chapter 1, the postsocialist celebrity must also encourage consumerism in addition to civic responsibility. Actors are not only expected to embody statist ideals, they become cautionary public examples if they violate them. In September 2018, for example, A-list actor Fan Bingbing, China's highest-paid performer, appeared to have gone missing for three months, alarming international news media. After Fan reemerged in early October 2018, it was revealed that the star was likely held in forced detention for failing to pay her taxes, after which she released a public apology and agreed to pay the equivalent sum of $130 million in back taxes.[11]

If pungent tastes provide aid to the body's circulation through forceful intensities, sweet tastes act as a tonic, calming irritation and inflammation.

In recent years, the volatility of popular martial arts and action films (flexing China's new muscle after the nation's 2001 entry into the World Trade Organization) seems to have given way to a sweeter and softer flavor palate: Chinese romance and comedy blockbusters. Playing an ambiguous, even complicit, role in attenuating China's hard ambitions for world power, mediated images of beautiful women circulate confectionary assurance and affective promise that China still intends to smell good and make good as a global leader. Beauty contests, which had been forbidden since the establishment of the PRC in 1949, began to flourish after the first pageant held in Guangdong Province in 1988. The opening of China's marketplace during Deng Xiaoping's reform era, strengthened by entry into the WTO, helped precipitate the breathtakingly quick and vast import of westernized beauty products and ideals. Although attention to feminine beauty was considered to be counterrevolutionary ideology and bourgeois decadence three decades earlier (recall Mao's description of women shackled and branded by jewelry and makeup), twenty-first-century Chinese officials radically changed their tune and advocated that pageants held propagandistic value as "symbols of women's liberation and modernization, rather than as tools of sexual repression and women's oppression," as Gary Xu and Susan Feiner note.[12] Since the 1980s, images of the good life and well-being disseminate through made-up, smiling faces, and toned, fashionably decorated bodies. Through the circulatory economies of fashion and beauty industries, as Sara Ahmed observes, "the figure of the woman is associated with beauty and appearance, and through her, the nation appears for and before others."[13] Embodying Chinese modernity and national health, female celebrities envisage modernity and encourage beauty consumerism. Feminine beauty, as circumscribed within disciplinary statist structures, conveyed through a recessive charm rather than an insistent charisma, assures its beholders of the nation's robustness through pleasing surfaces and their solicitation of pleasure. Moreover, Chinese feminine beauty and its mediated circulations throughout Greater China and the Chinese diasporas help bloom and reterritorialize Chineseness beyond national boundaries through migrating beauty acts (in locations like Taiwan, Hong Kong, and Singapore), demonstrating Vanita Reddy's observation that beauty "open[s] onto articulations of citizenship and belonging."[14]

Flavorful notions of feminine beauty also emerge in discursive metaphors of texture and ripeness. As Jie Yang observes, the constructions of the "tender" (*nennü*) young woman and the "ripe" (*shunü*) older woman in Chinese popular and consumer cultures advocate for the transformation of feminine ripeness into tenderness via appearance. As young, tender beauty becomes that which is natural and good, older women can only become retenderized through skin and body care, clothing, and cosmetic surgery. Such neoliberal techniques are viewed as youthful rejuvenation of the female body, returning it once again to a supple form that externalizes and gives proof to interior states of youth, wellness, and health. If young beauty is imagined through the feel of tender softness, then the weidao of charm is imagined through sweetness; if soft is an affective-aesthetic texture, sweet is its corresponding flavor. The mainlander gaze aimed at Taiwanese stars then is an appendage of diplomacy and soft power within changing political tides of cross-strait reconciliation, whereby sweetness encodes the promises of heterosexual romance and forms an affective anchor around which One China is forged and desired.

Knotted Feelings

The first blockbuster coproduction between mainland China, Taiwan, and Hong Kong was the 2006 *Yun shui yao* (The song of the clouds and water, English title *The Knot*). Produced by mainland China Film Group Corporation, Hong Kong's Emperor Classic Films Company, and Taiwan's Long Shong Entertainment Multimedia, the expensive joint collaboration (costing around 30 million yuan) reveals how ideological negotiations between the three geopolitical territories are subsumed within an allegory about romantic love and a negotiated historical consciousness that privileges the One China narrative. Rather than following in the international footsteps of Fifth Generation contemporary Zhang Yimou, Beijing Film Academy graduate Yin Li pursued a directing career in domestic *zhuxuanlü* production, or "main melody" (commercial propaganda), through a long-standing working relationship with the state-run China Film Group (CFG). A major state apparatus, CFG assists in ensuring what Emilie Yueh-yu Yeh and Darrell William Davis term the "re-nationalization and 'hyper-nationalization' of Chinese cinema," using the guises of marketization and internationalization to conceal the company's ideologico-economic interests.[15]

A saga spanning the 1940s to 2006, *The Knot* centers on a doomed love triangle that extends across Taiwan, Korea, and Tibet. The film's geopolitical wanderings through six decades of war and their resultant displacements produce a scattered plot with crosscutting timelines. The twenty-first-century present revolves around telephone conversations between Wang Biyun (Chang Gua Ahleh), a widowed painter in New York City, and her niece, Xiaorui (Isabella Leong), a young writer who is interviewing her aunt about her youthful love affair with a communist revolutionary. The historical timeline features a young Biyun (Vivian Hsu) in Taipei and her cross-strait love triangle, shaped by the forces of mid-twentieth-century political events. Medical student and covert communist Chen Qiushui (Chen Kun), whose grandparents migrated to Taiwan from the mainland, falls in love with high-schooler Biyun while tutoring her younger brother in English. After Biyun's mother discovers their romance and dismisses Qiushui, the slighted suitor retreats to his mother's home in the rural Taiwanese village of Xiluo. Biyun follows him, and a romance between the couple blossoms into engagement before their courtship is abruptly halted by the February 28 Incident of 1947, during which the KMT government violently purged its political dissenters, left-wing factions to which the fictional Qiushui belongs.

Qiushui then flees to fight in the Korean War with the People's Liberation Army, where he meets mainlander tomboy and fellow soldier Wang Jingdi (Li Bingbing). Jingdi quickly falls in love with Qiushui, but the steadfast young man remains committed to Biyun in body and mind. Meanwhile, Biyun, playing dutiful daughter while she awaits Qiushui's return, splits her time between Taipei and Xiluo, with her intended mother-in-law. As the years go by, Qiushui is relocated to Tibet, and this time it is Jingdi who follows him. Jingdi's persistence in loving Qiushui eventually wins him over; Jingdi even changes her name to Wang Biyun because Qiushui "only has Wang Biyun in his heart." After Jingdi's grand gesture of relinquishing her self through renaming, Qiushui agrees to wed her. Meanwhile, Biyun settles down in passionless matrimonial affection with Zilu (Steven Cheung), an insecure Taiwanese entrepreneur. In present day Tibet, Xiaorui meets Qiushui and Jingdi's adult son Chen Kunlun (also played by Chen Kun), and in the film's dénouement, she finds out that Qiushui and Jingdi died in an avalanche during a 1968 Tibetan snowstorm. An elderly Biyun is devastated upon finding out what happened to her lover, for whom she has waited her entire life, and the film ends with a long bird's-eye tracking shot following a hawk soaring over the Tibetan mountainside. Sublimating Biyun's grief into a picturesque vision of Tibet, and then of Earth, produced through an illusion of optical-digital mastery, the final sequence deflects the loss of love onto an omniscient image of a seamless, unified vision of China from above, implying an entitlement on the order of the divine.

The camera's final ocular ascension envisages the ideological belief system of *tianxia* (all under heaven), an ancient metaphysical concept related to what Chinese philosopher Tingyang Zhao describes as "an empire of world-ness responsible for the common happiness of all people," which he considers to be a family-based alternative to western conceptions of internationality premised on nation-states.[16] Reconstituting sublime rights within earthbound entitlements, the Qinghai-Tibet high-elevation train was constructed the year of the film's release, coincidentally, tethering Tibet to China through developmental modernization, technological dependency, and other forms of territorialization that further enable Han Chinese penetrative access and mobility into the autonomous region whose sovereignty, like that of Taiwan and Hong Kong, is denied by the PRC.

While the film's top-down view limns China's topographical, cosmological mastery, the ground is populated by the film's cosmopolitan casting: Taiwanese model-singer-actor Vivian Hsu, mainland actors Chen Kun and Li Bingbing, Macanese singer-actor Isabella Leong, and Hong Kong boyband member Steven Cheung. Similar to Ang Lee's *Crouching Tiger, Hidden Dragon* (2000), featuring actors from China, Taiwan, Hong Kong, and Malaysia and their divergent Mandarin accents, *The Knot* populates a vision of a unified "Sinophone," a term Shu-mei Shih uses to describe the post/neocolonial formations of peripheral areas like Taiwan and Hong Kong in relation to the PRC center, "where a historical process of heterogenizing and localizing of continental Chinese culture has been taking place for several centuries."[17] In *The Knot*, such tensions between center and periphery are played out through the manageable hostilities and subtle antagonisms underlying romantic (im)possibilities. In other words, the film explains that differences between Chinese subjects are ultimately familial—that is, invariably reconcilable because they are one family, bound by love. Reproducing the One China mythology, the casting of the actors suggests that anyone with a command of Mandarin can act Chinese. Such politics of absorption and linguistic assimilation stem from Confucianist principles dictating the superiority of the Han, which Melissa J. Brown traces to the belief (if not the actual practice) of Confucian "culturalism" whereby "a person or group can be considered Han as a result of their cultural practices *regardless of their ancestry.*"[18] Less about blood as an interior signifier of ethnicity, this returns us back to pliant gestures and soft surfaces. With the exceptions of mainland actors Chen Kun and Li Bingbing, the casting of Sinophone pop stars indicates soft power's important function to attract via what is pleasingly beautiful. Moreover, the film's knotted indexicality refers to Chen and Leong's actual names in order to confuse fiction and reality, further perpetuating the film's nationalistic con-fusions. Chen Kun plays Qiushui and Jingdi's son, who is named Chen Kunlun, and Xiaorui, upon meeting him, introduces herself as Isabella.

Nevertheless, whereas the film intends to pursue Zhao's recuperative notion of harmonious tianxia governance, the reception of *The Knot* outside of mainland China reaffirms Shih's assessment of peripheral resistance. Defending themselves against *The Knot*'s saccharine taste, reviewers criticized its melodramatic ploys. From the film's simplistic characterizations to its overdetermined and gushing orchestral score, wildly arrhythmic truncation of sequences containing important swaths of information, and Yin's unmotivated use of fades to black, the film is an aesthetic and critical failure by standard accounts. Even the Academy Awards, which characteristically favor the sentimental and superficial, refused to nominate *The Knot*, China's bid in its Best Foreign Language Film category. Although *The Knot* did well at the Chinese box office, its failure to draw moviegoing crowds in Taiwan and Hong Kong indicates local forms of resistance rooted in Sinophonic differences in politics and cinematic taste.[19]

My experience of the film aligns with that of viewers who found themselves irritated by *The Knot*. Pointing to the "uneasy zone" between irritation's cutaneous bodily experience and the internal psychological state, Sianne Ngai explains that being "rubbed the wrong way" refers to frictions and incongruities between interior and exterior.[20] Ngai demonstrates how, for instance, Nella Larson's *Quicksand* (1928) drew irritation from readers because of Helga Crane's "inadequate," banal responses of annoyance to racism. However, *The Knot*'s production of irritation stems from the characters' unrestrained outpouring of desiring feeling, wherein there is seemingly no cutaneous border between interior and exterior. Nevertheless, the film's lack of depth and radical superficiality chafes, particularly as its hardened ideological pit, rubbed against its soft sentimental surface, finally exposes itself through aesthetic and performative fissures. Moreover, the cloying performances in conjunction with the overt political conceit also "rubs the wrong way," as the political itself becomes an irritating exterior that tightly encases the film's domestic interior vignettes. The critical failure of *The Knot* produces its own disquieting, knotted feelings, which, in a way, rebounds de facto feelings of mutual suspicion within the stagnant cross-strait impasse.

The vulgar "obscenity" of *The Knot* then, which could also be said of "*soft*-core emotional porn for women," to draw upon Molly Haskell's description of melodrama, brings "soft" into the realm of "mush."[21] We already theorize the textural connections between sweetness and softness with terms like "sappy," "mushy," "corny," and "cheesy" to describe sentimental and melodramatic productions that have lost their sweet flavor and become formless, bland, and, in the case of "cheesy," even salty. The Chinese synonym *rouma* refers to the maudlin and fulsome, further explicating the dulling affectivity of oversentimentality. Consisting of the words "meat/flesh" and "numb," *rouma* describes the body's encounter with saccharine excess, which produces a sensation of numbness in one's flesh. Rather than a heightening of perception and sensitivity to touch, the overdone, overripe sentiment creates the opposite spectatorial response to toughen up one's own cutaneous and affective boundaries to prevent mushing into formlessness. An adversarial reaction to excessive sentiment (such as being grossed out or disgusted) thereby constitutes a numbing of flesh, representing the beholder's final line of intransigent defense against generic mimesis.

In addition to the reflection of one's own numbing flesh, we also refer to the mind-numbing quality of shallow objects. This hard-line propaganda film that masquerades as a sentimental melodrama flattens the political and the personal, and evacuates each realm of depth. The romance between Qiushui and Biyun, who fall in love at first sight, is conveyed through underdeveloped, clichéd montage and overwrought performances, particularly by Hsu, whose gestural outline for young Biyun is bulleted by infantilized giggling, crying, pouting, and foot stomping, demonstrating how the film's histrionics are ultimately entangled with its own speciousness in disruptive ways, an argument to which we will return. The film's exploitation of pathos and story of lost loves therefore result in too-predictable, diluted flavors of bittersweetness. Whereas bitter aesthetics correspond to desires for justice, and sweetness correlates with seductive persuasion, bitter and sweet's collusion seems salient for political projects aimed at convincing publics of violating inequities. As a charismatic, coercive politics, bittersweetness can be mobilized for the correction of wrongdoing through the management and tempering of outrage with melancholic and seductive geniality. Nevertheless, many critics agree that *The Knot*'s flavor palate tastes artificially sweetened, becoming disingenuous and unconvincing. A modern-day "Mandarin Duck and Butterfly" romance centering on tragic thwarted love, the film is critically despised, just like the populist Butterfly fictions of the late Qing and early Republican era by May Fourth intellectuals revolting against China's traditional and feudal systems. Mainland film critic Chi Meijian took issue with the film's dialectical tensions between soft melodramatic romance and hard-line wishes for Chinese unification: "Beneath the surface of a dream of love and longing lies a desire for national unification[;] the collective emerges through the individual."[22] Meanwhile, a commentator on Douban (China's most popular online film forum) protested, "Just as children know there are wolves in sheep's clothing, we all know this film is a 'united front' film cloaked in a pop star love story."[23] Similar to the founding Butterfly text, Wu Jianren's *The Sea of Regret* (1906), lovers are separated by history, which, as Haiyan Lee notes, "impinges on the imaginary autonomy and integrity of the self by inflicting on the body the cruel imprints of temporality (disease and death) and by assailing the virtue of constancy with the unbearable human tragedies of separation and betrayal."[24] The grief-stricken elderly Biyun at the film's end, becoming trace and marker of history's cruel temporalities, also embodies such consequences of separation and betrayal. However, such tragedies are not just human errors, they are political ones, mistakes like the February 28 Incident and the KMT's subsequent "white terror" reign of communist prosecution that compels Qiushui's exile. The Communist Party's bitterness, palpably resentful of the KMT, erupts through unfulfilled romance, metamorphosing political acrimony into thwarted love.

Indeed, the rheumatism that afflicts the elderly Biyun's leg joints, rendering her sedentary and requiring her to use a wheelchair in her later years, fittingly imagines bone and cartilage atrophy at the body's flexible contact points. Such a characterization also menacingly alludes to the aggravation of joint China-Taiwan relations. Widowed and increasingly silent, Biyun ultimately becomes overripe, inconsumable, and inconsolable. Where ripeness speaks to the maturation of female sexuality, as mentioned above, the "overripe image," according to Olivia Khoo, is one wherein the film frame is unable to contain its aesthetic and affective spillage, and gestures in particular to the "impossibility of rooted Chineseness."[25] *The Knot*'s effete overripeness, through acrobatic cinematography, visually dense historical texture, and overperformed sentimentality, produces the sensation of a sickening and stultifying sweetness that, rather than generating pathos, points to unrooted vacancy and spectral loss. This distasteful sweetness coalesces in Hsu-as-Biyun's melancholia, which Sigmund Freud describes as grieving over an object loss that is not consciously known but nevertheless reconstituted within the self as a diminishment of ego and self-esteem.[26] Biyun cannot actually "see clearly what it is that has been lost" because her attachment to the promise of "reunification" with Qiushui lays bare the film and CFG's ideological investments in Chinese renationalization (the wolf) cloaked in romantic wishes (sheep's clothing).[27] Biyun's melancholic misunderstanding of her loss in fact portends the film's ideological desires. As a vehicle through which to convey a political wish, Hsu's performance (exterior, gestural, and wholly superficial as it is) manifests the film's hardened political core.

Here we may slide again from the semiotic to the material to better understand the relation between sweetness and poison. When a fruit overripens, its sugars ferment into alcohol enzymes and carbon dioxide. The fruit's decay and bacterial rot transforms its matter into soft mushiness and a strongly sweet odor. As an object possessing (low) animacy, there nevertheless exists a continuum of life and death or decay for a piece of fruit, although at a certain point the fruit becomes unpalatable and disruptive to weak digestive systems. Too much sweetness can be nauseating or even toxic, and metaphors relating to density and emotion also relate to material toxicities. In curious relation to the "*soft*-core emotional porn for women," the inner "hard core" pits of stone fruits like peaches, cherries, and pears contain cyanogenic glycoside, a natural toxin that can turn into hydrogen cyanide, which is poisonous to humans. Some fruits like ackee even become toxic when they overripen, revealing the ways in which bitterness lies dormant in the sweet. In terms of texture, an overripe fruit becomes too soft, too responsive, becoming easily depressed to external touch. *The Knot*'s strong, smelly sweetness translates not only through its hard-core toxic ideology, but finds its visual correlate in Biyun's swollen arthritic body, which immobilizes her in a state of passive desire. The preoccupation with the melancholic Biyun is a fixation, as well, on the depressive qualities of the soft, impressionable woman, who becomes socially poisonous to those around her because of her unrelenting obsession with her childhood sweetheart.

The suggestion of overripeness also contains within it an intimation of the "too late!" temporal domain of melodrama, as Linda Williams discusses in her classic taxonomy of body genres. Williams argues that the fantasy of melodrama is concerned with the origin of selfhood through a return to "family romance" wherein the "quest for connection is always tinged with the melancholy of loss."[28] As a family romance, a Freudian fantasy of better birth, the film imagines "the replacement of both parents or of the father alone by grander people" through a *pater semper incertus est* fantasy of replacing one father with another: the KMT with the CCP.²⁹ Indeed, fathers in this film are by and large absent or inadequate. Qiushui's father is missing with no explanation, and Biyun's father becomes a depressive alcoholic after the unexplained loss of his wife. Biyun never bears a child by the frequently nosebleeding Zilu, who eventually dies of leukemia. Even as blood does not necessarily define Chineseness, dreams of better birth are nevertheless attached to the purity of blood. As such, the Taiwanese men in the film possess only polluted (via alcohol) or damaged blood (via mutated cells). Heroic bloodshed this is not. Meanwhile, the film's sole good father is Qiushui, who explicitly embodies the CCP because he is willing to shed blood for his political commitment, and implicitly because the Taiwanese is always already Chinese (the actor Chen Kun even rolls his *r*'s in a manner distinctly recognized as a mainlander's northern accent).

Unintentionally referencing Richard C. Bush's Brookings Institute white paper *Untying the Knot: Making Peace in the Taiwan Strait* (2005), which uses the emblem of the knot (the two strands represent sovereignty and security) to demonstrate the intractable entanglements between China and Taiwan, the film's clumsiness and achingly sweet love triangle betray the desperation, more than anything else, of soft power's cloying and calculating tendencies, particularly under the cover of artistic innocence.³⁰ While *The Knot* narrativizes cross-strait relationships as fraught, even unrequited, romance, the film's overripened formal language indicates the monolithic essentialism at the heart of the One China argument.

In the film's opening sequence, a cryptic phone conversation takes place between Biyun in Manhattan and Xiaorui, who has just traveled from Singapore to Taipei. One of the film's running motifs is established every time Xiaorui calls her aunt; she is always en route to another Chinese or Chinese-claimed territory (Taipei, Shanghai, Tibet), demonstrating the jet-setting rewards and benefits of "flexible citizenship," a term Aihwa Ong uses to describe Chinese geo-economic territorialization through travel and mobility.³¹ As the dramatic orchestral score plays, Xiaorui asks Biyun in a pleading tone, "What is it in this world that stands between the living and the dead? And what is it that sets apart people who love each other?" The camera zooms into a painted portrait of a young Qiushui by Biyun, and this aesthetic mediation of Biyun's fixed longing for Qiushui, fixed and fetishized in oil, cross-dissolves into what will be the film's most ambitious visual stunt: a three-minute tracking shot that establishes the historical setting of late 1940s Taipei after the KMT takeover. Beginning with a young boy selling newspapers in the foreground (evoking Benedict Anderson's national community imaginatively forged through print capitalism), a long single take winds through a darkened shoe shine parlor, onto narrow streets and balconies of Chinese singers and puppet performers, tracking airborne across a rooftop where a young boy and girl play, descending upon a red wedding sedan and celebration, glancing across students learning Mandarin tones, before pivoting to a bird's-eye view of Qiushui arriving for his interview at Biyun's home.[32] Similar to the film's final tianxia shot over Tibet, the depiction of a seamless and continuous practice of Chinese customs and traditions in Taiwan, reinforced by the single tracking shot, acts as a compressed image of the film's re-presentation of Chinese historical continuity via Mandarin and Han domination. Through such fluid reproductions of language and culture, Taiwan becomes an extension of China, and Chineseness persists seamlessly and without break (as the lack of visible cuts suggests), despite the political fracture of the two parties, each of which claimed at the time to be the sole guardian of an authentic China. This long shot functions as a stylistic counterpoint to the film's other prominent editing tic, the frequent use of fade-to-blacks to segue from one temporal or spatial sequence to the next, a technique that irritated reviewers.[33] Indeed, this transition inadvertently punctures the film's obsession with continuity; by visualizing the unrepresentable gaps in history that have been excised from the master narrative, the film's act of fading, or blinking, induces continuous unsuturing. This cinematic seizure suggests the unsustainability of the master narrative, stammering just like Biyun's stuttering and effeminate Taiwanese husband, Zilu, who is too soft to capture her heart. Meaghan Morris's vivid claim about the power of feminism to "make political discourse 'stammer'" resonates, even though it is not feminism that produces the effect here.[34] The film's stammering fades gesture to its rheumatic problem—it has a joint issue, in both formal and politico-ideological terms. Yin's inability to produce editing continuity across the dual story lines and various geopolitical locations constitutes a cinematic confession that its intended ideology—the fantasy of One China or tianxia—is full of holes, its stuttering a result of the unviable narrative that seeks to make Chinese national identity coherent and singular.

Unsurprisingly, filming in Taiwan was prohibited, likely because of the film's coercive and syrupy One China message. Consequentially, the notion of monolithic China is spatially reinforced by location substitutions of the mainland for Taiwan and Korea during principal photography: 1940s Taipei and Miaoli are re-created in the southeast Fujian Province city of Zhangzhou; Biyun's home is reproduced in Fujian's Gulangyu, and the Korean War is restaged in Beijing. Such spatial fungibility is also reproduced in the crisis of naming: Jingdi becomes Wang Biyun by legally changing her name. Thus although Qiushui and Biyun are separated from one another, new, albeit awkward and asymmetrical codependencies are forged, just as they are, increasingly, through joint cross-strait ventures. The film's political message ultimately emphasizes a lukewarm pragmatism and diplomacy: Qiushui and Jingdi's marriage is not a whirlwind and passionate romantic love, but it is a pragmatic and procreative relationship that endures. As Jingdi tells Qiushui after following him to Tibet, "You don't need to continue *bitterly* waiting for her. I am Wang Biyun," assigning the endless deferral of pleasure, the act of waiting, to the realm of bitterness. In contrast with the bitterness of past suffering and memory, the bitterness here is attached to thoughts of Qiushui's overripening body rendering him inedible/unlovable in the future. Thus Jingdi's palliative sweetness is the ostensible cure for Quishui's bitter lovesickness. Meanwhile, no such sentimental screen time is spent on the lukewarm Taiwanese coupling of Biyun and Zilu. The effeminately shy, nosebleeding Zilu, lacking conviction and passion for heroic sacrifice, only passively inherits his father's tea company—a characterization that betrays the film's perception of Taiwan as a territory that exploits the cloak of democracy only to pursue entrepreneurial capitalism.

Playing the hard-headed, self-sacrificing mainlander, Li Bingbing received praise for her performance, earning numerous domestic and Sinophone acting awards, whereas Hsu received none. Nevertheless, it is the curious case of Hsu's performance of perpetual waiting that illuminates the island's affective condition and political mood.[35] If Taiwan's liminality and persistent waiting for a permanent status of nationhood is inscribed in Biyun's character and story line, Hsu-as-Biyun's embodiment conveys China's apperception of Taiwan as a young and naive codependent.[36] However, a close reading of Hsu's aggressively superficial performance of cuteness reveals an undoing of the film's sweet-soft aesthetics, and a disabused softening of its intransigent politics, despite all of the aforementioned formal and narrative attempts to advance the One China myth as the film's sole heavenly body, or star.

Aggravated Cuteness

As Biyun (played by Hsu) overhears Qiushui's English language lesson for her brother, the young schoolgirl's gaze turns upward with reverence toward her soon-to-be lover's voice. Biyun's wonder is an image of political awakening, a glimpsing recognition of a cosmopolitan worldliness that hinges on a command of English. It is not merely coincidental that the United States figures indirectly here as a mediating presence in this cross-strait allegory, as also in Bush's overestimation of the United States as "the sole source of Taiwan's security and thus much of its psychological confidence."[37] English functions inspirationally, hinting at promises of global security and confidence through American tuition and epistemological capital. Biyun giggles as Qiushui teaches her brother word pairings: "Boy, girl. Shoes for men. Shoes for lady. Bathroom for men. Bathroom for lady," a statement signaling as much the impending romance between the two as an indoctrination of binarisms. Gender structures language, perspective, and worldview, as frictions and fictions of sexual difference between "boy" and "girl" form the basis for heterosexual romantic desire.

The sexual binary participates in larger dualistic epistemes within neocolonialism, for instance in strategies of classical nationalism, as June Yip observes of the Taiwanese anti-imperialist *hsiang-t'u* (native, "country-soil") literary movement of the 1960s and 1970s, which "envision[ed] a nation constructed on the dualism of self and other."[38] One imagines that if Qiushui's lesson carried on, he might eventually happen across the polar enunciations that structure the critical cultural-roots-seeking discourses and literary work in Yip's catalog: "Native versus foreign cultures, islanders versus mainlanders, Taiwanese dialect versus Chinese language, experiential versus cognitive knowledge, tradition versus modernity, age versus youth, village versus city, rural agrarianism versus industrial capitalism."[39] The film's proposition of a soft-sweet solution for the reconciliation of difference thus narrates that the One China mythology of sameness subsumes Taiwanese difference and nationalism through erotic substitution and romantic longing. "Versus" transmutes into "and" in heterosexual coupling, reconciling sexual difference by union. Read through the optics of allegory, the film, however, reveals the fractures and failures of the One China mythology, and the unhappy ending forecloses any possibility of Biyun-as-Taiwan's happy reunification with her love, while the coupling of Qiushui and Jingdi ends in sudden death when they perish in an avalanche. Despite the machinations of sweetness, the failed romances betray a much darker, more cynical, and embittered warning against Taiwan's desires for national solidarity, suggesting a stunted lifetime in longing and liminality through the final character iteration of exiled, widowed, and disabled Biyun.

Yet the film can be read not only through allegory, and here stardom helps us taste the recalcitrance embedded in the film's texture. Hsu's embodiment of Taiwaneseness signifies complex ways in which feminine softness and sweetness intersect with ethnic sexuality. With Taiwanese and Atayal Aborigine genealogy, Hsu's physical embodiment of Chineseness with Austronesian features signifies a deviation from the hypervisibility of Han Chinese in mainland publics, embodying instead Taiwan's polyglot multiculturalism and racial hybridity. Signifying a mixed racial and cultural inheritance, Hsu's physical look ruptures the Chinese masquerade-as-Han ethnicity, even as it serves to further attract the gaze of the pan-Asian male through its intimated promise of cross-racial and ethnic sexual encounter. Desires for Hsu-as-Biyun, both by Qiushui and the ostensible Chinese audience, exceed the film frame, and the impulse to assimilate the Taiwanese female body into Chinese partnership translates through (extra)diegetic longing for Hsu.

In addition to Hsu's complications of ethnic and racial homogeneity within Chineseness, Hsu's polysemic stardom signals a shift in the cultural sexualization of female adolescence in Taiwan, as the 1995 release of the actor's photo album, *Angel*, taken when she was nineteen years old, became the first time a teenage girl's images, marketed toward an adult demographic, were sold in regular Taiwanese bookstores. Taken by Chen Wen Ping, the erotic photographs reveal the model and singer (who was then part of the band Girls' Team) in various states of undress on a tropical beach. *Angel* and Hsu's second photography book, *Venus*, published in 1996, have since become rare, collectible items. Influenced by actor Rie Miyazawa's book of nude photographs, *Santa Fe*, published five years earlier, *Venus*'s limited Japanese and Hong Kong runs sold out immediately. The publisher explained, "[Hsu] represented a perfect mixture of teenage innocence and subtle but sophisticated sexual desire."[40] The perceived admixture of teenage innocence paired with sophisticated sexual desire represents contradictory ideologies in Hsu's brand of Taiwanese femininity, which signifies changing discourses surrounding female teenage-hood as well as Taiwan's own "budding" democracy in complex ways.[41] In 1995–96, tense cross-strait relationships leading up to and lasting through the first democratic Taiwanese election of native-born Lee Teng-hui escalated into the Third Taiwan Strait Crisis, during which the PRC engaged in provocative military exercises, including a series of missile tests and naval and air exercises to reinforce China's retaliatory force policy. Lee responded in like manner with missile and naval exercises. Hard power met with hard power, while questions of loyalty and fidelity were brought to the fore, illuminating the romantic undertones of international politics. Triangulating the tense relationship, the United States intervened to convey its dual deterrence diplomacy by deploying two carrier battle groups, bringing US-China relations to the lowest point since the 1960s Cold War era, and which resulted in China's loss of faith in American commitment to previous agreements. Emerging from this tense political love-hate triangle, Hsu's dualistic embodiment of "teenage innocence" and "sophisticated sexual desire" eroticized the native impulse to assert a new identity-in-development as well as its political maturation in soft power form.[42]

Hsu's adolescent sexuality packaged for public consumption signified a rejection of prudish Chinese sexual morality through a sensationalistic self-determination that celebrated the beauty, vitality, and promise of youth. Hsu's mediated foray into adult publics thus captured a deeper, libidinal impulse to celebrate Taiwan's young and youthful democracy in the utopian throes of an imagined independence just within grasp. Meanwhile the popularity of her erotic books also indicates the ways in which the Taiwanese marketplace, influenced by the United States and Japan, would fall in line with neoliberal image economies premised on the sexual commodification of young women.

The publication of *Venus* in the middle of this cross-strait flexing of military, masculine muscle therefore offered a feminized and eroticized desire for autonomy, softening and sublimating such impulses into sexual fantasy about and containment of the young, pliable girl-woman. The film returns us to this bristling moment, a decade after the fact, through the semiotics of Biyun's youthful schoolgirl uniform. A reminder of Hsu's teenage sexual debut, the audience re-*members* Hsu's provocative nude photography books through her historical costume. Doubly fashioned in subservience, through the desiring male gaze and the institutionalized population-marking of docile adolescent subjects through the appearance of conformity, Hsu-as-Biyun embodies the point where masculinist-nationalist desires converge.

At this point, however, let us turn to the vulgar disruptions of the actor's high-fructose performance in *The Knot*. Thirty-year-old Hsu's performance of cuteness as a lovestruck adolescent (giggling, flirting, pleading, crying) demonstrates Ngai's observations on the cute as a minor aesthetic category, as differentiated from the beautiful. Describing this diminutive aesthetic, Ngai emphasizes the perceived powerlessness and "unusual" responsiveness of the cute object.[43] In contrast with the awe-inspiring and moralizing effects of beauty's "untouchability," the cute welcomes touch and hapticity, imagined as desiring "ever more intimate, sensuous relation."[44] Hsu's receptive and infantilized lovelorn performance in *The Knot* seems to render her into an object of cuteness, one that minimizes distance with its beholder. However, it also bears noting that Hsu's nickname in the Chinese media, Xiao Nansheng Shashou (Little Boy Killer), suggests the threatening power of feminine seduction and empowerment, highlighting the potential of feminine embodiment to destabilize masculine strength through its destructive qualities. "Little Boy Killer" reveals the implicit anxiety surrounding soft power's force and the knowledge that, as Nye claims, "seduction is always more effective than coercion."[45] "Little Boy Killer" (a nickname that confuses the diminutive/diminished status of Hsu's male beholder with her own petite physicality) indicates a suspicion of cuteness as that which manipulates, and potentially injures, its beholder by seduction. Cuteness dangerously disarms and renders its observer defenseless against its charms. Although soft, feminine bodies like Hsu's are mobilized to envision Chinese reunification, aggression is always tacitly folded into their erotic appeal, what Ngai refers to as "cute eroticism," which she describes as "this 'sweet' but biting 'trimming' [that] underscores the extent to which the 'delightfulness' offered by cuteness is 'violent.'"[46] Relevantly, the name Little Boy also summons Japanese "superflat" artist Takashi Murakami's art exhibit *Little Boy: The Arts of Japan's Exploding Subculture* (2005), which referenced the code name of the atomic bomb the United States dropped on Hiroshima in 1945. As Christine R. Yano contends, Murakami's exhibit represents "the revenge of the 'little boy' nation of Japan, as it crawls out from under the hegemony of the west and asserts its own 'exploding subculture' soft power."[47] Likewise, Hsu's nickname Little Boy Killer also insinuates revenge by the objectified woman and the dangerous undercurrents of seduction wherein the enamored boy-nation cedes identity and power.

Since cuteness threatens to turn its onlooker into its parrot—for instance, we tend to coo and babble when in the company of a baby or puppy—by watching Hsu-as-Biyun perform vulnerable cuteness (giggling, pouting, stomping), we as the audience are in danger of responding in cute, that is to say, in diminutive and unusually responsive fashion. By watching cute, we risk becoming cute. However, Hsu's performance of cuteness-in-excess also contains bite in its passive aggressivity. In fact, it becomes a sickeningly sweet irritant, a sticky point that jams the film's efforts at formal and ideological continuity. Unlike Hello Kitty, the mute and mouthless animated character who plays a vital part in what Yano terms Japan's "pink globalization" soft power, Hsu's mouth loudly whines, pouts, cries, and wails Biyun's lovestruck desires.[48] Rather than ignoring Hsu's over-the-top performance or dismissing it as a failure of the film, only by recognizing it as fully intentional can we discover the insurgent vulgarity of cuteness.

Cuteness becomes a form of radical superficiality wherein both parties, the cute and the beholder, recognize its performance as artificially sweetened. Hsu-as-Biyun notably reproduces this behavior several times throughout the film, performing her limited autonomy and insistence on waiting as forms of resistance against her filial duties. Biyun's pouting cries and unhappy foot stomping can thus be perceived as a specious lie, an exaggeration that has the consequence of draining seriousness from the text and even provoking laughter. When, for instance, Biyun's mother fires Qiushui at the family dinner table, Hsu's turn of expression, anachronistically evocative of silent film performance, is jarring. Suspicion is aroused because of the anticipatory impatience of her response, and Hsu here is already signaling a (false) teleology. Flirtatiously grinning at Qiushui between popping food into her mouth, head and shoulders swaying with delight, Hsu's over-the-top contentedness prior to her mother's comments signals, in melodramatic fashion, that events will quickly sour (figure 4.1). After Biyun's mother fabricates a lie with which to dismiss Qiushui, the camera cuts to a close-up of Biyun bearing a crestfallen face. As tears gather in her eyes, visualizing in miniature the rain pitter-pattering upon the family home, a puckered Biyun looks into Qiushui's eyes before pleading with her mother, "Why are you being this way?" (figure 4.2) A point-of-view shot from her mother then reveals Biyun in full whine: "Ma, you're being so unfair to him!" (figure 4.3) After Qiushui makes his departing speech of gratitude, Biyun sobbingly apologizes to him, before finally covering her mouth as if trying to contain its confessional spillage, and runs out of the room. In breaking the fourth wall, and appearing to address the audience in the point-of-view shot, Hsu-as-Biyun becomes, in Jean-Louis Comolli's words, "a body too much" that "lapse[s] into the overcoded." Comolli aptly asks, "How can one play with a body too much? With one's own body too much? Why, by making this surplus visible, by disturbing the spectator's look with a bodily supplement."[49] Other characters in the scene inadvertently react to Hsu's overcoded bodily surplus. Biyun's mother restrains her wrist, as her younger brother asks, "What's wrong with my sister?"—a question with covertly humorous poignancy with regard to Hsu's tantrum-throwing performance of cuteness, or *sajiao* (the unleashing of tenderness), discussed in the introduction. The campiness in Hsu's exaggerations of a lovesick (historical) woman in turn chips away at, indeed dissolves, the film's hardened core, demonstrating Susan Sontag's contention that "camp is a solvent of morality…[that] neutralizes moral indignation, sponsors playfulness."[50] Neutralizing the film's moralistic ideology, Hsu's star body and campy melodramatics of excessive cuteness thus threaten to unravel the knotted Taiwan-China feelings and entanglements through a subversive play-acting of gender, love, and romantic sentiment.

If playing along with the One China/tianxia ideology implicitly precludes acting out against it, which would in turn reveal Chineseness itself as mere surface, then it is critical to address acting as an irritated site/sight, as surface abrasions of negotiation with PRC power. As Hsu illustrates, both through her polysemic stardom and excessive performance in *The Knot*, the Taiwanese female body (instrumentalized to convey sweetened assurance of China's promise to smell good in the world) can also become a sweet irritant, like a stultifying jam. Through aggravated cuteness and radical superficiality, the speciousness of Taiwanese complicity takes shape in Hsu's performance, engaging in a campy "mode of seduction—one which employs flamboyant mannerisms susceptible of a double interpretation: gestures full of duplicity, with a witty meaning for cognoscenti and another, more impersonal, for outsiders," as Sontag elaborates.[51] Hsu "acts Chinese" for multiple audiences and readings, enabling a "camp way of looking" through her histrionic performance.[52] That is, while her effusive emotionality can be interpreted by *The Knot*'s mainland director and audiences as acceptably and generically melodramatic, her excessiveness can also be interpreted as insincere by Sinophone viewers. This "witty meaning" thereby untangles Hsu's knotted complicity in a Chinese propaganda film. Indeed, her acting style is more Brechtian than Stanislavskian, which James Naremore clarifies as "deliberately calling attention to the artificiality of performance, foregrounding the staginess of spectacle, and addressing the audience in didactic fashion."[53] The didacticism in Hsu's overperformance therefore folds back onto itself, revealing its interior-ulterior subcutaneous motive.

Similar to the ways in which classical Korean American actor Philip Ahn engaged in what Hye Seung Chung refers to as an "Oriental masquerade," a performative technique in which Ahn used linguistic exaggeration in pidgin roles and spoke Korean in Japanese roles to draw attention to the artificial constructions of Orientalness, Hsu uses overstatement and over-embellishment in her cutesy performance to blunt and mitigate (sweeten and soften) the film's ideological persuasion and overt instrumentalization of feminine compliance.[54] In the case of Hsu, rather than a linguistic dupe, her hyperfeminine performance constitutes a complex swindle that relies on assessments of acting relative to persuasion, authenticity, and indexicality. Embodying the artifice of cuteness, Hsu exploits overwroughtness and sajiao flirtation to overripen the film's sweet-softness and render it unbelievably superficial and inconsumable.

In an off-screen but widely publicized display of tears several years later, Hsu passionately declared that she was "Taiwanese and not Chinese" at the 2010 Tokyo International Film Festival, after Taiwanese delegates were denied access to its red carpet for refusing to register as "Taiwan, China/Chinese Taipei." This public display turned many mainlanders against the actor and resulted in a temporary ban of her films on Chinese streaming websites. Revelatory of the stakes and consequences of acting Taiwanese, Hsu's tears in *The Knot* and at the Tokyo film festival perform the depressive bittersweetness of a leaky, soft body through which feminine vulnerability supplies the wetness of an extranational encounter. Hsu's tears in both cases sweeten and soften Chinese hard-line attitudes toward, and inflexible territorialization of, Taiwan. After all, if one is limited in hard-power options, why not weaponize feminine soft-sweetness as solvent of nationalist desire?

Tender Times

Whereas *The Knot* suffered from overripened aesthetics, allegorical irritation, and campy cuteness, all of which assisted in disabusing audiences of the film's One China politics, another contemporaneous Chinese film featuring a Taiwanese star became one of the most popular romantic comedies ever produced in China. Feng Xiaogang's 2008 film *Fei cheng wu rao* (*If You Are the One*) and its 2012 sequel *If You Are the One 2* also allegorize China-Taiwan relations through the device of the heterosexual love story, but these films are not recognized as a cross-strait metaphor by critics and audiences. Taiwanese reluctance to merge with China is again realized through a depressive female partner, in this case played by Taiwanese actor Shu Qi. While Hsu exteriorizes a Brechtian overperformance that

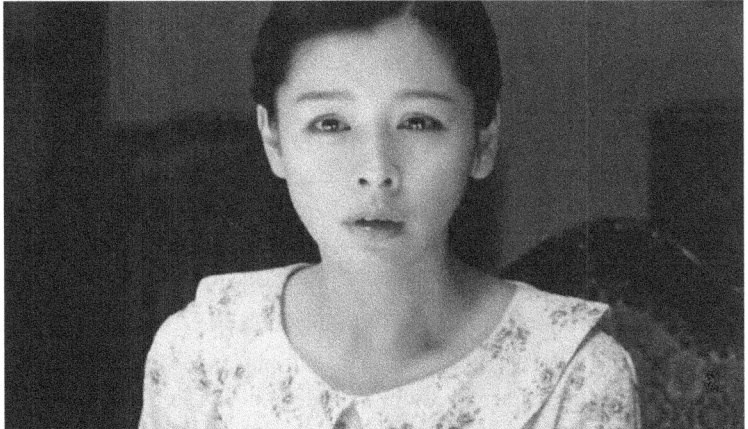

4.1–4.3

Hsu's infantilized cuteness, heightened by her direct address to the camera, enables a campy softening of the film's hardened ideology.

untangles knotted China-Taiwan relations, Shu's performance of hesitation embodies Taiwanese ambivalence toward Chinese partnership.

If You Are the One became the second highest-grossing film at the Chinese box office in 2008, following John Woo's *Chibi* (*Red Cliff: Part 1*), a masculinist imagining and spectacularization of militaristic hard power set in the ancient Han dynasty. Premiering a few months after Beijing's 2008 Summer Olympics, *If You Are the One* reiterated China's global ambitions through soft power. Its gentle creep of sweetness, constructed through space, sound, sentiment, and body, resonated with postsocialist Chinese publics who sought to demonstrate the ways in which, to quote Lisa Rofel, "postsocialist power operates on the site of 'desire.'"[55]

A commercial filmmaker whose works span the generic spectrum from epic melodramas like *Tangshan da dizhen* (*Aftershock*, 2012), propagandistic war films like *Ji jie hao* (*Assembly*, 2007), action films like *Tian xia wu zei* (*A World without Thieves*, 2004), and domestic dramedies like *Shouji* (*Cell Phone*, 2003), Feng is one of the PRC's most popular main-melody filmmakers and is often criticized or ignored by scholars for catering to populist appetites. Although Feng explores contemporary social issues, he often does so with an affectionately bemused tone that avoids direct institutional or political scrutiny, unlike his Sixth Generation contemporaries, independent filmmakers like Jia Zhangke, Wang Xiaoshuai, Lou Ye, and Li Yu who present more scathing and cynical portraits of contemporary China. Furthermore, while Sixth Generation filmmakers fix their gaze on marginalized communities like the migrant "floating population" and factory or service workers, Feng favors upwardly mobile middle-class subjects. Consequently, many of Feng's films themselves become objects of neoliberal pleasure, lined with conspicuous consumption, even as the director is softly and superficially critical of materialism. Feng is thus regarded as a duplicitous filmmaker by many critics because his films often spectacularly indulge in the lifestyles from which his characters morally suffer.[56] *Cell Phone*, for example, blames the adulterous behavior of its protagonist, Yan Shouyi (played by a younger Ge You, who also stars in *If You Are the One*), on the autonomy and secrecy afforded by his mobile phone. Meanwhile Feng, striking a promotional deal with Motorola, used the film to debut the latest MotoA79 cell phone model. Such deeply contradictory gestures exemplify the tensions of China's twenty-first-century "socialism with Chinese characteristics" wherein consumerist seductions and state morality coexist as forms of governmentality intended to produce embodied subjects of "high quality" (*suzhi*), an issue to which we later return.

Like Hsu, Taiwan-born Shu Qi (née Lin Li-hui) also began her career in erotica. Relocating to Hong Kong at the tender age of seventeen, Shu was quickly thereafter contracted to star in several quasi-pornographic Hong Kong Category III films (fare catering to "adults only," ages eighteen and older) like *Sex and Zen II* (Man Kei Chen, 1996). Although hard-core pornography is illegal in Hong Kong, Category III films, including exploitation and genre films, as well as a subset of soft-core pornography, are aptly described by Darrell William Davis and Yeh Yueh-yu as the intertextuality of Hong Kong styles and genres that involve "a promise of transgression: certain kinds of violence, sex, indecent language, blasphemy, brutality, and terror."[57] Shu's subsequent transition out of erotic Category III films through her breakthrough role in New Taiwanese Cinema auteur Hou Hsiao-hsien's *Millennium Mambo* (2001) suggests the possibility of permeable low- and highbrow demarcations within Sinophone cinemas, even as such movements reify the topographical unity of Greater China. As a flexible citizen, Shu negotiates the fluid boundaries of cinematic capital, continuing to act in mainstream Hong Kong and Chinese films, as well as Taiwanese art films directed by Hou (*Three Times*, 2005; *The Assassin*, 2015). With a transnational career that spans diverse genres and modes of filmmaking, local and global markets within the PRC and the Sinophone, Shu embodies the imagined cosmopolitan figure who moves with frictionless ease across geopolitical and cultural borders.

In *If You Are the One*, cross-strait cooperation through co-optation is inscribed in the film's preproduction. Inspired by the 2014 Taiwanese comedy series *Zhenghun qishi* (Mr. Right Wanted) about a woman writer who posts a marriage ad in order to research online dating culture, *If You Are the One* reverses gender roles in its adaptation (while subsuming its Taiwanese origins). Middle-aged entrepreneur Qin Fen (Ge You) decides to settle down after becoming wealthy by selling a patent for a "conflict resolution terminal," a plastic contraption that allows two individuals to conceal their hands while playing a game of rock-paper-scissors—thereby preventing cheating. After placing a newspaper ad for potential marriage candidates, he meets respondent Liang Xiaoxiao (whose personal name means Smiley), a flight attendant played by Shu. In juxtaposition with the easy promises of Fen's "conflict resolution" invention intended to unequivocally settle any dispute, the frictions that repeatedly arise during Fen and Xiaoxiao's courtship are not so easily resolved. Playing a melancholic "goddess"(a title Fen bestows upon Xiaoxiao for her beauty) who is in love with a married man, Shu's soft-sweet performance, delivering her lines in near-whispers, attracts the guilt-ridden Fen, who seeks his own redemption through love after a former lover committed suicide when he was unable to help her escape an abusive husband (figure 4.4).

After Fen and Xiaoxiao strike up a friendship, Xiaoxiao agrees to be Fen's girlfriend on the condition that she is allowed to preserve a space in her heart for her married ex-lover. When Fen asks if he might in turn be allowed to have sexual affairs while keeping only Xiaoxiao in his heart, she resolutely answers that although their hearts may drift, their bodies must remain faithful to one another. Xiaoxiao promises that she will dutifully act the part of a good girlfriend and eventual wife, as long as Fen accepts that she loves another man. Seemingly fulfilling Fen's desire for a woman who is "modern on the outside and traditional on the inside," Xiaoxiao's appearance complies with global trends of feminine hygiene and dress, whereas her traditional interior honors Chinese kinship practices via commitment to physical monogamy and spousal duty. As political discourse, this conversation demonstrates the possibility of a cross-strait negotiation wherein each side reveals its stakes and settles upon a satisfactory quid pro quo. One can easily read Xiaoxiao's desire to maintain autonomy and distance within a marriage of convenience as one possibility of Taiwanese compromise wherein economic interests (the faithful body) can merge with those of China, while Taiwan maintains its distinct democratic, cultural, and social identities (true love). To put it simply, if China accepts that Taiwan will never unequivocally merge as one nation, then Taiwan may agree to a "friends with benefits" situation.

Although he accepts, Fen also feels cheated, stating that he feels as though he has a "wallet full of borrowed money, which after spending it, he's in debt." The two then embark on a trip to Hokkaido, Japan, where Xiaoxiao attempts to reinscribe the place where her ex promised that he would leave his wife and marry her. Unable to move past the memories of her former love, however, Xiaoxiao unsuccessfully attempts suicide by jumping off a cliff into the ocean. Hokkaido is both overripe because it will always provoke an excess of desire in Xiaoxiao and already ruined because the second trip could never outperform Xiaoxiao's former affair. After Xiaoxiao's suicide attempt, Fen, having previously described his own morality grade at 50 percent, finally finds his redemptive opportunity and declares, "No matter what happens, I'll look after her," in an effort to pay back one guilty, historical debt with devotional futurity. *If You Are the One* advocates for a romance of pragmatic codependency, coded in flavorful promises of sweetness. "If you'll marry me, I'll make sure every day of yours will be as sweet as honey," remarks Fen, dressed in a bear costume during an outdoor drill exercise. Despite the film's sweet sentimentality, however, as in *The Knot*, the lead female character is debilitated and in a wheelchair by the end of the film. Unlike Biyun, with her tragic loneliness, however, the still-tender Xiaoxiao has a mainlander caretaker at her side, devoted and ready to fulfill the romantic comedy's heterosexual imperative.

As a texture of desirability, softness appears in the film's romantic discourses. A young widow in Hankou, one of Fen's seven marriage dates, inquires about his health. He responds that he is "a bit weak," and the woman suddenly perks up with a gleam in her eye: "Don't bother exercising. If you get sick, I'll take care of you." When Fen asks why she prefers a "softie," a "soft persimmon" (*ruanshi*), a fruit that outwardly resembles a tomato but tastes sweet, she retorts, "Soft persimmons taste the best!" In contrast with the undesired, overripe mush of certain fruits (bananas, for instance), persimmons, like kiwis, should be eaten when they are a little overripe, that is, when their flesh begins to soften and bloat, and they are most responsive to touch. The widow's prescriptive declaration that the soft persimmon tastes best reflects an intimate, acculturated knowledge of the fruit. Similarly, in his poem "Persimmons," Chinese/American poet Li-Young Lee utilizes the persimmon as an associative object through which to explore his memories and experiences of displacement and migration.[58] Lee describes the persimmon with an instructive tone:

> The sweet one
> will be fragrant. How to eat:
> put the knife away, lay down newspaper.
> Peel the skin tenderly, not to tear the meat.
> Chew the skin, suck it,
> and swallow. Now, eat
> the meat of the fruit,
> so sweet,
> all of it, to the heart.

An erotic encounter with the fruit is imaged through the prefatory gesture of laying down newspaper-like bedding, while the emphasis on "chew," "suck," and "swallow" performs a discursive, staccato foreplay before the speaker imagines "tenderly" peeling off the outer clothing and devouring the fruit's sweet meat. The poem encourages romantic timeliness; one must wait for the sweet ripeness of the persimmon. Further, the speaker's prescription for the proper treatment and practice of eating persimmons is starkly juxtaposed with the actions of his childhood teacher, Mrs. Walker, who brutalizes an unripe and surely astringent persimmon with a knife so that her class could experience eating a "Chinese apple." Not only by eating the persimmon the wrong way and calling it by an incorrect name, Mrs. Walker's cultural ignorance transmutes into material violence enacted against the body of the fruit, which the speaker imbues with animacy: "My mother said every persimmon has a sun / inside, something golden, glowing, / warm as my face." The fruit and the human body share a tender flesh, prompting its reciprocal caring treatment. Moreover, the speaker, punished by Mrs. Walker for not knowing the difference between the English words "persimmon" and "precision," demonstrates that epistemic stakes lie not only in language but also in "taste."

Like Lee's speaker, *If You Are the One*'s young widow envisions her lover's body as a tenderly soft persimmon. However, her attempt to invert the gender binarism of hard/man and soft/woman only indicates her disdain for sexual pleasure; the widow hopes to find a mate who wishes to have sex only once a year. She is not interested in the erotic possibilities of the sweet body, but rather in the rehabilitative potential posed by its sickly, ruined form (Munchausen syndrome by proxy). *If You Are the One*, however, suggests that it is women, not men, who should possess soft and ruined bodies, exemplified by Xiaoxiao's corporeal state in the film's final sequence. As she recovers in a wheelchair from her failed suicide attempt, Xiaoxiao becomes physically dependent upon Fen, who pushes her through the upper deck of a cruise ship heading to an unknown destination. Xiaoxiao's codependency on Fen and their anaclitic love reveals her ultimate submission to his desire, one initially based on Xiaoxiao's physical beauty (mentioned constantly). Only in ripened time does Fen discover Xiaoxiao's "good heart," Lee's persimmon core. Whereas Biyun's immobile condition signals Taiwan's perpetual waiting, Xiaoxiao's incapacitation relates to her acquiescence to Chinese masculine desire, a softening of her position forged through the tenderization of her body via cliff-side dive. Xiaoxiao's body, punished for her romantic reluctance, thus becomes a ruinous, tender bruise, an overripe soft persimmon, an unsutured wound. The architecture of Xiaoxiao's human form requires reassemblage. Contrastingly, when Fen and the audience first meet Xiaoxiao, we find her in an expensive restaurant surrounded by plush, womb-like, red pillows, suggesting passion, fecundity, and hunger. From an image of birth to one of death, Xiaoxiao's trajectory is framed through Fen's eyes, within his own trajectory from potential lover to paternalistic caretaker.

When Xiaoxiao recovers in the intensive care unit after her near-fatal jump, her body is bandaged and in a cast, her face exposed only above her mouth, holding a feeding tube, and evoking "vegetality," a condition that is perceived, in Mel Y. Chen's words, as "more than simply not being able to think, but a failure of lifeliness, of ability to act upon others" (figure 4.5).[59] Xiaoxiao's body achieves peak softness, wherein others may impress upon her, but she cannot "act upon others." Potentially but not actually vegetative, as we soon discover, Xiaoxiao's mouth is wrapped in layers of bandage. As Shu's most remarked-upon physical attribute is her full lips, her tender buttons, this scene acts as an austerity measure, a deprivation of her beauty. Only capable of listening, she becomes unusually responsive as Fen softly assures her, "I know you've been hurt. But with me here, there's nothing you can't overcome." Static, Xiaoxiao avoids eye contact, staring at the ceiling. As a tear descends her cheek, the image of Xiaoxiao's ruination enables a type of gaze that Brian Bergen-Aurand suggests recognizes failure as an ethical alternative to authenticity, as he contends that the "ruined bodies of transnational Chinese cinema" point to the dissolution of origins.[60] Xiaoxiao's failed suicide attempt places her romantic desires in question and exposes her inability to comprehend true love—thereby making Fen's unreciprocated love for her not only life-saving but also edifying. Violently decathecting Xiaoxiao of her melancholic fixation on her past love, the narrative hastens her codependency on Fen through her "failure of lifeliness." As in *The Knot*, the prickly edges of the film's hardened ideological pit wear through its superficial sweetness, revealing its fatalistic admonition against fixations on the past, and/or colonialist and indigenous complications of Chinese identity, which are viewed by the PRC as temporally lagging and uncivilized.

Whereas entrepreneur Fen is aligned with the rational, the fiscal, and the neoliberal—defined here as socioeconomic aspirations that align with nationalist-governmental projects to assign market/numeric value to individuals—Xiaoxiao is associated with the intuitive, the cosmological, and the animal. During Fen and Xiaoxiao's first conversation, she asks if he believes in "love at first sight" (*yijianzhongqing*), to which Fen jokes that he believed it when he met her. Xiaoxiao remarks that it is one's weidao, not appearance, that produces attraction: "It's not about sight. It's the smell. The other person's scent attracts you, enchants you. Some people are just made for one another." When Fen repudiates her claim by describing the absurd scenario of two people sniffing one another up and down upon first meeting, Xiaoxiao counters with a metaphysical account of scent:

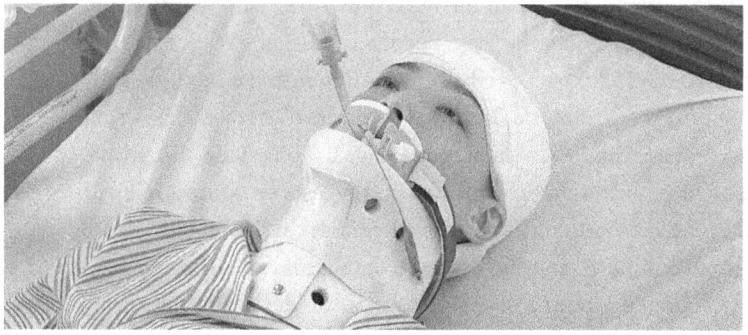

4.4–4.5

Shu's persistent melancholia throughout *If You Are the One* embodies Taiwanese recalcitrance, which eventuates in a ruined, silent compliance.

"If you're made for each other, then you could sense each other from far away." Xiaoxiao's description of an attraction grounded in a felt odor is a subjugated knowledge, one that is immediately disqualified as unscientific, but that nevertheless allows Xiaoxiao to articulate a sense of attraction through the vulgar episteme of smell. Unrelated to the scientific account of pheromones, a subclass of semiochemicals wherein bodily odors play a material role in attraction, Xiaoxiao's account of redolent attraction instead constitutes a type of popular knowledge that Michel Foucault defines as "a differential knowledge incapable of unanimity and which owes its forces only to the *harshness* with which it is opposed by everything surrounding it."[61] Observing an energetic dialecticism between subjugated knowing and hegemonic knowledge, Foucault notes that the friction or "harshness" of opposition is what grants differential knowledge its "force" or intensity, which thereby renders it attractive.[62] In return, "criticism" is spurred by inclinations to modulate, correct, and reject such knowledge. Xiaoxiao's subdermal account of attraction resists ocular, humanistic objectifications of sight, just as she resists the Greco-Roman mythological origins of love at first sight. Nevertheless, Xiaoxiao's differential knowledge of loving through animal instinct is met with the harshness of opposition in Fen's neoliberal metaphor of self. After a date with a stockbroker, Fen begins referring to himself as a declining stock who requires an investor as soon as possible. Asking Xiaoxiao to grade herself (she gives herself a seven for being damaged and emotionally unavailable), Fen grades her nine, solely based upon her beauty. Unsettling Fen's logocentric, self-made entrepreneurial Chinese identity modeled after western capitalist practice, Xiaoxiao's subjugated knowledge about odor or flavor-feeling gestures to a romantic exchange that escapes the visual and transactionary realm. Through the harshness of Fen's disdain for Xiaoxiao's theory of love, such a subjugated knowledge nevertheless gains its attractiveness, thinking with and through the animal to better understand human formation—a line of thought that appears across Darwinian biology, Chinese aesthetic theory, and critical and posthumanist theory.

Xiaoxiao's identification with the animal, rather than being positioned above the animal through a predatory or food-chain schema, on the one hand reproduces the association between femininity and a notion of natural sexuality. On the other, it allows the film to engage in a hierarchical speciesism whereby Xiaoxiao, as the representative Taiwanese (Shu's extradiegetic Taiwaneseness, the film's open secret) is aligned with the animal. Christopher Peterson observes that the "potency of the animal trope lies precisely in its fungibility, its potential as a placeholder for virtually any excluded other," and animality often stands in for minoritarian fungibility.[63] Fungibility also enables Fen and Xiaoxiao's romance. Were it not for a critical flaw in each of Fen's other dates (homosexual; doesn't like sex; early-onset Alzheimer's; must relocate to a remote village; already pregnant), all equally unsuitable, Fen and Xiaoxiao may not couple at all. Instead, they seem bound to one another with feelings caught between antagonistic friendliness and marital affection, an indeterminate state of in-betweenness that frames the China-Taiwan impasse as romance deferred, delayed, and yet inevitable.

Functioning as excess, Shu's Taiwaneseness, in addition to being imagined through the animal, is also narrativized through Xiaoxiao's occupation as a rootless flight attendant, with no mention of other family. The possibility of Xiaoxiao's Taiwaneseness is elided, and the diegetic

Xiaoxiao visually reconfigures Shu's extradiegetic Taiwaneseness into a fantasy of flight and ungrounded movement within utopic connotations of international airspace, complementing the film's reconciliatory fantasy of the couple on a ship cruising along international waters. In fact, Shu's Taiwaneseness becomes displaced and projected onto the body of the previously discussed Vivian Hsu, who appears in a cameo as Fen's sole Taiwanese respondent. Hsu's character is an unmarried, pregnant woman in Hangzhou for family business. During their coffee date, a joke is made at her expense when Fen refers to the "liberation" (*jiefang*) of China. With a wide-eyed, guileless expression, she asks, "What do you mean, 'liberation'?" Xiaoxiao, who is surreptitiously listening at a table nearby, chortles into her teacup, a minor act that betrays Feng's desire for the audience to read Xiaoxiao as mainland Chinese. Here the close-up of Xiaoxiao's mocking superiority is a disavowal, "not me," and Hsu's character is explicitly Taiwanese so that Xiaoxiao's Taiwaneseness can be repudiated. This moment therefore turns into a self-reflexive joke—Feng's witty duplicity emerges here to both install statist ideology and to satirize it. Xiaoxiao's nonverbal derision is polysemic: it can ridicule either Taiwanese political ignorance or the idea that China was ever indeed liberated.

When Hsu's nameless character and Fen discuss a recent earthquake on the mainland, after which many Taiwanese provided donations and relief, Feng begins speaking diplomatically through Fen: "Mainland people were very moved," to which Hsu's English subtitled response reads, "It pained us to see fellow Chinese suffering." Indeed, the term she uses, *tongbao*, refers to siblings or fellow citizens, but is composed of the words "same" and "womb." Whereas the film envisions Fen and Xiaoxiao's first meeting within a red, womb-like mise-en-scène, Hsu's character vocalizes the film's latent gynecological-ideological message: Chinese and Taiwanese share a womb. Although it serves as an ostensibly sweet reconciliation of difference, the discursive gesture to the matrixial relation is here wildly unstable and fickle. A few moments later, Hsu's character reveals that she is presently carrying a child "in her belly [*duzi*]" and that the father abandoned them. Although she has just used the word "womb," here she uses the word "belly," which by contrast sounds cutesy and naïve, and which invariably threatens to undermine her character's veracity and sincerity. Moreover, by revealing the semiotic instabilities of "womb" and "belly," Hsu indicates the arbitrary insincerity of their meanings. In other words, this may just be empty, surface talk. When she glibly proposes that Fen might be a good paternal candidate, he then exhibits his neoliberal values with a joke: "You can't just put a Mercedes Benz ornament on the hood of a BMW.... If it breaks down, Mercedes parts won't fit and BMW won't repair it." Fen's duplicitous turndown, in the same breath, both acknowledges Taiwanese difference through metaphor and reinstates Chinese sameness (BMW and Mercedes are both luxury cars, after all), thereby enabling this exchange to play to both desiring, capitalist sides of the strait.

The persistent structure of duplicity operating throughout the film engenders a collision of competing surfaces and superficial meanings. However, *If You Are the One*'s contradictory dualities (spectacle and moral message; diegesis and extradiegesis; China and Taiwan) are managed and subsumed within the film's presentation of beautiful spaces, and the film's incongruities become unified within its spatial aesthetics. Enlivened representational spaces produce topographies of desire that map onto sociopolitical structures of feeling, generating not only a diffuse longing for physical intimacy and romance, but also for certain types of physical space through an affective engagement, steeped in sentiment and sweetness. As Rofel notes, "If human nature has changed in China, this transformation takes place in the remaking of public spaces and stories through which human nature discovers itself."[64] The remaking of public spaces and stories is a deeply romanticized endeavor, finding its cultural complement in the romance genre, which is spatially aligned with what Henri Lefebvre refers to as the affective centers of "ego, bed, bedroom, dwelling, house."[65] As Jean Laplanche and J. B. Pontalis contend in their psychoanalytic account, fantasy is "not the object of desire, but its setting," insofar as the subject forms "no representation of the desired object" and is only "caught up... in the sequence of images" in which he or she participates.[66] Lauren Berlant similarly notes that "the *scene* of desire and the obstacles to it become eroticized, rather than the love that seems to motor it."[67] For contemporary Chinese audiences, futurism is deeply entangled with fantastic scenes, that is, the settings and locations of capitalist wealth and conspicuous consumption. Fen's superficial fixation on the surface of Xiaoxiao's body is echoed in Feng's preoccupation with the beautiful locations featured throughout the film.

Indeed, the act of loving is not only narratively thematized, it is readily accessible as a modality of fetishized looking through which to gaze upon, and linger in, the details of the film's beautiful indoor and outdoor spaces, illuminated by sunlight. This includes the various high-end cafés and restaurants in which courtship is staged between Fen and his dates, as well as the featured Xixi National Wetland, giving spectators occasion to experience cinephilic moments of becoming lost in "the wind in the trees," to evoke Christian Keathley's phrase.[68] Relatedly, Gilles Deleuze remarks upon Dutch filmmaker Joris Ivens's use of rain as "a set of singularities which presents the rain as it is in itself, pure power or quality which combines without abstraction all possible rains and makes up the corresponding any-space-whatever. It is rain as affect, and nothing is more opposed to an abstract or general idea, although it is not actualised in an individual state of things."[69] Likewise, sunlight itself becomes pure affect and quality, combining "all possible" sunlight in *If You Are the One*'s various locations, indexing actual places and generating touristic any-space-whatevers wherein climate produces pure affect and force.[70] In another sense, the sweet flavor-aesthetic is cinephilia itself as a mode of loving appreciation, remaking and re-presenting the world through an infatuation for background marginalia and sunny affect.

Despite the opportunity for revelatory cinephilia and commodified gazes, significantly, the film's spectacular pleasures are narratively attached to particular socioeconomic positions, and the romance between Fen and Xiaoxiao must also be read within a larger context of China's romance with neoliberalism and the accumulation of wealth. Specifically, the romance of *If You Are the One* centers on penetrative accessibility for the upwardly mobile Chinese heterosexual man to woman and space. Whereas *The Knot*'s superficiality glances off its unbridled displays of desiring, needy emotionality, *If You Are the One*'s surfaces flaunt the aesthetics of wealth and ornament. How do such desires take form within the mise-en-scène's various surfaces?

Anne Anlin Cheng's notes on glamour as "the last residue of aura or as a packaged, shining, and impenetrable mode of beauty" are salient, particularly in identifying shine as the "visual saturation" of Chinese celebrity and as a metaphor for cinematic sight in Anna May Wong's star vehicle *Piccadilly* (E. A. Dupont, 1929). As a particular type of ornamentation, shine lures its beholder by suggesting an "eruption of a body into a presence and a being that exists only in light."[71] In a dance sequence, Wong wears a short dress resembling metallic armor that reflects and refracts light in a frenzy of visibility that draws attention to her objectness as an Asian It Girl who is at once consumable and indigestible. If shine, what Cheng refers to as "glamour's shellacked beauty," brings to the fore tensions between object/subject, modernity/tradition, and sight/feeling that surface when dealing with racial/ethnic cinematic celebritization, then what can we make of *If You Are the One*'s repeated insistence on transparent glass as a surface upon which Chinese modernity is projected and ornamentalized? Noting that sugar glucose can dissolve into transparent liquids, precipitated by stirring and heat, an analysis of the film's use of glass must grapple with what is hidden in transparency, or hiding in plain sight.[72] The materiality of glass congruently and synchronously shapes how we see Shu-as-Xiaoxiao as a beautiful, diaphanous surface, envisaging the potentialities of sweet odorlessness and romance within the China-Taiwan unification.

The Quality of Glass and Body

If *The Knot*'s opening tracking shot visualizes Chinese historical singularity and continuity, *If You Are the One*'s opening credit sequence envisages the lure of Chinese modernity and development, as it tracks a svelte Chinese woman through an expansive, empty restaurant that flaunts an anodyne, modern design. She goes upstairs, where we see Fen standing in the middle of the room. It is similar to the opening tracking shot of Sixth Generation filmmaker Li Yu's independent film, notoriously banned in China, *Pingguo* (*Lost in Beijing*, 2007), released one year prior to *If You Are the One*, which follows an escort through a massage parlor to meet the parlor's owner. However, in contrast with Li's shot, which plunges the viewer into a subalternized sight of young, sexually commodified migrant women, *If You Are the One* utilizes the technique to flaunt a spacious dining room walled in by glass. The camera even pans gratuitously in order to better showcase white table-clothed tables and suede armchairs. Significantly, we note only a handful of patrons, signifying the restaurant's exclusivity, which immediately situates us as wealthy insiders. Abandoning the woman-as-lure on the restaurant's second floor, we see Fen in the final position of the camera. As Fen looks at the camera, we realize it is someone's point of view. Fen's first date is his former coworker, Ai Moli, a gay man infatuated with Fen who longed to see him again. As Moli flirts with Fen, insisting that his long bachelorhood indicates a repressed homosexuality, it becomes evident that the scene is intended to comically undermine Fen's heterosexual quest, beginning with the anonymous woman-as-bait. Yet what this transparently homophobic joke on the audience reveals is the obscured extent to which the film is more interested in producing a desiring gaze at lifestyle as the true object of romantic longing.

Glass architecture plays with a fascination with transparency and the collapse of inside/outside, displaying a vision of borderlessness between public and private spaces. It is another sort of "frenzy of the visible," to borrow Linda Williams's memorable phrasing of pornography.[73] Instead of the powerful intensity of shine that is light itself gleaming, bouncing, and shimmering off surface, glass, as a cool conduit, is able to convey the frenetic visibility of the world out there. Therefore, glass creates the illusion of borderlessness, even as it reinstates material boundary. Glass is a type of glamour that relies on trickery and deception; as a transparent, culturally odorless object, glass poses as neutral, pellucid, unmediating. However, its materiality only fosters apparitions of private/public collapse, actually situating those inside as voyeurs and audiences of the street and sidewalk. It is a position of affluence to be both in the world and separated from it, looking through the mastery and privilege of distance. Furthermore, the film's depopulated mise-en-scène of interiors and exteriors conveys a fantasy of urban China that is simultaneously unrealistic and highly suggestive of post-Mao political and cultural eugenics, specifically in regard to the concept of *suzhi*, a term suggesting an embodied quality or value that is believed to exteriorize transparently through one's appearance and behavior.

The notion of suzhi is vital to understanding *If You Are the One*'s sweet aesthetics and the pleasures it offers, particularly for upwardly aspiring, contemporary mainland audiences. Through capitalist discourse, suzhi is monetized and people are numerically appraised, as Fen demonstrates by taking stock of himself and grading Xiaoxiao. Lacking a concrete definition, suzhi is a product of Chinese developmental modernity, wherein improving the quality rather than quantity of Chinese people became a paramount concern. As a biopolitical concept used to describe and hierarchize an individual's social status, the concept of suzhi arose as a result of the movement from China's planned economy to a market economy, coinciding with the PRC's opening of economic, cultural, and social practices to other worldly influences beginning in the late 1970s.[74] In China's current sociopolitical environments of market privatization and rapidly expanding middle class, suzhi takes into account what Ann Anagnost notes as the "minute social distinctions defining a 'person of quality' in practices of consumption and the incitement of a middle-class desire for social mobility," similar to neoliberalism's abstraction of human value into capitalist discourse and consumerist self-making.[75] Indeed, such accounts of suzhi draw upon scent, as Yan Hairong notes that one Tianjin manager described poor rural migrants as "smelly hicks" (*lao ta'er*), while observing that the phrase "clean hands and feet" (*shoujia ganjing*) refers to a migrant domestic's unlikely propensity to steal from her or his employer.[76] If low suzhi is articulated through smelliness and uncleanliness, high suzhi is odorless and perhaps even sweet. Through visions of unaromatic glassed-in buildings and disinfecting sunshine, *If You Are the One* makes sense of suzhi through its sweetly sanitized spaces.

If You Are the One's emptying of space is intended to make even more room for its exemplar citizens of high suzhi (like Fen and Xiaoxiao), sweetening the deal of neoliberal desires to be both in and above the world occupied by lower-status, lower-quality individuals who remain on the other side of the glass (figure 4.6). In one scene, a real estate agent shows Fen a modernist glass home, with its own private lake access, in Hangzhou. Just as the agent continually refers to it as "your" home to Fen, similarly, the film draws upon real estate tourism to help mainland Chinese and Taiwanese envisage themselves as partakers in lifestyles of conspicuous consumption via illusory fantasy. In regard to wealth fantasies fostered by illusions of transparent mobility, Tansen Sen credits Deng Xiaoping's unofficial 1978 edict, "Let some people get rich first" (*rang yibufenren xian fuqilai*), along with his proclamation that "to get rich is praiseworthy" (*zhifuguangrong*) as the impetus which "sparked the transition from 'da shidai' [grand times] to 'xiao shidai' [small times]," suggesting that whereas a communal sense of progress marked Chinese socialist society, China's postsocialist ethos revolved around individualism and materialism, in which "the quintessential moral failure" is greed.[77]

Glorifying such ideals, the popular mainland film franchise *Xiao shidai* (*Tiny Times*, Guo Jingming), a series with four installments (2013, 2013, 2014, 2015) about four young, wealthy Shanghainese women (five out of the six main actors in the series are Taiwanese), has nevertheless been widely panned. Sen remarks that *Tiny Times* was "perhaps the worst Chinese film [he had] ever seen." Meanwhile, Hong Kong *Variety* reviewer Maggie Lee complains that "ultra-glossy production values will make audiences feel as if they've been trapped in a boutique or furniture showroom for two hours, but the aesthetic decisions are actually riddled with bad taste."[78] Touching on two sensorial qualities, ultra-glossy smoothness and bad taste, Lee's commentary encapsulates not only the big-budget conspicuous consumption film but also the qualities we often assign to the nouveau riche—a term some may use to describe China's twenty-first-century economic boom. Like *Tiny Times*, *If You Are the One* and its sequel are also guilty of being "ultra-glossy" productions that weave together an image of a life well lived by a few Chinese. Although catering to an older demographic than that of *Tiny Times*, *If You Are the One*'s thesis on suzhi equates it to territorializing access to certain bodies and spaces. By reproducing such visual access

4.6

If You Are the One assembles together Shu's body, glass, and decor to romanticize middle-class aspiration itself as the object of (cross-strait) love.

for its spectator, franchise films like *Tiny Times* and *If You Are the One* offer wealth tourism, romanticizing the image of suzhi itself. If the film's surface romance is invested in feminine beauty, its deep romance occurs between the spectator and the concept of suzhi. To wit, the film seduces the spectator to fall in love with the concept of remaking herself, using Fen and Xiaoxiao as suzhi ideals, in order to provoke desire for cosmopolitan mobility, wealth, and entry to exclusive public spaces. Unsurprisingly, the film was not only a Chinese box office hit over the New Year holiday, it is also credited for increased traffic to the film's locations by mainland Chinese vacationers, as it also prompted the creation of the most popular Chinese television dating game show, which bears the same title and features host Meng Fei, Fen's energetic televisual doppelganger.

If You Are the One constitutes a beauty film (a cinematic homology of the cosmetic beauty shot) of Chinese consumption, encouraging both a touristic gaze and a longing for wealth by embedding the sweetness of heterosexual romance within glassed-in restaurants and carefully groomed, depopulated public parks. Moreover, the tall glass windows, allowing in natural sunlight, outdoor greenery, and anonymous passersby, construct a world that appears transparent and seamlessly unified, producing within the consumerist sphere that which is absent in China's opaque political systems. That is, the film's representation of space envisions cooperation through seamless cohabitation and a collapse of indoor/outdoor and public/private. As a flavorless, odorless material, glass gives the fantasy of porosity, even though it can be hermetic and unyielding. Thus, as Hisham Elkadi notes, "glass panes cannot be marked by life. Glass does not soften with age nor can we observe the movement of time through it."[79] If cuteness is about formlessness and an unusual responsiveness (depression) to external pressure and touch, then the beautiful, like glass and like Shu's high-quality goddessness, transmits static sublimity and fantasies of transparency. Whereas the cross-strait political relationship is muddied and opaque, Taiwanese female bodies are indispensable operators within dreams of Chinese upward mobility, which long for cooperation, unity, and clarity, even if only illusorily and temporarily.

Dessert: The Sweet Taste of Autonomy

Female beauty is an everyday need. The pretty girl is the
prototype of erotic confection.
—Béla Balázs, *The Spirit of the Film*

Flavor denotes an affective and physiological orientation of the spectatorial body. While a bitter or pungent film increases the heartbeat, a sweet film washes over you with a soft lull. One is stimulating and the other is calming. When a person is described as sweet, it suggests a compliant position relative to the observer, satisfying a need that is only recognized as such through its evocation of pleasurable affects. Similarly, female beauty serves "an everyday need," according to Béla Balázs, and sweetness is an embodied performance of accommodation and care that is both Other-oriented and coercively seductive.[80] As dominant cultural productions draw upon beauty and romance to resolve conflict through mollifying fantasy, female celebrity is instrumentalized to sweetly embody reconciliatory nationalism and high-valued citizenry. For mainland Chinese audiences, the participation of Taiwanese superstars like Hsu and Shu in cross-strait romantic films envisions the possibility of China-Taiwan unification within imagined histories and modern aspirational settings. As *The Knot* and *If You Are the One* center on the romance of mobility that longs for Taiwanese cooperation, it also attempts to offer an anti-inflammatory fantasy, to draw on sweet's digestive effects, even as it recognizes the fatalistic potentiality and lack of reciprocation of these yearnings. Nevertheless, Hsu's overcoded cuteness and Shu's hesitation embody a beauty recalcitrance that disrupts and dissolves the hardened ideological core of Chinese soft-power films.

Alexander G. Weheliye crucially reminds us that the west's consumption of sugar and subsequent taste for sweetness is a direct result of transatlantic slavery. Caribbean slave plantations turned sugar from a luxury good into a commonplace commodity, enabling the British to develop their appetite for sweetness while it also helped to sweeten bitter colonial goods like tea, coffee, and chocolate, which provided "a caloric booster for the working class [because] it was cheap and filling."[81] After the abolition of slavery, Chinese, Portuguese, and Indian contract laborers came to the Caribbean to continue harvesting sugar. Abating the bitterness of human exploitation, the sugary commodity performs a double sleight of hand, first to allay the violence of slavery and then of indentured servitude, and second to fuel Britain's second-class citizens for increased labor extraction. Attending, however, to the beatitudes of flesh, even in conditions of slavery, internment, and exploitation, Weheliye poses the question, "When the hieroglyphics of the flesh are construed not merely as banishments but as transit visas to universes betwixt and between the jurisdictions of Man, they prompt the following question: how is it possible to politicize the 'natural sweetness' of the flesh without the limit imposed by the concepts of bare life and biopolitics?"[82] If sweetness is at once the smell of success and the taste of liberation, as Weheliye discusses, how might we manage the conflicting frictions between conceptions of success vis-à-vis wealth accumulation and suzhi, and freedom vis-à-vis states of nationhood and self-governance? As Hsu and Shu indicate, although they play female characters depressed by the weight of heteronationalism, they also load the position of sweet-softness with possibilities of subversion and subjugated knowledge, creating lines of flight away from political and capitalist capture.

Sour Laughter
Charlyne Yi and Ali Wong

I have tried to combat social awkwardness by the following:

1. *Drinking alcohol, despite my unusually low tolerance.*
2. *Playing in punk bands; hiding beneath the veneer of messy hair and loud music.*
3. *Not saying anything, to prevent saying something wrong.*
4. *Quickly excusing myself from a conversation in which I have said something wrong.*
5. *Silly dance moves, so others know that I mean to be weird.*

Everyone feels unbearably awkward at some point in their life, suddenly feeling like they don't belong in a particular space among particular people. A gulf suddenly opens; our difference tastes strange. Within this paranoid collision of narcissism and pathos, we momentarily unself and reencounter ourselves, our radical alterity, anew.

People of color sometimes recall this feeling when they are the only minorities in the room, and this becomes a frequent topic of conversation. But what does it mean to feel at home with awkwardness? What if a clumsy sense of unbelonging is one's baseline for social interaction? Some of the more charming among us become comedians, able to transform alienation into jokes and dispense the lemonade squeezed from life's sour pains.

Richard Dyer credits Elizabeth Taylor's star quality to her vinegary voice, writing, "Elizabeth Taylor was indeed a great beauty. All the same, that too is not enough for stardom; it needs to be offset by interest, even cut by something dissonant, the vinegar for the greens. With Elizabeth Taylor it is her voice."[1] In stand-up comedy, as well, the voice is the cutting instrument, acerbic and sparkling. In response, laughter resembles, in form if not function, the shape of a bite; the mouth looks as if preparing to eat. Even though comedy jostles rather than feeds the belly, some jokes and forms of comedy are said to be "biting." If pungent atmo(terrorist)spheres rely on unwitting complicity in breathing in one's own fatality, as discussed in chapter 3, laughter expels and discharges from the interior somatic envelope. Nevertheless, the act of laughing may be incapacitating in another way. As Norbert Elias notes, "Laughter, even though it might be hostile and aggressive, indicates to the beholder that the person who laughs is not in a state ready for physical attack.... Momentarily, laughter paralyzes or inhibits man's faculty to use physical force."[2] Laughter deflates animus. It is the threat of the bite, rather than its manifestation, that characterizes laughter, and both comic and spectator are imbricated in this sublimating exchange. As "laughter is the best medicine," comedy transmutes anger or provides its antidote. More than a defense mechanism, comedy provokes the exchange of shared air in our collective in/exhalation timed by jokes, providing a model of relationality that reveals a threatening promise (or a promising threat) whereby one reveals one's anger but orientates it toward nonviolent expressions and ends.

In traditional Chinese medicine, it is the sour flavor that rebalances the liver, where anger is stored. As opposed to the pungent, which limns the boundaries of tolerance through distinction and separation, comedy creates shared airspace. Drawing upon Elias's notion that invoking laughter is a means by which to disarm, this chapter examines various media forms (online satire, mockumentary, stand-up special) produced by Asian American comedians Charlyne Yi and Ali Wong. Returning to the United States, this book concludes with the flavor aesthetic of sourness and its relationship to minoritarian comedy, satire, and breath. Whereas sweet-softness takes shape through texture and density, the sour forms through rhythm and temporality. Demonstrating how offbeat improvisation and carnivalesque abjection constitute critical forms of vulgar materialism, Yi and Wong destabilize hegemonic ideals of love, work, and maternity.

Offbeat Tart

Among the flavors, discussions about sour often become eclipsed by the drama of bitterness, the seduction of sweet, the utility of salt, and the offense of pungency. Nevertheless, sour can produce the most comedic and exhilarating of facial expressions. Think of the YouTube trend "babies eating a lemon for the first time" (this search is so common that as soon as one begins to type in "babies eating," the rest is automatically populated in the search bar). As we assume that very young infants do not yet know how to lie, deceive, or act (in the sense of an artificial or insincere performance), their faces give away the intense surprise, thrill, pain, and betrayal of their first sour encounter—puckering in mimetic sympathy with the shriveling interior of their oral cavities. When watching such videos, one salivates involuntarily in touching sympathy. Insofar as the sour elicits a leaky body, it beckons a juicy encounter with the Other and world. Its taste is unmistakably impressive in its vibrancy and, like the pungent, it either is or it isn't. That is, as another signified that imparts immediacy, the insistent quality of the sour imputes singularity and distinction with the application of pressure and intensity. Although sour is often grouped with other difficult flavors like bitter and pungent, sour, like bitter, can also become collaborators with the sweet, as in tart.

In westernized versions of Chinese cuisine, sweet and sour become appetizing complements for various meat dressings. Addressing the "culinary ambivalence" Americans hold toward Chinese food, Robert Ku writes that Americans patronize Chinese restaurants to "consume simultaneously the foreign and familiar alongside a serving of sweet and sour."[3] The sour aesthetic, delivering both foreign and familiar connotations through its complementarity with sweet, seems uncertain and irresolute, not in the sense of the salty, whereby it holds on to a secret and performs ambivalence, but rather in the ways it denotes provisional hesitation. Despite its signified quality (sour taste is or it isn't), its contingency resides in preferential caprice. Thus when babies try lemons for the first time, they exhibit a wide range of expressions. Shuddering, eyes watering, faces crumpling, and verging on crying or laughing or both—then, just as abruptly, faces snapping back into neutrality. Part of sour's fun resides in its stunning immediacy and subsequent rapidity of departure. Tartness offers a piquant and enlivening thrill for taste buds, phenomenally—like a small kick to the mouth. However, it can be an acquired taste, and some are unable or unwilling to tolerate it. Sour can even become pungent. These premiere lemon encounters make clear the vicissitudes of affect's liquidity and indeterminacy, as well as the subordination of preferential taste making to the phenomenality of the event. Lagging behind the event itself, preference eventually arises in order to make sense from sensation. Meanwhile, as it is a comedic genre, the laugh track for babies eating lemons for the first time is often provided by the child's off-screen guardians, exhaling relief in having safely delivered their offspring to and from minor, minute trauma.

The deferral of preference, evinced in the babies' vacillating expressions, paired with the strange delightfulness of the experience, forms a breach through which difference can be intensely experienced, a priori to language, judgment, and valuation. In this sense, the sour relates to that which is offbeat and "quirky," defined as "a sharp or sudden movement; a twitch, a jerk; an unexpected change of position or direction."[4] The sour is capricious and unexpected; it goes off rhythm, off clock. Therefore, in contrast with the measured timing and beats of the stand-up routine—many say that comedy is all about timing, after all—there are those minor stars whom audiences find charming precisely because they seem to lack a certain sense of timing, or, to word it differently, they seem to possess a different cosmological sense of time. Relatedly, José Esteban Muñoz writes against the strong and paranoid current of antirelational queer theory and politics, proposing the generative concepts of the "not yet here" and the "not yet conscious" as a means of critically engaging with the aesthetic possibilities of queer utopia and hopefulness as anticipatory surplus.[5] Pace Muñoz, this chapter contends that the comic offbeat, specifying the quirky and unusual located at the margins of the margins, envisages charismatic refusal of neoliberal disciplinary rhythms. Racial sours, in other words, follow another tempo, pace, and beat that is out of step and misaligned with dominant demands of time.

Walter Benjamin, conversing with Karl Marx's concept of alienated labor, remarks on the uniform rhythms of modernity, noting that "in working with machines, workers learn to co-ordinate 'their own movements with the uniformly constant movements of an automaton.'"[6] Coinciding with the rhythms of a conveyor belt, the shocks of the classical cinematic spectacle also therein became measured and formalized. Post-Fordist production also abides by the rhythms of a reception that are rooted, if not in the beat of the factory, then in the tempo and patterns of the nine-to-five workday, which retains its own uniform pulse during diurnal hours. In response, the offbeat can be said to jam, hack, or play with capital reproduction by producing alternate and distracting temporal tracks that threaten to mislead and reroute subjects down different time tracks, pathways, and imaginings, as suggested by the term "quirky." Contesting the uniformity of rhythm, the quirky and offbeat aesthetic generates variable, changing, and disorderly temporalities. At the heart of the quirky resides a resistance to conformity and predictability, even if its form is speculative and not yet fully realized. The quirky offbeat therefore bears out the possibility of a possibility, and the unlearning of the metered, measured pace of production and social life. Moreover, as the disciplining of people of color is rooted in temporal normativity, a punctuality tethered to the institutional power that John Streamas refers to as "White People's Time," nonwhites who do not abide by such time, for instance, those who are late, are often disparagingly said to be on "C.P. time," or "Colored People time" or "CPT."[7] This CPT as a mode of offbeat timing is not an outright refusal of work but instead a way to poke, jab, and punch holes in the governmentality of work time.

Rethinking CPT as a strategic maneuver alongside W. E. B. Du Bois's "double consciousness" and Gary Saul Morson's concept of "sideshadowing," a "middle realm of real possibilities that could have happened even if they did not," Streamas proposes that CPT proffers a glimpse into alternative historical timelines for those whose temporal settings are misaligned with dominant time.[8] In Gregory Pardlo's account, it is the slaver's lash that produces an irregular time signature, forging through violence an otherworldly telos. Pardlo suggests that slaves who arrived in the late eighteenth and early nineteenth centuries "could have brought with them, on one hand, an *eidos* that viewed time as circular and ritualistic, past and present collapsing into one given" cyclic, African time. Instead slaves were forced to "accept the contrary view of time enforced by plantation rule, which is time-as-linear-duration, working from can't-see-in-the-morning until can't-see-at-night, as the saying goes, with only the most random of interruptions, marking time irregularly with the lash, their teleological sights trained on the singularly distant prospect of deliverance in the next world."[9] From this perspective, offbeat time, born from abuse, becomes a means through which to think extrinsically or outside enslaved brutality. Unfettering the enslaved body, offbeat time indulges chimerical investments in alternate realities and futurities. For the Asian American subject, whom the model minority myth depicts as punctual, hardworking, and obedient, the issue of timeliness is also significant. Opening onto the realm of the possible, CPT enables speculation about what could have been, the "not yet here," and in this way coincides with sour's provisional hesitation and sweet ambivalence.

With this in mind, we meet our first quirky comedic actor.

Arrhythmia, Anacrusis, Chaos

Charlyne Yi embodies offbeat, ill-timed, and awkward comic arrhythmia. Yi's comedic routines are not built around jokes and punch lines, but are instead constructed through their quirky persona, behavior, and absurdist observations. On a 2015 guest appearance on the eponymous talk show *Conan* hosted by comedian Conan O'Brien, Yi impersonates George W. Bush, Tracy Morgan, and a turtle, an amusing curation that recalls Michel Foucault's observation that "the mere act of enumeration that heaps [unusual juxtapositions] together has a power of enchantment all its own."[10] Foucault begins his preface to *The Order of Things* by quoting a passage in Jorge Luis Borges's "The Analytical Language of John Wilkins" (1942) in which Borges cites a "certain Chinese encyclopaedia" that categorizes animals by an absurdly random list of things: "A. belonging to the Emperor, B. embalmed, C. tame, D. sucking pigs, E. sirens, F. fabulous, G. stray dogs, H. included in the present classification, I. frenzied, J. innumerable, K. drawn with a very fine camelhair brush, L. *et cetera*, M. having just broken the water pitcher, N. that from a long way off look like flies."[11] This "exotic charm of another system of thought" is attributed to the Chinese and, as noted, evokes Foucault's laughter. The Chinese sour aesthetic is one that is sieved through absurdity, and that nevertheless is, at least partially (with a pinch of salt), believably Chinese. In other words, the western suspension of disbelief toward Chinese systems of thought can inadvertently authorize illicit, unpredictable, and random becomings through the reorder/disorder of things.

To substantiate Yi's bewildering impact, I offer the fact that when my then-partner found out that I was writing about Yi, he sought out the YouTube clip in question but claimed that he had to "stop watching" midway through it, because Yi was "too awkward." When further pressed, he conceded that Yi's impression, particularly of the turtle (for which they requested from O'Brien a plate of lettuce) was "too authentic," striking an uncomfortable uncanniness that bordered on what he admitted seemed "inappropriate," a misalignment of sorts. What is inappropriate is the apparent mismatch between Yi's lengthy and unselfconscious impression, paired unexpectedly with their cute, diminutive Asian Americanness. Perhaps even more unsettling is the way their performance resonates with Achille Mbembe's description of the multiply colonized body: "In this process during which human beings, animals, and plants are caught up in a series of metamorphoses, assume forms sometimes obscure, sometimes clear, hire their parts and their bodies and get them back, often at high price, exchange features, disguise themselves, and make their outlines tremble, the geography of existence vacillates and loses all stability and compartmentalization."[12] Yi's disassembled and reassembled body, through which they reimagine a former white male president, a Black male comedian, and a turtle, taxonomizes Yi's (dis)order of things as speculative posthumanism. Yi's unwavering commitment to the animal impression, down to the thoughtfully slow stretch of their neck, blunted, searching tongue, and screwed-tight shut eyes, illustrates Muñoz's notion that gesture itself, as ontological trace, "signals a refusal of a certain kind of finitude."[13] Rather than being in-finitude, Yi's commitment to quirkiness offers an off-finitude that qualifies the offbeat sour aesthetic as one that breaches the boundaries of the known vis-à-vis the socially legible/visible, offering a figure that dances to the beat of their own drum.

Best known for YouTube comedy and musical shorts; a feature-length mockumentary they wrote and starred in, *Paper Heart* (Nick Jasenovec, 2009); minor roles in Judd Apatow's *Knocked Up* (2007) and *This Is 40* (2012); repeated, rejected auditions for *Saturday Night Live*, which they post about on YouTube; and their recurring role on the television series *House* (Fox, 2011–12), Yi has become the type of minor star the entertainment industry likes to refer to as "singular," known for their distinct individualism, or what one online reviewer refers to as their "skin-curdling strangeness."[14] Yi's alienating quality stems from the fact that their humor does not elicit laughter so much as amusement and awe at the boldness with which they exhibit their strange quirks and idiosyncrasies. Rather than generating a communal relational space forged through laughter as a shared, timed exhalation, Yi's quirky film performances provoke an amused laughter that is gulped and swallowed, a variation on canned laughter whereby the body-as-can contains and suppresses laughter. Where early American television sitcoms beginning with *The Hank McCune Show* (NBC, 1950–53) were edited with canned laughter, or a laugh track, otherwise known as sweetening, the type of repressed chuckling elicited by Yi is more of a souring in response to the comedian's strange, curdling, oddball sensibility.

Rather than laughing out loud, one is more likely to smile, grimace, or giggle in response to Yi's mercurial behavior.

Onstage, Yi elicits scattered, arrhythmic laughter. Combining performance art with musical theater, in May 2010, Yi shaved their head for the nonprofit charity Locks of Love on the Upright Citizens Brigade stage. The task required several men, including their father, Luciano Yi, to use scissors and an electric razor to cut off all of Yi's medium-length hair, except for an off-center Mohawk strip that they wore for the remainder of the show, which consisted of musical numbers with other comedians and performers. Audience members laugh and giggle off-screen throughout the video, as Yi, in lieu of jokes and punch lines, blurts out random, impromptu commentary: "Demi Moore, *G.I. Jane*...help, somebody help me! He sedated me and I can't move my body!...I guess it's just really tough, my hair, kinda like, me." Offering a public spectacle in superficially disavowing their prescribed femininity, Yi reveals that they are the target of their own humor. Revealing their strangeness as a performance of feminine undoing, Yi garners encouraging cheers and support from the audience. Someone in the audience shouts, "You look awesome!"

In contrast with Yoko Ono's *Cut Piece*, related to the aesthetics of hospitality and pungent toleration discussed in chapter 3, Yi's cut displaces erotic risk and transposes it onto minor, harmless self-disfiguration. *Cut Piece* materialized sexual difference through the cutting of Ono's clothing and bra to reveal her breasts, prompting her to cover them with her hands (as we witness in Albert and David Maysles's filming of Ono's 1965 Carnegie Hall performance), pivoting upon the dangerous and damaging axes upon which feminine subjection and vulnerability are socially plotted. Yi's haircut, in contrast, signals an impermanent cut, beckoning a more playful and joyous engagement with gender fluidity and transformation. Yi even sets up the haircut by singing an upbeat version of Sinéad O'Connor's "Nothing Compares 2 U" (1990) with their backup band. O'Connor's memorably sincere music video showcases glamorous, softly filtered close-ups of the Irish singer-songwriter as she pleadingly narrates her breakup grief to her imaginary ex-lover. This video shares with "babies eating lemons" the promise of access to earnest feeling and sensational response, an affective indexicality. Whereas the babies show a range of genuine facial expressions, O'Connor's prodigious blue eyes moisten and tear on time by the song's culminating third chorus. Both videos are fixed upon facial expressivity to convey connotations of the sour (O'Connor's slighted amorous feelings; the babies' veracious encounters with sour taste) as signifers of different types of cut. Contrastingly, Yi's live event (despite being recorded and uploaded to YouTube) is cut neither in the sense of having been edited, nor in the psychoanalytical sense of the cut as a form of inhibiting castration. In fact, it is the exuberance with which Yi rids themself of their hair—their dimpled giggles to reassure the audience of their voluntary desire—that reaffirms Yi's performativity as a subjunctive form of side shadowing and sidestepping.

Giggling, as a type of nonlinguistic musicality, interrupts the speech act. In consideration of its affective quality, as well as the privilege and ease that it connotes, giggling is an antithesis to the scream, which Fred Moten contends is the phonic signature of Black dispossession.[15] In theorizing the resistance of the Black subject as object through a speculative Marxian twist that confers the possibility of the commodity's speech (which is an impossible prospect for Marx), Moten reimagines Frederick Douglass's account of his aunt Hester's screams while being beaten by her white slave owner as a type of "(phono-photo-porno-)graphic disruption" that can be traced in contemporary Black performance and musicality. Relevant to our discussion at hand, Moten's concept of anacrusis bears some similarity to what I have been referring to as the "offbeat":

> Having been called by call and response back to music, let's prepare our descent: let the call of call and response, passionate utterance and response—articulated in the scene Douglass identifies as "the bloodstained gate" through which he entered into subjection and subjectivity; articulated, more precisely, in the phonography of the very screams that open the way into the knowledge of slavery and the knowledge of freedom—operate as a kind of anacrusis (a note or beat or musicked word improvised through the opposition of speech and writing before the definition of rhythm and melody).[16]

As Moten argues, Aunt Hester's scream provided for Douglass the impassioned entry into the call-and-response structures undergirding Black subjectivity and knowledge formation. Anacrusis in music, also known as pickup, consists of an opening note or set of notes that precedes the first downbeat. As an anticipatory form, anacrusis is the aural canal through which the listener briefly passes in order to establish an origin point. It is an offbeat sound or set of sounds that do not count in the numerical scheme of the notes to follow, offering instead a breath-beat in suspended expectation of rhythm, tempo, and beat that will thereafter materialize. For Douglass and Moten, Aunt Hester's scream becomes the improvisational aural initiation, the anacrusis for a Black subjecthood borne of enslavement. Rather than co-opt Moten's argument as a blanket theory for all marginalized subjectivities born from racialized subjugation (as these are uneven, different historical, cultural, and political processes), it nevertheless bears asking how anacrusis as an aesthetic form can emerge through other minoritarian expressions of syncopation and rhythmic disruption. Can laughing or giggling also retain an "animative materiality—the aesthetic, political, sexual, and racial force—of the ensemble of objects" when it acts as irreducible vocality at the scene of comedic racial subjection?[17] What I would like to suggest is that the anticipatory, even hopeful qualia of anacrusis intimately relates to the sour, offbeat qualities of Asian American comedy.

Yi's comedic act rarely gets past its improvisational anacrusis though, leaving the audience in anticipation of measured jokes and punch lines that never arrive. In the first episode of *Bandmates*, a short YouTube series featuring Yi and comedian Fred Armisen (best known for *Saturday Night Live* [NBC, 2002–13] and *Portlandia* [2011–18]), the duo start a rock band. Seated behind a drum kit, Yi shows Armisen a song they have been working on, which consists of thirty preamble seconds of hitting their drumsticks together while interacting with an imagined audience ("Are you ready? I don't believe you. Prove it to me. Say, 'Oh yah,' say, 'Ooohhhhh yahhhh'") followed by fifteen seconds of wild (arrythmic) drumming as they glare at Armisen with a jutting jaw. Evincing the ways in which Yi is more interested in a call and response with the audience, this sketch demonstrates the extent to which Yi's offbeat humor resides in the contingent spaces of the not-yet, wherein improvisation toys with the deferral of resolution and closure. For the racialized subject, this temporal delay is a way in which they buy time, an appropriative gesture, like the cool, that generates an enigmatic secret around racial otherness. However, the sour does so distinctly through a comedic dexterity rooted in temporal disruption and a sense of chaotic play that does not abide by the metered rhythms of rule and law.

Parsing the rhythmic from the metric in Friedrich Nietzsche's *Thus Spoke Zarathustra*, Jan Hein Hoogstad and Birgitte Stougaard Pedersen observe the lines in which Zarathustra remarks upon the deficiencies of a shrunken town: "Ask my foot if it likes their melodies of praise and enticement! Truly, to such a measure and tick-tock beat it likes neither to dance nor to stand still," and "they would like to lure and commend me to a small virtue; they would like to persuade my foot to the tick-tock measure of a small happiness."[18] Hoogstad and Pedersen argue that the invocation of meter here (in German, "meter" also connotes "to conduct" and "to rule") expresses the submissive, domesticating, and governing qualities of virtue-as-meter. Accordingly, Hoogstad and Pedersen argue these "small people" possess meter but no rhythm, therefore, as they contend that whereas "meter is a conservative principle, rhythm is a critical or subversive political force."[19] Relatedly, Nietzsche's provocation in *Thus Spoke Zarathustra* that "one must still have chaos in oneself in order to give birth to a dancing star" suggests that chaos and disorder may be nourished in the force we call rhythm in order to produce the new.[20] Following Hoogstad and Pedersen, we can think of the pluralizing capacity of rhythm, which can harmonize not only through unifying but also through disruptive, even destructive, impulse. It is through these optics that the offbeat racial sour, which refuses the metered disciplinarity of the "tick-tock," can be reckoned as a stimulating novel force to lead us astray into pluralistic modes of being-in-the-world via giggling, improvising, and other performative acts of deferral and sidestepping. Yi's aesthetic is a chaotic dance steeped in childish delight.

Infantile Astringency

Yi was born and raised in Los Angeles by their Philippine/American mother and mixed-race father (purportedly Chinese, Mexican, Korean, Irish, German, French, and Native American). Yi's petite stature, dimpled, childlike expressions, and unselfconscious bursts of giggling have elicited descriptions of the minor star as "cute" and "adorable." Prior to Yi's nonbinary identification in 2021, they were associated with the child-woman archetype, forever suspended between adolescence and adulthood, which was also attached to Icelandic singer-actor Björk. The music video for Björk's rendition of "It's Oh So Quiet" (Spike Jonze, 1995), based on Betty Hutton's 1951 song and inspired by Jacques Demy's musical *Les Parapluies de Cherbourg* (*The Umbrellas of Cherbourg*, 1964), exemplifies the spirit and effervescence of childlike wonder. But she wasn't always so wholly cute. Karina Eileraas, quoting Joy Press and Simon Reynolds, describes Björk's vocalizations in her first punk-noise band the Sugarcubes as an "orgasmic, 'monstrous starburst gush of agony/ecstasy, a mix of...birth-pang, hiccup and mystic wonder that seems to explode in the listener's head.'"[21] Making sense of 1990s girl bands' performances of "ugliness as a resistant strategy," Eileraas contends that the scream, howl, wail, hiss, and shriek in vocal performances are disruptive subversions of phallogocentric language, and that "girl bands' strategic use of ugly voices seems to 'break up the "truth" with laughter' and to remind us that language is always pregnant with impurity."[22] Danish director Lars von Trier also instrumentalizes Björk's monstrous childishness in his cruel melodrama *Dancer in the Dark* (2000), in which Czech immigrant Selma (played by Björk) guilelessly attempts to escape her degenerating vision loss and impoverished blue-collar existence in rural America by restaging her life tragedies as musical numbers, to which the viewers are privy as diegetic material. Selma's foreigner status as an eastern European immigrant makes her a particularly naïve dupe for her neighbors and friends, and von Trier reveals the cruelty with which the American dream, vis-à-vis its hyperactively optimistic musicals, seduces foreign spectators into its machinic, capitalist folds. However, as she unlearns the automatic coordination Benjamin observed of workers' alignment with factory rhythms, she also submits to her offbeat yet dangerous fascination with Hollywood musicals (which abide by their own disciplinary rhythms of the preternaturally flexible body), resulting in Selma invariably losing her job along with her sight and ultimately her life. As with the "It's Oh So Quiet" music video, background characters become complicit collaborators in Björk's quirky beat and rhythm making, as her daydreams canvas over the stark and severe industrial American machinery.

In danger of presenting as naive or insincere, the minor acts of astonishment performed by such "child-women" as Björk model a type of social refusal that is nevertheless steeped in a sense of joy, utopic buoyancy, and vinegary effervescence. If Andy Warhol's propensity for speech acts such as "wow" and "gee" are manifestations of his utopic queer feelings, as Muñoz observes, Yi's ebullient bursts of giggling similarly exteriorize an ever-replenishing wondrous incredulity about the world.[23] Providing their own laugh track, Yi displays a narcissistic enjoyment of self, a libidinal form of self-preservation that Rey Chow argues is denied to ethnic subjects through the social forces that mediate and assail such self-love.[24] Moreover, Yi's weird expressions and impersonations are not about reversals and oppositions, but rather, about toying with those intractable and immovable structures. When one toys with something, it also, in turn, transforms that thing into a toy, draining seriousness and reverence from the object of play. Arbitrary seriality, a sense of gleeful wonder, and an absurdist sensibility mark Yi's comedic offbeat approach, which elicits a laughter steeped in uneasiness, just as Chinese encyclopedias generate a laughter that "shattered...all the familiar landmarks of my thought—*our* thought," and at the very ends of language itself.[25]

Aptly, in *Knocked Up*, Yi's film debut, they play a goofy stoner named Jodie whose speech is riddled with holes, in both logic and delivery. Rousing from a stoned slumber on the couch, Yi leans toward the pregnant Alison (whom the protagonist Ben "knocks up") and asks if she's afraid of vaginal birth and whether she is resentful about having to share her food with her baby. Yi, speaking in what sounds like their most baritone capacity, delivers the lines as if burping through laughter, a carbonated performance of marijuana-induced euphoria. Yi's vocality betrays a gaseous buoyancy of wonder about the world through belching, hiccupping exhalations. As Sara Ahmed notes, wonder enables us to take stock of pain and to ponder how the world took shape the way it has.[26] Therefore, "surprise engenders new forms of movement, and hence new forms of attachments."[27] If the mundane version of Ahmed's observation is expressed by babies eating lemons, whom we see negotiating novel discomforts through/of taste, then a feminist-political application of wonder might be oriented toward the creation of "new forms of movement" through the body's navigation of space and speech in novel ways. It is through this prism of affective possibility whereby we make sense of Yi's sour, quirky aesthetics. The offbeat, however, can also be off-putting, and it is by exploring this aspect of the offbeat, off-finitude that we witness Pierre Bourdieu's thought that "to introduce difference is to produce time."[28] Yi's production of offbeat time, one that does not accord with conventional comedic rhythms and timing, coupled with their perceived childish embodiment, has become, for some, an astringent difference.

Demonstrating the ways in which sour comedy can encourage a tightening, constricting impulse to firm up racialized, biosocial expectations, as astringency does, a *New York Times* article skewers the mockumentary *Paper Heart*, cowritten by and starring Yi:

> Your enjoyment of "Paper Heart" will hinge almost entirely on your receptiveness to Ms. Yi [*sic*] and the *extreme iteration of social awkwardness* she represents. Either naturally or as a manufactured comic persona (there's really no way to tell), she appears to be 23 going on 12. (When she dons a wedding dress, she's like a little girl playing dress-up.) Wearing a permanently baffled expression and a succession of androgynous jeans and hoodies, she shuffles through the movie without acting ability or, it seems, basic survival skills. Lost in the aisles of a supermarket, she [*sic*] and Mr. Cera (who have been romantically linked in real life) are as *helpless as kittens*; you would think neither had seen packaged food

before. Their *extreme lack of sophistication is faintly disturbing*, like a real-life example of one of Al Franken's "lowered expectations" skits from an old "Saturday Night Live."[29]

Troubled by both Yi and actor Michael Cera's social awkwardness, Jeannette Catsoulis claims that she is "disturbed" (sometimes a euphemism for "repulsed" for those wishing to sound authoritative) by what she perceives as the two young comedians' lack of social skills, framed as a life-or-death issue. Criticizing Yi's acting ability (or lack thereof), Catsoulis nevertheless contradicts this critique by admitting that she is unable to distinguish whether Yi's comic persona is natural or manufactured. Distressed by Yi's childishness, describing them as "23 going on 12," Catsoulis voices a white feminine anxiety surrounding the hypersexual infantilization of Asian women. By specifically bringing up that when Yi "dons a wedding dress, she's like a little girl playing dress-up," Catsoulis conjures the Asian child bride as an implied subterfuge through which to flaunt her assumed moral superiority. Despite the fact that Yi dresses down their prescribed femininity with androgynous clothing choices and refusals to groom and use makeup (at one point their lack of bathing is also commented upon in the film by Jake Johnson, who plays the film's diegetic director), Catsoulis feels the need to voice her discomfort over Yi's embodiment, affirming that the imagined crisis over Asian bodies is rooted in gendered and racialized ontologies of age, matter, and size. Yi's inalterable diminutive physicality, their brown skin, their cherubic cheeks—all of which are accentuated by Yi's refusal to mask or alter these attributes—are perceived by Catsoulis as a pathetic figure of enfleshed Asian infantilization. As evinced in this review, Yi cannot be thought of beyond their Asian flesh, in assemblage with their behavior and clothing choices (which signify and bring out their immaturity).

Catsoulis's strongly worded critique might also suggest another connotation of the sour, whereby one disparages something one does not/cannot possess. For Jon Elster, sour grapes is an "adaptation of preferences to what is seen as possible," an attempt to reconcile cognitive dissonance forged in part from religious indoctrination and Calvinist work ethic, and linked closely with Nietzsche's conception of ressentiment, or slave morality that is bitterly reactive and responsive.[30] Following this logic, disparaging what she perceives to be Yi's lack of social grace, immaturity, helplessness, and infantilism, might Catsoulis's snarky writing suggest the sour grapes she feels toward her perceived social inferior? Perhaps racial ontological matter is not lack but rather unattainable *objet petit a*, demonstrated in a sour grapes sentiment shrouded in accismus, which in fact reveals a disingenuous refusal of something one actually desires (youth, cuteness, Asianness). Reactive and resentful, Catsoulis's revulsion at *Paper Heart* is rooted in punitive desires provoked by Yi's childish appearance and behavior. Bearing the weight of this particular burden of infantilized representation, the Asian subject cannot escape this stereotype—thus, as Mbembe reminds us with regard to colonial structures, the better to play with such power in order to draw power out into the visible realm.[31]

Paper Heart revolves around the playful premise that Charlyne, who "plays" themself, "does not believe in love," but nevertheless sets out with director Nick Jasenovec (Jake Johnson) to interview several experts, couples, and kids across the United States about love. Testimonials by real-life couples are dramatized by cartoonish paper puppetry made by Yi and their father, further aestheticizing the film and Yi as credulously childlike. Along the way, Charlyne strikes up a romance with comedian Michael Cera, a white actor best known for starring in *Arrested Development* (Fox, 2003–6; Netflix, 2013–2019) and *Superbad* (Greg Mottola, 2007). The film's central conflict revolves around the tensions between Charlyne's commitment to the documentary and Michael's increasing desires for privacy around their budding relationship. After the two break up, Charlyne maintains that although they are not in love with Michael, they do not wish to lose him, and by the film's end the couple apparently reconcile at Michael's Toronto family home. Although the film earned Yi and cowriter Nick Jasenovec the Waldo Salt Screenwriting Award at the 2009 Sundance Film Festival, it also garnered harsh critique by other reviewers who felt duped and even offended by the possibility that the pair's ostensibly real courtship was manufactured for the sake of the film. Reviewers were angry either because the romance was fictional or because it was real and may have been restaged; the film was therefore doomed to fail. Although Yi insisted that the romance was fictional and written for the film, many were convinced by rumors that the two were dating and had been in a romantic relationship prior to *Paper Heart*'s production. Indeed, tartness is not for everyone, or, in this case, it is the particularly sweet and sour taste of "twee," a word that plays dyslexically on a child's pronunciation of "sweet," which repeatedly crops up in condescending reviews of the film. Like the formation of "twee," the couple's backward romantic teleology marks a disordered crisis. Critical reviews called the film a "crockumentary," a "crock of phony fluff," and "a Pirandellian funhouse mirror," referring to the Sicilian playwright Luigi Pirandello's metanarrative *Six Characters in Search of an Author* (1921) about the self-animation and insistence of an author's unfinished characters on representational animacy. The film, an invaginated Derridean text that collapses outside/inside, is a structure-en-abyme that intentionally blurs assumed boundaries between actor, celebrity, character, and individual, as talking-head interviews with real-life couples are interspersed with Charlyne speaking with fellow actor and comedian friends including Seth Rogen, Martin Starr, and Demetri Martin.[32]

Not only does the film attempt to overturn Charlyne's apparent disbelief in love through its romantic subplot with Michael, it also interrogates Charlyne's lovability in light of their disavowals of true love and apparent disinterest in femininity. The film begins with a scene of Charlyne standing alone in the middle of the Las Vegas strip asking passersby, "Has anyone been in love? Have you ever been in love?...There's not a soul in the world that wants to talk to me." Eventually a few people do speak with them, various individuals who have to stoop down to speak into their microphone, and the sequence concludes with Charlyne laughing heartily at being ignored once again, as the title appears one capitalized letter at a time in mustard yellow. Charlyne is, in fact, repeatedly "talked down to," literally because of their diminutive stature and figuratively by various experts and experiencers of love, including several male chemistry and biology professors who relay the molecular components of love sensations (serotonin and endorphins) and evolutionary-biological rationales for love (reproduction). Reaffirming Charlyne's undeveloped ideas about love, the juvenile sounds of a xylophone play as a chorus of youthful feminine voices eventually joins in on the nondiegetic soundtrack.

Charlyne's own unrecognizable charm even prompts friend and fellow comedian Demetri Martin to remark, "You've never been in love. And [chuckles], this is going to come out probably wrong, but, is it because you're not lovable?" The camera pans left to Charlyne, with whom he shares a restaurant booth, as they defensively retort, "You think I'm not lovable, Demetri?" Backpedaling, Martin suggests it is perhaps their own insecurity that is preventing them from finding true love and, using the language of material assessment, admits that he thinks they are "potentially valuable." Martin vocalizes what many, like Catsoulis and other critics, may be thinking—that is, how can Yi, an offbeat racial sour, be lovable? In other words, how are such qualities visible if they exist outside recognizable codes of the feminine lure? Charlyne's disavowal of love is intimately related to the ethnic subject's unfinished psychic project of narcissism, tied to the perpetuation of collective stereotype, as Chow illuminates in her question:

> Would it not be necessary to locate the loss and wounding of narcissism more specifically at the transindividual level of ethnicity, so as to clarify that what the "Asian American" feels she cannot love is not just any part of her but precisely her "Asian Americanness"—a mark that is not reducible to a single individualized self (because the identity it designates is collective by definition) yet meanwhile is a fluid, historical sign of difference, something that cannot be positivistically pinned down and categorized once and for all (as a statistical reality, for instance) without being turned into the most objectionable kind of cultural stereotype?[33]

That is, Charlyne's lovability and love-ability, which are entwined, speak to a wounded attachment to their Asian Americanness, a bad object (if it exists at all) or a cultural stereotype (if made legible), toward which a narcissistic engagement nevertheless persists. Saliently, Sigmund Freud's observation that "the charm of a child lies to a great extent in his narcissism, his self-sufficiency and inaccessibility" explains both Yi's childish charm and their apparent un-love-ability or inaccessibility to love.[34] And yet how to escape from such a bind? To quote Ru Paul, "If you can't love yourself, how the hell you gonna love anybody else?"

Even the film, which ostensibly seeks to repair this psychic loss, cannot help but reaffirm the Asian subject's value in a transactional manner. The film's sole inclusion of another interracial couple takes place in a Las Vegas chapel in which we see an older white man marrying a much younger Asian woman, apparently a marriage of convenience. Nick and Charlyne are seated toward the back, giggling at first, before earnestly taking in the spectacle. Because this scene shows the only other interracial couple in the film, *Paper Heart* invariably raises a question about the material exchange value of interracial romance. The contestations over *Paper Heart*'s authenticity belie the film's actual offense, to repeat Martin, which interrogates Charlyne's valuation—that the comedian, given their offbeat, awkward quirks and feminine disavowal, dares to become a desirable object of love in the first place (fictional or otherwise). Here we can thus take note that sweet and sour entanglements also apply to interracial seductions. As David R. Roedinger points out, "gook" and "tart" were interchangeable terms for "camp-following prostitutes" and "barrack hacks" during the Philippine-American War (1899–1902).[35]

Analogous to the ways in which offbeat, CPT, or anacrusic time deviates from racist capitalist time, awkward, gawky genderqueer embodiment disrupts the image of neoliberal envisionings of beauty and discipline, which ostensibly grant empowerment to women through illusions of consumer choice, self-creation, and governmentality through bodily and surface manipulation. As Adrienne Evans and Sarah Riley point out, "Given that desire is created but not sated within consumerism, making sense of oneself through a discourse of individualist consumption meant that these women could never be a finished product themselves."[36] Exemplifying the impulse to become oneself via consumption, one of *Paper Heart*'s interviewees recounts that she knew she had fallen for her husband when he drove his vehicle into a courthouse plaza so that she could avoid ruining her expensive Gucci shoes in the rain, reimagining modern chivalry through indemnity of luxury feminine goods.

If seduction is a type of feline grace, as we have seen with Maggie Cheung in her latex Catwoman suit, described by Jean Baudrillard as "all unfolding smoothly, without disruption," gawkiness is its antithesis, the repeated interruptions and staggering cessations of smooth movement.[37] As a mode of perforation, gawkiness pokes holes into grace, draining its seamless illusion of poise and finesse. As a form of offbeat timing, the spasmodic quality of gawkiness deracinates the tempo and temporality of hegemonic time, as prescribed by capitalist productivity and one's infinitude vis-à-vis the never-finished neoliberal project of self-making. Charlyne's sour performativity rejects the biopolitical dictates of consumption, Foucault's "homo economicus," as a self-conditioning mode.[38] When they don the aforementioned wedding dress and veil in Las Vegas, the comedian emerges from the dressing room with a self-conscious grin aimed at the camera, before waddling into a tentative spin, their encumbered toddling walk demystifying and making comic the fictions that women are comfortable in sexy attire and that they happily forgo comfort for the sake of obtaining sexual desirability (of course, in fact, many do). Expressing their failure to abide by the normative processes of gender iterability, Charlyne refuses to take the gown and its lacey materiality—signaling femininity's delicate ornamentality—seriously, and their waddling strut expresses a deliberate rhythmic slip from how one is supposed to walk in a wedding gown (figure 5.1). Failing to adhere to the pressures of neoliberal femininity, Charlyne offers the figure of an unfinished, racialized, gendered subjectivity. Driving home this point, midway through the

5.1
Yi's gawky movements in a wedding dress riddle the smooth fictions of heterosexual union and feminine seduction.

film, they share a nightmare with Nick in which they are on stage immobilized in a pink gown, to which he asks if Charlyne is afraid of being "all girly" since dating Mike. They reply, "I dunno. I've never been one of the girls, ya know?" and expresses that they are "one of the dudes." Reaffirming Charlyne's gender expression, Nick thereafter calls Charlyne "Chuck."

Cera and Yi's tentative romance, rendered through a hoodied slouch toward mutual affection, betrays uncertain feelings. Contrastingly, the film's documentary interviews of predominantly heterosexual couples giving their romantic testimonials envision an upright assuredness in their love, imputing decorum to their sanctimonious coupling. Oklahoma City high school sweethearts Mary Beth and Sid Hardy recount the memorable event of the birth of their son, as they stand in front of the National Cowboy and Western Heritage Museum's sculptural replica of Frederic Remington's 1902 *Off the Range (Coming through the Rye)*, of four exuberant cowboys pointing their guns straight up into the sky on galloping horses, an impassioned if frenzied image of love as conquest. Casting ex-army member Sid Hardy as a modern-day mythological cowboy, the film's choice of documentary subjects offers conventional, white coupledom (with notes of empire) as a romanticized counterweight to the strange and gawky sight of Cera and Yi's fumbling interracial romance. Indeed, the mockumentary sets up Yi as the object of desire who inevitably fails, by dint of contrasting romanticizations of white, heterosexual couples through which masculine pursuit, courtly love, and male subjects (an army reserve member, a Texas courthouse judge, a Hells Angels biker) uphold patriarchal Law. The types of men represented here as models of upright (phallic) love serve only to aggravate the contrasting portrait of Michael as an effeminate, gawky hipster love interest, as well as reaffirming Yi's impossible access to such traditionally love-able men—the cowboys and outlaws.

In the final sequence of *Paper Heart*, a paper puppet show reverses Charlyne and Michael's assumed gender roles in a fantasy inscribed through metered transgression. Remaking an earlier sequence in which a Hells Angels biker takes Charlyne on the back of his motorcycle, Michael rides pillion as Charlyne recklessly drives a motorcycle across the United States, facing down policemen who shoot at the couple for speeding. In violation of velocity as a metered constraint, Charlyne as biker-outlaw defies the statist metric of the law: "I don't care! Life is too short to be wondering 'what if'! Sometimes, you just gotta live, see what happens, even if you get hurt. Sometimes, you can only feel something if you take a risk, and I, Charlyne Yi, am taking a risk." The speech moves the policemen to tears, an affective opening that permits the couple to escape without consequence. Silly, yes. Childish, yes. And yet, offbeat fantasy prompts an engagement with metric-defying chaos that can produce critically subversive rhythms, or what Nietzsche calls a "dancing star."[39] In fact, it is minor star Yi's awkward genderqueerness and the film's suggestion of an interracial (un)love that most effectively sours the film's attempts to sentimentalize white heteronormative romance, even as Cera's brand of white slacker hipsterdom presents itself as a potential means through which to stabilize and normalize Yi's offbeat rhythms under the guise of an alternative neoliberal counterculture. However, if Yi's sour aesthetic, rendered through androgyny and articulated through the quirky and offbeat, twists time and its disciplinary power by perforating the mating rituals of heterosexual reproduction, comedian Ali Wong further refuses temporal supremacies in the domain of capital re/production. Wong's vulgar desires inscribe the Asian American female body as a sensually noncompliant plaything within Mikhail Bakhtin's conception of the carnivalesque in which "Time plays and laughs!"[40]

Radical Raunch

A 2016 *New Yorker* article titled "Ali Wong's Radical Raunch" describes one white woman's exhilarated experience watching Wong's star-making stand-up special: "'Baby Cobra' [Netflix, 2016] is an hour of often extremely filthy material delivered by a tiny, foxy, Vietnamese-Chinese-American wearing a short, tight, black-and-white dress that hugs the balloon of her belly. There is a bracing thrill to watching a woman so manifestly gravid being irreverent and lewd."[41] *Baby Cobra* centers around bodily topics and themes too vulgar for polite dinner conversation, including defecating at work, initiating prostrate stimulation on her male lovers, having anal sex, leaking vaginal discharge and mucus, miscarrying twins over the toilet, and having HPV. Moreover, much of Wong's act revolves around the leaky, porous Asian body and the many objects entering and exiting it. Maintaining the spirit of Wong's fixation with what comes out of her own body, Ariel Levy notes that the comedian experiences nosebleeds when she is excited. Wong's somatic disclosures are antithetical to cool, racial secrets—even her body cannot but secrete her interiority. There is also a thrill in the racial spectacularity of such irreverent, lewd talk. As a petite Asian American woman, Wong's "radical raunch" is a doubled transgression against decorous expectations of women and of model minoritized Asian Americans. Unlike many of the other stars discussed in this book, it is Wong's apparent scrutability, her unsanitized observations of her body and desire, that has garnered her sudden and explosive burst of popularity since 2016. Referring to herself as a "pervert, a gross, filthy animal," Wong unabashedly recounts stories about her abundant sexual activity in her twenties, and explicitly confesses on stage her desires for diverse and unconventional sexual experiences in her thirties. On the one hand, Levy's excitement in watching Wong resides in the vicarious delight of seeing another woman vocalizing "dirty" observations without repercussion, a type of transgression that takes pleasure in displays of feminine unruliness, as noted by Kathleen Rowe.[42] Focusing on Wong's various achievements and material successes, Levy's article explicates sociocultural reasons for Wong's sudden breakthrough, surmising that "Wong can get away with a considerable amount of vulgarity—and hollering—because she is funny, but it also helps that she uses her differences, as she put it, to destabilize her audience's expectations." That is, Wong reveals the false fictions of the Lotus Blossom stereotype that Asian women are quiet, docile, and subservient. Moreover, Wong ironically displays her enceinte seven-months-pregnant belly as she unceremoniously desecrates the unspoken, hallowed idealizations of femininity and motherhood. Neither proud nor precious about her abundant carriage, Wong eagerly throws her weight around the stage, stomping, jogging, dancing, and kicking in ballet-style flats. Drawing upon her differences only to explode many of the deleterious stereotypes surrounding Asian femininity, Wong is shamelessly matter-of-fact about her bountiful sexual appetite. In contrast with Bai Ling's overembodied gifting of inscrutable sex appeal, Wong announces without equivocation her desire to "colonize the colonizer," modeled by a gesture in which she imagines fatally crushing with her thighs the head of a white man who is giving her cunnilingus. Rather than acting ashamed of her numerous and diverse sexual experiences, Wong touts her hypersexuality and even its potentially infectious consequences: "If you don't have HPV yet, you're a fucking loser. That's what it says about you." If on the one hand Wong rejects the deferential stereotype about Asian women, on the other she fully embraces the cliché of the rude Chinese who lacks self-consciousness and volume control in shared public spaces. Evoking both laughter and yelling, Wong's voice has been characterized by journalists as "a loud, staccato honk" and "like a delighted tantrum."[43]

Indeed, Wong's postures, movements, and gestures reveal the antagonism and hostility fueling her comedy. For instance, one of Wong's frequent poses, slightly bending over with one hand gesticulating as she glares at a fixed spot in the audience, adapts an instructive and pedagogical posture—her stance suggesting that if you don't agree with her, then "you're a fucking loser" (figure 5.2). This type of gesture, as distinct from the "act," is what Henri Bergson describes as the expression of a mental state "from no other cause than a kind of inner itching" that aligns the comic with the automaton, giving us a humorous image of "something mechanical encrusted on the living."[44] As corrective response, laughter is an expression of flexibility bestowed upon the rigid or unbending display.[45] In stark contrast with other contemporary Asian American celebrities, like the popular Asian fashion blogger who, as Minh-Ha T. Pham describes, generally constructs "a visual rhetoric of cuteness...suggest[ing] youthfulness, modesty, informality, and guilelessness," Wong's gesture of mechanical injunction suggests that we, as her audience, have much to learn from the comedian.[46] Frequent cutaways to audience members, particularly of white spectators smiling and laughing, assure the white spectator at home that they can be in on the joke, rather than feeling antagonized, insulted, or othered. After Wong's joke about crushing the cunnilingus-giving colonizer ("I could just crush your head at any moment, white man! I could just kill you right now! Crush those brains! Colonize the colonizer!"), the special cuts to a middle-aged, balding white man laughing and clapping, apparently delighted by Wong's cute aggression. What makes Wong's hostility palatable is that her petite physicality appears so nonthreatening that it seems unlikely that she could fulfill her dangling threats. Although Wong overtly bares her bite, conviviality is imputed to Wong's small frame. As the title of her special suggests, through the image of a baby cobra, the rhythm of Wong's comedic presence vacillates between coiling and springing, her various comic observations and complaints vaulting forth in short bursts and proclamations. If the model of the jack-in-the-box toy demonstrates the material form of comedy wherein a spring, as a "moral type," becomes "an idea that is first expressed, then repressed, and then expressed again…the vision of one stubborn force, counteracted by another, equally pertinacious," as Bergson suggests, then the fact that the moral is both rigid and springy indicates the extent to which its formal quality invites a buoyant sense of play or manipulation.[47] Wong's comedy specials seem particularly interested in trifling with two "moral types" through the sour, one premised on gendered conventions of sexuality, marriage, and parenthood, and the other on the notion of work as a moral ideal.

Don't Breathe, Can't Breathe…Just Laugh

Invoking synesthesia in her review, Inkoo Kang characterizes Wong's second stand-up special, *Hard Knock Wife* (Netflix, 2018), by listing the various smelly objects provoked in the olfactory imagination: "a combination of baby head, breast milk, sex fluids and that acrid, vinegary extreme perspiration that either comes from bodily trauma or not sleeping for three days straight."[48] In contrast with Elizabeth Taylor's vinegar-for-the-greens vocality, Kang's evocation of vinegar to describe a type of perspiration under duress (bodily trauma or sleep deprivation) aptly reveals the relationship between stress and comedy. Rather than invoking pungency or rottenness per se—although Wong uses the language of putrefaction in describing her desperation to be married ("I was ready. I was ripe. I was *rotten*")—Wong's comic performance demonstrates sourness as a mode through which tensions between comedy's Janus faces of bitter hostility and sweet resignation are stressed to produce the release of laughter.

Laughter assists and breaks up the respiratory system's natural cycle by compelling exhalation, leaving us, as Elias notes, "refreshed, with the aftertaste of the pleasurable experience still on our tongue," so that we may "return to the business at hand."[49] According to Mladen Dolar, laughter is the most valuable cultural production due in part to the fact that it elicits animality, which is always present in and coterminous with the human, as Dolar observes that "there is again the amalgamation of the highest and the lowest, culture and physiology; the inarticulate quasi-animal sounds coincide with quintessential humanity—and, after all, can culture offer anything better than laughter?"[50] As with beauty, which palpitates the heart and circulates the blood, laughter is also life-saving through its respiratory, oxygenating resuscitations.[51]

Relevantly, the vitality of Wong's comedy comes to the fore when we take a lateral glance at the horror-thriller sleeper hit *Don't Breathe* (Fede Álvarez, 2016), which came out a few months after *Baby Cobra*. The film nightmarishly envisions conservative backlash in a story about three juvenile delinquents who attempt to rob the home of a blind ex–Army Special Forces veteran, who in turn invokes the full capacity of American "stand your ground" legality that permits one to use deadly force against unlawful intruders in twenty-five states. The man, a tight-lipped Clint Eastwood figure, relies on preternatural hearing to hunt down his intruders. Eventually he kills the two delinquent men and attempts to capture and impregnate the woman with a "semen baster" in order to produce a child to replace the one he lost in a car accident. North American critics were, by and large, delighted by the effectively disturbing home invasion flick, happily gratifying their wits with breathing puns; the film leaves the audience "gasping for air," "breathing a sigh of relief," and afterward, "you'll need a breather."[52] Allegorizing the year's volatile debates over immigration and state abortion funding (both of which, from a conservative perspective, envision the home/nation and the womb as sanctified, impermeable enclosures), *Don't Breathe* blurs the boundaries between victim and perpetrator through embodied appeal and visceral intersubjectivity, thus playing to both ideological sides of the rancorous 2016 American political debates. Were one to sympathize with the youths, one might be horrified by the vindictive nature of the blind veteran and his monstrous strength. Meanwhile, others with more conservative sympathies could feel impressed and awed by the man's relentlessly muscular embodiment, and defend the stoic man's violent retaliation. Regardless of political affiliation, *Don't Breathe* envisaged a nightmare that allegorized white fears about invasive, nonwhite Others.

This dark fantasy, however, becomes particularly poignant in light of the 2014 murder of Black American Eric Garner by New York City police officers, infamously captured on cell phone video as Garner is audibly heard protesting "I can't breathe" eleven times during the fifteen to nineteen seconds during which he was choked to death by four officers.[53] Garner's final words become a spectral trace in the 2016 film's titular invocation of breath, shifting the blame for police brutality onto the victim's own responsibility—Garner's "I *can't* breathe" deforms into the authoritative injunction *"Don't* breathe." Consistent with the horrors of atmoterrorism, the youths become complicit in their own brutal murders when the blind man hears their involuntary breaths, their exhalations. Either way they cannot but die. Whereas *Don't Breathe* performed a histrionic, even if ambivalent, indication of the American Right's triggering reactions around the perceived trespass and violation of borders and boundaries by outsiders, Wong's comedic invitation to laugh and loudly exhale offers a counteract, one that imagines a shared communality of air and space. Both 2016 texts (*Don't Breathe* and *Baby Cobra*) captured atmospheric tensions that revolved around the vulgar politics that took the public stage throughout the year's campaigning, televisual news and entertainment, social media exchanges, and online discourses. Moreover, the affective landscapes of American imperialism and the reentrenchment of nationalist sentiment beckoned new types of engagement with racial comedy with a sour bite.

Vulgar Materialisms

The sonic quality of laughter, mirroring the puncturing blows of anger in aural form, constitutes a particular type of orality and voice. Unlike Jiazhi's piquant song in *Lust, Caution*, which penetrates her enemy-lover's psyche, the buoyancy of laughter generates its own vibrational disturbance, an interior rumble that jostles the gut. In addition to circulating blood to our heads, laughter alters the body's contours and borderlines, stretching its elastic skin. Laughter assists in the body's reach toward the Other by constituting touch via breath, whereby the atmospherics of breath surround others. Clearing the head, as Elias notes, laughter also engages the lower bodily stratum. Similarly, Rachel Lee observes that belly laughs create a reverse peristalsis similar to vomiting, thereby staging a kind of corporeal choreography that "jiggles in all sorts of directions, which may be a queer refusal of normative argumentation as political critique, but is critical nonetheless."[54] Like Wong, Korean American comedian Margaret Cho is also loud, her vociferous bursts resembling, as Lee points out, "the basic biological action of peristalsis (shitting, vomiting, swallowing, passing gas)."⁵⁵ Neither oral nor anal, Cho's subversive comedy emanates from the "pussy," as seen in her comedy special *Revolution* (2003), which circles around various punch lines involving the vagina's multifarious capacities (to explode, eat, play, write, change oil, crack corn). Such "pussy ballistics," to quote Lee, "incite rhythmic waves of (commercial) terrorism that first register below the belt as belly-shaking laughter, the felt actions of the viscera intrude into cognitive registers where apparent rationality does not rule as much as (imperialist) disavowal and contradiction."⁵⁶ Therefore, locating Cho's activism throughout her comedic routine, Lee situates Cho's politics between the Thai sex worker who shoots Ping-Pong balls from her pussy and a Third World feminist alliance that critiques US market and military capitalisms. Meanwhile Cho's admission that she has no "maternal instincts whatsoever" and that she "ovulate[s] sand" aligns Cho with the queer rejection of heteronormative futurity, as articulated in Lee Edelman's refusal to envision futurity through protections and projections of the child.⁵⁷ While Wong is working in Cho's genealogical-gynecological comedic tradition, there are remarkable differences between the two Asian American comedians that suggest vital changes in Asian American representation. In one of Cho's most memorable bits, she recalls that the producers of her show *All-American Girl* (ABC, 1994–95), the first Asian American television sitcom, told her that she was neither skinny enough nor "Asian enough" to hold the American public's interest. As a result, the show was canceled after one season. In her 2015 Netflix special *PsyCHO*, Cho revisits this experience and self-deprecatingly remarks in the first few opening minutes, "I fucked it up so badly, they had to wait for an entire generation of Asian Americans to be born and grow up to be Nielsen voting age." Ostensibly faulting herself for her show's demise, rather than revisiting the network executives' short-sighted, superficial demands that she lose weight and appear more Asian, Cho misses an opportunity to challenge the underlying premise of Asian American visibility via the American sitcom format, which simultaneously reifies racial/ethnic stereotypes while modeling a colorblind sensibility that can laugh off such representations because of postracial assumptions that they are no longer authentic, injurious, and/or socially consequential. Nor does Cho take up the issue of work itself as problematic. Whereas Cho laments the ways in which she was excluded from work, Wong laments that she has to work at all.

Wong was born and raised in the San Francisco Bay Area along with three siblings by her Chinese American anesthesiologist father and Vietnamese American mother. Majoring in Asian American studies at UCLA as an undergraduate, Wong flirted with the idea of becoming a professor, but changed her mind when one of her colleagues asked her, "Do you want to study, or do you want to *be* studied?"[58] Wong decided to pursue the latter "because it sounded more glamorous," and then in her early twenties moved to New York City, where she began performing stand-up comedy. While regularly guest starring on television shows including *Are You There, Chelsea?* (NBC, 2012), *Black Box* (ABC, 2014), and *Inside Amy Schumer* (Comedy Central, 2013–16), Wong also began writing for the Asian American family comedy *Fresh Off the Boat* (ABC, 2015–20), based upon celebrity chef Eddie Huang's eponymously titled memoir. *Baby Cobra* debuted on Netflix on May 6, 2016, shortly after Donald J. Trump became the presumptive Republican nominee for the American presidency, and Wong's escalation in the public eye coincided with an electional year during which racist, misogynist, and xenophobic sentiments flowed directly and unapologetically from the eventual president. What had formerly been too ob/scene, that which is typically relegated off-screen, to borrow Linda Williams's pornographic term, had become on/scene and at the forefront of political conversations.[59] It was the first time political on/scenities involved a presidential candidate who bragged that he grabs women "by the pussy," undoubtedly imagined as a passive object in contrast to Cho's indomitable "pussy ballistics." During a time of political foment and ferment, Wong's accounts of pain, felt in and through bodily evacuations, vocalized a soured discontent that became attached to the collective discomfort of progressive audiences who found themselves in shock over America's reemergent pungent ethno-nationalism that sought to, in the words of Trump's campaign slogan, "make America great again."

Thus 2016 was a year of contestations over the vulgar. As political theater collided with the realm of populist crudity via the unequivocal back-and-forth exchange of insults from one candidate to the other, one political group to the other, cinematic production became particularly interested in masculinized expressions of the crude. In addition to *Don't Breathe*, two other vulgarly masculinist films broke into the year's top-ten box office: *Deadpool* (Tim Miller) and *Suicide Squad* (David Ayer), both of which recast vengeful post 9/11 male superheroes as highly ironic and self-aware narcissists. Meanwhile, niche audiences patronized *Sausage Party*, an animated film that brandished a litany of phallic and sexual innuendos, as its title suggests. Appropriating vulgar masculine codes (potty humor and dick jokes) to demystify the figures of the docile Asian American woman and the cherished mother, Wong's focus on the body's basic needs offers an abject intervention that refuses to sanitize or accommodate the racial body for the sake of majoritarian comfort, against the backdrops of the political mainstreaming of right-wing vulgarity and renewal of American empire. Conveyed through an unruly Asian American femininity, Wong's brand of humor struck a nerve in American audiences because of its synchronous appeal to cynicism and vulgarity, and her special felt doubly transgressive because the comic's antagonistic display also stood in stark contrast with the mainstream political posture espoused by the Democratic Party. Nominee Hillary Clinton plainly distinguished herself from the vulgar when she denounced half of Trump supporters as "a basket of deplorables" at a New York fundraiser, a sentiment reinforced by First Lady Michelle Obama's plea for civility at the Democratic National Convention: "When they go low, we go high." Whereas "going high" ultimately proved to be politically ineffectual, the cultural realm moved in to reclaim the crass and vulgar for its own purposes, fulfilling a desiring impulse to "go low."

Indeed, populist escape valves often mirror that which they claim to elude, providing illusions of determinacy and order. Drawing from Sigmund Freud's observations that the "joke work" betrays repressed aggression, sexual or otherwise, John Limon describes comedy's relationship with, and apparent aggression toward, authority: "The process is to convert Audience to Law for the purpose of winning the Law back as Audience."[60] Nevertheless, "what is stood up in stand-up comedy is abjection," and Limon contends that "American abjectness taken to its extreme is a craving for abstraction," whereby stand-up comedy plays with both surfacing and obfuscating our psychic ambivalences and anxieties.[61] In this conception, stand-up comedy creates a childish/childlike interaction with the authoritarian father, toward whom the comic is both aggressive and aspiring to displace. In Limon's account, Richard Pryor, identifying with the abjection of race, draws upon the repudiated body through an "excremental vision" that unites white and Black audiences. Although white and Black audiences may laugh at Pryor for different reasons (the first to disavow their own complicity in racism, and the latter through identificatory pain), the shared convulsions of laughter merge in oceanic possibilities of the abject. Through the aesthetics of vulgarity, both Pryor and Wong shamelessly reveal the ways in which race/ethnicity itself is deplorably abject, that is, evacuated from the symbolic order as the undesirable, the indecipherable, and the excremental.

Moreover, the turn to comic racial abjection resides in a kind of bitter ressentiment whereby the racial subject must overperform his or her narcissistic self-love in order to rescue it from its social disavowal. As

Chow points out in her reading of ethnic abjection, narcissism becomes a "transindividual issue of attachment and belonging" when marginalized groups like Asian Americans are barred from loving their own Asian Americanness.[62] Thus Chow traces racial abjection in Asian American autobiographical writing as caught between inaccessible narcissism and self-hatred, another internalization of social exclusion. By way of an example, in John Yau's short story "A Little Memento from the Boys" (1995), three mixed-race men deposit their secret/ion (semen) into a white liquid mixture with which they paint the walls of a white woman's renovated apartment. Where Chow reads this secret/ing act as inaccessible narcissism's by-product of racial abjection, a performance of self-loathing and humiliated narcissism, Wong's explicit overattachment to her own waste rescues the abject from pathology and shame, as it revels in the various kinds of discharge emitted from the suspect Asian female body. Wong, for instance, nostalgically remembers her abundant vaginal secretions at age eighteen: "You just took it for granted that you could just reach your hand down your pants at any given moment, you throw up the peace sign afterwards, and there would be that snail-trail in between your fingers. Oh, my God, it was so juicy. You could just blow a bubble wand with it, just... 'I slime you, I slime you. Ghostbusters!'" In contrast with Yau's aggrieved men, who secrete in order to reveal their interior wounded secret as racial abjects, Wong gleefully relishes in her genital fluids. Rather than viewing her vaginal discharge as a vengeful trace of racial self-hatred, she offers it as delightful gift of slime.

To make sense of sour's vulgar materialisms, we can reflect on vinegar production, which involves a two-step conversion of sugar into alcohol, then alcohol into vinegar by acetic acid bacteria. Less sweet than sour, satirical comedy by minoritarian figures is a process of fermentation whereby a doubled conversion can be said to take place. First, the comedian reflects upon his or her own struggle of being-in-the-world as a minority figure. Second, the comedian transforms and transubstantiates such narratives into jokes, with the understanding that such comedy ought to be consumed cynically. Exemplifying Audre Lorde's comment that "anger is loaded with information and energy," Wong remarks on the role of affective channeling in her writing process: "Sometimes when the audience is so shitty... when the circumstances are so shitty, you get that anger and then blurt out things. That's how I write. I only write on stage.... It has to come from like pure emotion. Yah, and you just feel like something streaming out of your mouth and you have no pause between your brain and your mouth.

And it's delivered."[63] For Wong, humor is a defense mechanism, and the joke is the comeback, or the come-around of the clever, witty speech act as anger's recoil. Wong's best work comes from returning an insult in the style of a tennis serve's ballistic force, replete with its server's accompanying effortful grunts. Returning to alchemical processes and disknowledge, discussed in chapter 2, comedy requires the spectator to both believe the speaker and disavow their speech acts. Humor resides in the disjunctures between perception and recollection, and truth and perception. When a comic shares an anecdote with her audience, stand-up sociality impels the spectator to maintain a certain dubious skepticism and ability to "disknow" the entertainer's statements, which is meanwhile encouraging the spectator to embrace what Peter Sloterdijk refers to as an "enlightened false consciousness," defined as "that modernized, unhappy unconsciousness, on which enlightenment has labored both successfully and in vain," which carries a "certain chic bitterness" in its undertone.[64] That is, in the post-1960s wake of political disillusionment, we live and work under the pervasive knowledge of the failures of reason and ideology critique, but nevertheless seek to carve out enjoyment. A return to the body and its sensual pleasures, even while cynically reflecting upon what Andreas Huyssen aptly describes as "a modernity gone *sour* and a postmodernity unable to stand on its own feet without constant groping back to what it ostensibly opposes" is necessary.[65] Therefore, as a social response, laughter acknowledges the partial truth, the saltiness, of the comic's utterances, of which sarcasm is the plainest example of comedic disknowledge, as meaning is formed in opposition to, or in tension with, utterance. Wong's joke about feminism in *Baby Cobra* offers a fecund example:

> I've been reading that book by Sheryl Sandberg, she's the COO of Facebook, and she wrote that book that got women all riled up about our careers. Talking about how we as women should challenge ourselves to sit at the table and rise to the top. And her book is called *Lean In*. Well, I don't wanna lean in, OK? I wanna *lie down*.
>
> I want to lie the fuck down. I think feminism is the worst thing that ever happened to women. Our job used to be no job. We had it so good. We could have done the smart thing, which would have been to continue playing dumb for the next century and be like, "We're dumb women. We don't know how to do anything. So, I guess we better just stay at home all day and eat snacks and watch *Ellen*. 'Cuz we're too stupid to have any real responsibility."

The comedian's superficial critique of feminism is undermined by the fact of her apparent professional success and fame. Furthermore, Wong's final joke in *Baby Cobra* overturns one of her running gags that she trapped her husband, a Harvard Business School graduate, so that she would never have to work again. In the final minutes of the show, Wong reveals that during their home escrow process, she was shocked to learn about her husband's $70,000 debt, which she nevertheless paid off entirely using her hard-earned salary from *Fresh off the Boat*. In her closing joke, Wong remarks, "So, as it turns out, he's the one who trapped me. How did he do it? How did he bamboozle me? Oh! Maybe because he went to Harvard Business School, the epicenter of white-collar crime. He Enron'd my ass." Rather than subscribing to the spiritual ethics of hard work, which, as Max Weber argues underwrites the logic of capitalism, Wong characterizes elite white-collar employment as the obtainment of economic profits by scamming and bamboozling. Following Weber's thesis, if spiritual/religious forms of conduct have been adapted for capitalist doctrine, then signs of God's grace emerge in the unquestioning diligence and endurance of hard work. Wong's dis-grace of work, then, not only performs the captive role Chow observes by suggesting that "to be ethnic is to protest," but does so through discourses of abjection, which reframes the biopolitics of labor struggle in ways that are not easily recuperated by capitalist sanitizations of a disembodied calling.[66] Wong grabs the "dirt" that, as McKenzie Wark describes, "sticks to [laboring peoples] one way or another" and, in turn, smears it onto the Harvard-educated bourgeois body.[67] Moreover, the cynical spectator (dis)knows that Wong is not in fact criticizing feminism. Rather, in following the logic that feminism empowers women through increased employment, then it also follows that women are subjugated to the hegemonic dictates of work as a rigid and oppressive sociopolitical structure. Thus Wong offers the anticapitalist countersuggestion that women should not work at all. In other words, Wong's critique of work is buried within her sarcastic critique of feminism. Even more crucially, Wong's antiwork jokes cynically subvert the stereotype of the Asian American model minoritarian subject who increases his or her socioeconomic status through hard work, labor, and merit.

Wong's repeated returns to the physical body—and particularly its mechanisms of ingestion and evacuation—sabotages the Protestant ethic of work as inherently good, virtuous, or moral. As Kathi Weeks contends, "The problem with work is not just that it monopolizes so much time and energy, but that it also dominates the social and political imaginaries."[68]

Wong's comedic routine demonstrates the very dominance of work in such imaginaries, even while she advocates for women to play dumb and not work. Wong's resentment about work, as a recurring narrative, becomes a testament to the overbearing and dominant status of work in our lives. Weeks, joining other feminist political theorists like Wendy Brown and Linda Zerilli, therefore views work as a political problem of freedom.[69] Leaning in bars Wong from the freedom to lie down. For Wong, work prevents one from fully enjoying one's sensuous/sensual body, of which resting, eating, defecating, and sex constitute its most enjoyable acts.

Unable to rest at work, Wong is also ambivalent about standing up as a comic form. Just as Pryor performs a heart attack on stage as a form of standing-up abjection, as Limon contends, Wong also vibrantly animates the prostrate form during her act, most notably in re-creating onstage sexual and postcoitus positions when she and her husband try to conceive.[70] Descending to the stage on her hands and knees, Wong demonstrates how she "twerk, twerk, twerk[s] the shit out of [her husband]," before lowering herself to a dorsal position and elevating her legs straight into the air, "to make sure all of that Harvard nectar would just drain inside [of her]" (figure 5.3). Most of Wong's physical comedy stems from reproducing intimate acts, her sexual immodesty on display as a carnivalesque body descending to earth in its pursuit of sensual pleasure, as opposed to work. In fact, she makes it a point to seem unimpressed by money. Although the phrase "double-income household" makes Wong "wanna throw up," a few moments later, Wong is already thinking about eating (again), as she says, "Do you know how much shittier food tastes when you know you have to earn it?" Then, a few beats later, "Housewives get to shit in their house." Wong plays with the Marxist presupposition that alienated labor is estranging and unfulfilling. Here, the food one earns by working, the fruits of one's labors so to speak, taste "shitty." Working inverses the relationship between what is consumed and what is eliminated, reversing the oral-fecal route, as Wong's own rapid vacillations between eating and shitting reveal such a confusion.

By pointing out the ways in which work is unnatural and detrimental to the body's organic needs, Wong's comedic act echoes hedonistic Marxist expressions, articulated, for instance, by Paul Lafargue, Karl Marx's disavowed son-in-law, who offered *The Right to Be Lazy*, which touted the "virtue of laziness" as a response to socialist Louis Blanc's 1848 "Right to Work." Lafargue, who wrote, "in capitalist society, work is the cause of mental deterioration and physical deformity," offers a tragic vision of Bergson's "mechanical encrusted on the living" (prior to Bergson) with

5.2–5.3

Wong vacillates between rigid authoritative poses and fluid abject postures.

his description of "machine slaves" and "women and girls in the factory, stunted flowers with pale complexion, colorless blood, poor stomachs and exhausted limbs."[71] Invoking a woman coworker's gastrointestinal failure, Wong jokes about a coworker with a "poor stomach" having diarrhea; the same coworker later criticized Wong for not arriving to work on time. Wong's comeback, as she recounted it to the audience, was, "Don't try to tell me to get my shit together when I heard you not have your shit together," gesturing to the multiple significations of "shit" whereby having one's shit together in the workplace denotes professionalism, punctuality, and responsibility, corresponding to the body's healthy disposal of excreta.[72] Fixated on shit, Wong says the word no fewer than forty times during *Baby Cobra*. Indeed, Wong's value system revolves around the ways in which the mundane body is less of a desiring machine than a surviving machine: one that vomits, eats, shits. Through a psychoanalytic perspective, Wong returns to a pre-Oedipal, precastration period of infantilism, vacillating between need and want.

Aptly, Deborah Vargas's concept of *lo socio* as a queer analytic, derived from *suciedad*, a "Latino vernacular for dirty, nasty, and filthy," upholds the figure of *sucias* who is "boldly commit[ed] to making filthy love and creating new modes of transactions that refuse capital's self-disciplining."[73] Sour, vulgar comedy as another such low theory pathway can also enable us to contemplate new undisciplined futurities, as we evacuate valuation and insult from vulgarity. Although Wong does not identify as queer, the comedian similarly advocates for sexual promiscuity and spending time on, as Vargas says, "pointless doings." Like other comedians, Wong is not only against, she is also confounded by, the concept of work. Writing about Paula Poundstone and her bit where she asks audience members what they "do," Limon observes that "stand-ups at their deepest are in awe of the fact that people do *anything*. Stand-up, in the minds of comedians, is a way of continuing to do nothing."[74] Hence, stand-up comedy, which is not work, offers a labor whose exploitation might be contested and contestable. The commodity of stand-up comedy (the Netflix special, a DVD boxset, for instance) is a material object, but the act itself, reliant on affective labor and performance, is located in individual expression and expressability—a pleasurable "doing nothing."

Thinking about other pleasurable "doing nothings," Wong also obsesses over the quotidian lives of housewives, tampering with their ostensibly modest masquerade by vividly elaborating on their pungent anal pleasures:

> Housewives, they don't gotta muffle their shit, too. They don't gotta worry about the velocity with which their doo doo comes out. They don't gotta try to, you know, squeeze their butt cheeks together to make sure that the doo doo comes out at a slow and steady pace, so that no unpredictable noise suddenly escapes and brings you deep, deep shame. Housewives are free to just blow ass into the toilet and let it echo and reverberate to the ends of their hallways while watching as much Netflix on their iPad as they want. They don't gotta take these boring, repressed shits. They can listen to podcasts. *Planet Money*. They can do whatever they want.

Wong's ostensible resentment of housewives stems from social repressions of basic, even if infantile, pleasures, making her both an especially enlightened Freudian analysand and an underdeveloped adult according to rigid social conventions, for which laughter becomes the corrective. Returning to laughter as a shared air, the laughter elicited by Wong's crude observations resides in Bergson's comment that "it is the faults of others that make us laugh, provided we add that they make us laugh by reason of their *unsociability* rather than of their *immorality*."[75] Wong's unsociable interest in polluting the imaginative sensorium's shared air with the body's putrefied and abject productions of gas and shit pursues a crass aesthetics that reaffirms the body's abjection, allowing it to rise and become hypervisible.[76] Nevertheless, because it is always affirmative and right, laughter forms a kind of common sense, an agreement of sorts. As Sianne Ngai and Lauren Berlant write, "Comedy helps us test or figure out what it means to say 'us.' Always crossing lines, it helps us figure out what lines we desire or can bear."[77] Similarly Limon asserts that "laughter, like pain, is incorrigible: pain is the thing about which I cannot be wrong, and laughter is the thing about which *we* cannot be wrong."[78] Less reluctant than anticipatory, comedic spectatorship generates what Ngai and Berlant refer to as "a socially lubricating mood."[79] In contrast with the pungent aesthetic, which limns the reluctant boundaries of tolerance for the majoritarian collective, as we saw in chapter 3, the comedic sour experience is forged upon the rewards of envisioning "us" through laughter. Although Wong invokes the pungent in her act, the aesthetic-affective experience provoked by her comic act cultivates affability and enjoyment, lubrication rather than separation.

Still, despite its collectivizing effect, the vulgar insult derives from a particular form of carnivalesque hostility that stages verbal, discursive assault—thus the punch line is both directly and indirectly aimed at the audience itself as the hypothetical target of jokes. In so doing, the stand-up routine becomes a kind of individuated appeal to the mass through a testimony sieved through cynicism, doubt, and irony, all methods to circumvent becoming the direct target. Like a painless punch to the gut, the concluding line of a joke is intended to trigger the exhalation of breath vis-à-vis laughter. Comedy, like beauty, is breath*taking*, lifesaving. One's breath commingles breath with others within laughter's material, even if ephemeral, atmospheres, generating a Deleuzian assemblage, an affective "multiplicity which is made up of many heterogeneous terms and which establishes liaisons, relations between them, across ages, sexes and reigns— different natures."[80] Imputing risk, transgression, and atmospheric chaos to the notion of symbiosis through his metaphorical uses of "contagions, epidemics, the wind," Deleuze explains, "the assemblage's only unity is that of a co-functioning: it is a symbiosis, a 'sympathy.' It is never filiations which are important, but alliances, alloys; these are not successions, lines of descent, but contagions, epidemics, the wind."[81] Laughter, a contagious wind kindly punched out of us, creates an assemblage out of disparate bodies in respiratory sympathy. What draws us together, what generates alliances and alloys, is precisely those phenomena that threaten to contaminate and rend. To this end, sour, as an astringent, both possesses a contracting function, creating a puckering mouthfeel, and denotes a caustic, acerbic manner. In other words, even as sour may bring multiplicities into tighter, closer proximities, it is not through filiations or identifications, but rather, sympathies drawn by trenchant, out-of-bounds happenings, none of which can be controlled by any individual, but all of which bring us back to the collective atmospherics of shared air.

Toying Around

Wong says that her preferred destiny is to "turn into a circle with eyelashes. Like Mrs. Pacman." Instead of enacting a politically ambiguous erosion between play and work, a characteristic of what Ngai refers to as the zany, Wong posits play as an alternative to work, turning her flexing, fluctuating body into a toy, a source of diversionary pleasure and amusement.[82] Playing house ("Let's decorate") means Wong can enjoy sensuous pleasures without restraint or judgment, unbounded by the nine-to-five workday. Moreover, Wong's interests in playing house are steeped in the carnivalesque and what Bakhtin refers to as the "lower bodily stratum," referring to the activities and pleasures of the belly, womb, and genitals.[83] If work deprives one of freedom, laughter holds "an indissoluble and essential relation to freedom," as the displays of the grotesque and obscene bodies during carnival upend official hierarchies, turning officials into objects of ridicule.[84]

In contrast with the pungent femme fatale who stands at the fatalistic formations of political identities and tolerances, Wong's sour maternity makes life, not death, the grounds upon which to return to everyday, fundamental material being. Whereas sm/Othering is a pungent form of feminine desire, Wong's vulgar displays of mothering, including what comes before (sex) and after (feeding), enable us to revisit the underlying feminine and maternal metaphors in Bakhtin's carnivalesque conception. Bakhtin, after all, refers first to "the carnival, ritual, and spectacle" as the "maternal womb" for the humorous Rabelaisian literature that would emanate from such inspirations.[85] Moreover, the carnivalesque is itself a return to belly, bowels, and what Bakhtin refers to as "the fruitful womb of earth."[86] The carnival enables body and world to engage in a material exchange through orifices and interpenetration. Therefore, the fecund relationship between freedom and the carnivalesque relates back to the body of the mother, a point Wong makes clear when elaborating upon maternal vulgarities in *Hard Knock Wife*:

> Nobody told me about all the crazy shit that comes out of your pussy after you give birth. You know what happens after the baby comes out? You know what else exits? Her house. Her living room, her pillows…the Bob Marley poster…all the food that went bad in her refrigerator…for months! So then you have to wear this cartoonishly large pad that's like the size of a toddler mattress, and it's only held up by the strength of this mesh fishnet underwear that's exclusively available at the hospital. You can't get that shit on Amazon or anything, so you gotta snatch that shit every day. It's made out of the same material that they package fancy Korean pears in. It's very *dac biet* [special], okay? Number one extra large dac biet hospital underwear. For three months, I was walking around my house with a top knot, giant diaper, nipples bleeding. Like a defeated sumo wrestler.

Entertaining the literal implications of playing house, Wong describes how her body evicted her baby, along with all her wombly furnishings. Relevantly, Bakhtin recounts the Italian commedia dell'arte scene wherein the comic servant Harlequin helps deliver the word "born" from a stuttering man's mouth after ramming his head into his abdomen. Reversing the birth-oral canals and relocating pregnancy in the male body, the scene helps Bakhtin conceptualize the grotesque body, as encapsulated by this movement from the "upper" speech apparatus to the "lower bodily stratum."[87] The stutterer chokes on the word "born," only to have Harlequin deliver another kind of punch line to his gut in order to free it from thought. This *tête-à-intestin* contact not only brings forth the word, but "born" also becomes a kind of exhaled laughter, aligning with Bakhtin's conceptualization of the vulgar carnivalesque as subversive comedy. This fantasy is inscribed in a misrecognition whereby the stuttering man "looks as if he were in the throes and spasms of childbirth." Although he does not produce a child, the grotesque figure (with eyes bulging, mouth agape, and sweaty body), produces himself through the inability or unwillingness to speak, becoming porous and earthly in extending himself through protrusions and perspiration. Whereas the men in Bakhtin's example (the stutterer, Harlequin, and even Bakhtin as the interpreter) each metaphorically conceive of pregnancy and delivery in relation to something else (word, thought, the grotesque), in Wong's carnivalesque reversal, she invokes the image of the sumo wrestler, who through comedic distortion inverts the appearance of mother with that of an overgrown toddler. After describing various physical effects of giving birth that both she and her friends have experienced ("demolished-ass bodies"), Wong makes her politicized assertion that "this is why women need maternity leave. In every other First World country…Canada, France, Germany…women get up to three years off paid maternity leave when they have a new baby. In the US, we get jack shit."

In a 2018 *New Yorker* essay, Rebecca Mead compares Wong's comedic advocacy for mothers with "First Daughter" Ivanka Trump's "insipid" attempts to represent working mothers.[88] Trump's flavorless version of maternity has mothers drawing from their Social Security benefits to fund their own maternity leave, a soft cruelty when compared with her father's overt gestures of hatred toward foreigners and immigrants, but a cruelty nonetheless. Mead for instance points out the ill-timed coincidence of Ivanka's Instagram photo on May 27, 2018, in which she embraces her son Theodore, with the Trump administration's new policies forcibly separating children from their parents at the Mexican border. In contrast, Mead reads Wong's silence about her second pregnancy as a willful omission, "because, in so many ways, the structure of our society, in its scandalous lack of support for new mothers, persists in doing exactly the same." Although Wong is silent about her second pregnancy, Wong's graphic descriptions offer a master narrative about birth that demystifies the spiritual calling that underwrites maternal and domestic labors, which have become part and parcel of capitalist function and reproductive nationalism.

It must also be said then that Wong's comic vulgarity is also rooted in her performative play with power and, in particular, her sexual proprietariness over men's bodies. In *Baby Cobra*, Wong shares her premarital thrill in being able to introduce men to the pleasures of their "magical clit" located in their prostates, turning her finger into a penetrating phallus. In *Hard Knock Wife*, she jokes about her territorial title over her husband:

> I'm very lucky to have gotten to marry my best friend, and our whole dynamic confuses my mother because it's the inverse of what she had

with my father. She was like, "Your father was not my best friend. I cannot believe how comfortable you guys are around each other. Do you fart in front of your husband?"

[Glaring] I fart *in* my husband. 'Cause we are best friends. I hope that he and I always stay together, truly, you know?

Throughout *Hard Knock Wife*, although the very title of the special stipulates Wong's self-definition as (someone's) wife, Wong focuses on imagining the male body as a playground for power play. Wong's most memorable and humorous character performance emerges when she envisions an alternate universe in which teenage girls coerced boys into sex: "But as a teenage girl, you never just casually got your pussy eaten behind the bleachers. [With a nasal, insistent tone] 'Come on, Gary. Come on... come on, Gary. Come on. Just lie down on your back, Gary. Come on, like you're gonna change oil. Come on, Gary!'"

Reimagining the sexual politics of the playground, Wong delights in envisioning nonnormative acts of seduction. Raising the hemline of her skirt and flashing her white-and-black striped underwear to the audience, Wong squats down and flashes her covered genitals, imagining the male body as the object of harassment. Not merely an inversion of oppositions, Wong's embodied performativity surfaces the quality of "conviviality" that Mbembe describes of the intimacy between ruled and ruler, whereby the familiarity and domesticity inscribed within the relationship (here, it is heterosexual rather than colonial-statist) generates what he describes as mutual "zombification," wherein "each has robbed the other of vitality and left both impotent."[89] What Wong calls into question through her unseductive techniques and mockery of power embedded in heterosexual rituals of sexual pressure is the adolescent male entitlement to sexual favor, evoking Mbembe's observation that the *commandement* (referring to both the commander and the command) "had a right to enjoy everything—which is why, of the elements that make up post-colonization, one is always banditry."[90] Thieving the codes of sexual demand, Wong's illicit act draws boundaries around the absurd "confines of this intimacy" between men and women, rendered visual by Wong's striped undergarment (both barred in the psychoanalytic sense of that which is inaccessible to the subject, and in visually evoking prison bars). Power structures are not reinvented, as Mbembe argues, but rather, they must exist precisely so that subjects can play within them. The postcolonial condition is also manifest in American racial contexts, particularly in terms of Albert Memmi's codependent portraits of the colonizer and the colonized. It is the very "bond" that Memmi argues connects the ostensibly opposed subjects that also continually "destroys and re-creates" both partners.[91] Wong pithily acknowledges this destructive colonial entanglement as well when she cautions her Asian American spectators: "I have some useful advice for all my Asian American brothers and sisters. Yeah! Never go paintballing with a Vietnam veteran." The joke rests upon the fact that Wong need not build up to the punch line nor explicate it; its epigrammatic appeal depends on the audience apprehending the United States' violent imperialistic histories, their compulsory hostile entrapments, and their lingering racial aftertastes.

Acid Burns

Yi and Wong sour the charm of the ornamental Asian beauty by humorously over- and underperforming their sexuality. Contrastingly, we can consider the physical charisma of comedian Jim Carrey, whom Vivian Sobchack characterizes as possessing the ability to "*transform space* with his body and voice…and thus constituting the world as infinitely capacious and able to entertain and combine an infinite number of actual and virtual scenarios."[92] Contrary to the exuberant possibilities embedded in Carrey's performances of rubber virtuosity, what Sobchack refers to as "unlimited development," Yi and Wong can be interpreted as developments of another kind, one that becomes through constraints and limitations concerning work, time, and order. Nevertheless, even the sour possesses a kind of beautiful charm that induces a familiar attachment once it becomes assimilated over time. The lack of videos showing babies eating lemons for the second, third, or fortieth time (as opposed to the first time) on YouTube, for instance, suggests that the sour aesthetic does not induce significant interest or enthusiasm for watching the processual mechanics of toleration or acclimation. As novelty loses its charm over time, what takes the place of the stun or stammer is a less intense form of charm. Charisma, embodied force itself, transmutes into a milder appeal, which is pleasant, easygoing, and digestible. Deleuze writes, "In life there is a sort of *awkwardness*, a delicacy of health, a frailty of constitution, a vital stammering which is someone's charm. Charm is the source of life just as style is the source of writing. Life is not your history—those who have no charm have no life, it is as though they are dead. But the charm is not the person. It is what makes people be grasped as so many combinations and so many unique chances from which such a combination has been drawn."[93] In contrast with charisma, charm's awkward delicacy and frailty, its somatic stammering, is about a lessening of affect, a presence that does not insist, but invites. As Yi and Wong become increasingly popular, their once-becoming charismatic intensity may invariably devolve into a type of acceptable, recognizable raciality, which will thereby necessitate novel forms of charismatic becoming as "new forces or new weapons."

conclusion

Aftertaste

Quite a lot of indigestion, not to mention excretion, is the natural result, some of which is the vehicle for new sorts of complex patternings of ones and manys in entangled association.
—Donna J. Haraway, *When Species Meet*

There is a tendency to regard beauty as both/contradictorily potently ruthless and astonishingly passive, an object unable to think or act. *Vulgar Beauty* has argued otherwise, contending that un/feminine beauty is a vivifying force, a potentially disruptive and transformative agent. As such, I invite us to contemplate our own attachments to beauty—wounded, passionate, curious, fraught—a priori and anterior to its commoditization, circulation, and exploitation. Toward this end, bell hooks's remarks are well taken: "One can critique modes of glamour and still appreciate glamour. It's not a binary either or world. That is why we have a feminist politics that works to liberate the female gaze, so we need never choose who is more committed to being beautiful."[1] Although I am not necessarily interested in convincing readers to embrace different types of beauty, that is a welcome and, I hope, inevitable side effect. This project elaborates upon the ways in which we sense beauty, specifically through our mediated encounters with screen beauty, and it is concerned with appreciating beauty as a kind of glamour, not simply as surface or simulacra, but rather, to honor the original Scottish denotation of "glamour" as "a corrupt form of grammar" or deviant structure of enchantment.[2] Such a frame enables us to critically confront our coterminous fondness for, and suspicion of, beauty. Why and how does the phenomenality of beauty matter?

Race, gender, sexuality, and nationality materialize through the vulgar Chinese body. Ontologies of marginalized identity are sensualized at the tender points of sociocultural uncertainty, hesitation, and bewilderment during irregular times and offbeat rhythms. Forged from promiscuous interactions between western philosophy and Chinese epistemologies, I propose a methodology of tasting flavors as a means through which to critically sense, interpret, and describe a film performer's affect. Weidao provides us with a new analytic frame, one that bypasses object-subject ocular binarisms, with which to better comprehend Asian stardom, popular cultures, and cinemas. In this way, we also contest the Euro-American presupposition that beauty is a universal, stable object diagnosed within the visual realm. Flavor affective-aesthetics are felt through liquidity, texture, velocity, breath, and atmosphere. Vulgar charisma's energetic material exudes from the bones, by way of musculature, through the lips, upon the skin, and by virtue of exquisite eyes. Moreover, this book demonstrates how film acting is a system of intelligence that participates in epistemological production through beauty. Minor acts of beauty not only render legible our affective investments in ideology and common sense, they may renew such attachments or even offer glimpses of new possibilities and futurities. Although the book's organization ostensibly aligns flavors with specific historical temporalities and cultural sites, it is the interpenetration of aesthetic flavors that best reveals the body's affective surplus and the generative hermeneutics of reading the body's gestures as form. Rather than advocate for a rigid or deterministic model of flavor as form, *Vulgar Beauty* encourages an attunement to the ways in which the lower senses (taste, smell, touch) produce viscous intimacies with star bodies. As coincidental exchanges between star and beholder lubricate a kind of enworlding together, sites of racialized, gendered subjection also produce cuts and fractures that dehydrate and disjoin us from one another.

Nevertheless, the attempt to understand beauty's polyvalent feeling has returned us to the etymological root of *aesthesis*, the holistic perception of the senses. Beauty is lifesaving because it palpitates the heart and adrenalizes the body. As a stimulant, beauty increases one's alertness to the animations of others and to the environment. Explaining beauty's perceptual effects/affects, Elaine Scarry also holds that encounters with beauty, defined capaciously by its aesthetic symmetry, inspire longings for justice and fairness. Scarry writes, "Beauty seems to place requirements on us for attending to the aliveness or (in the case of objects) quasi-aliveness of our world, and for entering into its protection."[3] Tearing into the world's surface, beauty's creation of a vaster territory relocates its beholder to a space where one unbodies forth, ceding the self's terrestrial center to an/other's image before them. As an absorbent worldly guardian, beauty summons us to attend to and care for peoples, animals, environments, and objects. Because beauty galvanizes individuals to move toward acts of custody, it concerns ethics of the highest order. Critiques of Scarry's proposition do not unsettle or challenge her phenomenological observations of beholding beauty, and our submission to beauty remains a guilty pleasure. Beauty happens, whether or not we agree that it is fair. Nevertheless, I am in agreement with Scarry's critics that we also need to attend to the biosocial, cultural, and political ways in which beauty is recognized, named, and experienced. It is for this reason that it is important to consider beauty as a racialized and gendered technique of seduction. Vulgar beauty in particular is the underthought of sexuality, and I would contend, perhaps polemically, that as social and academic persons, we are oversexed and underseduced. Thus, let us pursue seduction once more.

Seduction is not best understood through sexuality, but rather as a vital and vibrant practice of not only being-in-the-world but also strategically navigating in and through the world (both for the beautiful and the beholder). Beauty, as a mode of passing, carves new grooves and pathways into calcified structures, and it is via beauty's lead and summon that we are permitted to peer into new vistas. Attending to beauty's seductions requires thinking through fetishizations of flesh and surface to investigate beauty's animate and animating ontologies, ultimately to help us better understand how screen bodies beckon, interpellate, and seduce spectators into relationality via fantasy and through the affective structures of desire and love. Star beauty and charisma participate in what Jean-Louis Comolli refers to as the lure of cinema itself, which, taken from the Lacanian principle "I know very well…but all the same," denotes the lack operating at the center of the spectatorial suspension of dis/belief.[4] In this way, beauty and cinema are akin to fantasies of love, which Lauren Berlant describes as "the misrecognition you like, can bear, and will try to keep consenting to."[5] Simply put, it is precisely beauty's deceptive quality that continually restores and replenishes desire itself, as well as the desire for attachment to shared myths, histories, worlds, and identities.

In his controversial work *Seduction*, Jean Baudrillard is fixated on the heterosexual relation, which he describes as a Nietzschean master-slave dynamic, insisting that it is the radical sexual difference performed through ritual and game that generates the lure of seduction. Critical of identitarian political movements that take as their primary motivation the equalizations of sex and power among men and women, Baudrillard claims that the only alternative for thinking outside such limiting constructs is seduction, a force that is disinterested in power and can transcend the masculine/feminine opposition. Thus he argues that "this strength of the feminine is that of seduction."[6] However, Baudrillard only acknowledges feminine seduction in dialectical relation to the masculine, as he imagines "a universe that can no longer be interpreted in terms of structures and diacritical oppositions, but implies a seductive reversibility—a universe where the feminine is not what opposes the masculine, but what seduces the masculine."[7] Women do not gain power by mimicking the actions and gestures of men—they can only reverse it by playing with male desire, offering not the pleasures of the flesh but the overpowering forces of the "glamour of seduction," glimmering with the lure of enchanting secrets and illusions.[8] Baudrillard therefore wishes that women's seduction remain undomesticated, feral, and inscrutable—a term that bears distinctly racialized Chinese and Asian/American signification.

Although Baudrillard's concept explains the ways in which seduction operates through a subject's defiant play with feminine signs, a feminist appropriation of Baudrillard's concept necessitates a cynical suspension of the expectation of gender equality (at least in "the now"), a deep reckoning with the concept of equality itself, and an understanding that the only way out is through the ludic, a state of enchantment generated by a giddy observation of the rule of the game as obligation as opposed to a prohibitive adherence to the linear universality of law. As Baudrillard states, "By choosing the rule one is delivered from the law."[9] On the one hand, this distinction enables us to understand that the nature of feminine beauty's circumvention is neither routed through nor transgressive of the male gaze, which institutes patriarchal Law through the power dynamics of gendered relations and looks. This argument enables us to revisit feminine etiquette vis-à-vis the geisha and courtesan, for instance, as a type of rule-based game of seduction, operating outside of masculinist, statist, patriarchal

Law, even though the acquiescence of male patrons within such cultures seems to overtly contradict this contention. Moreover, it bears noting that Baudrillard does not consider the relationality between women, and his discussion does not consider the ways women seduce other women, erotically or otherwise. Unable to attend to the collective dynamics of the game and the law, this oversight produces a blind spot in Baudrillard's theory of seduction whereby gamers/players are never on the same team, so to speak.[10] Should we expand the ludic principle to an understanding of a game whereby players cooperate rather than compete, where tension is shared and orientated toward the game itself, then the concept of seduction becomes generative for feminist appropriation. And here, we take liberty with and depart from Baudrillard's account of games. In a cooperative game, teams delight in finding and exploiting loopholes in the rules—and one might argue, after all, that breaking a rule is merely another rule that should be followed. To be clear, I am not suggesting that feminists ought to be complacent or abstain from making interventions in law; rather, this approach pursues the radical notion of an underappreciated sovereignty of the feminine that exists in the ludic play with boundary. In other words, is it possible to make the game more seductive than the law? If the game constitutes the domain of feminine seduction, whereby rules are observed through a giddy and passionate complicity with enchantment, in contrast with the pleasure that arises from obedience to law (which we understand through psychoanalysis as the symbolic enactment of castration, which eludes the female subject), then a feminist politics of seduction and beauty should aim to destabilize and rewrite the rules by playing with the energetic and unpredictable volatilities of charisma and passion, rather than reproducing the digestible qualities of charm and pleasure. Is it possible to queer heterosexuality without appropriating queer theory's radical, marginal politics to inadvertently reify and reproduce the domination of heteronormativity? What other post/humanist, material, and animal pathways and theories can we uncover and mobilize in pursuing such a question? What does it mean to wild or undomesticate feminine seduction? These questions remain provocatively unanswered, because beauty's existence in the global sensorium lives and thrives, relentlessly and inexplicably, and the topics of beauty are inexhaustible.

Nevertheless, in closing, I wish to briefly discuss a final film in relation to wilding femininity, a postmeal dessert for the lactose intolerant. Korean Canadian actor Sandra Oh frequently embodies a savory Asian American femininity that is indigestibly delightful and vibrantly vulgar. In

Alexander Payne's *Sideways* (2004), depressed, divorced writer Miles (Paul Giamatti) and Jack (Thomas Haden Church), a concupiscent actor about to be married, revitalize their libidos and taste palates with a trip to Santa Ynez wine country. Determined to have a final fling or two before his wedding, Jack picks up wine-pourer Stephanie (played by Oh), who responds to his characterization of her as a "bad, bad girl" (after an exceedingly generous pour) with a confident wink: "I know. I need to be *spanked*." She is game, illustrating Baudrillard's observation that one can only become seduced if one is himself or herself seductive.[11] Nevertheless, it is neither Stephanie's effervescent charisma nor her hypersexuality flaunted through tight, midriff-revealing clothing that constitutes the vulgar beauty act that persists in the film's aftertaste. It is not even that, according to Jack, "nasty" Stephanie "fucks like an animal" (another connotation of sexual predation and game). Beauty compels that which is animal in us; rather than viewing this statement as derogatory and dehumanizing, we might instead raise the human to the esteemed position of the animal, who is incapable of feeling shame about its sexual appetite. As Jacques Derrida aptly reminds us, the animal "is not naked because it is naked."[12]

When Stephanie finds out that Jack is to be wed, the pot-smoking, motorcycle-riding, single mom wilds out on him with the rawness of an unselfconscious animal. Beating Jack with her helmet, she shouts, "You're getting married on Saturday? What's with all that shit you said to me?" She sobs, "You said you loved me," then with a quick affective pivot, growls, "I hope you die!" Stephanie then jumps onto her bike and points at Miles: "Fuckface, you too!" As with Ali Wong's sour cynicism, Stephanie's bite is not taken as a serious threat, and the scene, despite Jack's bloodied face, is played for comedic effect at the philanderer's expense. And we do not see Stephanie again. However, notwithstanding her unpalatable act of violence, it is the velocity of her rage, the guttural baritone with which she spews her insults, and the way she throws (un)like a girl that serve to limn a racial monstrosity that is bitterly honest about the pain of being other, a pungently seductive fantasy for the Asian/American woman, who is often contained and deanimated in western cinema's representational politics. If Stephanie is "an animal," her affective performance insists that she cannot be caged. If she is animal, let her provoke a crisis on par with Derrida's epistemological quandary when his little cat sees him naked.[13] Rather than securing heteronormativity or white civility, and the social gifts they bestow, Stephanie, like many of the characters discussed in this book, is forced to exist outside of such a frame, her abject jouissance creating something to be enjoyed in its corporeal residues—a kind of discordant, out-of-step dance with bedlam. To sense Stephanie's vulgar, flavorful beauty is to perceive the charismatic ways in which she liberates both her racial pleasures and injuries (which are intimately coiled) through traversals of space and speed—her rapid escape from the film's diegesis connoting the possibilities of undomesticated ways of knowing and becoming.

But Stephanie's pain lingers, and it is this aftertaste that bleeds through into other realms of discomfort. A cursory familiarity with the US health care system, and the politics and legislation that never cease to assail it, which puts the most marginalized and vulnerable among us at mortal risk, indicates that, as a society, we do not care about the pain of certain bodies. I am continually reminded of this stunning fact when I enter the sanctity of a women's writing salon of which I am a part. In the cozy, creaky quarters of an old house, my colleagues and I discuss, in the confines of our safe space and professional privilege, the ways in which our stresses and pains, including our bodily aches and dislocated bones, miscarriages and undiagnosable infections, have become the shameful, even chronic conditions that we must repeatedly sanitize and bury. If civility is the properly posed, hygienic, perfumed, watertight, and poreless body, then corporeal abjection may help reimagine an alternative, uncivilized game—a carnival. Indeed, it is through vulgarity, in connection with the feral "undercommons," to draw on Stefano Harney and Fred Moten's beautiful concept of a relational space for radical thought, whereby we act out and make visible our pain through the wayward animal.[14] Constructed from racialized-gendered injury, vulgarity insists that we take pain and beauty seriously. Although I conclude here with visibility, what I really mean is a permeable surface whose flavorful depths are not only seen but chaotically tasted. Whether that means (not): yelling, smiling, slouching, flirting, wearing too much/little makeup, showing too much skin, driving too fast, glaring, crying, waddling, burping, bleeding, stammering, talking too much—such bodily stylizations only remain on the surface if we neglect the materiality of charismatic force. We must do these things, but do them with the naked intention and fiery interior of Sandra Oh's Stephanie.

Stephanie is not vulgar because she is vulgar.

notes

Introduction

1 *Oxford English Dictionary*, s.v. "vulgar," https://www.oed.com.
2 Baudrillard, *Seduction*, 158.
3 For more on Zhang's pungent reception in mainland China, see Zuo, "Sensing 'Performance Anxiety.'"
4 Haraway, *When Species Meet*, 17.
5 Haraway, *When Species Meet*, 19.
6 Massumi, *Parables for the Virtual*, 36.
7 Massumi, *Parables for the Virtual*, 36, emphasis in original. In other words, the autonomic affect that Massumi describes precedes the formation of social emotion and emotion as a cultural politics, as explored by other scholars. See for example Ahmed, *The Cultural Politics of Emotion*; Berlant, *The Female Complaint*; Stewart, *Ordinary Affects*.
8 Tompkins, *Racial Indigestion*, 7.
9 Pham, *Asians Wear Clothes on the Internet*.
10 See "creative contagion" in Massumi, *Parables for the Virtual*, 19.
11 Shimizu, *The Hypersexuality of Race*, 3.
12 With this observation, Feng counters the remark made in *The Joy Luck Club* (Wayne Wang, 1993) that *The World of Suzie Wong* is a "film that Asian Americans love to hate." Feng, "Recuperating Suzie Wong," 40.
13 Palumbo-Liu, *Asian/American*.
14 Duggan and McHugh, "A Fem(me)inist Manifesto," 153–54, emphasis in original.
15 Baudrillard, *Seduction*, 85.

16 Baudrillard evokes Paul Virilio's concept of an "aesthetics of disappearance." Virilio uses the condition of "picnolepsy," wherein a person briefly loses consciousness, as a metaphor to comment on the powers and realities of the unseen, the invisible and of disappearance. Virilio's inquiries into the picnoleptic experience urge us to consider the disappearance of time in its various permutations as meaningful, albeit misunderstood, experiences. The "aesthetics of disappearance" are themselves productions of meaning. Virilio, *The Aesthetics of Disappearance*.
17 Doane, *Femmes Fatales*, 2.
18 Baudrillard, *Seduction*, 117.
19 Mulvey, "Visual Pleasure and Narrative Cinema."
20 Garland-Thomson, *Staring*.
21 Baudrillard, *Seduction*, 34.
22 See Chow, *Woman and Chinese Modernity*; Cheng, *Ornamentalism*; Khoo, *The Chinese Exotic*.
23 For example, demonstrating the etymological resonance of *detail* ("to cut in pieces"), Chow gives the example of breasts in Mao Dun's *Hong* (*The Rainbow*, 1930) in which the "narrative gaze returns obsessively" to the cerebral protagonist's bodiliness, with the effect of producing sensuous, erotic gaps in language, analysis, and political intent. Through the superfluous recurrence of Mei's breasts, Mao Dun demonstrates the limits of cerebral, revolutionary thought. Chow, *Woman and Chinese Modernity*, 114.
24 Manning, *The Minor Gesture*, 23–24.
25 See for example Ang, "The Differential Politics of Chineseness"; Chun, "Fuck Chineseness"; Ang, "Can One Say No to Chineseness?"; Chow, "Introduction."
26 Chow, *Primitive Passions*, 9.
27 Chow, *Primitive Passions*, 145.
28 Cheng, *Ornamentalism*, xi.
29 Cheng, *Ornamentalism*, 70.
30 Cheng, *Ornamentalism*, 208.
31 Scarry, *On Beauty and Being Just*.
32 Scarry, *On Beauty and Being Just*, 100.
33 del Río, *Deleuze and the Cinemas of Performance*, 21, 6.
34 Gunning, "The Cinema of Attractions"; Gunning, "An Aesthetic of Astonishment."
35 Sobchack, "Cutting to the Quick," 340.
36 For a similar argument, see Barthes, "The Face of Garbo," 84.
37 Farquhar, *Appetites*, 75.
38 Farquhar, *Appetites*.
39 Farquhar, *Appetites*, 67.
40 Jullien, *In Praise of Blandness*, 42.

41 Jullien, *In Praise of Blandness*, 52.
42 Jullien, *In Praise of Blandness*, 81.
43 Xue, "Cotton Candy," 111.
44 Jullien, *In Praise of Blandness*, 62.
45 Jullien, *This Strange Idea of the Beautiful*, 214.
46 See for example Shah, *Contagious Divides*.
47 Sohn, "Introduction."
48 Although it is beyond the purview of this book to revisit such histories, I nonetheless join scholars like Shimizu and Karen Shimakawa to embrace "abjection" and "perversity" as a way to critically wrestle with the racial circumscriptions that produce the Chinese body politically, socially, and aesthetically. See Shimizu, *The Hypersexuality of Race*; Shimakawa, *National Abjection*.
49 Sedgwick, *Touching Feeling*, 150.
50 Hegel, *Aesthetics*, 138.
51 Chow, *The Protestant Ethnic and the Spirit of Capitalism*, 141.
52 Quoted in Zhang, *Shengti Zhengzi*, 228.
53 See Classen, Howes, and Synnott, *Aroma*; Corbin, *The Foul and the Fragrant*.
54 Korsmeyer, *Making Sense of Taste*, 11.
55 Zehou, *The Chinese Aesthetic Tradition*, 1.
56 Zehou, *The Chinese Aesthetic Tradition*, 7.
57 A "snout-to-belly-to-bowel" route also appears in Indian Vedic aesthetic notions of *rasa* or "rasaesthetics," a term coined by performance scholar Richard Schechner to refer to the ways in which live performance can vividly arouse one's enteric nervous system. Drawing upon the *Natyasastra*, an ancient handbook written by Bharata-muni on Sanskrit theater and in which rasa appears, Schechner explains that rasa "is sensuous, proximate, experiential. Rasa is aromatic. Rasa fills space, joining the outside to the inside.... What was outside is transformed into what is inside." Drawing correlations between flavor and performance, rasa is starkly contrasted with the western performance aesthetic, which is founded on the "'theatron,' the rationally ordered, analytically distanced panoptic." Schechner, "Rasaesthetics," 29.
58 Perullo, *Taste as Experience*, 8.
59 Perullo, *Taste as Experience*, 10.
60 Brinkema, *The Forms of the Affects*, xv.
61 Jullien, *Living Off Landscape*.
62 Jullien, *In Praise of Blandness*, 42.
63 See Eng, Ruskola, and Shen, "Introduction," 6; Yapp, "Chinese Lingering."
64 Han, *Shanzhai*, 4.
65 Han, *Shanzhai*, 6.
66 Han, *Shanzhai*.

67 Christina A. León contends that in order to point to the constitutive losses which mediate racialized referentiality through a "grid of intelligibility that is profoundly racist," one must pursue the risks of a catachrestic deconstruction, one that embraces the abuse and monstrosities of language, which "acknowledges violence, undoes mastery, shows need, and allows for uncanny hauntings," even as those overdetermined claims are revealed in and by linguistic processes as false and/or insufficient. For example, León offers the improper use of metaphor in Raquel Salas Rivera's poem *The Tertiary/ Lo Terciario*, which names untranslatable and impossible objects like "pink plaintains" in order to underscore the various, unequivocal losses of Puerto Rican indebtedness. Moreover, as León suggests, to "read identitarian terms as catachrestic would mean to read the contexts within which such terms make claims born out of the tense relationship between a lack of a proper word and a need to make a claim." León, "Raciality's Referential Interruption."

68 Foucault, "Two Lectures," 94.

69 To evacuate chance and accident from the "co-incidence," a suitable synonym for assemblage, and to regard it as isomorphic, cosmic homology is itself a radical hermeneutic gesture, particularly in light of the global domination of western sciences, which emphasize, among other principles, linear-temporal causality, analytical and reductionist methods, objectivity and quantitative results, and the denaturalized isolation and control of studied objects.

70 As recalled in Keathley, *Cinephilia and History*, 6.

71 See Sobchack, *The Address of the Eye*; Sobchack, *Carnal Thoughts*; Marks, *Touch*; del Río, *Deleuze and the Cinemas of Performance*; Barker, *The Tactile Eye*.

72 Baudrillard, *Seduction*, 64.

73 Harman, *Guerrilla Metaphysics*, 44.

74 Contemporary critics of beauty are justified in many of their charges and concerns over the uncritical esteem and reverence of beauty, particularly from a biopolitical point of view. The injurious effects of beauty have been well documented in feminist accounts elaborating upon Simone de Beauvoir's contention that women voluntarily perpetuate their own subjugation by engaging in beauty care as a "kind of work." Naomi Wolf's *The Beauty Myth: How Images of Beauty Are Used against Women* (1990) and likeminded studies demonstrate correlations between material gain and perceived attractiveness. Feminist scholars including Mimi Thi Nguyen, Rita Barnard, and Sianne Ngai launch compelling criticisms of Elaine Scarry's universalizing account of beauty for glossing over the uneven distributions and normative constructions of beauty that exclude and provoke hatred and disgust toward bodies deemed unbeautiful and ugly, premised on racism, sexism, sizeism, classism, ableism, ageism, and other forms of biosocial-structural discrimination. Nguyen's work in particular describes

the ways in which beauty biopolitically organizes worlds, how beauty as a Foucauldian form of governmentality "is war by other means" by becoming one of the stakes upon which liberal humanism is imperialistically enforced. It is difficult to contest the fact that beauty lubricates the wheels of capitalist-consumerist-imperialisms, greasing their wildly destructive, disciplinary capabilities. The cultivation of socially acceptable feminine beauty takes time, money, and labor, involving (neo)liberal ideological complicity and generic rites of cosmetic passage. As Kant's own racist and rigid aesthetic criteria for beauty reflect, it is also indisputable that white-supremacist biosocial politics, which constitute dominant beauty ideals, govern much of the ways we in the west recognize and consume beauty, thereby causing many deleterious material effects. See Nguyen, "The Biopower of Beauty"; Barnard, "The Place of Beauty." Sianne Ngai criticizes what she views as Scarry's "fairly aggressive claims against feminist, queer, and postcolonial critiques of beauty (and, perhaps most aggressively, never identifies any of them by name)," in Ngai, *Our Aesthetic Categories*, 316–17n25).

75 Adorno, *Minima Moralia*, 111.
76 Massumi, "Translator's Foreword," xiii.
77 Kant, *Critique of Judgement*.
78 Quoted in Lindholm, *Charisma*, 19.
79 Lindholm, *Charisma*, 20.
80 Lindholm, *Charisma*, 6.
81 Musser, *Sensual Excess*, 5.
82 See Bennett, *Vibrant Matter*; Chen, *Animacies*; Jackson, "Animal"; Jackson, "Outer Worlds."
83 Chen, *Animacies*, 5.
84 Ngai, *Ugly Feelings*, 93.
85 Huang, "Inscrutably, Actually," 198.
86 Cheng, *Ornamentalism*.
87 Jullien, *In Praise of Blandness*, 51.
88 In distinguishing charm from the transcendental essence of beauty as an impure distraction, Kant also found it to be basically stupid, aligning it with emotion and "barbarism." Insofar as charm, charisma, and beauty are often means through which to obtain desired objects and ends, it would be erroneous to insist that such affective-aesthetics are unintelligent, particularly when we understand intelligence to mean an "exchange of knowledge, information, opinion" (*Oxford English Dictionary*, s.v. "intelligence"). I further add that intelligence also involves an exchange of energy, affect, and intensity through which we make sense of and understand the world. Kant, *Critique of Judgement*, 69.
89 Deleuze, *Cinema 1*, 101. One is also reminded of Ingmar Bergman's proclamation that "the possibility of drawing near to the human face is the

primary originality and the distinctive quality of cinema." Bergman quoted in Deleuze, *Cinema 1*, 99.
90 Doane, *Femmes Fatales*, 47.
91 Gottfried Semper quoted in Cheng, *Ornamentalism*, 79–80.
92 Levinas, *Totality and Infinity*.
93 Levinas, *Totality and Infinity*, 193.
94 Goffman, "On Face-Work."
95 Goffman, "On Face-Work," 8.
96 Dyer, *Heavenly Bodies*, 7.
97 Deleuze and Parnet, *Dialogues*, 4–5.
98 Freud, *Civilization and Its Discontents*, 62.
99 Shaviro, "Beauty Lies in the Eye," 19.
100 See Ahmed, *Living a Feminist Life*; Cvetkovich, *An Archive of Feelings*; Sedgwick, *Touching Feeling*; Stewart, *Ordinary Affects*.
101 Cvetkovich, *An Archive of Feelings*.
102 Barthes, *A Lover's Discourse*, 193, emphasis in original.

Chapter One: Bitter Medicine, Racial Flavor

1 Han, *Shanzhai*, 4.
2 Nietzsche, *The Genealogy of Morals*, 42–43.
3 Deleuze, *Nietzsche and Philosophy*, 130.
4 Drawing upon metaphors of indigestion, Nietzsche writes, "On the road to angel-hood (not to use in this context a harder word) man has developed that dyspeptic stomach and coated tongue, which have made not only the joy and innocence of the animal repulsive to him, but also life itself." Nietzsche, *The Genealogy of Morals*, 42–43.
5 Zhang, *Shengti Zhengzi*, 213.
6 Author's translation. The Chinese quotation is: 她在外表上很纯，不张扬，不夸张，但内心和性格里却有一种泼辣可以表达出来，这样在戏里出现会更好。
7 Zhang, *Shengti Zhengzi*, 214.
8 Chen, *Zhongguo Dianying Mingxing Yanjiu Bianji*, 412.
9 Classen, Howes, and Synnott, *Aroma*, 4.
10 Dyer, *Stars*, 3.
11 Iwabuchi, *Recentering Globalization*, 27.
12 Original emphasis in Lu, "Zhang Ruifang," 114.
13 Clark, *The Chinese Cultural Revolution*, 257.
14 Clark, *The Chinese Cultural Revolution*.
15 Ban Wang notes that "overcoming and sublimating the feminine" became an aesthetic concern which manifested in revolutionary politics and media through a libidinal identification with the motherland and a symbolic release of psychic energy to the sublime order of law, the father. See Wang, *The Sublime Figure of History*, 103.

16 Mao Zedong quoted in Otis, *Markets and Bodies*, 18.
17 Otis, *Markets and Bodies*.
18 Man, "Female Bodily Aesthetics, Politics, and Feminine Ideals of Beauty in China," 190.
19 Quoted in Clark, *The Chinese Cultural Revolution*, 200n22.
20 She wears this floral blouse in several other scenes during which she exercises morally correct behavior, for instance, when she reports to the town clerk that many villagers (including her husband) are abusing the system to gain more points by privileging speed over quality.
21 Tang, "Rural Women and Social Change in New China Cinema," 653.
22 Tina Mai Chen's study of Maoist dress contends that aesthetically pleasing patterns inscribed the "historical progress and prosperity" of the Chinese Communist Party onto its disciplined and loyal subjects. See Chen, "Dressing for the Party," 151.
23 Lu, "Zhang Ruifang," 119.
24 Lu Ren quoted in Hang, *Literature the People Love*, 76.
25 Chen, "Proletarian White and Working Bodies in Mao's China," 367.
26 Quoted in Hang, *Literature the People Love*, 83–84, emphasis added.
27 Zehou, *The Chinese Aesthetic Tradition*, 177.
28 hooks, *Black Looks*, 14; Kierkegaard, *Repetition and Philosophical Crumbs*, 60.
29 Clark points out this possibility when he writes, "With its carefully crafted close-ups and travelling shots, the film captures every quiver of her red tunic as she mimes her resistance to being bound in chains by the landlord's men.... An appreciation of ballet was probably not the motivation for sticking up such stills for many eager (mostly male) viewers." Clark, *The Chinese Cultural Revolution*, 155.
30 Barthes, "Romans in the Movies," 21.
31 Nietzsche, *The Genealogy of Morals*, 59.
32 Bitterness is foregrounded in historiographical titles like Mitter, *A Bitter Revolution*; and Manning and Wemheuer, *Eating Bitterness*.
33 Flatley, "How a Revolutionary Counter-mood Is Made," 503.
34 Mao, "The Law of the Unity of Contradictions [on Contradiction]," 194.
35 Wu, "Speaking Bitterness," 10.
36 In one manifestation of the party's virtuous turn to bitterness, privileged families no longer held the same degree of political favor as before, and power dynamics between classes and social groups were upturned. My mother, daughter of high-ranking government cadres in Changchun, along with her siblings, was one of the youths who were sent down to labor in the countryside and to become reeducated/"rehabilitated" by farmers. She lived in the rural Qian Gorlos Mongol autonomous county in Songyuan, Jilin Province, for five years before being allowed to return to the city. She remembers "recalling bitterness" meetings during which peasants and

farmers recounted their pain and struggles. However, she noticed that they would often conflate their experiences, for instance recounting their difficulties during the 1960 famine but falsely displacing those memories onto a pre-Liberation timeline. Corroborating this phenomenon, Guo Wu writes about how, "very often, an invited bitterness speaker confused pre-Liberation bitterness and post-Liberation suffering," which had the potential consequence of destroying the "youthful dream of revolution *in toto*," as it did for sent-down youth and historian Zhu Xueqin. The slippage of facts reinforces the affective quality of bitterness as an intensity that can be decoupled from its cause and yet still retain its force. Wu, "Recalling Bitterness," 264.

37 Wemheuer, "'The Grain Problem Is an Ideological Problem,'" 113.
38 Wemheuer, "'The Grain Problem Is an Ideological Problem,'" 126.
39 Deleuze, *Nietzsche and Philosophy*, 123.
40 Li Lifeng quoted in Wu, "Speaking Bitterness," 13.
41 This sequence elicited mainland feminist critic Dai Jinhua's observation of the camera as "greedily fix[ing] itself on this woman's face," framing Zhang's desiring gaze as ravenously hungry. This signature shot reappears in nearly all of Zhang and Gong's filmic collaborations (even in the documentary-esque *The Story of Qiu Ju*, 1992). Dai, "Severed Bridge," 35.
42 Deleuze, *Cinema 1*; Balázs, *Early Film Theory*, 109.
43 Phillips, *On Kissing, Tickling, and Being Bored*, 97.
44 Zhang, *Chinese Modernism in the Era of Reforms*, 327.
45 For mainland film critics like Yao Xiaomeng, "New Chinese Cinema [Fifth Generation cinema] is fundamentally antilinguistic, as long as the linguistic is understood as the ideological structure of the status quo." Quoted in Zhang, *Chinese Modernism in the Era of Reforms*, 234.
46 Zhang departs from Mo Yan's novel in which Grandma's feet are perfect examples of "lotus blossoms," his adaptation effacing this gesture to China's feudal past and replacing it with a vision of feminine naturalness and corporeal desire.
47 For a sustained study on the filmic engendering of China and the nationalization of women throughout the twentieth century, see Cui, *Women through the Lens*.
48 Chouy, "Asia's Movie Queen."
49 Pan, "Chinese Master."
50 Brook, "To Live and Dye in China," 21.
51 Nietzsche, in *The Birth of Tragedy*, invokes Dionysus, the ancient Greek god of wine, to describe the aesthetic of dissolution or transgression of boundaries, as in choral music, which ushers in ecstatic intoxication (*Rausch*).
52 I am here appropriating James Hillman's description of salt as "human brine" in "Salt," 157.

53 Nietzsche, *The Genealogy of Morals*, 37; Bachelard, *The Psychoanalysis of Fire*, 7.
54 Deleuze, *Nietzsche and Philosophy*, 30.
55 Scarry makes mention of this Platonic "requirement" that we move from eros to caritas, arguing that this notion appears throughout early aesthetic thought. Scarry, *On Beauty and Being Just*, 81.
56 Scarry, *On Beauty and Being Just*, 57.
57 Roland Barthes explains the punctum as a detail in the photograph that pricks its spectator in Barthes, *Camera Lucida*, 27.
58 Mavor, *Black and Blue*, 15.
59 Chen, *Animacies*, 211, 15.
60 Chow, *Primitive Passions*.
61 Chow, *Primitive Passions*, 213. Gong herself is also quick in interviews to assert that women's condition has changed in China, disassociating herself from the feudal characters she often played.
62 Despite the tumultuous end of the New Era and the banning of their films, neither Gong's nor Zhang's careers suffered in the long run. Gong's rising celebrity also coincided with a larger shift in feminine publics, evinced in part by the creation of new women's magazines like *Jiating* (Family) beginning in 1982; *Zhiyin* (Bosom friend) in 1985; and *Xiandai Jiating* (Modern family) in 1985. Gong's celebrity correlated with the new identity politics of a Chinese womanhood that departed from state feminism's creation of the *funü* (woman) subject position, which emphasized women's categorical roles alongside worker and proletariat as a collectivist participant rather than as biological and/or essentialist identity.
63 Griffin, "Acclaimed Concubine Is Not That Likeable."
64 Benjamin, "The Task of the Translator," 78.
65 hooks, *Black Looks*, 21
66 Classen, Howes, and Synnott, *Aroma*, 4.
67 Classen, Howes, and Synnott, *Aroma*.
68 German studies scholar Hans Rindisbacher quoted in Classen, Howes, and Synnott, *Aroma*, 174.
69 Writing about the powerfully "entrancing" effect the "blond angel" had on the internees during her daily visits, Lengyel testifies to the ways in which the woman's perfume caused the prisoners to inhale "these fragrances joyfully," only to become even more keenly aware of their suffering after she left the room. Lengyel, *Five Chimneys*, 160.
70 Williams, "The Care and Feeding of a Young Cannibal."
71 In *Homo Sacer*, Giorgio Agamben describes western biopolitics as a process of exclusions and exceptions, which in the extreme manifested in Nazi concentration camps, which governed life through sovereign violence.
72 Drobnick, "Introduction," 14.
73 Nietzsche, *The Genealogy of Morals*, 42–43.

74 "According to Buffon, it was the sense of animality. Kant excluded it from aesthetics. Physiologists later regarded it as a simple residue of evolution. Freud assigned it to anality. Thus discourse on odors was indicted." Corbin, *The Foul and the Fragrant*, 229.

75 Analyzing Freud's "olfactory marginalia," which discusses the significance of smell in neurosis, Mavor contends that "the bottom line for Freud was that no matter who smelled what, it had something to do with the mother/feminine. Smell was to the feminine what the visual was to the masculine: odor, indeed, separated the girls from the boys." Because the child identifies the mother through scent prior to the development of sight, the "body of the mother and the coprophilic pleasures of a long lost childhood" are later fetishized through odorous body parts like feet and hair. Mavor, "Odor di Femina," 65.

76 Williams, *Hard Core*.

77 Sobchack, "The Dream Olfactory," 137.

78 Deleuze and Guattari, *A Thousand Plateaus*, 88–89; Kohn, "'Mirror of Auras,'" 227.

79 Chen, *Animacies*, 89.

80 Tompkins writes about the commodified enjoyment of Black and Asian bodies as "that [which] seem to enjoy what whiteness is meant to disavow." Tompkins, *Racial Indigestion*, 150.

81 In addition to Tompkins, see Ku, *Dubious Gastronomy*; Ku, Manalansan, and Mannur, *Eating Asian America*; Wu, "The Best 'Chink' Food."

82 Marks, *Touch*.

83 Barker, *The Tactile Eye*, 147.

84 Barker, *The Tactile Eye*.

85 Lorde, "The Uses of Anger," 280.

Chapter Two: Salty-Cool

1 Jung, "Sal, Salt as the Arcane Substance," 130–31.

2 Quoted in Frijda and Sundararajan, "Emotion Refinement," 228.

3 Jung, *Aion*.

4 References to eastern man and traditional Chinese thought abound in Jung's *Psychology and Alchemy* (1944), for instance, in Jung's description of alchemy as the purifying merging of "supreme opposites, male and female (as in the Chinese *yang and yin*)." Jung, *Psychology and Alchemy*, 43.

5 Jung and Sigmund Freud split because of Jung's disagreement that the libido was purely sexual, a split Terrie Waddell characterizes as an "intensely emotional 'father-son' relationship [that] ended bitterly in 1912." Waddell, *Mis/Takes*, 10.

6 In film studies, Jungian film theory is perceived, as Luke Hockley describes with odorous appeal, "diffuse and unfocused—a *miasma* that floats

alongside the more concrete and structural presence of psychoanalysis." Hockley, "Jungian Screen Studies," 56, emphasis added. As an unpleasant, amorphous vapor that floats alongside psychoanalysis, a substantive and substantial production of humanistic knowledge, the flavor-scent of Jungian theory is regarded as an abrasive fume. Undoubtedly, film studies have been dominated by Freudian and Lacanian psychoanalytic theory, deepening our interrogations of the subjective, gendered, sexualized, and desiring dimensions of cinema, in particular, delivering to us such useful concepts as the gaze, desire and fantasy, and loss and lack. Nevertheless, even the foremost film scholars working with Jungian ideas concede that there really is no such thing as Jungian screen studies, and that Jung's theories of the unconscious, archetype, and nonsexual libidinality occupy a dark continent in film studies. As Jung's most significant cultural contributions center the collective unconscious and transindividual, transpersonal ontologies of being, such premises may seem unfashionably out of step in a post-1960s era of cynical individualisms and self-motivated neo/liberalisms.

7 Burton, "*Batman Returns* at 25."
8 Huang, "A Question of Appearance."
9 Hillman, "Salt," 118.
10 Hillman, "Salt," 153.
11 The remark in full is "When translating from one medium to another, specifically from the relatively more sensuous audiovisual media to the relatively more symbolic medium of words, the task is to make the dry words retain a trace of the wetness of the encounter." Marks, *Touch*, x.
12 Hillman, "Salt," 148.
13 Rich, *Wrong Place, Wrong Time*, xvi.
14 Ashley and Billies, "The Affective Capacity of Blackness," 64.
15 Eggert, *Disknowledge*, 4.
16 Eggert, *Disknowledge*, 5.
17 Sontag, "Notes on 'Camp,'" 291.
18 Sontag, "Notes on 'Camp.'"
19 Cheung quoted in Reynaud, "Maggie Cheung," 34.
20 Naficy, *An Accented Cinema*, 23.
21 Barthes, "Inaugural Lecture, Collège de France," 465.
22 Romney, "Maggie Cheung."
23 Romney, "Maggie Cheung."
24 Hudson, "'Just Play Yourself, Maggie Cheung,'" 10.
25 Helena Bassil-Morozow, for instance, point outs that the Jungian archetype has "been appropriated by popular culture and used to describe the idea of an object or phenomenon being a typical representative of its class," and contends that archetype is now used in place of "stereotype." Bassil-Morozow, "Using Jung to Analyse Visual Narratives," 38.

26 Chow, *The Protestant Ethnic and the Spirit of Capitalism*, 66.
27 Badiou, *In Praise of Love*, 26.
28 Shimizu, *The Hypersexuality of Race*, 5.
29 Nguyen, *A View from the Bottom*.
30 Khoo, *The Chinese Exotic*, 92.
31 See hooks, *We Real Cool*; Hebdige, *Subculture*; Thompson, "An Aesthetic of the Cool"; Pountain and Robins, *Cool Rules*; Winnubst, *Way Too Cool*. In her conceptualization of Black male cool, hooks also draws upon alchemical and thermal metaphors when she writes, "Once upon a time black male 'cool' was defined by the ways in which black men confronted the hardships of life without allowing their spirits to be ravaged. They took the pain of it and used it alchemically to turn the pain into gold. That burning process required high heat. Black male cool was defined by the ability to withstand the heat and remain centered." hooks, *We Real Cool*, 138.
32 Thompson, "An Aesthetic of the Cool," 41, 42.
33 Thompson, "An Aesthetic of the Cool," 67.
34 Donnell, "Cool Like Me."
35 Deleuze, *Cinema 1*, 103, emphasis added.
36 Eagan, "Coming Clean."
37 Žižek, *The Metastases of Enjoyment*, 96, emphasis in original.
38 See Doyle, *Hold It against Me*.
39 Wollen, "Godard and Counter-cinema," 123.
40 Shimizu, *Hypersexuality of Race*, 97.
41 She substitutes one "placeholder of ideology" for another, to draw from Shimizu, *Hypersexuality of Race*.
42 Although Han is talking about social media likes, I am applying it to the wider phenomenon of "being liked" as part and parcel of being a successful neoliberal subject. See Han, *Neoliberalism and New Technologies of Power*.
43 Baudrillard, *Cool Memories* (London: Verso, 1990), 6.
44 TheEnglish subtitled translation substitutes "animal" for "feline."
45 Deleuze and Guattari, *A Thousand Plateaus*, 274–75.
46 Ashley and Billies, "The Affective Capacity of Blackness," 12, 16.
47 Hudson, "'Just Play Yourself, Maggie Cheung,'" 225.
48 McLuhan, "Media Hot and Cold," 29.
49 Cheng, "Ornamentalism," 415–16.
50 Kim, *Ends of Empire*, 8, 4.
51 Deleuze and von Sacher-Masoch, *Masochism*, 71.
52 Williams, "Film Bodies," 7.
53 Berlant, *The Female Complaint*, 2.
54 Berlant, *The Female Complaint*, 20.
55 Deleuze and von Sacher-Masoch, *Masochism*, 52.
56 Celebrity Face-to-Face, "Joan Chen."
57 Appadurai, *Modernity at Large*, 33.

58 Quoted in Lavery, "Introduction," 3–4.
59 Kelley, "The Turncoat."
60 Klein, *Cold War Orientalism*, 7–8.
61 Koshy, *Sexual Naturalization*, 22.
62 Kim, *Ends of Empire*, 8.
63 Liu, *The Laws of Cool*, 179.
64 Liu, *The Laws of Cool*.
65 Pountain and Robins, *Cool Rules*, 26.
66 Other Asian/American actors on American television playing series regulars predating Chen include Miyoshi Umeki in *The Courtship of Eddie's Father* (ABC, 1969–72); George Takei in *Star Trek* (NBC, 1966–69); Victor Sen Yung in *Bonanza* (NBC, 1959–73); Bruce Lee in *The Green Hornet* (ABC, 1966–1967); Kim Miyori in *St. Elsewhere* (NBC, 1982–88); Keye Luke and Philip Ahn in *Kung Fu* (ABC, 1972–75); Pat Morita in *Mr. T and Tina* (ABC, 1976) and *Happy Days* (CBS, 1974–84); and Jack Soo in *Barney Miller* (ABC, 1975–82). Many thanks to Peter X. Feng for helping me compile this comprehensive list.
67 Dolar, "I Shall Be with You on Your Wedding-Night," 13.
68 Dolar, "I Shall Be with You on Your Wedding-Night."
69 Corliss, "West to East."
70 León, "Raciality's Referential Interruption," 14.
71 McGowan, "Looking for the Gaze," 32.
72 McGowan, "Looking for the Gaze."
73 This deferral is constitutive of desire.
74 Deleuze and von Sacher-Masoch, *Masochism*, 94.
75 Deleuze and von Sacher-Masoch, *Masochism*, 66.
76 Deleuze and von Sacher-Masoch, *Masochism*, 51.
77 Yeats's poem in full:

   A Drinking Song
   Wine comes in at the mouth
   And love comes in at the eye;
   That's all we shall know for truth
   Before we grow old and die.
   I lift the glass to my mouth,
   I look at you, and I sigh.
   (Yeats, "A Drinking Song")

78 Bruce Fink points out that, despite the fact that the quotation is often attributed to Lacan by Žižek and others, this statement was in fact made by someone in the audience. Fink, *Lacan on Love*, 215–16n15).
79 del Río, *Deleuze and the Cinemas of Performance*, 41.
80 del Río, *Deleuze and the Cinemas of Performance*.
81 Deleuze, *Difference and Repetition*, 90.

82 McGowan, "Looking for the Gaze," 40.
83 McGowan, "Looking for the Gaze," 42.
84 Deleuze and von Sacher-Masoch, *Masochism*, 31, emphasis added.
85 Studlar, "Masochism and the Perverse Pleasures of the Cinema," 275.
86 Dyer, *White*, 122.
87 Zehme and Rolston, "Babes in the Woods."
88 Lynch quoted in George, "A Feminist Reading of *Twin Peaks*," 111.
89 Muñoz, "Feeling Brown, Feeling Down."
90 Deleuze and Guattari, *A Thousand Plateaus*, 287.

Chapter Three: Pungent Atmospheres

1 Byrnes and Hayes, "Personality Factors Predict Spicy Food Liking and Intake."
2 Byrnes and Hayes, "Personality Factors Predict Spicy Food Liking and Intake," 10.
3 Derrida and Dufourmantelle, *Of Hospitality*, 45.
4 Brown, *Regulating Aversion*.
5 This notion of disgust also appears in Ngai, *Ugly Feelings*; Brinkema, *The Forms of the Affects*; Ahmed, *The Cultural Politics of Emotion*.
6 Hsu, "Naturalist Smellscapes and Environmental Justice," 801.
7 Sloterdijk, *Terror from the Air*, 20.
8 Sloterdijk, *Terror from the Air*.
9 Sloterdijk, *Terror from the Air*, 50.
10 *Oxford English Dictionary*, s.v. "pungent," https://www.oed.com.
11 Getino and Solanas, "Toward a Third Cinema," 124.
12 Kurlansky, *Salt*, 389.
13 Debord and Wolman, "A User's Guide to Détournement," 14.
14 Dyer, "Monroe and Sexuality," 225.
15 Dyer, "Monroe and Sexuality."
16 Quoted in Meyer, "Rock Hudson's Body," 265, emphasis added.
17 Meyer, "Rock Hudson's Body."
18 Huang, "Inscrutably, Actually," 191.
19 Ngai, *Ugly Feelings*, 201.
20 Sunderland, "Bai Ling Is Still Alive."
21 For instance, "When the body of another becomes an object of disgust, then the body *becomes* sticky." Ahmed, *The Cultural Politics of Emotion*, 92.
22 I am drawing here on Giorgio Agamben's concept of "bare life" (exposure of life to death) within states of exception to think about the ways presumed death circulates as a discursive, symbolic form of biopolitics within celebrity economies. Agamben, *Homo Sacer*.
23 Huang, "Inscrutably, Actually," 198.
24 Radin, "Rot."

25 Maslin, "Film Review."
26 English Language and Usage, "'Hot Mess' Meaning and Etymology," https://english.stackexchange.com/questions/118204/hot-mess-meaning-and-etymology. Accessed July 14, 2021.
27 *Oxford English Dictionary*, s.v. "hot mess," https://www.oed.com.
28 McLuhan, "Media Hot and Cold," 27.
29 McLuhan, "Media Hot and Cold."
30 The term "racial capitalism" comes from Cedric Robinson's study on the coconstitutions of racialism, "the legitimation and corroboration of social organization as natural by reference to the 'racial' components of its elements," and capitalism in modern European history. Robinson, *Black Marxism*, 2.
31 "If they would but suffer to be melted in the pot, then they would become just as American as anyone else." Wattenberg, "The First Measured Century."
32 Meanwhile, the concept of "wrong place, wrong time," an alchemical-pyschological concern of salt, as discussed in chapter 2, has also become part of *The Crow*'s mythology. Brandon Lee's on-set death, a freak accident in which he was shot by part of a bullet that was lodged in the gun's barrel, has caused the film to be regarded as one of the most cursed Hollywood productions of all time and an extraordinarily superstitious bad object.
33 Chow, *Ethics after Idealism*, 16.
34 Chow, *Ethics after Idealism*, 32.
35 Brown, *Regulating Aversion*, 18.
36 This logic also undergirds the majority of post-9/11 superhero movies, all of which center on justifying retaliatory state violence against terrorism.
37 Culp, *Dark Deleuze*, 37.
38 Culp, *Dark Deleuze*, 58.
39 Culp, *Dark Deleuze*, 69.
40 Sloterdijk, *Terror from the Air*, 25.
41 Sloterdijk, *Terror from the Air*, 56.
42 Žižek, *The Metastases of Enjoyment*, 117.
43 Dolar, *A Voice and Nothing More*, 15.
44 Dolar, *A Voice and Nothing More*, 20.
45 Žižek, *The Metastases of Enjoyment*, 104.
46 Žižek, "Tolerance as an Ideological Category."
47 Nakamura, *Cybertypes*, 21.
48 Ontologies of skin color saturate the film's gothic, Manichean contrasts. Even though Brandon Lee was mixed race, his character not only passed as white, whiteness as artificial mask became foregrounded in the posthumous Crow's stark white-and-black makeup, inspired by the fixed smile of a marionette mask.
49 Brown, *Regulating Aversion*, 13.

50 Higgins and Swartz, "The Knowing of Monstrosities," 97.
51 Mbembe, "Necropolitics," 28.
52 Mbembe, "Necropolitics," 21. See also Higgins and Swartz, "The Knowing of Monstrosities," for more elaboration between the American gothic tradition and slavery.
53 Brown, *Regulating Aversion*, 17.
54 Camilli, "Bai Ling Admits."
55 AP Reuters, "Bai Ling Says She's from the Moon"; Sohn, "Introduction."
56 Sohn, "Introduction," 7. See also Nakamura, *Cybertypes*; Nishime, "Whitewashing Yellow Futures"; Roh, Huang, and Niu, *Techno-Orientalism*.
57 Ku, *Dubious Gastronomy*, 163.
58 Lacan, *Anxiety*, 54.
59 Lacan, *Anxiety*.
60 Demanding love, the sm/Other simulates the child's performance of need and even displaces the child in his or her demonstrative need.
61 Lacan, *Anxiety*, 67.
62 Adey, "Air/Atmospheres of the Megacity," 292.
63 Ettinger, *The Matrixial Borderspace*.
64 Ettinger, *The Matrixial Borderspace*, 117.
65 Gumbs, Martens, and Williams, *Revolutionary Mothering*, 21.
66 Ettinger, *The Matrixial Borderspace*, 106.
67 Ettinger, *The Matrixial Borderspace*, 107.
68 Ettinger, *The Matrixial Borderspace*, 97.
69 Ettinger, *The Matrixial Borderspace*.
70 Ettinger, *The Matrixial Borderspace*, 147.
71 Wang, *High Culture Fever*, 73, emphasis added.
72 Mooney, "Chinese Not Surprised by Zhang Ziyi Scandal"; see also Zuo, "Sensing 'Performance Anxiety.'"
73 Even prior to the establishment of the People's Republic, pungent punishments have historically been dealt to Chinese women stars like Ruan Lingyu, the "Chinese Garbo" of 1930s Chinese cinema, who famously played the self-sacrificing maternal prostitute in Wu Yonggang's *The Goddess* (1934). Ruan tragically committed suicide at age twenty-four because of a public scandal sparked by an ongoing affair during her marriage. Her suicide hauntingly recalled her final film role in *New Women* (1935), a role inspired by another actress, Ai Xia, who also took her life because of a scandal over adultery.
74 Dai, "Gender and Narration," 116.
75 Yang, "From Gender Erasure to Gender Difference," 50.
76 "Tang Wei Fengsha De Zhenzheng Yuanyin?"
77 See Brook, *Collaboration*.
78 Davies, "Should We Worry about Chinese Patriotism?"
79 Sun, "Two Versions of *Sejie*," 46.

80 Brook explains how male and female bodies received differing treatments from the Japanese Imperial Army: "During the first assault, both sexes were equally vulnerable to aerial attack, bombardment, and fire. Thereafter gender mattered, for Japanese soldiers treated the bodies of Chinese men and women differently. Both could be damaged, but for different symbolic purposes. Men of fighting age were shot or conscripted for labor because they were, or stood in for, the soldiers of the nation. Women of childbearing age were raped or forced into prostitution because they were, or stood in for, the body of the nation." Brook, *Collaboration*, 23.

81 Ng, "Eleven Days in Hell," 255.

82 Chi, "Exhibitionism," 180; see also Huang, "Sejie Sisui Renxing Hong Hui Yishu."

83 For more on the geographical distinctions and nuances within the trans/national discourses surrounding the film, see Lee, "Ang Lee's *Lust, Caution* and Its Reception."

84 Tam, "Boycott."

85 As Rey Chow notes, "The appeal of *Lust, Caution* lies in the scandal—and truth—of this liberation of the flesh on the part of the woman, which brings about a fatal reversal of her patriotic act." Chow, "Guest Column," 558.

86 Chen, "Eros Impossible and Eros of the Impossible in Lust/Caution," 87.

87 Tang Wei describes the actor's eyes as quoted in Hu, "Lust, Caution, and Tony Leung's Eyes."

88 Chang, "'Lust, Caution,'" 36.

89 Freud, *Beyond the Pleasure Principle*, 43.

90 Freud, *Beyond the Pleasure Principle*, 58.

91 It is also worth noting that "zaiyiqi" (together) in Chinese combines the words for "be at," "one," and "rise," perhaps suggesting both a singularity of being and witness with the other, and notions of rising and erection as well. Moreover, Yi's surname, although not the character for "one" (*yi*) but rather for "easy" or "amiable," could be regarded capaciously as a homonym for one, phallic singularity. Thanks to William Brown for raising this line of thought.

92 McGowan, *The Impossible David Lynch*, 153.

93 Lee, "Enemy under My Skin," 653.

94 Stoler, *Imperial Debris*, x.

95 Roquet, *Ambient Media*, 8.

96 Ebert, "The Night Porter."

97 Lacan, *The Seminar of Jacques Lacan, Book XX*, 144.

98 Shaviro, "Beauty Lies in the Eye," 19.

99 Schamus, "Introduction," xii.

100 Huang, "China Has Stood Up, But Ang Lee and Company are Still Kneeling," in Chi, "Exhibitionism"; and Tam, "Boycott."

101 Zhang et al., *Zhongguo Keyi Shuo Bu*.

102 Ng, "Mai Tai-Tai, Pleased to Meet You!," 249.
103 Dargis, "A Cad and a Femme Fatale Simmer."
104 "Anything but 'Blacklisted.'"
105 Jullien, *The Impossible Nude*, 37.
106 The full passage reads, "However, on reading Chinese treatises on aesthetics it becomes clear that priority is given to the resonances of the figuration (*qiyun*), the radiance that emanates from it (*shencai*), and the atmosphere it diffuses (*fengshen*)." Jullien, *The Impossible Nude*, 38.

Chapter Four: Sweet and Soft Coupling

1 Contrastingly, Taiwanese women's literature since the 1980s, like that of Li Ang and Ping Lu, represents and allegorizes ambivalences toward cross-strait politics from the perspective of Taiwanese women. Lin Pei-yin, for example, notes that mainland lover Wang Yang's erectile dysfunction in Li Ang's *Seven-Generation Predestined Relationship* (2009), his inability to "get hard," constitutes an ironic comment on his arrogant support of China's peaceful rise and rigid nationalism. Pei-yin, "Gendering Cross-Strait Relations."
2 Nye, *Soft Power*.
3 Kurlantzick, *Charm Offensive*.
4 Kurlantzick, *Charm Offensive*, 42.
5 Liao Ping-hui and David Der-Wei Wang describe Taiwan's history in four colonial stages: Dutch conquest (1622–61), Chinese settlement (1661–1895), Japanese occupation (1895–1945), and nationalist recovery (after 1945). Liao and Wang, *Taiwan under Japanese Colonial Rule*, 4.
6 Zhang, *Pacific Asia*, 79.
7 Nye, *Soft Power*, xvi.
8 Writing about the rise of Chinese soft or "ideational" power from an American perspective, Michael Barr and David M. Lampton generously and uncritically use words like "attraction" and "seduction." See Barr, *Who's Afraid of China?*; Lampton, *The Three Faces of Chinese Power*.
9 Niou, "The China Factor in Taiwan's Domestic Politics," 168.
10 Jonathan Sullivan and Tricia Kehoe write, "Celebrity is also a powerful component in the discursive and symbolic armory used by China's one-party-state to promote regime goals and signal accepted modes of behavior for emulation by the masses. The development and instrumentalization of celebrity by the Chinese Communist Party, the state, and business actors is motivated and sustained by the 'spiritual vacuum' created by the emerging market socialist system and its associated societal dislocations and aspirations. Chinese celebrities are vehicles for the Party-state's inculcation of nationalism, traditional virtues, and the pursuit of modernity." Sullivan and Kehoe, "Chinese Celebrity and the Soft Power Machine."
11 Thanks to Jon Lewis for reminding me about the relevance of this incident.

12　Xu and Feiner, "*Meinü Jingji*/China's Beauty Economy," 314.
13　Ahmed, *The Cultural Politics of Emotion*, 136.
14　Reddy, "Jhumpa Lahiri's Feminist Cosmopolitics and the Transnational Beauty Assemblage," 29. See also Shirley Tate on "Black beauty citizenship" in Tate, *Black Beauty*; and Reddy, *Fashioning Diaspora*.
15　As an example of CFG's ambitions, both in reaching a vaster Chinese-language market and in producing ideological content, *The Knot* "unites melodrama subplots from both Taiwan and Tibet that powerfully fantasize the sublime, all-embracing One China principle." Yeh and Davis, "Re-nationalizing China's Film Industry," 38, 45.
16　Zhao, "Rethinking Empire from a Chinese Concept," 34.
17　Shih, *Visuality and Identity*, 4.
18　Brown, *Is Taiwan Chinese?*, 24.
19　In Hong Kong and Taiwan that year, audiences preferred Hollywood blockbusters, and only one mainland "pungent" blockbuster emerged in the box office top ten, Zhang Yimou's cynical critique of patriarchal rule set in a morally decadent and declining imperial China, *Manchengjindai huangjinjia* (*Curse of the Golden Flower*), which featured an embittered Gong Li as a righteously vindictive matriarch. Sinophone audiences preferred Zhang's hard-power extravaganza over China's soft-power romantic coproduction; it would appear that bitterness still held purchase over global Chinese imaginaries, replenished by new twenty-first-century nationalistic discourses that continued to embolden ressentiment over past injustices.
20　Ngai, *Ugly Feelings*, 174–208.
21　Haskell, *From Reverence to Rape*, 155, emphasis added.
22　Author's translation. Chi, "Yun Shuiyao."
23　Author's translation. Ma Te, "Fei Exin Yingping Wu Yi Pei Exin Dianying."
24　Lee, *Revolution of the Heart*, 74.
25　Khoo, "Love in Ruins," 244.
26　Freud, "Mourning and Melancholia."
27　Freud, "Mourning and Melancholia," 21.
28　Williams, "Film Bodies," 11.
29　Freud cites an old Roman legal principle, *pater semper incertus est, mater semper certa est*, to emphasize the pronounced and dubious role of the father within the family romance. Freud, "Family Romances," 239.
30　Bush, *Untying the Knot*.
31　Ong, *Flexible Citizenship*.
32　Anderson, *Imagined Communities*.
33　Shaoyi Sun, for instance, writes, "[Yin] frequently used fade-to-black transitions between sequences and shots, even in its two-second cut-aways, however, are hard to swallow." Sun, "Review of *The Knot*."
34　Morris, *Too Soon Too Late*, x.

35 For more on Taiwanese cinema in relation to its contested nationhood, see Yip, *Envisioning Taiwan*.
36 Hsu, whose Chinese name is Xu Ruoxuan, contains the implication of "softness," as Ruo (若), the first character of her given name, is a tonal homonym for the character for "weak," "fragile," or "delicate" (弱).
37 Bush, *Untying the Knot*, 11.
38 Yip, *Envisioning Taiwan*, 29.
39 Yip, *Envisioning Taiwan*.
40 Quoted in Ho, "From Spice Girls to Enjo Kosai," 3.
41 On stardom and social contradictions, see Dyer, "Stars as Images," 153.
42 Such imagined independence also appeared in concurrent Taiwanese film cultures, as New Taiwan Cinemas featuring male auteurs Hou Hsiao-hsien, Edward Yang, and Tsai Ming-liang elevated the cinematic movement to a global platform, bringing their films to the international festival circuit.
43 Ngai, *Our Aesthetic Categories*, 54.
44 Ngai, *Our Aesthetic Categories*.
45 Nye, *Soft Power*, x.
46 Ngai, *Our Aesthetic Categories*.
47 Yano, "Wink on Pink," 686.
48 See Yano, *Pink Globalization*.
49 Comolli, "Historical Fiction," 49.
50 Sontag, "Notes on 'Camp,'" 290.
51 Sontag, "Notes on 'Camp,'" 281.
52 Sontag, "Notes on 'Camp,'" 277.
53 Naremore, *Acting in the Cinema*, 3.
54 Chung, *Hollywood Asian*.
55 Rofel, *Desiring China*, 6.
56 Rui Zhang, drawing from Stuart Hall, contends that Feng's representations of modern society attest to the "'doubleness' of popular culture, exemplifying a 'double movement of containment and resistance.'" Zhang, *The Cinema of Feng Xiaogang*, 2.
57 Davis and Yeh, "Warning! Category III," 14.
58 Lee, "Persimmons," 46.
59 Chen, *Animacies*, 41.
60 Bergen-Aurand, "The Ruined Bodies of Transnational Chinese Cinema."
61 Writing in the wake of Gilles Deleuze and Felix Guattari's groundbreaking, unconventional *Anti-Oedipus: Capitalism and Schizophrenia* (1972), Foucault grapples with the failure in "totalitarian theories," noting that "to think in terms of totality has in fact proved a hindrance to research." Foucault, "Two Lectures," 81–82, emphasis in original.
62 "That is through the re-appearance of this knowledge, of these local popular knowledges, these disqualified knowledges, that criticism performs its work." Foucault, "Two Lectures."

63   Peterson, *Bestial Traces*, 7–8.
64   Rofel, *Desiring China*, 6.
65   Lefebvre, *The Production of Space*, 42.
66   Pontalis and Laplanche, "Fantasy and the Origins of Sexuality," 17.
67   Berlant, *Desire/Love*, 73.
68   Keathley, *Cinephilia and History*.
69   Deleuze, *Cinema 1*, 111.
70   The sequel, *If You Are the One 2* (Feng Xiaogang, 2010), is preoccupied with rain as an affective force through which to make sense of death.
71   Cheng, "Shine," 1028.
72   Thanks to Elizabeth Sheehan for this observation about sugar.
73   See Williams, *Hard Core*.
74   Anagnost, "The Corporeal Politics of Quality," 189.
75   Anagnost, "The Corporeal Politics of Quality," 190.
76   Hairong, "Neoliberal Governmentality and Neohumanism," 511.
77   Sen, "Tiny Times and the Dream of a '*Xiaokang*' Society' in China," 20–21.
78   Lee, "Film Review."
79   Elkadi, *Cultures of Glass Architecture*, 13.
80   Balázs, *Early Film Theory*, 105.
81   Weheliye, *Habeas Viscus*, 129.
82   Weheliye, *Habeas Viscus*, 127.

Chapter Five: Sour Laughter

1   Dyer, *Only Entertainment*, 113.
2   Elias, "Essay on Laughter," 288.
3   Ku, *Dubious Gastronomy*, 52.
4   *Oxford English Dictionary*, s.v. "quirky," https://www.oed.com.
5   Muñoz, *Cruising Utopia*.
6   Benjamin, "On Some Motifs in Baudelaire," 184.
7   Streamas, "Closure and 'Colored People's Time,'" 233.
8   Streamas, "Closure and 'Colored People's Time,'" 232.
9   Pardlo, "Colored People's Time," 370.
10 Foucault, *The Order of Things*, xvii.
11 Foucault, *The Order of Things*.
12 Mbembe, *On the Postcolony*, 204.
13 Muñoz, *Cruising Utopia*, 80.
14 Greenwald, "Charlyne Yi Inexplicably Joins House."
15 Moten, *In the Break*.
16 Moten, *In the Break*, 21–22.
17 Moten, *In the Break*, 7.
18 Quoted in Hoogstad and Pedersen, "Introduction," 20–21.
19 Hoogstad and Pedersen, "Introduction."

20 Nietzsche, *Thus Spoke Zarasthustra*, 9.
21 Eileraas, "Witches, Bitches and Fluids," 125–26.
22 Eileraas, "Witches, Bitches and Fluids," 126.
23 Muñoz, *Cruising Utopia*, 5.
24 Chow, *The Protestant Ethnic and the Spirit of Capitalism*.
25 Foucault, *The Order of Things*, xv.
26 Ahmed, "Feminist Futures," 249.
27 Ahmed, "Feminist Futures."
28 Bourdieu, *The Field of Cultural Production*, 106.
29 Catsoulis, "Out on the Highways in Search of Love," emphasis added.
30 Elster, *Sour Grapes*.
31 Mbembe, *On the Postcolony*.
32 The ontological veracity of documentary film has long been debated. Much ink has been spilled over the fact that the "father of documentary," Robert Flaherty, for instance, fictionalized and staged sequences in some of the first documentary features. There are many cinematic cues that suggest the fictional constructions of Charlyne and Michael's on-screen romance. To name two: Michael speaks to "Nick," played by actor Jake Johnson, as if he were actually Nick Jasenovec the documentarian, and the use of multiple takes in a single-camera setup. And there are even subtler cues of the film's artifice. For instance, when they are speaking with a Las Vegas Elvis impersonator, he shows a Photoshopped picture of a baby onto which his sunglasses and hairline were copied and pasted. "Elvis," as an inauthentic fake, commenting upon the digital manipulation of the photograph, imagines an angered response by the baby's parents should they ever see the photo: "What'dya do to my baby?" This affective response anticipates the outrage *Paper Heart* reviewers later expressed.
33 Chow, *The Protestant Ethnic and the Spirit of Capitalism*, 142.
34 Freud, "Part One on Narcissism," 19.
35 Roediger, "Gook."
36 Evans and Riley, *Technologies of Sexiness*, 136.
37 Baudrillard, *Cool Memories*, 6.
38 See Foucault, *The Birth of Biopolitics*.
39 Nietzsche, *Thus Spoke Zarathustra*, 9.
40 Bakhtin, *Rabelais and His World*, 82.
41 Levy, "Ali Wong's Radical Raunch."
42 Rowe, *The Unruly Woman*.
43 Reynolds, "In Ali Wong's *Hard Knock Wife* Special"; Zinoman, "The Strategic Mind of Ali Wong."
44 Bergson, *Laughter*, 144, 37.
45 As Bergson notes in his essay on laughter, "As soon as our attention is fixed on gesture and not on action, we are in the realm of comedy," that is, when we are engaged with unconscious behavior. Bergson, *Laughter*, 144.

46　Pham, *Asians Wear Clothes on the Internet*, 47.
47　Bergson, *Laughter*, 70–71.
48　Kang, "With *Hard Knock Wife*."
49　Elias, "Essay on Laughter," 283.
50　Dolar, *A Voice and Nothing More*, 29.
51　See Scarry, *On Beauty and Being Just*.
52　Dowd, "*Don't Breathe* during This Tense Thriller"; Nordine, "'Don't Breathe' Review"; Graham, "Review."
53　My appreciation to Celine Parreñas Shimizu for reminding me of this crucial connection.
54　Lee, "Pussy Ballistics and the Queer Appeal of Peristalsis," 513.
55　Lee, "Pussy Ballistics and the Queer Appeal of Peristalsis," 510.
56　Lee, "Pussy Ballistics and the Queer Appeal of Peristalsis," 493.
57　Edelman, *No Future*.
58　Maron, "Ali Wong."
59　Williams, *Hard Core*.
60　Limon, *Stand-Up Comedy in Theory*, 26.
61　Limon, *Stand-Up Comedy in Theory*.
62　Chow, *The Protestant Ethnic and the Spirit of Capitalism*, 141.
63　Lorde, "The Uses of Anger," 280; Maron, "Ali Wong."
64　Sloterdijk, *Critique of Pure Reason*, 5.
65　Huyssen, "Foreword," xiii, emphasis added.
66　Chow, *The Prostestant Ethnic and the Spirit of Capitalism*, 48.
67　Wark, "Four Cheers for Vulgar Marxism!!!!"
68　Weeks, *The Problem with Work*, 36.
69　See Brown, *Undoing the Demos*; Brown, *States of Injury*; Zerilli, *Feminism and the Abyss of Freedom*.
70　Limon, *Stand-Up Comedy in Theory*, 87.
71　Lafargue, *The Right to Be Lazy*, 5, 6, 11.
72　Weeks, who views Lafargue's critique as less serious than other Marxist critiques of work, offers a counterargument to his antiwork conception, clarifying that "it is not a renunciation of labor *tout court,* but rather a refusal of the ideology of work as highest calling and moral duty, a refusal of work as the necessary center of social life and means of access to the rights and claims of citizenship, and a refusal of the necessity of capitalist control of production." Nevertheless, Lafargue and Weeks both advocate for a three-hour work day. Weeks, *The Problem with Work*, 99.
73　Vargas, "Ruminations on *Lo Sucio* as a Latino Queer Analytic," 715, 718.
74　Limon, *Stand-Up Comedy in Theory*, 111.
75　Bergson, *Laughter*, 139.
76　Limon, *Stand-Up Comedy in Theory*, 4.
77　Berlant and Ngai, "Comedy Has Issues," 235.
78　Limon, *Stand-Up Comedy in Theory*, 104.

79 Berlant and Ngai, "Comedy Has Issues," 236.
80 Deleuze and Parnet, *Dialogues*, 69.
81 Deleuze and Parnet, *Dialogues*.
82 Ngai, *Our Aesthetic Categories*.
83 Bakhtin, *Rabelais and His World*.
84 Bakhtin, *Rabelais and His World*, 87.
85 Bakhtin, *Rabelais and His World*, 17.
86 Bakhtin, *Rabelais and His World*, 23.
87 Bakhtin, *Rabelais and His World*, 303–67.
88 Mead, "Ali Wong's Comedy, Ivanka Trump's Instagram, and the Rights of Mothers."
89 Mbembe, *On the Postcolony*, 104.
90 Mbembe, *On the Postcolony*, 125.
91 Memmi, *The Colonizer and the Colonized*, 89.
92 Sobchack, "Thinking through Jim Carrey," 280.
93 Deleuze and Parnet, *Dialogues*, 5.

Conclusion

1 hooks, "Femme Feminista." hooks, in *Black Looks*, also explains that the motto "Black is beautiful" became a significant revolutionary understanding of the valuation of Black bodies, and suggests that if we fail to understand beauty, we lose the opportunity to comprehend its power over us.
2 *Oxford English Dictionary*, s.v. "glamour," https://www.oed.com.
3 Scarry, *On Beauty and Being Just*, 90.
4 Comolli, *Cinema against Spectacle*.
5 Berlant, *Desire/Love*, 106.
6 Baudrillard, *Seduction*, 7.
7 Baudrillard, *Seduction*.
8 Baudrillard, *Seduction*, 22.
9 Baudrillard, *Seduction*, 133.
10 Although it may seem like Baudrillard's *Seduction* fortifies or galvanizes the misogynistic games or player behavior popularized by celebrity male seducers who have monetized teaching other men how to score sex from women, Baudrillard's passage on cheaters in fact reveals that the player is, in fact, not playing the game, instead relinquishing the possibility of mutual enchantment and reinstating Law because "he is afraid of being seduced." Baudrillard, *Seduction*, 140–41.
11 Like Gong and Zhang, and Cheung and Assayas, Oh and Payne were also in a relationship during filming. They were married from 2003 to 2006.
12 Derrida, "The Animal That Therefore I Am," 374. For other engagements with Derrida's essay, see Donna Haraway's critique of the philosopher's lack of critical curiosity and missed opportunity to "other-world" with

his cat when she sees him naked. Haraway, *When Species Meet*, 19–23. See also William Brown's short film *Clem* (2018) and its elaboration on transspecies encounters and sexual shame, in particular. Brown, "Clem."
13 Derrida's little female cat makes him blush, a pivotal moment of embarrassment that ushers in a lengthy treatise on discursive, mythological, and philosophical divisions of animal and human. Derrida and Dufourmantelle, "The Animal That Therefore I Am," 374.
14 Harney and Moten, *The Undercommons*.

bibliography

Adey, Peter. "Air/Atmospheres of the Megacity." *Theory, Culture and Society* 30, nos. 7–8 (2013): 291–308.
Adorno, Theodor W. *Minima Moralia: Reflections on a Damaged Life*. New York: Verso, 2005.
Agamben, Giorgio. *Homo Sacer: Sovereign Power and Bare Life*. Translated by Daniel Heller-Roazen. Stanford, CA: Stanford University Press.
Ahmed, Sara. *The Cultural Politics of Emotion*. Edinburgh: Edinburgh University Press, 2014.
Ahmed, Sara. "Feminist Futures." In *A Concise Companion to Feminist Theory*, edited by Mary Eagleton, 236–54. Oxford: Blackwell, 2003.
Ahmed, Sara. *Living a Feminist Life*. Durham, NC: Duke University Press, 2017.
Anagnost, Ann. "The Corporeal Politics of Quality (*Suzhi*)." *Public Culture* 16, no. 2 (2004): 189–208.
Anderson, Benedict. *Imagined Communities: Reflections on the Origin and Spread of Nationalism*. 1983. Reprint, London: Verso, 2006.
Ang, Ien. "Can One Say No to Chineseness? Pushing the Limits of the Diasporic Paradigm." *boundary 2* 25, no. 3 (1998): 223–42.
Ang, Ien. "The Differential Politics of Chineseness." *Asian Journal of Social Science* 22, no. 1 (1994): 72–79.
"Anything but 'Blacklisted.'" *China Daily*, April 1, 2010. http://www.chinadaily.com.cn/cndy/2010-04/01/content_9672211.htm.
Appadurai, Arjun. *Modernity at Large: Cultural Dimensions of Globalization*. Minneapolis: University of Minnesota Press, 1996.
AP Reuters. "Bai Ling Says She's from the Moon." *Hollywood Reporter*, April 18, 2009.

Ashley, Colin Patrick, and Michelle Billies. "The Affective Capacity of Blackness." *Subjectivity* 10, no. 1 (2017): 63–88.

Bachelard, Gaston. *The Psychoanalysis of Fire*. Translated by Alan C. M. Ross. Boston: Beacon, 1964.

Badiou, Alain. *In Praise of Love*. New York: New Press, 2012.

Bakhtin, Mikhail. *Rabelais and His World*. Translated by Helene Iswolsky. Bloomington: Indiana University Press, 1984.

Balázs, Béla. *Early Film Theory: Visible Man* and *The Spirit of Film*. Translated by Rodney Livingstone. Oxford: Berghahn, [1924, 1930] 2010.

Bardsley, Jan, and Laura Miller. *Manners and Mischief: Gender, Power, and Etiquette in Japan*. Berkeley: University of California Press, 2011.

Barker, Jennifer M. *The Tactile Eye: Touch and the Cinematic Experience*. Berkeley: University of California Press, 2009.

Barnard, Rita. "The Place of Beauty: Reflections on Elaine Scarry and Zakes Mda." In *Beautiful/Ugly: African and Diaspora Aesthetics*, edited by Sarah Nuttall, 102–21. Durham, NC: Duke University Press, 2006.

Barr, Michael. *Who's Afraid of China? The Challenges of Chinese Soft Power*. London: Zed, 2011.

Barthes, Roland. *Camera Lucida: Reflections on Photography*. Translated by Richard Howard. New York: Hill and Wang, 1981.

Barthes, Roland. "The Face of Garbo." In *A Barthes Reader*, edited by Susan Sontag, 82–84. New York: Hill and Wang, 1982.

Barthes, Roland. "Inaugural Lecture, Collège de France." In *A Barthes Reader*, edited by Susan Sontag, 457–78. New York: Hill and Wang, 1982.

Barthes, Roland. *A Lover's Discourse: Fragments*. Translated by Richard Howard. New York: Hill and Wang, 1978.

Barthes, Roland. "Romans in the Movies." Translated by Richard Howard and Annette Lavers. In *Mythologies*, edited by Roland Barthes, 19–21. New York: Hill and Wang, 2013.

Bassil-Morozow, Helena. "Using Jung to Analyse Visual Narratives: Tools and Concepts." In *Jungian Film Studies: The Essential Guide*, edited by Helena Bassil-Morozow and Luke Hockley, 27–62. New York: Routledge, 2016.

Baudrillard, Jean. *Cool Memories*. London: Verso, 1990.

Baudrillard, Jean. *Seduction*. Translated by Brian Singer. New York: St. Martin's, 1990.

Benjamin, Walter. "On Some Motifs in Baudelaire." In *Illuminations: Essays and Reflections*, edited by Hannah Arendt, 155–200. New York: Schocken, 2007.

Benjamin, Walter. "The Task of the Translator: An Introduction to the Translation of Baudelaire's 'Tableaux Parisiens.'" In *Illuminations: Essays and Reflections*, edited by Hannah Arendt. New York: Schocken, 2007.

Bennett, Jane. *Vibrant Matter: A Political Ecology of Things*. Durham, NC: Duke University Press, 2009.

Bergen-Aurand, Brian. "The Ruined Bodies of Transnational Chinese Cinema." In *Transnational Chinese Cinema: Corporeality, Desire, and Ethics of Failure*, edited by Brian Bergen-Aurand, Mary Mazzilli, and Hee Wai-Siam, 27–50. Piscataway, NJ: Bridge 21, 2014.

Bergson, Henri. *Laughter: An Essay on the Meaning of the Comic*. Translated by Cloudesley Brereton and Fred Rothwell. Norwood, OR: Norwood, 1911.

Berlant, Lauren. *Desire/Love*. New York: Punctum, 2012.

Berlant, Lauren. *The Female Complaint: The Unfinished Business of Sentimentality in American Culture*. Durham, NC: Duke University Press, 2008.

Berlant, Lauren, and Sianne Ngai. "Comedy Has Issues." *Critical Inquiry* 43, no. 2 (2017): 233–49.

Bourdieu, Pierre. *Distinction: A Social Critique of the Judgement of Taste*. Translated by Richard Nice. 1979. Reprint, New York: Routledge, 2013.

Bourdieu, Pierre. *The Field of Cultural Production: Essays on Art and Literature*. New York: Columbia University Press, 1993.

Brinkema, Eugenie. *The Forms of the Affects*. Durham, NC: Duke University Press, 2014.

Brook, Timothy. *Collaboration: Japanese Agents and Local Elites in Wartime China*. Cambridge, MA: Harvard University Press, 2005.

Brook, Vincent. "To Live and Dye in China: The Personal and the Political in Zhang Yimou's *Judou*." *Cineaction*, January 1, 2003, 21–29.

Brown, Melissa J. *Is Taiwan Chinese? The Impact of Culture, Power, and Migration on Changing Identities*. Berkeley: University of California Press, 2004.

Brown, Wendy. *Regulating Aversion: Tolerance in the Age of Identity and Empire*. Princeton, NJ: Princeton University Press, 2009.

Brown, Wendy. *States of Injury: Power and Freedom in Late Modernity*. Princeton, NJ: Princeton University Press, 1995.

Brown, Wendy. *Undoing the Demos: Neoliberalism's Stealth Revolution*. New York: Zone, 2015.

Brown, William. "Clem." *[in]Transition: Journal of Videographic Film and Moving Image Studies* 7, no. 2 (2020). http://mediacommons.org/intransition/clem.

Brown, William. "A (Mush)Room of One's Own: Feminism, Posthumanism and Race in Sofia Coppola's *The Beguiled*." *Aniki: Revista Portuguesa da Imagem em Movimento* 7, no. 1 (2020): 71–95.

Burton, Byron. "*Batman Returns* at 25: Stars Reveal Script Cuts, Freezing Sets and Aggressive Penguins." *Hollywood Reporter*, June 19, 2017.

Bush, Richard C. *Untying the Knot: Making Peace in the Taiwan Strait*. Washington, DC: Brookings Institution, 2005.

Byrnes, Nadia K., and John E. Hayes. "Personality Factors Predict Spicy Food Liking and Intake." *Food Quality and Preference* 28, no. 1 (2013): 213–21.

Camilli, Doug. "Bai Ling Admits She Has a Multiple-Little-Spirit Personality." *National Post*, May 10, 2005.

Catsoulis, Jeannette. "Out on the Highways in Search of Love, an Endlessly Elusive Quest." *New York Times*, August 6, 2009.

Celebrity Face-to-Face 名人面对面. "Joan Chen: 'Little Flower' as Dazzling as Before" 名人面对面2008–07–20 陈冲—'小花'绚烂依. Celebrity Face-to-Face. Accessed July 17, 2021. https://www.bilibili.com/video/av26092961/.

Chang, Eileen. "*Lust, Caution*: A Story." In *Lust, Caution: The Story, the Screenplay, and the Making of the Film*, 1–48. New York: Pantheon, 2007.

Chen, Hsiang-yin Sasha. "Eros Impossible and Eros of the Impossible in Lust/Caution." In *From Eileen Chang to Ang Lee: Lust/Caution*, edited by Peng Hsiao-yen and Whitney Crothers Dilley, 81–100. New York: Routledge, 2014.

Chen, Mel Y. *Animacies: Biopolitics, Racial Mattering, and Queer Affect*. Durham, NC: Duke University Press, 2012.

Chen, Tina Mai. "Dressing for the Party: Clothing, Citizenship, and Gender-Formation in Mao's China." *Fashion Theory* 5, no. 2 (2001): 143–71.

Chen, Tina Mai. "Proletarian White and Working Bodies in Mao's China." *positions: east asia cultures critique* 11, no. 2 (2003): 361–93.

Chen, Xiaoyun. *Zhongguo Dianying Mingxing Yanjiu Bianji* [Analysis of Chinese film stars]. Beijing: Zhongguo dianying banshe [China Cinema Press], 2012.

Cheng, Anne Anlin. *Ornamentalism*. Oxford: Oxford University Press, 2019.

Cheng, Anne Anlin. "Ornamentalism: A Feminist Theory for the Yellow Woman." *Critical Inquiry* 44, no. 3 (2018): 415–16.

Cheng, Anne Anlin. "Shine: On Race, Glamour, and the Modern." PMLA 126, no. 4 (2011): 1022–41.

Cheng, Anne Anlin. "Wounded Beauty: An Exploratory Essay on Race, Feminism, and the Aesthetic Question." *Tulsa Studies in Women's Literature* 19, no. 2 (2000): 191–217.

Chi, Meijian. "'Yun Shuiyao': Lishi Waiyi Xia De Yuanyanghudie" ["Cloud water ballad": Mandarin duck and butterfly under the cloak of history]. QQ.com, December 11, 2006. http://ent.qq.com/a/20061211/000060.htm.

Chi, Robert. "Exhibitionism: Lust, Caution." *Journal of Chinese Cinemas* 3, no. 2 (2009): 177–87.

Chouy, Lee San. "Asia's Movie Queen." *Straits Times*, July 23, 1993.

Chow, Rey. *Ethics after Idealism: Theory, Culture, Ethnicity, Reading*. Bloomington: Indiana University Press, 1998.

Chow, Rey. "Guest Column—Framing the Original: Toward a New Visibility of the Orient." PMLA 126, no. 3 (2011): 558.

Chow, Rey. "Introduction: On Chineseness as a Theoretical Problem." *boundary 2* 25, no. 3 (1998): 1–24.

Chow, Rey. *Primitive Passions: Visuality, Sexuality, Ethnography, and Contemporary Chinese Cinema*. New York: Columbia University Press, 1995.

Chow, Rey. *The Protestant Ethnic and the Spirit of Capitalism*. New York: Columbia University Press, 2002.

Chow, Rey. *Sentimental Fabulations, Contemporary Chinese Films: Attachment in the Age of Global Visibility*. New York: Columbia University Press, 2007.

Chow, Rey. *Woman and Chinese Modernity: The Politics of Reading between West and East*. Minneapolis: University of Minnesota Press, 1991.

Chun, Allen. "Fuck Chineseness: On the Ambiguities of Ethnicity as Culture as Identity." *boundary 2* 23, no. 2 (1996): 111–38.

Chung, Hye Seung. *Hollywood Asian: Philip Ahn and the Politics of Cross-Ethnic Performance*. Philadelphia: Temple University Press, 2006.

Clark, Paul. *The Chinese Cultural Revolution: A History*. Cambridge: Cambridge University Press, 1987.

Classen, Constance, David Howes, and Anthony Synnott, eds. *Aroma: The Cultural History of Smell*. New York: Taylor and Francis, 1994.

Comolli, Jean-Louis. *Cinema against Spectacle: Technique and Ideology Revisited*, edited by Daniel Fairfax. 1971. Reprint, Amsterdam: Amsterdam University Press, 2016.

Comolli, Jean-Louis. "Historical Fiction: A Body Too Much." *Screen* 19, no. 2 (1978): 41–54.

Corbin, Alain. *The Foul and the Fragrant: Odor and the French Social Imagination*. Cambridge, MA: Harvard University Press, 1986.

Corliss, Richard. "West to East." *Time*, April 5, 1999.

Cui, Shuqin. *Women through the Lens: Gender and Nation in a Century of Chinese Cinema*. Honolulu: University of Hawai'i Press, 2003.

Culp, Andrew. *Dark Deleuze*. Minneapolis: University of Minnesota Press, 2016.

Cvetkovich, Ann. *An Archive of Feelings: Trauma, Sexuality, and Lesbian Public Cultures*. Durham, NC: Duke University Press, 2003.

Dai, Jinhua. "Gender and Narration: Women in Contemporary Chinese Film." Translated by Jonathan Noble. In *Cinema and Desire: Feminist Marxism and Cultural Politics in the Work of Dai Jinhua*, edited by Jing Wang and Tani E. Barlow, 99–150. London: Verso, 2002.

Dai, Jinhua. "Severed Bridge: The Art of the Sons' Generation." In *Cinema and Desire: Feminist Marxism and Cultural Politics in the Work of Dai Jinhua*, edited by Jing Wang and Tani E. Barlow, 13–48. London: Verso, 2002.

Dargis, Manohla. "A Cad and a Femme Fatale Simmer." *New York Times*, September 28, 2007.

Davies, Gloria. "Should We Worry about Chinese Patriotism?" Harvard University Press Author Forum: Off the Page, May 28, 2008. https://harvardpress.typepad.com/off_the_page/2008/05/should-we-worry.html.

Davis, Darrell W., and Yeh Yueh-Yu. "Warning! Category III: The Other Hong Kong Cinema." *Film Quarterly* 54, no. 4 (2001): 12–26.

de Beauvoir, Simone. *The Second Sex*. Translated by H. M. Parshley. New York: Alfred A. Knopf, 1957.

Debord, Guy, and Gil Wolman. "A User's Guide to Détournement." Translated by Ken Knabb. In *Situationist International Anthology*, edited by Ken Knabb, 14–20. Berkeley, CA: Bureau of Public Secrets, 2006.

Deleuze, Gilles. *Cinema 1: The Movement-Image*. Translated by Hugh Tomlinson and Barbara Habberjam. Minneapolis: University of Minnesota Press, 1986.

Deleuze, Gilles. *Difference and Repetition*. Translated by Paul Patton. 1968. Reprint, New York: Columbia University Press, 1994.

Deleuze, Gilles. *Nietzsche and Philosophy*. Translated by Hugh Tomlinson. 1962. Reprint, New York: Columbia University Press, 1983.

Deleuze, Gilles, and Félix Guattari. *A Thousand Plateaus: Capitalism and Schizophrenia*. Translated by Brian Massumi. Minneapolis: University of Minnesota Press, 1987.

Deleuze, Gilles, and Claire Parnet. *Dialogues*. Translated by Hugh Tomlinson and Barbara Habberjam. New York: Columbia University Press, 1987.

Deleuze, Gilles, and Leopold von Sacher-Masoch. *Masochism: Coldness and Cruelty and Venus in Furs*. Translated by Jean McNeil. 1967. Reprint, New York: Zone, 1991.

del Río, Elena. *Deleuze and the Cinemas of Performance: Powers of Affection*. Edinburgh: Edinburgh University Press, 2008.

Derrida, Jacques. "The Animal That Therefore I Am (More to Follow)." Translated by David Wills. *Critical Inquiry* 28, no. 2 (2002): 369–418.

Derrida, Jacques, and Anne Dufourmantelle. *Of Hospitality: Anne Dufourmantelle Invites Jacques Derrida to Respond*. Translated by Rachel Bowlby. Stanford, CA: Stanford University Press, 2000.

Doane, Mary Ann. *Femmes Fatales: Feminism, Film Theory, Psychoanalysis*. New York: Routledge, 1991.

Dolar, Mladen. "'I Shall Be with You on Your Wedding-Night': Lacan and the Uncanny." *October* 58 (1991): 5–23.

Dolar, Mladen. *A Voice and Nothing More*. Cambridge, MA: MIT Press, 2006.

Donald, Stephanie Hemelryk. "Tang Wei: Sex, the City and the Scapegoat in *Lust, Caution*." *Theory, Culture and Society* 27, no. 4 (2010): 46–68.

Donnell, Alexander. "Cool Like Me: Are Black People Cooler Than White People." In *Shiny Adidas Tracksuits and the Death of Camp*, edited by *Might Magazine*, 46–58. New York: Berkley Boulevard, 1988.

Dowd, A. A. "*Don't Breathe* during This Tense Thriller from the Maker of the New *Evil Dead*." *A.V. Club*, August 25, 2016. https://film.avclub.com/don-t-breathe-during-this-tense-thriller-from-the-maker-1798188642.

Doyle, Jennifer. *Hold It against Me: Difficulty and Emotion in Contemporary Art*. Durham, NC: Duke University Press, 2013.

Drobnick, Jim. "Introduction: Olfactocentrism and Preface." In *The Smell Culture Reader*, edited by Jim Drobnick, 1–17. Oxford: Berg Oxford, 2006.

Duggan, Lisa, and Kathleen McHugh. "A Fem(me)inist Manifesto." *Women and Performance: A Journal of Feminist Theory* 8, no. 2 (1996): 153–59.

Dyer, Richard. *Heavenly Bodies: Film Stars and Society*. London: Routledge, 1986.

Dyer, Richard. "Monroe and Sexuality: Desirability." In *The Film Cultures Reader*, edited by Graeme Turner, 223–27. London: Routledge, 2002.

Dyer, Richard. *Only Entertainment*. 1992. Reprint, New York: Routledge, 2002.
Dyer, Richard. *Stars*. London: British Film Institute, 1979.
Dyer, Richard. "Stars as Images." In *The Celebrity Culture Reader*, edited by P. David Marshall, 153–76. New York: Routledge, 2006.
Dyer, Richard. *White*. London: Routledge, 1997.
Eagan, Daniel. "Coming Clean: Olivier Assays Directs Maggie Cheung in an Addict's Tale." *Film Journal International*, April 19, 2006.
Ebert, Roger. "The Night Porter." *Chicago Sun-Times*, February 10, 1975.
Edelman, Lee. *No Future: Queer Theory and the Death Drive*. Durham, NC: Duke University Press, 2004.
Eggert, Katherine. *Disknowledge: Literature, Alchemy, and the End of Humanism in Renaissance England*. Philadelphia: University of Pennsylvania Press, 2015.
Eileraas, Karina. "Witches, Bitches and Fluids: Girl Bands Performing Ugliness as Resistance." TDR: *The Drama Review* 41, no. 3 (1997): 122–39.
Eisenstein, Sergei. *Film Form: Essays in Film Theory*. Translated by Jay Leyda. New York: Harcourt, Brace and World, 1949.
Elias, Norbert. "Essay on Laughter." *Critical Inquiry* 43, no. 2 (2017): 281–304.
Elkadi, Hisham. *Cultures of Glass Architecture*. New York: Routledge, 2016.
Elster, Jon. *Sour Grapes: Studies in the Subversion of Rationality*. 1983. Reprint, Cambridge: Cambridge University Press, 2016.
Eng, David L., and Shinhee Han. "A Dialogue on Racial Melancholia." *Psychoanalytic Dialogues* 10, no. 4 (2000): 667–700.
Eng, David L., Teemu Ruskola, and Shuang Shen. "Introduction: China and the Human." *Social Text* 29, no. 4, 109 (2011): 1–27.
Ettinger, Bracha. *The Matrixial Borderspace*. Minneapolis: University of Minnesota Press, 2006.
Evans, Adrienne, and Sarah Riley. *Technologies of Sexiness: Sex, Identity, and Consumer Culture*. Oxford: Oxford University Press, 2015.
Farquhar, Judith. *Appetites: Food and Sex in Post-Socialist China*. Durham, NC: Duke University Press, 2002.
Feng, Peter X. "Recuperating Suzie Wong: A Fan's Nancy Kwan-Dary." In *Countervisions: Asian American Film Criticism*, edited by Darrell Y. Hamamoto and Sandra Liu, 40–56. Philadelphia: Temple University Press, 2000.
Fink, Bruce. *Lacan on Love: An Exploration of Lacan's Seminar VIII, Transference*. Cambridge: Polity, 2017.
Flatley, Jonathan. "How a Revolutionary Counter-mood Is Made." *New Literary History* 43, no. 3 (2012): 503–25.
Fleetwood, Nicole R. *On Racial Icons: Blackness and the Public Imagination*. New Brunswick, NJ: Rutgers University Press, 2015.
Foucault, Michel. *The Birth of Biopolitics: Lectures at the Collège de France, 1978–1979*. Edited by Michael Senellart, translated by Graham Burchell. New York: Palgrave Macmillan, 2008.

Foucault, Michel. *The History of Sexuality, Volume I: An Introduction.* Translated by Robert Hurley. 1978. Reprint, New York: Vintage, 1990.

Foucault, Michel. *The Order of Things: An Archaeology of the Human Sciences.* 1966. New York: Routledge, 2005.

Foucault, Michel. "Two Lectures." In *Power/Knowledge: Selected Interviews and Other Writings, 1972–1977*, edited by Colin Gordon, translated by Colin Gordon, Leo Marshall, John Mepham, and Kate Soper, 78–108. New York: Pantheon, 1980.

Freeman, Elizabeth. *Time Binds: Queer Temporalities, Queer Histories.* Durham, NC: Duke University Press, 2010.

Freud, Sigmund. *Beyond the Pleasure Principle.* New York: Norton, 1961.

Freud, Sigmund. *Civilization and Its Discontents.* Translated by James Strachey. New York: Norton, 1989.

Freud, Sigmund. "Family Romances." In *The Standard Edition of the Complete Psychological Works of Sigmund Freud, Volume IX (1906–1908): Jensen's "Gradiva" and Other Works*, edited by J. Strachey, 235–42. London: Hogarth, 1959.

Freud, Sigmund. "Mourning and Melancholia" (1917). In *On Freud's "Mourning and Melancholia,"* edited by Leticia Glocer Fiorini, Thierry Bokanowski, and Sergio Lewkowicz, 19–36. New York: Routledge, 2018.

Freud, Sigmund. "Part One on Narcissism: An Introduction" (1914). In *Freud's "On Narcissism: An Introduction,"* edited by Joseph Sandler, Ethel Spector Person, and Peter Fonagy, 1–32. London: Karnac, 2012.

Frijda, Nico H., and Louise Sundararajan. "Emotion Refinement: A Theory Inspired by Chinese Poetics." *Perspectives on Psychological Science* 2, no. 3 (2007): 227–41.

Garland-Thomson, Rosemarie. *Staring: How We Look.* Oxford: Oxford University Press, 2009.

George, Diana Hume. "A Feminist Reading of *Twin Peaks*." In *Full of Secrets: Critical Approaches to* Twin Peaks, edited by David Lavery, 109–19. Detroit: Wayne State University Press, 1995.

Getino, Octavio, and Fernando Solanas. "Toward a Third Cinema." *Tricontinental* 14 (1969): 107–32.

Goffman, Erving. "On Face-Work: An Analysis of Ritual Elements in Social Interaction." *Psychiatry* 18, no. 3 (1955): 213–31.

Grace, Victoria. *Baudrillard's Challenge: A Feminist Reading.* London: Routledge, 2000.

Graham, Adam. "Review: No Catching Your Breath in Wild *Don't Breathe*." *Detroit News*, August 25, 2016. https://www.detroitnews.com/story/opinion/columnists/adam-graham/2016/08/25/movie-review-catching-breath-wild-breathe/89384192/.

Greenwald, Andy. "Charlyne Yi Inexplicably Joins *House*." *Grantland*, August, 3, 2011. http://grantland.com/hollywood-prospectus/charlyne-yi-inexplicably-joins-house/.

Griffin, John. "Acclaimed Concubine Is Not That Likeable." *Gazette*, November 6, 1993.

Gumbs, Alexis Pauline, China Martens, and Mai'a Williams. *Revolutionary Mothering: Love on the Front Lines*. Oakland, CA: PM Press, 2016.

Gunning, Tom. "An Aesthetic of Astonishment: Early Film and the (In)Credulous Spectator." In *Viewing Positions: Ways of Seeing Film*, edited by Linda Williams, 114–33. New Brunswick, NJ: Rutgers University Press, 2004.

Gunning, Tom. "The Cinema of Attractions: Early Film, Its Spectator and the Avant-Garde." *Wide Angle* 8, no. 3–4 (1986): 63–70.

Hairong, Yan. "Neoliberal Governmentality and Neohumanism: Organizing *Suzhi*/Value Flow through Labor Recruitment Networks." *Cultural Anthropology* 18, no. 4 (2003): 493–523.

Han, Byung-Chul. *Neoliberalism and New Technologies of Power*. Translated by Erik Butler. London: Verso, 2017.

Han, Byung-Chul. *Shanzhai: Deconstruction in Chinese*. Translated by Philippa Hurd. Boston: MIT Press, 2017.

Hang, Krista Van Fleit. *Literature the People Love: Reading the Chinese Texts from the Early Maoist Period (1949–1966)*. New York: Palgrave Macmillan, 2013.

Haraway, Donna J. *When Species Meet*. Minneapolis: University of Minnesota Press, 2007.

Harman, Graham. *Guerrilla Metaphysics: Phenomenology and the Carpentry of Things*. Chicago: Open Court, 2005.

Harney, Stefano, and Fred Moten. *The Undercommons: Fugitive Planning and Black Study*. New York: Autonomedia, 2013.

Harris, Daniel. *Cute, Quaint, Hungry, and Romantic: The Aesthetics of Consumerism*. New York: Basic Books, 2000.

Haskell, Molly. *From Reverence to Rape: The Treatment of Women in the Movies*. Chicago: University of Chicago Press, 1973.

Hebdige, Dick. *Subculture: The Meaning of Style*. 1979. Reprint, New York: Routledge, 2012.

Hegel, G. W. F. *Aesthetics: Lectures on Fine Art*. Translated by T. M. Knox. Oxford: Oxford University Press, 1975.

Heidegger, Martin. *Being and Time: A Translation of Sein und Zeit*. Translated by Joan Stambaugh. 1953. Reprint, Albany: State University of New York Press, 1996.

Higgins, Ethan M., and Kristin Swartz. "The Knowing of Monstrosities: Necropower, Spectacular Punishment and Denial." *Critical Criminology* 26, no. 1 (2017): 91–106.

Hillman, James. *Alchemical Psychology*. Putnam, CT: Spring, 2010.

Hillman, James. "Salt: A Chapter in Alchemical Psychology." In *Salt and the Alchemical Soul: Three Essays by Ernest Jones, C. G. Jung, and James Hillman*, edited by Stanton Marlan. Woodstock, CT: Spring, 1995.

Ho, Josephine. "From Spice Girls to Enjo Kosai: Formations of Teenage Girls' Sexualities in Taiwan." *Inter-Asia Cultural Studies* 4, no. 2 (2003): 325–36.

Hockley, Luke. "Jungian Screen Studies—'Everything Is Awesome...'?" *International Journal of Jungian Studies* 7, no. 1 (2015): 55–66.

Hoogstad, Jan Hein, and Birgitte Stougaard Pedersen. "Introduction." In *Off Beat: Pluralizing Rhythm*, edited by Jan Hein Hoogstad and Birgitte Stougaard Pedersen. Amsterdam: Rodopi, 2013.

hooks, bell. *Black Looks: Race and Representation*. Boston: South End, 1992.

hooks, bell. "Femme Feminista." bell hooks Books. https://bellhooksbooks.com/femme-feminista/.

hooks, bell. *We Real Cool: Black Men and Masculinity*. New York: Routledge, 2004.

Hsu, Hsuan L. "Naturalist Smellscapes and Environmental Justice." *American Literature* 88, no. 4 (2016): 787–814.

Hu, Brian. "Lust, Caution, and Tony Leung's Eyes." UCLA Asia Pacific Center, October 3, 2007. http://www.international.ucla.edu/apc/article/79221.

Huang, Jisu. "Sejie Sisui Renxing Hong Hui Yishu" [*Lust, Caution* shreds humanity, explodes art]. Huang Jisu's blog. Accessed September 5, 2012. http://blog.voc.com.cn/blog_showone_type_blog_id_411306_p_1.html.

Huang, Vivian L. "Inscrutably, Actually: Hospitality, Parasitism, and the Silent Work of Yoko Ono and Laurel Nakadate." *Women and Performance: A Journal of Feminist Theory* 28, no. 3 (2018): 187–203.

Huang, Vivian L. "A Question of Appearance: Kathy Change, Soomi Kim, and Asian Femme Study." Paper presented at the Association for Asian American Studies Conference, San Francisco, 2018.

Hudson, Dale. "'Just Play Yourself, Maggie Cheung': *Irma Vep*, Rethinking Transnational Stardom and Unthinking National Cinemas." *Screen* 47, no. 2 (2006): 213–32.

Huyssen, Andreas. "Foreword: The Return of Diogenes as Postmodern Intellectual." In *Critique of Cynical Reason*, by Peter Sloterdijk, ix–xxv. Translated by Michael Eldred. Minneapolis: University of Minnesota Press, 1987.

Iwabuchi, Koichi. *Recentering Globalization: Popular Culture and Japanese Transnationalism*. Durham, NC: Duke University Press, 2002.

Jackson, Zakiyyah Iman. "Animal: New Directions in the Theorization of Race and Posthumanism." *Feminist Studies* 39, no. 3 (2013): 669–85.

Jackson, Zakiyyah Iman. "Outer Worlds: The Persistence of Race in Movement 'beyond the Human.'" GLQ*: A Journal of Lesbian and Gay Studies* 21, no. 2 (2015): 215–18.

James, Susan. *Passion and Action: The Emotions in Seventeenth-Century Philosophy*. Oxford: Clarendon, 1997.

Jeong, Seung-hoon. *Cinematic Interfaces: Film Theory after New Media*. New York: Routledge, 2013.

Jullien, François. *The Impossible Nude: Chinese Art and Western Aesthetics*. Translated by Maev de la Guardia. Chicago: University of Chicago Press, 2007.

Jullien, François. *In Praise of Blandness: Proceeding from Chinese Thought and Aesthetics*. Translated by Paula M. Varsano. New York: Zone, 2007.

Jullien, François. *Living Off Landscape: Or the Unthought-of in Reason.* Translated by Pedro Rodriguez. Lanham, MD: Rowman and Littlefield, 2018.
Jullien, François. *This Strange Idea of the Beautiful.* Translated by Michael Richardson and Krzysztof Fijałkowski. Chicago: University of Chicago Press, 2014.
Jung, C. G. *Aion: Researches into the Phenomenology of the Self.* New York: Routledge, 2014.
Jung, C. G. *The Archetypes and the Collective Unconscious.* Translated by R. F. C. Hull. 1959. Princeton, NJ: Princeton University Press, 1969.
Jung, C. G. *Psychology and Alchemy.* Translated by R. F. C Hull. 1944. Reprint, Princeton, NJ: Princeton University Press, 2014.
Jung, C. G. "Sal, Salt as the Arcane Substance." In *Salt and the Alchemical Soul: Three Essays by Ernest Jones, C. G. Jung, and James Hillman*, edited by Stanton Martin, 101–44. Woodstock, CT: Spring, 1995.
Kang, Inkoo. "With *Hard Knock Wife*, Ali Wong Is More Ferocious Than Ever." *Miami New Times*, May 9, 2018. https://www.miaminewtimes.com/film/with-hard-knock-wife-the-ali-wong-show-smells-like-success-10329116.
Kant, Immanuel. *Critique of Judgement.* 1790. Translated by James Creed Meredith. Oxford: Oxford University Press, 2007.
Keathley, Christian. *Cinephilia and History, or the Wind in the Trees.* Bloomington: Indiana University Press, 2005.
Keeling, Kara. *The Witch's Flight: The Cinematic, the Black Femme, and the Image of Common Sense.* Durham, NC: Duke University Press, 2007.
Kelley, John T. "The Turncoat" [television episode script]. *Hong Kong*. Aired November 23, 1960. UCLA Film and Media Archives, Los Angeles,.
Khoo, Olivia. *The Chinese Exotic: Modern Diasporic Femininity.* Hong Kong: Hong Kong University Press, 2007.
Khoo, Olivia. "Love in Ruins: Spectral Bodies in Wong Kar-Wai's *In the Mood for Love*." In *Embodied Modernities: Corporeality, Representation, and Chinese Cultures*, edited by Fran Martin and Larissa Heinrich, 235–52. Honolulu: University of Hawai'i Press, 2006.
Kierkegaard, Søren. *Repetition and Philosophical Crumbs.* Translated by M. G. Piety. Oxford: Oxford University Press, 2009.
Kim, Jodi. *Ends of Empire: Asian American Critique and the Cold War.* Minneapolis: University of Minnesota Press, 2010.
Klein, Christina. *Cold War Orientalism: Asia in the Middlebrow Imagination, 1945–1961.* Berkeley: University of California Press, 2003.
Kohn, Livia. "'Mirror of Auras': Chen Tuan on Physiognomy." *Asian Folklore Studies* 47, no. 2 (1988): 215–56.
Korsmeyer, Carolyn. *Making Sense of Taste: Food and Philosophy.* Ithaca, NY: Cornell University Press, 1999.
Koshy, Susan. *Sexual Naturalization: Asian Americans and Miscegenation.* Stanford, CA: Stanford University Press, 2004.

Kristeva, Julia. *Powers of Horror*. New York: Columbia University Press, 1982.
Ku, Robert Ji-Song. *Dubious Gastronomy: The Cultural Politics of Eating Asian in the USA*. Honolulu: University of Hawai'i Press, 2014.
Ku, Robert, Martin Manalansan, and Anita Mannur, eds. *Eating Asian America: A Food Studies Reader*. New York: New York University Press, 2013.
Kurlansky, Mark. *Salt: A World History*. New York: Penguin, 2002.
Kurlantzick, Joshua. *Charm Offensive: How China's Soft Power Is Transforming the World*. New Haven, CT: Yale University Press, 2007.
Lacan, Jacques. *Anxiety: The Seminar of Jacques Lacan, Book X*. Translated by Adrian Price. London: Polity, 2014.
Lacan, Jacques. *The Seminar of Jacques Lacan, Book XX: On Feminine Sexuality, the Limits of Love and Knowledge, Encore 1972–1973*. Translated by Bruce Fink. New York: Norton, 1998.
Lafargue, Paul. *The Right to Be Lazy: Being a Refutation of the "Right to Work" of 1848*. Translated by Harriet E. Lothrop. Colorado Springs, CO: Standard Publishing, 1904.
Lampton, David M. *The Three Faces of Chinese Power: Might, Money, and Minds*. Berkeley: University of California Press, 2008.
Lan, Feng. "Zhang Yimou's *Hero*: Reclaiming the Martial Arts Film for 'All under Heaven.'" *Modern Chinese Literature and Culture* 20, no. 1 (2008): 1–43.
Lavery, David. "Introduction: *Twin Peaks*' Interpretive Community." In *Full of Secrets: Critical Approaches to Twin Peaks*. Detroit: Wayne State University Press, 1995.
Lee, Haiyan. "Enemy under My Skin: Eileen Chang's *Lust, Caution* and the Politics of Transcendence." PMLA 125, no. 3 (2010): 640–56.
Lee, Haiyan. *Revolution of the Heart: A Genealogy of Love in China, 1900–1950*. Stanford, CA: Stanford University Press, 2006.
Lee, Leo Ou-fan. "Ang Lee's *Lust, Caution* and Its Reception." *boundary 2* 35, no. 3 (2008): 223–38.
Lee, Li-Young. "Persimmons." *American Poetry Review* 10, no. 6 (1981): 46.
Lee, Maggie. "Film Review: *Tiny Times*." *Variety*, July 13, 2013. http://variety.com/2013/more/global/film-review-tiny-times-1200563190/.
Lee, Rachel. "Pussy Ballistics and the Queer Appeal of Peristalsis, or Belly Dancing with Margaret Cho." GLQ: *A Journal of Lesbian and Gay Studies* 20, no. 4 (2014): 491–520.
Lefebvre, Henri. *The Production of Space*. Translated by Donald Nicholson-Smith. Oxford: Blackwell, 1991.
Lengyel, Olga. *Five Chimneys: A Woman Survivor's True Story of Auschwitz*. 1947. Reprint, Chicago: Chicago Review, 2005.
León, Christina A. "Raciality's Referential Interruption: Grammar, Risk, and Catachresis." Unpublished manuscript, October 25, 2020.
Levinas, Emmanuel. *Totality and Infinity: An Essay on Exteriority*. Translated by Alphonso Lingis. 1961. Reprint, Boston: Martinus Nijhoff, 1979.

Liao, Ping-hui, and David Der-wei Wang, eds. *Taiwan under Japanese Colonial Rule, 1895–1945: History, Culture, Memory*. New York: Columbia University Press, 2006.

Limon, John. *Stand-Up Comedy in Theory, or, Abjection in America*. Durham, NC: Duke University Press, 2000.

Lindholm, Charles. *Charisma*. Hoboken, NJ: Basil Blackwell, 1990.

Liu, Alan. *The Laws of Cool: Knowledge Work and the Culture of Information*. Chicago: University of Chicago Press, 2004.

Loesberg, Jonathan. *A Return to Aesthetics: Autonomy, Indifference, and Postmodernism*. Stanford, CA: Stanford University Press, 2005.

Lorde, Audre. "The Uses of Anger." *Women's Studies Quarterly* 9, no. 3 (1981): 7.

Lu, Xiaoning. "Zhang Ruifang: Modelling the Socialist Red Star." *Journal of Chinese Cinemas* 2, no. 2 (2008): 113–22.

Ma Te. "Fei Exin Yingping Wu Yi Pei Exin Dianying—'Yun Shuiyao'" [Nauseated movie critic's film commentary on disgusting film "Cloud Water Ballad" (The Knot)]. Douban.com, March 8, 2007. https://movie.douban.com/review/1131648/#comments.

MacCormack, Patricia. *Cinesexuality*. New York: Routledge, 2016.

Man, Eva Kit Wah. "Female Bodily Aesthetics, Politics, and Feminine Ideals of Beauty in China." In *Beauty Matters*, edited by Peggy Zeglin Brand, 169–96. Bloomington: Indiana University Press, 2000.

Mao Zedong. "The Law of the Unity of Contradictions [on Contradiction]." In *Mao Zedong on Dialectical Materialism: Writings on Philosophy, 1937*, edited by Nick Knight, 154–229. Armonk, NY: M.E. Sharpe, 1990.

Manning, Erin. *The Minor Gesture*. Durham, NC: Duke University Press, 2016.

Manning, Kimberley Ens, and Felix Wemheuer, eds. *Eating Bitterness: New Perspectives on China's Great Leap Forward and Famine*. Vancouver: University of British Columbia Press, 2011.

Marks, Laura U. *Touch: Sensuous Theory and Multisensory Media*. Minneapolis: University of Minnesota Press, 2002.

Maron, Marc. "Ali Wong." WTF *with Marc Maron* [podcast], episode 704, May 5, 2016.

Maslin, Janet. "Film Review: Lady Killer? Beijing Is Not Charmed." *New York Times*, October 31, 1997.

Massumi, Brian. *Parables for the Virtual: Movement, Affect, Sensation*. Durham, NC: Duke University Press, 2002.

Massumi, Brian. "Translator's Foreword: Pleasures of Philosophy." In Gilles Deleuze and Félix Guattari, *A Thousand Plateaus: Capitalism and Schizophrenia*, ix–xv. Minneapolis: University of Minnesota Press, 1987.

Mavor, Carol. *Black and Blue: The Bruising Passion of* Camera Lucida, La Jetée, Sans Soleil, *and* Hiroshima Mon Amour. Durham, NC: Duke University Press, 2012.

Mavor, Carol. "Odor di Femina: Though You May Not See Her, You Can Certainly Smell Her." *Cultural Studies* 12, no. 1 (1998): 51–81.

Mbembe, Achille. "Necropolitics." *Public Culture* 15, no. 1 (2003): 11–40.

Mbembe, Achille. *On the Postcolony*. Berkeley: University of California Press, 2001.

McGowan, Todd. *The Impossible David Lynch*. New York: Columbia University Press, 2007.

McGowan, Todd. "Looking for the Gaze: Lacanian Film Theory and Its Vicissitudes." *Cinema Journal* 42, no. 3 (2003): 27–47.

McLuhan, Marshall. "Media Hot and Cold." In *Understanding Media: The Extensions of Man*. Cambridge, MA: MIT Press, 1994.

Mead, Rebecca. "Ali Wong's Comedy, Ivanka Trump's Instagram, and the Rights of Mothers." *New Yorker*, June 5, 2018.

Memmi, Albert. *The Colonizer and the Colonized*. Translated by Howard Greenfeld. Boston: Beacon, 1965.

Merleau-Ponty, Maurice. *Phenomenology of Perception*. Translated by Colin Smith. 1945. Reprint, London: Routledge, 2002.

Merleau-Ponty, Maurice. *Sense and Non-sense*. Evanston, IL: Northwestern University Press, 1964.

Meyer, Richard. "Rock Hudson's Body." In *Inside/Out: Lesbian Theories, Gay Theories*, edited by Dianna Fuss, 259–88. New York: Routledge, 1991.

Miller, Laura. *Beauty Up: Exploring Contemporary Japanese Body Aesthetics*. Berkeley: University of California Press, 2006.

Mitter, Rana. *A Bitter Revolution: China's Struggle with the Modern World*. Oxford: Oxford University Press, 2004.

Mooney, Paul. "Chinese Not Surprised by Zhang Ziyi Scandal." Daily Beast, June 9, 2012.

Morris, Meaghan. *Too Soon Too Late: History in Popular Culture*. Bloomington: Indiana University Press, 1998.

Moten, Fred. *In the Break: The Aesthetics of the Black Radical Tradition*. Minneapolis: University of Minnesota Press, 2003.

Mulvey, Laura. "Visual Pleasure and Narrative Cinema." *Screen* 16, no. 3 (1975): 6–18.

Muñoz, José Esteban. *Cruising Utopia: The Then and There of Queer Futurity*. New York: New York University Press, 2009.

Muñoz, José Esteban. *Disidentifications: Queers of Color and the Performance of Politics*. Minneapolis: University of Minnesota Press, 1999.

Muñoz, José Esteban. "Feeling Brown, Feeling Down: Latina Affect, the Performativity of Race, and the Depressive Position." *Signs: Journal of Women in Culture and Society* 31, no. 3 (2006): 675–88.

Murdoch, Iris. *The Sovereignty of Good*. 1970. Reprint, London: Routledge, 2013.

Musser, Amber Jamilla. *Sensual Excess: Queer Femininity and Brown Jouissance*. New York: New York University Press, 2018.

Naficy, Hamid. *An Accented Cinema: Exilic and Diasporic Filmmaking*. Princeton, NJ: Princeton University Press, 2001.

Nakamura, Lisa. *Cybertypes: Race, Ethnicity, and Identity on the Internet*. New York: Routledge, 2013.

Naremore, James. *Acting in the Cinema*. Berkeley: University of California Press, 1988.

Negri, Antonio. *Spinoza for Our Time: Politics and Postmodernity*. New York: Columbia University Press, 2013.

Ng, Roseanna. "Eleven Days in Hell." In Lust, Caution: *The Story, the Screenplay, and the Making of the Film*, 255–58. New York: Pantheon, 2007.

Ng, Roseanna. "Mai Tai-Tai, Pleased to Meet You!" In Lust, Caution: *The Story, the Screenplay, and the Making of the Film*, 248–50. New York: Pantheon, 2007.

Ngai, Sianne. *Our Aesthetic Categories: Zany, Cute, Interesting*. Cambridge, MA: Harvard University Press, 2012.

Ngai, Sianne. *Ugly Feelings*. Cambridge, MA: Harvard University Press, 2009.

Nguyen, Mimi Thi. "The Biopower of Beauty: Humanitarian Imperialisms and Global Feminisms in an Age of Terror." *Signs: Journal of Women in Culture and Society* 36, no. 2 (2011): 359–83.

Nguyen, Tan Hoang. *A View from the Bottom: Asian American Masculinity and Sexual Representation*. Durham, NC: Duke University Press, 2014.

Nietzsche, Friedrich. *The Genealogy of Morals*. 1913. Translated by Horace B. Samuel. Mineola, NY: Dover, 2003.

Nietzsche, Friedrich. *Nietzsche: The Anti-Christ, Ecce Homo, Twilight of the Idols: And Other Writings*. Translated by Judith Norman. Cambridge: Cambridge University Press, 2005.

Nietzsche, Friedrich. *Nietzsche: The Birth of Tragedy and Other Writings*. Edited by Raymond Geuss and Ronald Speirs. Cambridge: Cambridge University Press, 1999.

Nietzsche, Friedrich. *Thus Spoke Zarasthustra: A Book for All and None*. Edited by Adrian Del Caro. Cambridge: Cambridge University Press, 2006.

Niou, Emerson. "The China Factor in Taiwan's Domestic Politics." In *Democraticization in Taiwan*, edited by Paul Paolino and James Meernik, 167–82. New York: Routledge, 2008.

Nishime, LeiLani. "Whitewashing Yellow Futures in *Ex Machina*, *Cloud Atlas*, and *Advantageous*: Gender, Labor, and Technology in Sci-Fi Film." *Journal of Asian American Studies* 20, no. 1 (2017): 29–49.

Nordine, Michael, "*Don't Breathe* Review: Home-Invasion Thriller Outstays Its Welcome." The Wrap, August 25, 2016. https://www.thewrap.com/dont-breathe-review/.

Nye, Joseph S. *Soft Power: The Means to Success in World Politics*. New York: PublicAffairs, 2004.

Ong, Aihwa. *Flexible Citizenship: The Cultural Logics of Transnationality*. Durham, NC: Duke University Press, 1999.

Otis, Eileen. *Markets and Bodies: Women, Service Work, and the Making of Inequality in China*. Stanford, CA: Stanford University Press, 2011.

Palumbo-Liu, David. *Asian/American: Historical Crossings of a Racial Frontier.* Stanford, CA: Stanford University Press, 1999.

Pan, Lynn. "Chinese Master." *The Guardian*, March 21, 1992.

Pardlo, Gregory. "Colored People's Time." *Callaloo* 39, no. 2 (2016): 361–71.

Park, Jane Chi Hyun. *Yellow Future: Oriental Style in Hollywood Cinema.* Minneapolis: University of Minnesota Press, 2010.

Pei-yin, Lin. "Gendering Cross-Strait Relations: Romance and Geopolitics in Li Ang's Seven-Generation Predestined Relationship and Ping Lu's East and Beyond." *Archiv Orientalni* 81, no. 3 (2013): 515.

Perullo, Nicola. *Taste as Experience: The Philosophy and Aesthetics of Food.* New York: Columbia University Press, 2016.

Peterson, Christopher. *Bestial Traces: Race, Sexuality, Animality.* New York: Fordham University Press, 2013.

Pham, Minh-Ha T. *Asians Wear Clothes on the Internet: Race, Gender, and the Work of Personal Style Blogging.* Durham, NC: Duke University Press, 2015.

Phillips, Adam. *On Kissing, Tickling, and Being Bored: Psychoanalytic Essays on the Unexamined Life.* Cambridge, MA: Harvard University Press, 1993.

Pippin, Robert. *Introductions to Nietzsche.* Cambridge: Cambridge University Press, 2012.

Pollack, Griselda. "The Visual." In *A Concise Guide to Feminist Theory*, edited by Mary Eagleton, 173–94. Hoboken, NJ: Wiley-Blackwell, 1993.

Pontalis, Jean-Baptiste, and Jean Laplanche. "Fantasy and the Origins of Sexuality." *International Journal of Psycho-analysis* 49 (1968): 1.

Pountain, Dick, and David Robins. *Cool Rules: Anatomy of an Attitude.* London: Reaktion, 2000.

Radin, Joanna. "Rot." In *The Multispecies Salon: A Companion to the Book.* Accessed May 19, 2021. http://www.multispecies-salon.org/rot/.

Reddy, Vanita. *Fashioning Diaspora: Beauty, Femininity, and South Asian American Culture.* Philadelphia: Temple University Press, 2016.

Reddy, Vanita. "Jhumpa Lahiri's Feminist Cosmopolitics and the Transnational Beauty Assemblage." *Meridians: Feminism, Race, Transnationalism* 11, no. 2 (2011): 29–59.

Reynaud, Bérénice. "Maggie Cheung: Icon of Modernity." *Cineyama* 37 (1997): 32–36.

Reynolds, Megan. "In Ali Wong's *Hard Knock Wife* Special, Motherhood Is a Queef-Filled Adventure." *Jezebel*, May 14, 2018. https://themuse.jezebel.com/in-ali-wongs-hard-knock-wife-special-motherhood-is-a-q-1825994867.

Rich, John A. *Wrong Place, Wrong Time: Trauma and Violence in the Lives of Young Black Men.* Baltimore, MD: Johns Hopkins University Press, 2009.

Robinson, Cedric J. *Black Marxism: The Making of the Black Radical Tradition.* Chapel Hill: University of North Carolina Press, 1983.

Roediger, Dave. "Gook: The Short History of an Americanism." *Monthly Review* 43, no. 10 (1992): 50–55.

Rofel, Lisa. *Desiring China: Experiments in Neoliberalism, Sexuality, and Public Culture*. Durham, NC: Duke University Press, 2007.

Roh, David S., Betsy Huang, and Greta A. Niu. *Techno-Orientalism: Imagining Asia in Speculative Fiction, History, and Media*. New Brunswick, NJ: Rutgers University Press, 2015.

Romney, Jonathan. "Maggie Cheung: The Lady Is a Vamp." *Independent*, June 26, 2005.

Roquet, Paul. *Ambient Media: Japanese Atmospheres of Self*. Minneapolis: University of Minnesota Press, 2016.

Rowe, Kathleen. *The Unruly Woman: Gender and the Genres of Laughter*. Austin: University of Texas Press, 1995.

Salvato, Nick. *Obstruction*. Durham, NC: Duke University Press, 2016.

Scarry, Elaine. *On Beauty and Being Just*. Princeton, NJ: Princeton University Press, 2013.

Schamus, James. "Introduction." In Lust, Caution: *The Story, the Screenplay, and the Making of the Film*, xi–xv. New York: Pantheon, 2007.

Schechner, Richard. "Rasaesthetics." TDR: *The Drama Review* 45, no. 3 (2001): 27–50.

Sedgwick, Eve Kosofsky. *Touching Feeling: Affect, Pedagogy, Performativity*. Durham, NC: Duke University Press, 2003.

Sen, Tansen. "Tiny Times and the Dream of a '*Xiaokang* Society' in China." *Economic and Political Weekly* 49, no. 21 (2014): 19.

Shah, Nayan. *Contagious Divides: Epidemics and Race in San Francisco's Chinatown*. Berkeley: University of California Press, 2001.

Shaviro, Steven. "Beauty Lies in the Eye." In *A Shock to Thought: Expression after Deleuze and Guattari*, edited by Brian Massumi, 9–19. London: Routledge, 2002.

Shaviro, Steven. *The Cinematic Body*. Minneapolis: University of Minnesota Press, 1994.

Shih, Shu-mei. *Visuality and Identity: Sinophone Articulations across the Pacific*. Berkeley: University of California Press, 2007.

Shimakawa, Karen. *National Abjection: The Asian American Body Onstage*. Durham, NC: Duke University Press, 2002.

Shimizu, Celine Parreñas. *The Hypersexuality of Race: Performing Asian/American Women on Screen and Scene*. Durham, NC: Duke University Press, 2007.

Sloterdijk, Peter. *Critique of Pure Reason*. Translated by Michael Eldred. Minneapolis: University of Minnesota Press, 1987.

Sloterdijk, Peter. *Terror from the Air*. Los Angeles: Semiotext(e), 2009.

Smith, Andrew. *Gothic Literature*. Edinburgh: Edinburgh University Press, 2007.

Smith, Sheila Cornelius, and Ian Haydn. *New Chinese Cinema: Challenging Representations*. London: Wallflower, 2002.

Sobchack, Vivian. *The Address of the Eye: A Phenomenology of Film Experience*. Princeton, NJ: Princeton University Press, 1992.

Sobchack, Vivian. *Carnal Thoughts: Embodiment and Moving Image Culture*. Berkeley: University of California Press, 2004.

Sobchack, Vivian. "'Cutting to the Quick': Techne, Physis, and Poiesis and the Attractions of Slow Motion." In *The Cinema of Attractions Reloaded*, edited by Wanda Strauven, 337–51. Amsterdam: Amsterdam University Press, 2006.

Sobchack, Vivian. "The Dream Olfactory: On Making Scents of Cinema." In *Carnal Aesthetics: Transgressive Imagery and Feminist Politics*, edited by Betinna Papenburg and Marta Zarzycka, 121–43. London: I. B. Tauris, 2013.

Sobchack, Vivian. "Thinking through Jim Carrey." In *More Than a Method: Trends and Traditions in Contemporary Film Performance*, edited by Cynthia Baron, Diane Carson, and Frank P. Tomasulo, 275–96. Detroit: Wayne State University Press, 2004.

Sohn, Stephen Hong. "Introduction: Alien/Asian: Imagining the Racialized Future." *Melus* 33, no. 4 (2008): 5–22.

Song Qiang, Zhang Zangzang, Qiao Bian, Tang Zhengyu, and Gu Qingsheng. *Zhongguo Keyi Shuo Bu* [China can say no]. Beijing: Zhonghua Gongshang Lianhe Chubanshe, 1996.

Sontag, Susan. "Notes on 'Camp.'" In *Against Interpretation and Other Essays*, 275–92. London: Pengiun, 2009.

Sontag, Susan. "Writing Itself: On Roland Barthes." In *A Barthes Reader*, edited by Susan Sontag, vii–xxxvi. New York: Hill and Wang, 1982.

Stewart, Kathleen. *Ordinary Affects*. Durham, NC: Duke University Press, 2007.

Stoler, Ann Laura. *Imperial Debris: On Ruins and Ruination*. Durham, NC: Duke University Press, 2013.

Streamas, John. "Closure and 'Colored People's Time.'" In *Time: Limits and Constraints*, 219–40. Leiden: Brill, 2010.

Studlar, Gaylyn. "Masochism and the Perverse Pleasures of the Cinema." *Quarterly Review of Film and Video* 9, no. 4 (1984): 267–82.

Sullivan, Jonathan, and Tricia Kehoe. "Chinese Celebrity and the Soft Power Machine." *China Film Insider*, April 3, 2016. http://chinafilminsider.com/chinese-celebrity-soft-power-machine/.

Sun, Cecile Chu-chin. "Two Versions of *Sejie*: Fiction and Film—Views from a Common Reader." In *From Eileen Chang to Ang Lee: Lust/Caution*, edited by Peng Hsiao-yen and Whitney Crothers Dilley, 35–50. New York: Routledge, 2014.

Sun, Shaoyi. "Review of *The Knot*." Shaoyi Sun's Film Review Blog, October 23, 2009. https://shaoyis.wordpress.com/2009/10/23/review-of-the-knot-%E4%BA%91%E6%B0%B4%E8%B0%A3-mainland-chinahong-kongtaiwan-2006/.

Sunderland, Mitchell. "Bai Ling Is Still Alive." *Vice*, April 13, 2016. https://www.vice.com/en/article/bmwqav/bai-ling-broadly-profile.

Tam, Bill. "Boycott: *Lust, Caution*. An Lee [*sic*]: Cultural Traitor" [press release]. Traditional Family Coalition, September 29, 2007. http://tfcus.homestead.com/boycott_lust_caution.pdf.

"Tang Wei Fengsha De Zhenzheng Yuanyin?" [What is the real reason for Tang Wei's ban?]. *Baidu zhidao*, 2010. http://zhidao.baidu.com.

Tang, Xiaobing. "Rural Women and Social Change in New China Cinema: From Li Shuangshuang to Ermo." *positions: east asia cultures critique* 11, no. 3 (2003): 647–74.

Tate, Shirley. *Black Beauty: Aesthetics, Stylization, Politics*. Farnham, UK: Ashgate, 2009.

Thain, Alanna. *Bodies in Suspense: Time and Affect in Cinema*. Minneapolis: University of Minnesota Press, 2017.

Thompson, Robert Farris. "An Aesthetic of the Cool." *African Arts* 7, no. 1 (1973): 41–91.

Tierney, Robert. *Tropics of Savagery: The Culture of Japanese Empire in Comparative Frame*. Berkeley: University of California Press, 2010.

Tomlinson, John. *Globalization and Culture*. Chicago: University of Chicago Press, 1999.

Tompkins, Kyla Wazana. *Racial Indigestion: Eating Bodies in the 19th Century*. New York: New York University Press, 2012.

Vargas, Deborah R. "Ruminations on *Lo Sucio* as a Latino Queer Analytic." *American Quarterly* 66, no. 3 (2014): 715–26.

Virilio, Paul. *The Aesthetics of Disappearance*. Translated by Philip Beitchman. Los Angeles: Semiotext, 2006.

Waddell, Terrie. *Mis/Takes: Archetype, Myth and Identity in Screen Fiction*. New York: Routledge, 2012.

Wang, Ban. *The Sublime Figure of History: Aesthetics and Politics in Twentieth-Century China*. Stanford, CA: Stanford University Press, 1997.

Wang, Jing. *High Culture Fever: Politics, Aesthetics, and Ideology in Deng's China*. Berkeley: University of California Press, 1996.

Wark, McKenzie. "Four Cheers for Vulgar Marxism!!!!" *Public Seminar*, April 25, 2014. http://www.publicseminar.org/2014/04/four-cheers-for-vulgarity/.

Wattenberg, Ben J., host. *The First Measured Century: The Other Way of Looking at American History*. PBS, 2001.

Weeks, Kathi. *The Problem with Work: Feminism, Marxism, Antiwork Politics, and Postwork Imaginaries*. Durham, NC: Duke University Press, 2011.

Weheliye, Alexander G. *Habeas Viscus: Racializing Assemblages, Biopolitics, and Black Feminist Theories of the Human*. Durham, NC: Duke University Press, 2014.

Wemheuer, Felix. "'The Grain Problem Is an Ideological Problem': Discourses of Hunger in the 1957 Socialist Education Campaign." In *Eating Bitterness: New Perspectives on China's Great Leap Forward and Famine*, edited by Kimberley Ens Manning and Felix Wemheuer, 107–29. Vancouver: University of British Columbia Press, 2011.

Williams, Joe. "The Care and Feeding of a Young Cannibal." *St. Louis Post-Dispatch*, February 9, 2007.

Williams, Linda. "Film Bodies: Gender, Genre, and Excess." *Film Quarterly* 44, no. 4 (1991): 2–13.

Williams, Linda. *Hard Core: Power, Pleasure, and the "Frenzy of the Visible."* Berkeley: University of California Press, 1999.

Wilson, Elizabeth A. *Gut Feminism*. Durham, NC: Duke University Press, 2015.

Wilson, Flannery. *New Taiwanese Cinema in Focus*. Edinburgh: Edinburgh University Press, 2015.

Winnubst, Shannon. *Way Too Cool: Selling Out Race and Ethics*. New York: Columbia University Press, 2015.

Wolf, Naomi. *The Beauty Myth: How Images of Beauty Are Used against Women.* New York: Random House, 2013.

Wollen, Peter. "Godard and Counter-cinema: *Vent D'est*." In *Narrative, Apparatus, Ideology: A Film Theory Reader*, edited by Philip Rosen, 120–29. New York: Columbia University Press, 1986.

Wu, Frank H. "The Best 'Chink' Food: Dog Eating and the Dilemma of Diversity." *Gastronomica: The Journal of Critical Food Studies* 2, no. 2 (2002): 38–45.

Wu, Guo. "Recalling Bitterness: Historiography, Memory, and Myth in Maoist China." *Twentieth-Century China* 39, no. 3 (2014): 245–68.

Wu, Guo. "Speaking Bitterness: Political Education in Land Reform and Military Training under the CCP, 1947–1951." *Chinese Historical Review* 21, no. 1 (2014): 3–23.

Wyatt, Tristram D. *Pheromones and Animal Behaviour: Communication by Smell and Taste*. Cambridge: Cambridge University Press, 2003.

Xu, Gary, and Susan Feiner. "*Meinü Jingji*/China's Beauty Economy: Buying Looks, Shifting Value, and Changing Place." *Feminist Economics* 13, no. 3–4 (2007): 307–23.

Xue, Can. "Cotton Candy." In *Vertical Motion*, 110–120. Rochester, NY: Open Letter, 2011.

Yang, Mayfair Mei-hui. "From Gender Erasure to Gender Difference: State Feminism, Consumer Sexuality, and Women's Public Sphere in China." In *Spaces of Their Own: Women's Public Sphere in Transnational China*, edited by Mayfair Mei-hui Yang, 35–67. Minneapolis: University of Minnesota Press, 1999.

Yano, Christine R. *Pink Globalization: Hello Kitty's Trek across the Pacific*. Durham, NC: Duke University Press, 2013.

Yano, Christine R. "Wink on Pink: Interpreting Japanese Cute as It Grabs the Global Headlines." *Journal of Asian Studies* 68, no. 3 (2009): 681–88.

Yapp, Hentyle. "Chinese Lingering, Meditation's Practice: Reframing Endurance Art beyond Resistance." *Women and Performance: A Journal of Feminist Theory* 24, no. 2–3 (2014): 134–52.

Yeats, W. B. "A Drinking Song." In *Yeats's Poems*, edited by A. Norman Jaffares. London: Macmillan, 1989.

Yeh, Emilie Yueh-yu, and Darrell William Davis. "Re-nationalizing China's Film Industry: Case Study on the China Film Group and Film Marketization." *Journal of Chinese Cinemas* 2, no. 1 (2008): 37–51.

Yip, June. *Envisioning Taiwan: Fiction, Cinema, and the Nation in the Cultural Imaginary*. Durham, NC: Duke University Press, 2004.

Zehme, B., and M. Rolston. "Babes in the Woods." *Rolling Stone*, October 4, 1990, 68.

Zehou, Li. *The Chinese Aesthetic Tradition*. Translated by Maija Bell Samei. Honolulu: University of Hawai'i Press, 2009.

Zerilli, Linda M. G. *Feminism and the Abyss of Freedom*. Chicago: University of Chicago Press, 2005.

Zhan, Mei. "Worlding Oneness: Daoism, Heidegger, and Possibilities for Treating the Human." *Social Text* 29, no. 4, 109 (2011): 107–28.

Zhang, Caihong. *Shengti Zhengzi: Bainian Zhongguo Dianying Nü Mingxing Yanjiu* [Body politics: Analysis of a hundred years of Chinese female film stars]. Beijing: Zhongguo guangbodianshi chuban she [China Broadcast and Television Publishing Society], 2011.

Zhang, Rui. *The Cinema of Feng Xiaogang: Commercialization and Censorship in Chinese Cinema after 1989*. Hong Kong: Hong Kong University Press, 2008.

Zhang, Xudong. *Chinese Modernism in the Era of Reforms: Cultural Fever, Avant-Garde Fiction, and the New Chinese Cinema*. Durham, NC: Duke University Press, 1997.

Zhang, Yumei. *Pacific Asia*. New York: Routledge, 2003.

Zhang, Zangzang, Song Qiang, Qiao Bian, Tang Zhengyu, and Gu Qingsheng. *Zhongguo Keyi Shuo Bu* [China can say no]. Beijing: Zhonghua Gongshang Lianhe Chubanshe, 1996.

Zhao, Tingyang. "Rethinking Empire from a Chinese Concept 'All-under-Heaven' (Tian-Xia, 天下)." *Social Identities* 12, no. 1 (2006): 29–41.

Zinoman, Jason. "The Strategic Mind of Ali Wong." *New York Times*, May 3, 2018.

Zitong, Qiu. "Cuteness as a Subtle Strategy: Urban Female Youth and the Online *Feizhuliu* Culture in Contemporary China." *Cultural Studies* 27, no. 2 (2013): 225–41.

Žižek, Slavoj. *The Metastases of Enjoyment: Six Essays on Women and Causality*. London: Verso, 2005.

Žižek, Slavoj. "Tolerance as an Ideological Category." *Critical Inquiry* 34, no. 4 (2008): 660–82.

Zuo, Mila. "Sensing 'Performance Anxiety': Zhang Ziyi, Tang Wei, and Female Film Stardom in the People's Republic of China." *Celebrity Studies* 6, no. 4 (2015): 519–37.

index

Page numbers in italics refer to figures.

abject epistemologies, 23, 30, 78
abjection: biopolitics of labor struggles, 223; carnivalesque, 195; comedy, 17, 35, 219–21, 224, *225*, 227; ethnic, 18, 221, 223; racial, 17–18, 220–21; saltiness, 78; witnessing, 60
acting Chinese, 4–11, 77, 173
Adey, Peter, 136
Adorno, Theodor W., 25
aesthetics: atmosphere, 151, 258n106; beauty, 16; bitterness, 72, 75; blandness, 14–16, 50, 71; *The Crow*, 123–24, 126, 255n48, 132; Cultural Revolution, 45–46, 50–51, 71, 246n15; feminine beauty, 16; flavor, 14; *If You Are the One*, 186–91; Indian rasa, 243n57; matrixial, 138; pungency, 227; rasa, 243n57; saltiness, 75, 79; sourness, 198, 232; spatial, 185; sweetness, 188
affect, 3, 20, 78, 85–86, 89, 241n7
Agamben, Giorgio, 132, 249n71, 254n22
Ahmed, Sara, 120, 157, 205, 254n21
Ahn, Philip, 173–74
Ai Xia, 256n73
alchemy, 78–79

anacrusis, 35, 201–2, 209
Anagnost, Ann, 188
animacy, 27–28
anxiety, 114, 134–35, 139, 171
Appadurai, Arjun, 94
archetypes: child-woman, 203–4, 206; *versus* stereotypes, 83, 251n25
Armisen, Fred, 202
Ashley, Colin Patrick, 78, 89
Asian/American television actors, 97, 253n66
Asian financial crisis of 1997, 153
Assayas, Olivier, 81–83, 86, 90–91. See also *Irma Vep*
As Tears Go By (Wong), 80
atmosphere: aesthetics, 151, 258n106; anxiety and charisma, 114; pungent, 134, 136, 151, 194
atmoterrorism, 117, 127, 137, 217
awkwardness, 210. See also *Paper Heart*

Baby Cobra (Wong, Ali), 213–17, 219–20, 222–23, 226, 230
Bachelard, Gaston, 61
Badiou, Alain, 84

Bai Ling, 35; inscrutability, 120–21, 124, 150; life and career, 120–22; notoriety, 122, 133; pungency, 129–30, 132, 134, 150–51; in *Red Corner*, 122; self-presentation, 133–34; shamelessness, 120–21; white anxieties, 139. *See also* Bai Ling in *The Crow*

Bai Ling in *The Crow*, 114; close-ups, 129, *130*; death, 132–33, 145; fire, 127, 129; inscrutability, 124; minor acts, 120, 124, 129; ornamentation, 129–30; pungency, 129–30, 132; sexualization, 124, 128, 130, 132, 151; voice, 127–28, *130*

Bakhtin, Mikhail, 212, 228–30

Balázs, Béla, 55, 191

Barnard, Rita, 244n74

Barr, Michael, 258n8

Barthes, Roland, 36, 51, 80–81, 248n57

Bassil-Morozow, Helena, 251n25

Baudrillard, Jean, 2, 7, 14, 24, 28, 88, 210, 237–39, 242n16, 264n10

beauty: affects, 3, 20; biopolitics, 28; captivating power, 24; Chinese aesthetic theory, 16; Chinese etymology, 19; Chinese ideologies, 157; and cinema, 12–13, 24; consumption (eating), 19; criticisms of, 244n74; cultural theories, 24–25; deceptive qualities, 236–27; effects, 235–36; encounters, 3; ethics, 236; feminist politics, 238; flavors of, 4–5, 14; gestural expression of, 12; guilt and loss, 148–49; and justice, 12, 62, 162, 236; Kantian, 26, 244n74; performativity as worldling, 3; production, 7; racialized embodiment, 28; *Red Sorghum*, 57, 62, 248n46; screen, 30, 32, 36; sensory perception of, 19; subject formation, 11–12; as surface ornament, 30; tasting, 20, 23; tender *versus* ripe, 157–58; as vivifying force, 234; vulgar, 7, 16–18, 28, 41–42; white supremacy, 244n74; as withdrawn, 24

beauty pageants, 157

Beauvoir, Simone de, 244n74

becoming-animal, 88–89

Benjamin, Walter, 65, 196, 204

Bergen-Aurand, Brian, 181

Bergman, Ingmar, 245n89

Bergson, Henri, 214–15, 227, 262n45

Berlant, Lauren, 93, 185, 227, 236

Billies, Michelle, 78, 89

bitterness, 34, 40; aesthetic, 72; and the color red, 58–59; Cultural Revolution, 52–53, 247n36; desire for, 64; Gong Li, 40, 42, 112; Jung, 75–77; *The Knot*, 163, 167; Mao Zedong, 52; *Red Sorghum*, 55, 57, 59–62, 64, 77; Reform era, 54, 64, 71; ressentiment, 51; saltiness, 75; speaking, 52–53; and sweetness, 162; in Traditional Chinese Medicine, 40–41; translation across borders, 65; twentieth-century China, 51; vulgar feminine beauty, 41–42; women speaking, 52–53

bittersweetness, 162

Björk, 203–4

Black Americans, 85, 252n31

Blackness's affective capacities, 89

blandness, 14–16, 50, 71, 73

bodies: Chinese, 16–17; Chinese medicinal, 14, 17; colonized, 133, 199; consumption fantasies, 4, 70, 250n80; pains, 240; porous, 62, 71, 77, 144–45, 213; post-socialist era women's, 138–39; racialized in *Hannibal Rising*, 69–70; racialized stereotypes, 28. *See also* Taiwanese female bodies

Borges, Jorge Luis, 198

Bourdieu, Pierre, 205

breath, 227

Brinkema, Eugenie, 20

Brook, Timothy, 257n80

Brown, Melissa J., 160

Brown, Wendy, 116, 126, 131

Bush, Richard C., 165, 168

camp, 79, 173

Can Xue, 15

carnivalesque, the, 35, 59, 195, 212, 224, 227–30

Carrey, Jim, 232

Catsoulis, Jeannette, 206–7
Cavani, Liliana, 148
celebrity, political uses of, 156–57, 191, 258n10
Center Stage (Kwan), 80
Cera, Michael, 206–7, 211–12, 262n32
Chang, Eileen (Zhang Ailing), 139, 145
Chang Gua Ahleh, 159
charisma, 26; atmospheric anxiety, 114; *versus* charm, 29, 232–33; and desire, 26–27; feminine, 27; gender and race, 27; Gong Li, 43; pungency, 136, 151; vulgar, 29; Ali Wong, 233
charm, 157, 245n88; *versus* charisma, 29, 232–33; Deleuze on, 232–33; Kant on, 245n88; Charlyne Yi, 209, 233
Chen, Hsiang-yin Sasha, 144
Chen, Joan, 34; coolness, 105; in *The Last Emperor*, 73, 94–95; life and career, 94; minor acts, 34, 92; saltiness, 74; *Tian Yu (Xiu Xiu: The Sent Down Girl)*, 95. *See also* Chen, Joan, in *Twin Peaks*
Chen, Joan, in *Twin Peaks*: coldness, 96–98, 102, 112; death, 105–7; as decoration, 98; gaze, 101; historical significance, 95; inscrutability, 100–1, 111; maid scene, 103–5, *106*; mirror scene (close-up), 98–103; objectification, 105–111; ornamentation, 103–5, *106*, 112; paratextual absences, 109; saltiness, 93, 98, 105; sexualization, 95–96, 104–5, 107–9; speech, 99–100; transformation, 109, 111
Chen, Mel Y., 27, 64, 131, 181
Chen, Tina Mai, 48, 247n22
Cheng, Anne Anlin, 10–12, 30, 92, 186
Chen Kun, 160–61
Chen Tuan, 69
Chen Xiaoyun, 43
Cheung, Maggie, 34; and Olivier Assayas, 81–82, 86, 90–91; in *Center Stage,* 80, 82; life and career, 79–80; minor acts, 34; saltiness, 74, 134. *See also* Cheung, Maggie, in *Irma Vep*
Cheung, Maggie, in *Irma Vep*, 10, 32, 81; close-ups, 86; coolness, 85–91, 111–12; doubling, 82; felinity, 88–89; latex costume, 76–77, 84, 89, 91, 112, 210; racial tricks, 89–90; saltiness, 77, 85, 87–88, 90–91, 111–12; sexualization, 84–87, 89, 91; as surface, 76, 81–82, 85–87, 90–91, 125; transnational cosmopolitanism, 83
Cheung, Steven, 159–60
Chiang Kai-shek, 155
child-woman archetypes, 203–4, 206
Chi Meijian, 163
China: Asian financial crisis of 1997, 153; Communist Party (CCP), 52, 154, 165; consumerism, 176; feminine beauty ideologies, 157; Hong Kong relations, 160, 259n19; international film collaborations, 158; international policies, 153–54; Kuomintang Nationalist Party (KMT), 154–55, 159, 163, 165–66; market economy transition, 188; post-socialist era, 138–39; post-Tiananmen cultural production limits, 64–65; shame, 140; soft power, 155–56, 258n8; Taiwan relations, 154–56, 158, 160, 169–70, 259n19. *See also* Cultural Revolution
China Film Group (CFG), 158, 259n15
Chinese Communist Party (CCP), 52, 154, 165
Chinese cool, 74
Chinese femininity, 8–9, 33
Chinese medicine. *See* Traditional Chinese Medicine (TCM)
Chineseness: as abstraction, 11; acting Chinese, 4–11, 77, 173; beauty affects producing, 3; flavor, 4; as *quan*, 22
Cho, Margaret, 217–19
Chow, Rey: captivity, 223; ethnic abjection, 18, 221; fascism and multiculturalism, 124–26; Gong Li, 43–44; *Lust, Caution*, 257n85; narcissism, 204, 209, 221; performativity of Chineseness, 9–10; representations of Chinese femininity, 8–9, 242n23; stereotypes, 83–84; women's stories in Chinese cinema, 64
cinema's lure, 236
Clark, Paul, 45, 50, 247n29

Classen, Constance, 44, 66–67
Clean (Assayas), 82–83
Clinton, Bill, 125–26, 153
close-ups: Bai Ling in *The Crow*, 129, *130*; Joan Chen in *Twin Peaks*, 98–103; Maggie Cheung in *Irma Vep*, 86; as consumption, 56; Deleuze on, 30, 55; faces, 30, 55, 245n89; Gong Li in *Red Sorghum*, 55–56, 130, 248n41; *Red Sorghum* (others), 55–56, 61–62, 248n41
Cold War, 96–97
colonialism, 145–48
colonization, 60, 133, 144, 147, 155, 199, 214–15, 231–32
Colored People Time (CPT), 197–98, 209
comedy, 194; and abjection, 17, 35, 219–21, 220, 224, *225*, 227; and authority, 220; Margaret Cho, 217–19; jokes, 227; laughter, 194, 214–17, 222, 227–28, 262n45; minoritarian, 221; offbeat, 196; sour, 205; spectators, 222, 227; spring metaphor, 215; stand-up, 226; and stress, 215; timing, 196. *See also* Wong, Ali; Yi, Charlyne
Comolli, Jean-Louis, 172, 236
Confucianism, 160
consumerism, 210
consumption (eating): blandness, 53; body edibility fantasies, 4, 70, 250n80; cannibalism, 66–67; close-ups as, 56; *Lust, Caution*, 141, 143; of the Other, 60, 70; racial fantasies, 71; sexual fantasies of ease, 118–19; spicy foods, 118
coolness, 85–92, 95, 97
Corbin, Alain, 68, 250n74
cosmologies, 20–21, 23
"Cotton Candy" (Can), 13, 15
Crow, The (Proyas), 123–24; aesthetics, 123–24, 126, 255n48, 132; animality, 131; fire, 127–28; multiculturalism and tolerance critiques, 124–26, 130–32, 151; production, 255n32; pungency, 124, 151; racial politics, 124; reception, 125; ressentiment, 131; skin color ontologies, 131, 255n48. *See also* Bai Ling in *The Crow*
Culp, Andrew, 126–27

Cultural Revolution: actors and cinema, 45–51, 246n15; aesthetics, 45–46, 50–51, 71, 246n15; bitterness, 52–53, 247n36; blandness, 71; famine, 52–53, 56–57; feminine beauty, 45–46, 246n15; *Li Shuangshuang*, 45–50, 247n20, 247n22, 247n29; spicy food, 117–18
Curse of the Golden Flower (*Manchengjindai huangjinjia*, Zhang), 259n19
cuteness, 170–75, 191–92
Cut Piece (Ono), 200
Cvetkovich, Ann, 34

Dai Jinhua, 139, 248n41
Dargis, Manohla, 150
Davies, Gloria, 140
Davis, Darrell William, 177
Davis, William, 158
Debord, Guy, 118
deconstruction theory, 21–23, 41, 244n67
Dee, Sandra, 104–5
Deleuze, Gilles: affect, 85–86; assemblages, 227–28; becoming-animal, 88–89; charm, 232–33; close-ups, 30, 55; dark readings of, 126–27; faceification, 80; fetish objects, 107; individuality and non-sense, 105–6; masochism, 93–94, 101–2; materialist correspondence, 69; Nietzsche, 41, 61; object relationships in cinema, 19; rain in cinema, 186; ressentiment, 53; secrets, 112; style, 33; waiting, 93
Deng Xiaoping, 189
Derrida, Jacques: animal nakedness, 239, 264n12, 265n13; deconstruction theory, 83; hospitality, 35, 115, 119, 131
Der-wei Wang, David, 258n5
desire: for bitterness, 64; and charisma, 26–27; feminine, 137, 139; *Lust, Caution*, 148; matrixial, 137, 151; morality, 148; Oedipal, 102; pungency, 136, 139; *Red Sorghum*, 56
disknowledge, 79
Doane, Mary Ann, 7, 30
documentary film veracity debates, 262n32

Dolar, Mladen, 98, 128, 216
Donnell, Alexander, 85
Don't Breathe (Álvarez), 216–17
"Drinking Song, A" (Yeats), 103, 253n77
Drobnick, Jim, 67–68
Du Bois, W. E. B., 197
Duggan, Lisa, 6–7
Dyer, Richard, 31, 44, 109, 118, 194

eating. *See* consumption
Ebert, Roger, 148
Edelman, Lee, 218
Eggert, Katherine, 79
Eileraas, Karina, 203–4
elemental thinking, 21
Elias, Norbert, 194, 215–17
Elkadi, Hisham, 191
Elster, Jon, 206
ethnic abjection, 18, 221
Ettinger, Bracha, 136–37
Evans, Adrienne, 210

face-giving, 31
face reading (*mian xiang*), 30
faces: cinematic, 245n89; face-work, 31; high-key lighting, 32; legibility, 30; and the Other, 30–31; stars, 32. *See also* close-ups
Fan Bingbing, 156
fantasies of love, 236
Farquhar, Judith, 14, 17, 52
fascism, 124–25
Feiner, Susan, 157
female sexuality, social anxieties over, 138–39
femininity as object, 10
femme, the, 6–7
femme fatales, 7
Feng, Peter X., 5, 253n66
Feng Xiaogang, 153, 176, 260n56. See also *If You Are the One*
Fifth Generation cinema, 43, 54, 58, 248n45
film's sensory experiences, 23–24
film workers, 45
Fink, Bruce, 253n78
Five Chimneys (Lengyel), 67, 249n69

Flaherty, Robert, 262n32
Flatley, Jonathan, 51
flavor, 4–5, 14–15, 44, 235. *See also* bitterness; pungency; saltiness; sourness; sweetness; weidao
flavorful embodiment, 44
force *versus* power, 25
foreign identity, 80
Foucault, Michel, 23, 160nn61–62, 182
Freud, Sigmund: beauty, 33; death instinct, 145; family romance, 259n29; feminine desire, 137; fetish, 109; homo economicus, 210; joke work, 220; juxtaposition, 198; melancholia, 163–64; narcissism, 209; Oedipal desires, 102; sexuality, 75; smell, 68, 250n75; split from Jung, 75, 250n5
Fu Manchu, 82

Garland-Thomson, Rosemarie, 8
Garner, Eric, 216–17
gawkiness, 210
Gee Jon, 127
Getino, Octavio, 117
giggling, 200–1, 204
glamour, 186, 234–35
glass, 186–91
glimpses, 138
global sensorium, 12
glow of white women, 109
Goffman, Erving, 31
Gong Li, 18, 34; American career, 66; beauty, 65; bitterness, 40, 42, 112; career reception, 43–44, 54; character deaths, 64; charisma, 43; *versus* Cultural Revolution actors, 44–46; in *Curse of the Golden Flower*, 259n19; erotic-exoticness, 44–45; in *Hannibal Rising*, 66, 71; *Ju Dou*, 71–72; life and career, 42–43; in the Red Trilogy, 58–59; stardom, 65–66, 71; on women in China, 249n61; and Zhang Yimou, 42–43. *See also* Gong Li in *Red Sorghum*
Gong Li in *Red Sorghum*: casting, 18; close-ups, 55–56, 130, 248n41; desire, 56; stills, *58*, *61*

Griffin, John, 65
Griffith, D. W., 96
Guattari, Félix, 69, 88–89, 112
Gumbs, Alexis Pauline, 136–37
Guo Jingming, 189

Hairong, Yan, 188
Han, Byung-Chul, 21–22, 41, 88, 252n42
Hannibal Rising (Webber), 66–71
Haraway, Donna J., 3, 234, 264n12
Hard Knock Wife (Wong, Ali), 215, 229–31
Harlequin (*commedia dell'arte* character), 229–30
Harman, Graham, 24
Harney, Stefano, 240
Haskell, Molly, 162
Hayworth, Rita, 31
heat, 122–23
Hegel, Georg Wilhelm Friedrich, 17
Higgins, Ethan M., 132
high culture fever, 138
Hillman, James, 77, 248n52
Hitchcock, Alfred, 101
Hockley, Luke, 250n6
Hong gao liang. See *Red Sorghum*
Hong Kong: *2046*, 3; Maggie Cheung, 79–80; Chineseness, 10–11, 157; Chinese relations, 154, 160, 259n19; film audience tastes, 161, 259n19; international film collaborations, 158; pornography, 177; stars, 33
Hong Kong television show, 96
Hoogstad, Jan Hein, 202–3
hooks, bell, 50, 66, 234, 252n31, 264n1
hospitality, 35, 115, 119, 131, 138
hot and cold media, 90
hot messes, 122–23, 133–34
Hou Hsiao-hsien, 177
Hour of the Furnaces, The (Solonas and Getino), 117
Howes, David, 44, 66–67
Hsu, Hsuan L., 116
Hsu, Vivian, 35; acting Chinese, 11; career, 153; cultural-racial heritage, 169; erotic photo albums, 152–53, 169–70; in *If You Are the One*, 184; name, 260n36; politics, 174; sexuality, 169–70. See also Hsu, Vivian, in *The Knot*
Hsu, Vivian, in *The Knot*, 159; acting Chinese, 173; bodily surpluses, 172–73; cuteness, 170–75, 191–92; performance, 162, 164, 167, 173–74, 176; sexuality, 170; softness, 169, 174, 192; sweetness, 169, 192
Huang, Vivian L.: on inscrutability, 28, 121; racial bodies and comfort, 119; racial cheer, 77
Huang Jisu, 143
Hudson, Dale, 83, 90
Hudson, Rock, 118–19
hunger, 27
Huyssen, Andreas, 222
hypersexuality, 5, 84. See also sexuality
hypersexualization. See sexualization

identification, 5, 10, 84, 116
identity, 3, 6, 80, 82. See also Chineseness
If You Are the One (*Fei cheng wu rao*, Feng), 174, 177–78; glass and wealth aesthetics, 186–91; Vivian Hsu, 184; politics, 178, 181–85, 191; sequel, 189, 271n70; smell, 181–83; softness, 179–81; spatial aesthetics, 185–86, 191; success, 176, 190; *suzhi*, 188–89; sweetness, 178–79, 181, 185–86, 188, 190–91. See also Shu Qi in *If You Are the One*
Imitation of Life (Sirk), 104–5
ingestion. See consumption
inscrutability, 28–29; Bai Ling, 120–21, 124, 150; Joan Chen in *Twin Peaks*, 100–1, 111; stereotypes of, 83–84, 86; Tang Wei in *Lust, Caution*, 150–51
interracial romance, 96
Irma Vep (Assayas), 74, 78, 81–83, 86–87; fantasy, 81–82, 86–87; and French national cinema, 82–83; identity, 82; saltiness, 78. See also Cheung, Maggie, in *Irma Vep*
irritation, 120
Iwabuchi, Koichi, 44

Japanese colonialism, 148. *See also* Second Sino-Japanese war
Japanese odorlessness, 44
Jia Zhangke, 176
Jie Ying, 157
Johnson, Jake, 206–7, 262n32
Ju Dou (Zhang), 71–72
Jullien, François, 14–16, 20, 24, 28, 151, 258n106
Jung, Carl Gustav, 75–77, 250nn4–6
justice, 12, 51–52, 62, 162, 236

Kang, Inkoo, 215
Kant, Immanuel, 26, 244n74, 245n88
Keathley, Christian, 186
Kehoe, Tricia, 258n10
Keller, Helen, 40
Khoo, Olivia, 85, 163
Kim, Jodi, 92–93, 96
Klein, Christina, 96
Knocked Up (Apatow), 199, 205
Knot, The (*Yun shui yao*), 158–59; bitterness, 163, 167; cast, 160–61; editing, 166, 259n33; English language, 168; failings, 161–62, 165; as family romance, 164–65; fathers, 165; historical setting tracking shot, 165–66; melodrama, 35, 161–63, 172–73, 259n15; One China/tianxia ideology, 159–60, 163–68, 173–74, 187, 191; reception, 161, 163, 259n19, 259n33; sexual binaries, 168; sweetness, 163–65, 167–69, 174, 191. *See also* Hsu, Vivian, in *The Knot*
Korsmeyer, Carolyn, 19
Koshy, Susan, 96
Ku, Robert, 134, 195
Kuomintang Nationalist Party (KMT), 154–55, 159, 163, 165–66
Kwan, Nancy, 5
Kwan, Stanley, 80

Lacan, Jacques, 98, 101, 103, 121, 135, 137, 253n78
Lacanian mirror stage, 98
Lafargue, Paul, 224–25, 263n72
Lampton, David M., 258n8
Laplanche, Jean, 185
Last Emperor, The (Bertolucci), 73, 94–95
laughter, 194, 214–17, 222, 227–28, 262n45
Lee, Ang, 140–41, 150. See also *Lust, Caution*
Lee, Brandon, 123–24, 255n32, 255n48
Lee, Haiyan, 147, 163
Lee, Li-Young, 179–80
Lee, Maggie, 189
Lee, Rachel, 217
Lee Teng-hui, 169–70
Lefebvre, Henri, 185
Lengyel, Olga, 67, 249n69
León, Christina A., 23, 100, 244n67
Leong, Isabella, 159–60, 159–61
Leung, Tony Chiu-wai, 140, 143, 150
Le Vent d'Est (Godard), 87
Levinas, Emmanuel, 30–31, 36, 147
Levy, Ariel, 213
Liao Ping-hui, 258n1
Li Bingbing, 159–60, 167
Li Bo, 15–16
Li Lifeng, 53
Limon, John, 220, 224, 226–27
Lindholm, Charles, 26–27
Lin Pei-yin, 258n1
Li Shuangshuang (Lu), 45–50, 247n20, 247n22, 247n29
"Little Memento from the Boys, A" (Yau), 221
Liu, Alan, 96–97
Li Yin, 153
Li Yu, 176, 187
Logan, Joshua, 96
Lorde, Audre, 72, 221
Lost in Beijing (*Pingguo,* Li), 187
Lou Ye, 143, 176
love, 36–37
Lu, Xiaoning, 45
Lu Ren. See *Li Shuangshuang*
Lust, Caution (Lee), 113–14, 138; appeal, 149, 257n85; colonialism, 145–47; consumption (eating), 141, 143; desire, 148; diamond ring and the death drive, 146–47; Tony Leung Chiu-wai, 140, 143, 150; minor acts, 144–45; moral outrage over, 139–40, 143, 149;

Lust, Caution (Lee) (continued)
  phallic language, 147, 257n91; plot summary, 141–42; pungency, 138, 140, 144, 147–48, 151; ressentiment, 149; saltiness, 147; sex, 140–41, 143–45, 149–50; themes, 141–42. *See also* Tang Wei in *Lust, Caution*
Lu Xun, 52
Lynch, David, 111. See also *Twin Peaks*

Madonna, 31
male gaze, 7
Man, Eva Kit Wah, 46
Manning, Erin, 9
Mao Zedong, 45–46, 52, 117–18
Marks, Laura U., 71, 77, 251n11
Martens, China, 136–37
Martin, Demetri, 208–9
Marx, Karl, 224
masculinity and spicy foods, 115
masochism, 93–94, 101–2, 107, 109
Massumi, Brian, 3, 25, 241n7
matrixial aesthetics, 138
matrixial desire, 137, 151
Mavor, Carol, 63, 250n75
Mbembe, Achille, 132–33, 199, 231
McGowan, Todd, 101, 107, 147
McHugh, Kathleen, 6–7
McLuhan, Marshall, 90, 122
Mead, Rebecca, 230
melodrama: *The Knot*, 35, 161–63, 172–73, 259n15; masochism, 93; softness and sweetness, 162; temporality, 164; *Twin Peaks*, 97, 102
melting pot, 123, 255n31
Memmi, Albert, 232
Meyer, Richard, 119
mind-body holism, 13–14
minor acts, 9, 44; astonishment, 204; Bai Ling in *The Crow*, 120, 124, 129; of beauty, 235; Joan Chen, 34, 92; Maggie Cheung, 34; Chineseness, 33; *Lust, Caution*, 144–45; Shu Qi, 11, 184; Tang Wei in *Lust, Caution*, 120
misogyny and heat, 122–23
modernity, 196–97, 222
monosodium glutamate (MSG), 134

Monroe, Marilyn, 118
Morris, Meaghan, 166
Morson, Gary Saul, 197
Moten, Fred, 35, 201–2, 240
m/Other, 135–36
mothers, 135–37
Mo Yan, 54, 248n46
multiculturalism, 124–26, 130–32, 151. *See also* tolerance
Mulvey, Laura, 7
Muñoz, José Esteban, 111, 196, 199, 204
Murakami, Takashi, 171
Musser, Amber Jamilla, 27

Naficy, Hamid, 80–81
Nakadate, Laurel, 119
Nakamura, Lisa, 131, 134
Naremore, James, 173
neo-Confucianism, 138–39
New Era, 249n62
Ng, Roseanna, 150
Ngai, Sianne: Asian stereotypes, 28; beauty, 244n74; comedy, 227; coolness, 97; cuteness, 170–71; irritation, 120, 161; ugly feelings, 29; zaniness, 228
Nguyen, Mimi Thi, 244n74
Nietzsche, Friedrich: aesthetic of boundary transgression, 248n51; bad conscience, 41, 53, 148, 246n4; beauty, 28; chaos, 35; charisma, 26; guilt and smell, 68; memory, 61; ressentiment, 51, 206; subversive rhythms, 212; *Thus Spoke Zarathustra*, 202–3
Nightmare, The (painting by Fuseli), 107, 108
Night Porter, The (Cavani), 148
Niou, Emerson, 156
Nishime, Leilani, 134
Nye, Joseph S., 154–55
Nyugen, Tan Hoang, 84–85

O'Connor, Sinéad, 200
odor, 68. *See also* smell
odorlessness, 44
offbeat, 197, 201, 203, 210
Oh, Sandra, 238–40, 264n11

One China mythology, 11, 35, 153–54, 160. See also *The Knot*
Ong, Aihwa, 165
Ono, Yoko, 119, 200
ornamentation and ornamentalism, 30; Bai Ling in *The Crow*, 129–30; Joan Chen in *Twin Peaks*, 103–5, *106*, 112; objectification via, 92; salt as, 92; shine, 186; *Twin Peaks*, 103
Other, the: anxiety, 135–36, 256n60; consumption of, 60, 70; faces, 30–31; the m/Other, 135–36; saltiness, 81, 111; smell, 68, 129; the sm/Other, 135–37, 228, 256n60
overkills, 132
over-ripeness, 163
oversentimentality (*rouma*), 162

Palumbo-Liu, David, 6
Paper Heart (Yi), 199, 205–12, 262n32
Pardlo, Gregory, 197
Payne, Alexander, 239–40
Pedersen, Birgitte Stougaard, 202–3
People's Liberation Army (PLA), 52
"Persimmons" (Lee), 179–80
Perullo, Nicola, 19–20
Peterson, Christopher, 183
Pfeiffer, Michelle, 76, 84, 89
Pham, Minh-Ha T., 4, 214
Phillips, Adam, 56
physiognomy, 31, 55
picnolepsy, 242n16
Pondering Sweetness campaign, 53
Pontalis, J. B., 185
pornography, 177
post-socialist era (China), 138–39
Poundstone, Paula, 226
Pountain, Dick, 97
pregnancy, 136–37
Proyas, Alexander, 123. See also *The Crow*
Pryor, Richard, 220, 224
psychoanalysis, 136–37. *See also* Freud, Sigmund; Lacan, Jacques
public spaces, 185
pungency, 34–35, 114, 116–18; aesthetics, 227; agit-prop documentary examples, 117; atmospheric, 134, 136, 151, 194; Bai Ling, 129–30, 132, 134, 150–51; bodily acts, 135–36; charismatic, 136, 151; Chinese women, 118; and desire, 136, 139; disgust, 116; disidentification, 116; as environmental, 116–17; and health, 116–17; *Lust, Caution*, 138, 140, 144, 147–48, 151; nudity, 151; rot, 118; sexuality, 121; as signified matter, 118; sm/Othering, 228; sour, 196; temporality, 117; Traditional Chinese Medicine, 119; western culture, 138; yellow peril fantasies, 134. See also *The Crow*; *Lust, Caution*
Purple Butterfly (*Zi Hudie*, Lou), 143
putrefaction, 121

quan, 22
Quine, Richard. See *The World of Suzie Wong*
quirkiness, 196–97, 199, 203–5, 209

race: abjection, 17–18, 220–21; affect theories, 78; beauty, 28; bodies and comfort, 119; and charisma, 27; consumption, 4–5, 71; *The Crow*, 124; materialist theory, 78; risk differences, 119; sexualization, 5, 66, 68; stereotypes, 28; *Twin Peaks*, 78, 93–94, 97; yellow peril fantasies, 134. *See also* racism
racial capitalisms, 122, 255n30
racial cheer, 77
racial humor. *See* Wong, Ali
racialized Others's saltiness, 81, 111
racialized-sexualized subjection, 84
racialized violence, 78
racial tricks, 84, 89–90
racism, 67, 116, 122–23
Radin, Joanna, 121
rain, 186, 271n70
Rainbow, The (*Hong*, Mao), 242n23
rasa aesthetics, 243n57
Recollecting Bitterness campaign, 53
red (color), 58–60, 63–64
Red Detachment of Women, The (*Hongse niangzi jun*, Pan), 45
Reddy, Vanita, 157

Red Sorghum (*Hong gao liang,* Zhang), 54–55; bitterness, 55, 57, 59–62, 64, 77; close-up sequences, 55–56, 61–62, 248n41; *versus* Cultural Revolution films, 62–63; earthly bodies, 41–42; eroticism, 56–57, *58*, 62; feminine beauty, 57, 62, 248n46; reception, 58; ressentiment, 41, 60, 62; saltiness, 77; Second Sino-Japanese war, 60–63, 143; sweat, 48, 50, 56, 59–60; sweetness, 60; urine, 59–60, 62; use of red, 56, 58–59, 63. *See also* Gong Li in *Red Sorghum*

Reform era (China), 54, 64, 71

relationality, 3

representations of Asian people in western cinema, 28–29

ressentiment: bitterness, 51; comic racial abjection, 220–21; *The Crow*, 131; *Hannibal Rising*, 68; *Lust, Caution*, 149; Nietzschean, 51, 206; *Red Sorghum*, 41, 60, 62; sour, 17; spread of, 52–53

Revolution (Cho), 218

rhythm: pluralizing capacity, 203; subversive, 212. *See also* temporality

Rich, John A., 78

Right to be Lazy, The (Lafargue), 224–25, 263n72

Riley, Sarah, 210

Río, Elena del, 12, 24, 104–5

risk, 115, 119

Robins, David, 97

Roedinger, David R., 209

Rofel, Lisa, 176, 185

Roh, David, 134

Romney, Jonathan, 81

Roquet, Paul, 148

rot, 121, 148, 164

rouma (oversentimentality), 162

Ruan Lingyu, 80, 256n73

Rui Zhang, 260n56

sajiao (unleashing tenderness), 1–2, 173–74

salt: abject epistemologies, 78; aesthetics of, 79; in alchemical psychology, 77; as caution against literality, 78; connotations, 79; necessity for survival, 74; ornamental functions, 92; of words, 80–81. *See also* saltiness

saltiness, 34, 74; and abjection, 78; aesthetics, 75, 79; bitterness, 75–77; Joan Chen, 74, 93, 98, 105; Maggie Cheung, 74, 77, 85, 87–88, 90–91, 111–12, 134; cooling effects, 92–93; gender, 75; *Irma Vep*, 78; Jung, 75–77; *Lust, Caution*, 147; misfortune connotations, 78; and Othering, 81, 111; *Red Sorghum*, 77; as signifier, 118; *versus* sourness, 195; *Twin Peaks*, 78, 102, 104–5, 147; yellow peril fantasies, 134. See also *Irma Vep*; *Twin Peaks*

Sayonara (Logan), 96

Scarry, Elaine, 12, 62, 236, 244n74, 249n55

Schamus, James, 149

Schechner, Richard, 243n57

screams, 201

Second Sino-Japanese war, 140; Chinese complicity, 149; rape, 140–41, 257n80; *Red Sorghum*, 60–63, 143. See also *Lust, Caution*

Sedgwick, Eve Kosofsky, 17

seduction: in *2046*, 1–3; absence and presence, 7–8, 24; Baudrillard's theory, 2, 7, 14, 24, 28, 88, 210, 237–39, 242n16, 264n10; and beauty, 236; feminist, 237–38; *versus* gawkiness, 210; ludic aspects, 237–39; reversibility of power, 7; *sajiao* (unleashing tenderness), 1–2, 173–74

Sen, Tansen, 189

sentimentality, 93–94, 162

Severino, Rodolfo, 153

sexuality: fantasies of easy consumability, 118–19; Freud, 75; heat, 123; Vivian Hsu, 169–70; pungency, 121; social anxieties, 138–39; Ali Wong, 214, 232; Charlyne Yi, 232. *See also* sexualization

sexualization: Bai Ling in *The Crow*, 124, 128, 130, 132, 151; Joan Chen in *Twin Peaks*, 95–96, 104–5, 107–9; Maggie Cheung in *Irma Vep*, 84–87, 89, 91;

identification, 84; and infantilization, 206; Michelle Pfeiffer in *Batman Returns*, 76; race, 5, 66, 68; Tang Wei in *Lust, Caution*, 140; *Twin Peaks*'s parody, 104–5
shame, 120–21
Shaoyi Sun, 259n33
Shaviro, Steven, 34, 148–49
Shih, Shu-mei, 160–61
Shimizu, Celine Parreñas, 5, 84, 87, 243n48
shine, 186
Shu Qi, 35; acting Chinese, 11; career, 153, 177; in *If You Are the One*, 174, 176; minor acts, 11, 184. *See also* Shu Qi in *If You Are the One*
Shu Qi in *If You Are the One*, 174, 176; beauty, 180, 183, 192; hesitation, 176, 192; minor acts, 184; soft-sweetness, 177–78, 180, 192; Taiwaneseness, 183–84
Sideways (Payne), 239–40
Sirk, Douglas, 104–5
Sixth Generation filmmakers, 176
Sloterdijk, Peter, 116–17, 127, 222
smell: European epistemologies, 66–68; Freud, 68, 250n75; *Hannibal Rising*, 67–71; ideology, 128–29; *If You Are the One*, 181–83; memory, 67; the Other, 68, 129; racial discrimination, 116; racial politics, 67; and *suzhi*, 188–89; and voice, 129
sm/Other, the, 135–37, 228, 256n60
smothering, 135
soap operas, 93. *See also Twin Peaks*
Sobchack, Vivian, 13, 24, 69, 232
socialism. *See* Cultural Revolution
social media likes, 88, 252n42
softness, 153; Vivian Hsu in *The Knot*, 169, 174, 192; *If You Are the One*, 179–81; Shu Qi in *If You Are the One*, 177–78, 180, 192; and sweetness, 162
soft power, 154–56, 160, 171, 258n8
Sohn, Stephen Hong, 17, 133–34
Solanas, Fernando, 117
Sontag, Susan, 79, 173
sour grapes, 206–7

sourness, 35, 194–95; aesthetics, 198, 232; collectivizing functions, 228; comedy, 205; facial expressions, 195; offbeat, 203; *Paper Heart*, 199, 205, 208, 210; pungent, 196; ressentiment, 17; and sweetness, 195, 209; temporality, 195–96; traditional Chinese medicine, 194; twee, 207; vulgar materialism, 221; Ali Wong, 215, 219, 228, 232; Charlyne Yi, 199–200, 205, 208, 210, 232. *See also* comedy
spiciness, 115–19. *See also* pungency
stares and staring, 7–9
stars, 31–32; acting Chinese, 10; beauty, 32, 36; behavioral rules, 156; faces, 32; and the gaze, 7–8; meaning accumulation, 44; on-screen charisma, 27; political uses of, 156–57, 191, 258n10; as public objects, 139; public scrutiny, 138–39, 256n73; and spectators creating meaning, 44; staring at, 7–9; term connotations, 45; vulgar beauty acts, 7. *See also* Bai Ling; Chen, Joan; Cheung, Maggie; Gong Li; Hsu, Vivian; Shu Qi; Tang Wei
stereotypes: *versus* archetypes, 83, 251n25; Asian people, 28; Chinese inscrutability, 83–84; *versus* fantasies, 111; as surface encounters, 83–84; visual nature, 83
Stoler, Ann Laura, 148
Streamas, John, 197
Studlar, Gaylyn, 107
Sullivan, Jonathan, 258n10
Sunderland, Mitchell, 120
Sun Tzu, 75
surfaces: Maggie Cheung in *Irma Vep*, 76, 81–82, 85–87, 90–91, 125; faces, 31; inscrutability stereotypes, 84, 86; stereotypes, 83–84
suzhi, 188–89
Swartz, Kristin, 132
sweetness, 35, 153, 191; aesthetics, 188; and bitterness, 162; calming, 156; cute, 172; Vivian Hsu in *The Knot*, 169, 192; *If You Are the One*, 178–79, 181, 185–86, 188, 190–91; images of beautiful

sweetness (continued)
women, 157; irritating, 173; *The Knot*, 163–65, 167–69, 174, 191; and poison, 164; *Red Sorghum*, 60; rot, 164; Shu Qi in *If You Are the One*, 177–78, 180, 192; and softness, 162; soft power, 156; and sourness, 195, 209; sugar as commodity, 192; and *suzhi*, 189; twee, 207

Synott, Anthony, 44, 66–67

Taiwan: anti-imperialist literary movements, 168; Chineseness, 10–11, 157; Chinese relations, 154–56, 158, 160, 169–70, 259n19; demographics, 155; femininity, 169; film audience tastes, 161, 259n19; film cultures, 260n42; history, 155, 258n5; international film collaborations, 158, 161; in mainland films, 153; stars, 33, 156, 158; women's literature, 258n1. See also *If You Are the One*; *The Knot*

Taiwanese female bodies, 153, 169, 173, 191. See also Hsu, Vivian; Shu Qi

Tam, Bill, 143

Tang, Xiaobing, 47

Tang Wei, 35; audience interest in, 149; life and career, 139–40, 150–51. See also Tang Wei in *Lust, Caution*

Tang Wei in *Lust, Caution*, 114; backlash, 139–40, 143; casting, 150; inscrutability, 150–51; minor acts, 120; sex scene filming, 150; sexualization, 140

tartness, 207

taste and subject-object relations, 19–20

TCM. See Traditional Chinese Medicine

temporality: Colored People Time (CPT), 197–98, 209; melodrama, 164; modernity, 196–97; offbeat, 197, 201, 203, 210; pungency, 117; sourness, 195–96, 202; White People's Time, 197

Thailand, 153

Third Taiwan Strait Crisis, 169–70

Thompson, Robert Harris, 85

tianxia (all under heaven), 160

Tibet, 160

Tingyang Zhao, 160

Tiny Times (*Xiao shidai*, Guo), 189

tolerance, 81; *The Crow*, 124–26, 130–32, 151; governmentality, 125; liberal, 126, 134; and smell, 128; of the unpleasant, 116

Tompkins, Kyla Wazana, 4, 70, 250n80

Traditional Chinese Medicine (TCM), 14, 21; bitterness, 40–41; flavors, 33; methodology, 23; pungency, 119; sourness, 194

Trier, Lars von, 204

Trump, Donald, 219–20

Trump, Ivanka, 230

Twin Peaks (Lynch), 74, 93, 95; coolness, 95; female doubles, 100–2, 111; historical contexts, 95, 97; male tears, 102; melodrama, 97, 102; ornamentation, 103; race, 78, 93–94, 97; *Rolling Stone* coverage, 109, *110*; saltiness, 102, 104–5, 147; sentimentality, 93–94; sexualized Chinese parody, 104–5; sound, 99–100. See also Chen, Joan, in *Twin Peaks*

2046 (Wong Kar-wai), 1–3, 6–7, 28, 32

Vargas, Deborah, 226

Venus with a Mirror (Titian), 102, 107

vermilion, 63–64

Vertigo (Hitchcock), 101

Virilio, Paul, 242n16

visual shocks, 13

voice, 194; Bai Ling in *The Crow*, 127–28, *130*; comedy, 194, 217–18; cultural odorlessness, 44; female jouissance, 137; laughter, 217; piercing function, 127–28; and smell, 129, 144; ugly, 203–4; Ali Wong, 214; Zhang Ruifang in *Li Shuangshuang*, 47

vulgar beauty, 7, 16–18, 28, 41–42

vulgarity: beauty, 7, 16–18, 28, 41–42; charisma, 29; Chinese body associations, 16–17; collectivizing effects, 227; decay, 17; definitions, 1–2, 16; epistemologies, 17; and identity, 3; and pain, 240; sourness, 221; Ali Wong, 212–14, 219–21, 230

Waddell, Terrie, 250n5
Wang, Ban, 246n15
Wang, Jing, 138
Wang Xiaoshuai, 176
Warhol, Andy, 204
Wark, McKenzie, 223
waste, 17
weak theory, 17
wealth tourism, 190
Weber, Max, 223
Weeks, Kathi, 223–24, 263n72
Weheliye, Alexander G., 192
weidao, 18–20, 33–34, 235. See also flavor
Wemheuer, Felix, 52
western sciences, 244n69
White-Haired Girl, The (*Bai mao nü*, Yan), 45
White People's Time, 197
Williams, Linda, 69, 93, 164, 188, 219
Williams, Mai'a, 137
Wolf, Naomi, 244n74
Wollen, Peter, 87
womb, 136, 138, 145
wonder, 205
Wong, Ali, 35; antiwork ideology, 223–24, 226; Asian American stereotype subversion, 223; *Baby Cobra*, 213–17, 219–20, 222–23, 226, 230; charisma, 233; *versus* Margaret Cho, 218; fecal comedy, 224–27; feminism, 222–23; *Hard Knock Wife*, 215, 229–31; life and career, 218–19; maternity and childbirth, 228–30; physicality, 214–15, 224, *225*; play, 228; racial humor, 214–15; sexuality, 214, 232; sexual power inversion, 230–31; sourness, 215, 219, 228, 232; voice, 214; vulgarity, 212–14, 219–21, 230; writing process, 221–22
Wong, Anna May, 28–29, 95, 186
Wong Kar-wai, 80. See also *2046*
work, 223–26, 228, 263n72

World of Suzie Wong, The (Quine), 5, 96, 241n12
"wrong place, wrong time," 78, 93, 255n32
Wu, Guo, 247n36
Wuxing cosmology, 21

Xiu Xiu: The Sent Down Girl (*Tian Yu*, Chen), 95
Xu, Gary, 157

Yang, Mayfair, 139
Yano, Christine R., 171–72
Yao Xiaomeng, 248n45
Yau, John, 221
Yeats, W. B., 103, 253n77
Yeh Yueh-yu, 177
yellow peril fantasies, 134
Yi, Charlyne, 35; career, 199; charm, 209, 233; child-woman archetype, 203; giggles, 200–1, 204; impressions, 198–99; in *Knocked Up*, 199, 205; lovability, 208–9; non-binary, 203; offbeat approach, 199, 202, 204–5, 209; *Paper Heart*, 199, 205–12, 262n32; performativity, 200–1; quirkiness, 199, 205, 209; sexuality, 232; sourness, 199–200, 205, 208, 210, 232
Yin Li, 158
Yip, June, 168

Zehou, Li, 19, 50
Zhang, Xudong, 56
Zhang Caihong, 43
Zhang Ruifang, 45–48, *49*, 51, 247n29
Zhang Yimou, 18; banned films, 64; career status, 43; Cultural Revolution, 59; and Gong Li, 42–43; *Ju Dou*, 71–72; use of red, 58–59. See also *Red Sorghum*
Zhang Ziyi, 1–2, 7, 143
Žižek, Slavoj, 86–87, 127–29

www.ingramcontent.com/pod-product-compliance
Lightning Source LLC
Chambersburg PA
CBHW051049230426
43666CB00012B/2620